Constitutional Theocracy

CONSTITUTIONAL THEOCRACY

Ran Hirschl

HARVARD UNIVERSITY PRESS
Cambridge, Massachusetts
London, England
2010

Library of Congress Cataloging-in-Publication Data

Hirschl, Ran.
Constitutional theocracy / Ran Hirschl.
p. cm.
ISBN 978-0-674-04819-5
1. Constitutional law—Religious aspects.
2. Theocracy—Political aspects. I. Title.
K3280.H57 2010
342—dc22 2010000963

Contents

Constitutional Theocracy

CHAPTER ONE

The Rise of Constitutional Theocracy

The Holy One, blessed be He, waits for the nations of the world in the hope that they will repent, and be brought beneath His wings.

NUMBERS RABBAH (JEWISH MIDRASH, CIRCA SECOND CENTURY C.E.)

RELIGION and the belief in God have made a major comeback. Over the last few decades principles of theocratic governance have gained enormous public support worldwide.[1] From the fundamentalist turn in predominantly Islamic polities to the spread of Catholicism and Pentecostalism in the global South and to the rise of the Christian Right in the United States, it is hard to overstate the significance of the religious revival in late twentieth- and early twenty-first-century politics. Parties that advance religion-infused agendas have gained a tremendous popular following in polities as diverse as India, Israel, Malaysia, and Turkey. Christianity, meanwhile, has been growing exponentially in the so-called developing world.[2] The Roman Catholic population in Africa alone more than doubled between the mid-1970s and the mid-1990s, and in Asia it increased by 90 percent during that period.[3] Religion-based morality continues to hover over much of the Catholic "old world," from Latin America to the Philippines. The Orthodox Church has enjoyed a big resurgence in parts of Eastern Europe just as Russia has been struggling to control the spread of Islam in the northern Caucasus. The changing demographics of French society have given rise to serious challenges, raucous at times, to France's assertive secularism. And one only needs to reach for the television remote control to appreciate the prevalence of Evangelical, born-again Christianity in the United States, with its scores of pastors, churches, and televised salvation ceremonies. All of this happens, lest we forget, as newspaper headlines report on religion-based insurgency from Iraq and Afghanistan to Pakistan, Yemen, Somalia, and Indonesia on a near-daily basis; on how Hezbollah (the "party of God") has effectively erected its own governing apparatus within Lebanon; on how the struggle between the nationalist Fatah movement and the religious Hamas movement has effectively split the Palestinian people; and on struggles between clerics and reformists in Iran. In short, the reports of God's death, to paraphrase Mark Twain's remark, have been greatly exaggerated.

At the same time, the world has witnessed the rapid spread of constitutionalism and judicial review. Constitutional supremacy, a concept that has long been a major pillar of the American political order, is now shared, in one form or another, by over 150 countries and several supranational entities across the globe. Most of these countries can boast the recent adoption of a constitution or a constitutional revision that contains a bill of rights and enshrines some form of active judicial review. Consequently, constitutional courts and judges have emerged as prominent translators of constitutional provisions into guidelines for public life. The international migration of constitutional concepts and structures has grown exponentially. At the uneasy intersection of these two sweeping trends—the tremendous increase of popular support for principles of theocratic governance and the global spread of constitutionalism—a new legal and political order has emerged: *constitutional theocracy.*

What is constitutional theocracy? In a pure theocracy (e.g., the Islamic state envisioned by the Prophet Muhammad in the early seventh century or its emulation in Mahdist Sudan of the late nineteenth century) the supreme religious leader is also the highest political leader. Law proclaimed by the ruler is also considered a divine revelation and hence the law of God. In a closely related ecclesiocracy (e.g., the Vatican) an ensconced institutional religious leadership is at the helm; the religious leaders assume a leading role in the state but do not claim to be instruments of divine revelation. In contrast, formal separation exists in constitutional theocracy between political leadership and religious authority. Power in constitutional theocracies resides in political figures operating within the bounds of a constitution rather than from within the religious leadership itself. Basic principles such as the separation of powers are constitutionally enshrined. The constitution also typically establishes a constitutional court that is mandated to carry out some form of active judicial review.

At the same time, constitutional theocracies defy the Franco-American doctrine of strict structural and substantive separation of religion and state. Like models of "establishment" or "state religion," constitutional theocracies both formally endorse and actively support a single religion or faith denomination. Moreover, that state religion is enshrined as the principal source that informs all legislation and methods of judicial interpretation. Unlike the handful of European countries that grant exclusive recognition and support to a given state religion, the designated state religion in constitutional theocracies is often viewed as constituting the foundation of the modern state; as such, it is an integral part, or even the metaphorical pillar, of the polity's national metanarrative. In this way religion often determines the polity's boundaries of collective identity, as well as the scope and nature of some or all of the rights and duties assigned to its residents.

Constitutional theocracies, however, do more than grant exclusive recognition and support to a given state religion: laws must conform to principles of religious doctrine, and no statute may be enacted that is repugnant to these principles. In most instances a well-developed nexus of religious bodies, tribunals, and authorities operates in lieu of, or in tandem with, a civil court system. The opinions and jurisprudence of these authorities and tribunals carry notable symbolic weight and play a significant role in public life. Importantly, however, this nexus of laws and institutions is subject to judicial review by a constitutional court or tribunal. This tribunal consists of judges who are often well versed in both general and religious law and can speak knowledgeably on pertinent matters of law to jurists at Yale Law School, as well as at al-Azhar, the center of Islamic learning in Cairo.

The ideal model of a constitutional theocracy can be summarized by outlining four main cumulative elements: (1) adherence to some or all core elements of modern constitutionalism, including the formal distinction between political authority and religious authority and the existence of some form of active judicial review; (2) the presence of a single religion or religious denomination that is formally endorsed by the state, akin to a "state religion"; (3) the constitutional enshrining of the religion and its texts, directives, and interpretations as *a* or *the* main source of legislation and judicial interpretation of laws—essentially, laws may not infringe on injunctions of the state-endorsed religion; and (4) a nexus of religious bodies and tribunals that often not only carry tremendous symbolic weight but are also granted official jurisdictional status on either a regional or a substantive basis and operate in lieu of, or in uneasy tandem with, a civil court system. Most important, their jurisdictional autonomy notwithstanding, some key aspects of religious tribunals' jurisprudence are subject to constitutional review by higher courts, often state created and staffed.

In all, hundreds of millions of people, perhaps as many as a billion, now live in polities or subnational units that either fall squarely within the definition of a constitutional theocracy or that feature many of the substantive characteristics and tensions of this legal order.[4] From the early 1970s to

2000 alone, at least two dozen predominantly Muslim countries, from Egypt to Pakistan, declared Shari'a (Islamic law) "a" or "the" source of legislation.[5] The more recent new constitutions of Afghanistan (2004) and Iraq (2005) reflect precisely that type of dual commitment to principles of Shari'a and to principles of human rights, constitutional law, and popular sovereignty.[6] Although virtually none of these polities' constitutions was adopted in an authentic bottom-up, "we-the-people" fashion—in fact, quite the opposite is true in most cases—Islamization does reflect a set of values that a large portion of the population in these countries seems to support. In several other countries precepts of Islam have been incorporated into the constitution, penal code, and personal-status laws of subnational units, most notably in twelve Nigerian states, Pakistan's North-West Frontier Province, and Indonesia's Aceh, to varying degrees in two Malaysian states, and to an increasing extent in Russia's Chechnya and Dagestan. Much like the considerable variations within the so-called liberal democratic world, wide variation exists within the constitutional theocratic world in how central religion is in public life. Granted, Malaysia and Tunisia are a world apart from Iran or the Vatican in how lax or rigid the actual translation of religious principles into public life is. But in virtually all these countries religion not only plays a key collective-identity role but is also granted a formal constitutional status, serves as a source of legislation, whether symbolically or practically, and, more important, enjoys jurisdictional autonomy in matters extending from education and personal-status law to essential omnipresence in every aspect of life, law, and politics.

The prevalence of variations on constitutional theocracy in the predominantly Islamic world points to an interesting constitutional trajectory—perhaps anomalous from a Western hegemonic perspective—in such settings. Whereas much of the Western world has undergone a gradual political and constitutional confinement of religion since early modern times, the Islamic world of the last forty years seems to have taken the opposite route. Throughout most of the twentieth century nationalism and socialism were the two pillars of political discourse in North Africa, the Middle East, and Southeast Asia. With few exceptions, polities in these regions emerged from colonialism with surprisingly little reliance on religion or religious authorities. The secularist nationalism of Mahatma Gandhi and the leftist revolutionary independence movement in Algeria are two prominent examples. But religion has made a major comeback over the last few decades and is now a de facto and often a de jure pillar of collective identity, national metanarrative, and constitutional law in many predominantly Muslim countries in Asia, Africa, and the Middle East.

A further two billion people, perhaps as many as three billion, live in countries such as India, Indonesia, and Turkey where no particular religion is granted formal status, but where religious affiliation is a pillar of collective identity. The struggle to establish uniform personal-status law in formally secular but markedly religious India has been a perennial bone of contention in Indian constitutional law and politics. In half a dozen Indian states, to pick another example, strict restrictions on conversion from Hinduism have been introduced into law by the Hindu nationalist Bharatiya Janata Party (BJP). The fundamental mismatch between Turkey's constitutionally enshrined secularism and the manifested religious inclinations of most Turks has given rise to a frenzy of political and constitutional maneuvering in that country. In countries such as Israel, Sri Lanka, or parts of the former Yugoslavia religious affiliation is closely entangled with definitions of ethnicity, nationality, and citizenship. To that count one may add polities where, despite formal separation of church and state, long-standing politically systemized Catholic Church preeminence and religion-centric morality continue to loom large over the constitutional arena. The de facto, as opposed to de jure, boundaries of religion and state in these countries can be described as being blurred at best and are continually contested in both the political and the judicial spheres.

Regimes in these and other countries throughout the new world of constitutional theocracies have been struggling with questions of a profoundly foundational nature and have been forced to navigate between cosmopolitanism and parochialism, modern and traditional metanarratives, constitutional principles and religious injunctions, contemporary governance and ancient texts, and judicial and pious interpretation. More often than not, the clash between these conflicting visions results in fierce struggles over the nature of the body politic and its organizing principles. These tensions are evident in virtually every aspect of public life, from court hearings to university lectures, from crowded soccer stadiums to secluded board meetings, and from casual conversations in markets and street eateries to maneuvers in the upper echelons of politics.

All these countries face the sources of friction inherent in a constitutional theocracy—a potentially explosive combination by its very nature, and one that poses new challenges to conventional constitutional ideas about secularism, religious freedom, and the relationship between religion and the state. How, therefore, can a polity reconcile the principles of accountability and separation of powers and the notion of "we-the-people" as the ultimate source of sovereignty when the fundamental notion of divine authority and holy texts constitutes the supreme governing norm of the state? Who should be vested with the ultimate authority to interpret the divine text, and on what grounds? What ought to be done when principles of modern constitutionalism and human rights collide with religious injunctions and support for theocratic governance? More generally, how can a polity advance principles of twenty-first-century government or run a modern economy when it treats ancient texts and pious authorities as a main source of legislation? And what is the place of courts in the new matrix of religion, state, and constitutionalism in a nonsecularist world?

Like early writings about the postcolonial world that tended to view postcolonial countries as a homogeneous bloc, populist academic and media accounts in the West tend to portray the spread of religious fundamentalism in the developing world as a near-monolithic, ever-accelerating, and all-encompassing phenomenon.[7] The frequent formulation of this supposed dichotomy is that the West is largely secular and modernist, whereas the non-West is largely religious and traditionalist. According to this "civilizational" approach, a distinction between religion and state is deeply rooted in Christendom but does not exist in other major religions, certainly not in Islam. Moreover, in contrast to the Western portrayal of religion as private and relatively benign, "politicized" religions are depicted as a threat to reason and a hindrance to progress.[8] The Islamic world, in particular, has been the target of much of this critique. Whereas the West is characterized as driven by a constant quest for modernism and progressiveness, Islam and Muslims have increasingly been depicted as insular and anticosmopolitan.[9] The post-9/11 popular media followed suit by portraying Islamic societies as united by their religious zeal and antiliberal sentiment.

The reality, however, is more complex and nuanced, for the secular/religious divide is a continuum, not a binary, dichotomous classification. Europe has been the birthplace of secularism and the separation of church and state, but at the same time it has maintained, and is reluctant to forgo, its ultimate Christian predominance. And just as American society has multiple traditions and defining characteristics and thus may not be easily labeled either "modern" or "parochial," most polities where principles of theocratic governance have gained public support may not be easily defined as fundamentalist, reactionary, or ultrareligious. Egypt, to pick one example, has witnessed tremendous growth in popular support for the Muslim Brotherhood. The prospects of further Islamization are real; even under extreme duress—the regime is doing everything it can, often at the expense of civil liberties and democracy, to contain the theocratic threat—political Islam was able to garner one-fifth of the votes in the 2007 parliamentary elections. But this is the same Egypt that attracts millions of tourists every year to some of the world's cultural and natural wonders, as well as millions more to party at the beaches of Sharm el-Sheikh, and that produced Anwar al-Sadat, initiator of the historic peace accord with Israel, Naguib Mahfouz, winner of the Nobel Prize in Literature, and Boutros Boutros-Ghali, former secretary general of the United Nations, among other world-class luminaries. Cairo is one of the most culturally vibrant cities in the Middle East. In 1980 Egypt's constitution was amended to introduce Shari'a as *the* (instead of "a") source of legislation. But this is also the Egypt that on December 31, 1999, hosted the world's largest outdoor concert to celebrate the new millennium, as well as five thousand years of Egyptian civilization—an audiovisual megaspectacle by French electronic music icon Jean Michel Jarre performed at the Grand Pyramids of Giza. Although the literary scene is regulated by government-appointed religious clerics, *The Yacoubian Building* by Alaa Al Aswany freely depicts homosexuality, corruption, and illegal abortion in Cairo and has become the best-selling Arabic novel in recent history.

These intriguing amalgams are widespread in religion-laden polities. The Justice and Development Party (Adalet ve Kalkınma Partisi, AKP), a moderately religious party, is now governing Turkey, a country whose constitution is arguably one of the most militantly secularist constitutions on offer. Iran—commonly perceived as a strict, fundamentalist Islamic republic—is the country where the first major antimonarchist constitutional revolution in the Middle East, dating back to 1906, took place. In 1993 the Iranian Majlis (parliament) approved the Free Zones Act, which established Kish Island, Qeshm Island, and the Port of Chabahar as the Free Zones of Iran: free-trade zones in Iran, each of which offers various perks to the international investor, such as full exemption from "Islamic banking" hurdles, tourist attractions, guaranteed repatriation of capital and accumulated profit in case of nationalization, and other benefits that are, by any stretch of the imagination, not fully compatible with a straightforward reading of Shari'a. In a much-heralded move in 2005, neighboring Kuwait adopted a law that for the first time in its history allows women to vote and to run for parliament. The new law also added, in a generic fashion, that both women voters and candidates must comply with Shari'a law norms. In 2009, four women, two of whom are vocal advocates of women's rights, were elected to the Kuwaiti parliament. Conservatives argued that women who serve in office must dress in accordance with Muslim religious law, with their heads covered. The struggle over women's dress code in parliament even found its way to Kuwait's Constitutional Court (I discuss this case in some detail in Chapter 4). The court had to determine the meaning of the requirement that women voters and elected representatives comply with Shari'a norms. More generally, it had to rule whether Kuwait is governed by religious law, or whether Islam is merely the state religion. (The Constitution of Kuwait [1962] establishes that Islam is "the religion of the state," and that Shari'a is "a main source of legislation.")

Such existential tensions, of course, are not confined to the Islamic world. Israel is arguably one of the world's capitals of embedded, near-oxymoronic contradictions of that nature. The very title of the utopian novel *Altneuland* (The Old New Land, 1902) by Theodor Herzl, the founder of political Zionism, captures some of these existential paradoxes. Israel defines itself as a Jewish and democratic state. Much has been written about this duality, how logically plausible it may be, given the fact that non-Jews make up approximately one-fifth of Israel's citizenry, and how these two foundational tenets may be translated into a fairly coherent set of guidelines for public life. The Supreme Court of Israel has developed rich jurisprudence (which I discuss in some detail in Chapter 4) on formative questions such as "Who is a Jew?" for conversion purposes, the scope of naturalization rights for non-Jewish spouses of Israeli citizens, or the jurisdictional boundaries of rabbinical courts. But everyday-life episodes of the close entanglement of state and religion in Israel seem to tell the story of these complexities better than any grand philosophical accounts. In 2004 Professor Avram Hershko and Aaron Ciechanover of the Technion in Haifa, Israel, won the Nobel Prize in Chemistry for their discovery of ubiquitin-mediated protein degradation. This was the first-ever Nobel Prize awarded to a scientist working in an Israeli university and a foundational event for Israel's scientific community, no doubt. (Israelis had won Nobel Prizes in Literature and Peace; Daniel Kahneman, an Israeli, had won the Nobel Prize in Economic Sciences while he was working at Princeton.) The Swedish Royal Academy happened to announce Hershko and Ciechanover's prize on a Jewish holiday. Instead of holding a major press conference at the Technion, as one would expect, given the moment's grandeur, Technion authorities had to host the press conference with the two laureates at Hershko's private home. It was later revealed that the Technion's rabbi would not allow the university to hold a press conference on the university's premises during the Jewish holiday because by law all public institutions must remain closed on such days. Not even a historic Nobel Prize could change that divine call.

Meanwhile, several notable scholars and prominent politicians have argued that the preamble of a new European constitution should contain a reference to Europe's "Judeo-Christian tradition" so as to avoid an artificial "Christian deficit" that would in turn hinder efforts to create an authentically European political community.[10] In Catholic Europe, the continued prevalence of religious morality sends Poland and Ireland to frequent rendezvous with the European Court of Human Rights (ECtHR). One had only to listen to the reaction of Prime Minister Silvio Berlusconi of Italy to the ruling of the ECtHR in November 2009 (discussed in some detail in Chapter 5) that called for ubiquitous crucifixes to be removed from Italian classrooms—he described it as a "nonsensical attempt to deny Europe's Christian roots" and thus "unacceptable for us Italians"—to understand how Swiss voters' 2009 endorsement of a constitutional amendment that bans the construction of new minarets in that country is anything but an idiosyncratic manifestation of embedded Christian dominance in Europe. And lest we forget, steps from where Berlusconi was speaking in Rome stands the Vatican, the world's undisputed bastion of Catholicism. It has recently reformed its legal system so that as of January 1, 2009, Italian laws no longer apply automatically to the Vatican state (the Holy See). Instead, pertinent Italian laws will be examined by Vatican clerics to determine their compatibility with canon law and Catholic moral principles. This transformation alters the Lateran Pacts of 1929 that made Italian laws automatically applicable in the Vatican state. A senior Vatican canon lawyer, Monsignor José María Serrano Ruiz, has gone on record as saying that Italian laws are too many and too unstable and too often conflict with the moral teachings of the Catholic Church.[11]

Another telling illustration of mixed commitments heralds from South East Asia. A person's wish to convert from one religion to another is considered a private matter in most secular states. However, in Malaysia, things are not that simple. Malaysia is a multiethnic yet formally Islamic state that grants ethnic Malays (all of whom are Muslims) preferential treatment and protects the jurisdictional autonomy of Shari'a courts in an expansive list of personal-status matters pertaining to Muslims, including the politically sensitive issue of conversion to and from Islam. At the same time, religious freedoms for members of all other denominations are constitutionally guaranteed, as interracial harmony has long been the country's official stance. This framework is inherently prone to existential constitutional clashes between the state religion and the rights of non-Muslims. A unique jurisprudential landscape has inevitably formed. In 2007, for example, Malaysia's Federal Court held in the *Lina Joy* case that a Muslim-born woman who claimed to have converted to Christianity cannot convert from Islam to another religion at her own will but must ask the Syariah (Bahasa Malaysia or Malay for Shari'a) courts to contemplate her request and possibly risk a designation as an apostate. Confused? In Chapter 4 I discuss the war currently being waged between Malaysia's Federal Court in charge of enforcing the constitution and its rights provisions and the Syariah courts, which, by law, adjudicate all matters pertaining to personal status, inheritance, apostasy, child custody, and conversion to and from Islam.

The same year that *Lina Joy* was decided a Catholic newspaper in Malaysia used the word "Allah" to refer to God in its Malay-language edition. A controversy arose regarding who may use the word "Allah"—whether it is an exclusively Muslim word as some Muslim leaders in Malaysia suggest or a neutral term referring to One God that may be used by all regardless of their religion as the newspaper argued. A law to ban the use of the term in reference to God by non-Muslims was enacted in the 1980s, but had seldom been enforced prior to 2007. On December 31, 2009 (quite symbolically), the high court in Kuala Lumpur ruled that the ban on non-Muslims using the word "Allah" to refer to God was unconstitutional as it infringed on freedom of expression and freedom of religion principles. The court went on to state that the word "Allah" is the correct word for "God" in various Malay translations of the Bible, and that it has been used for centuries by Christians and Muslims alike in Arabic-speaking countries. This ruling was viewed by radical Islamists as a legitimation of deceitful attempts to convert Muslims to Christianity. Riots and church burning ensued. The government appealed the high-court ruling, and the implementation of the decision has been suspended until the appeal is heard.

Although core predicaments and jurisprudential clashes of that sort may be captivating, they do not capture all the complexities in such settings. The secular/theocratic rift itself is often not only about worldviews, modernism versus tradition, or sources of authority but also about distribution of material resources, access to government funding, and employment opportunities. To begin with, the potential of desecularized laws is in many respects bad for business. Religious directives are generally not very conducive to a modern market economy. Islam's prohibition of interest or usury is only one illustration. Some religious directives are simply old, obsolete, or irrelevant in today's high-tech markets. Others are based on individual or small-scale economic premises that are not suitable for a multitrillion-dollar, interconnected, globalized economy. Still others advance restrained or collectivist normative stands that are not in line with prevalent notions of megacapitalism, individualism, and conspicuous consumerism.

Because most religion-based economics are not in accord with modern economic theory, international markets, monetary bodies, and financial institutions—the World Trade Organization, the World Bank, and the International Monetary Fund, for example—are not keen on them. The tourism industry, perhaps with the exception of a few chain hotels in Rome, Jerusalem, or Mecca, resents it. (If one looks at the other side's perspective, it is little wonder that the targets of so many incidents of sectarian violence have been fancy hotels and resorts, from Sharm El-Sheikh to Mumbai and from Bali to Islamabad to Mombasa.) More generally, strict religious law is not helpful, to put it mildly, in supporting a country's international economic reputation. It would be reasonable to assume, for example, that despite the formal constitutional entrenchment of Shari'a precepts, most upper-class Qataris are not very enthusiastic about turning their heavenly paradise—Qatar is one of the most affluent places on earth—into a distinctly more religious polity that would require them to give up much of its impressive economic and international success. In Dubai, a member of the United Arab Emirates (UAE), Islam is a marker of collective identity, but ultra-conservative Islamic morality is not exactly the mantra Dubai's politicians or its investors and high-end commercial managers (for example, of Burj Khalifa, the tallest free-standing structure in the world, or Dubailand, the world's largest amusement park, twice as big as Disney World) wish to recite. Abu Dhabi (capital of the UAE) and Bahrain are two of the glossy locations of the Formula One world racing tour, with all the ultracommercialization that comes with it. Fly Emirates, as the commercial slogan goes. And, despite all the differences, the image of a predominantly religious polity clearly does not aid Turkey's bid to join the European Union.

But the political economy of the secular/religious divide stretches well beyond the apparent incompatibility of a conservative reading of religious precepts with principles of modern economy. As Ernest Gellner famously observed, the ruling classes in what he called agroliterate states often control state institutions and use artifacts like high culture or modernism to underwrite social structure, distancing themselves from nonmembers of the national elite.[12] This logic sheds light on some of the interests at play in the secularist/religious divide. A plausible but often-overlooked reason that secularists or moderates resent theocratic government is the potential redistributive implications of such a regime. In countries such as Israel, Malaysia, Turkey, and Egypt the clash between secularists and religionists has an important center-versus-periphery economic-distribution dimension to it. In terms of demographic indicators, support for religious parties in these countries is often closely associated with the relative have-nots and is distinctly more prevalent among occupiers of the sidelines, economic and cultural. Secularism and cosmopolitanism, on the other hand, are often associated with the metaphorical center. It often comprises old elites, the urban intelligentsia, and the managerial class and is characteristic of the relative haves, members of the upper socioeconomic echelons. Granted, support for religion-infused political agendas has not been confined to lower socioeconomic groups. In several instances religious parties, perhaps by virtue of their participation in the formal political process, are led by pragmatic moderate leaders, not by fundamentalist zealots. Turkey's AKP and the similarly named Justice and Development Party in Morocco (Parti de la Justice et du Développement, PJD) illustrate this trend. Still, in virtually all pertinent settings religious parties draw many more followers from denizens of the political, economic, and cultural periphery than from occupants of the political, economic, and cultural core.

In short, principles of theocratic governance may pose a threat to the cultural propensities and policy preferences of secular-nationalist elites and the often-pragmatist bureaucracy and state apparatus, as well as of powerful economic stakeholders in these countries. Theocratic governance has seldom appealed to members of the often-cosmopolitan urban intelligentsia and the managerial class. At the same time, theocratic governance is also often at odds with principles of modern economics and may threaten the interests of major economic sectors and stakeholders. The contrast between the "Muezzin's call" and the "Dow Jones bell" is a telling metaphor in that respect.[13] Pragmatic state bureaucrats may see theocratic governance as an impediment to progress and modernization. It would be an understatement to say that theocratic governments are not the type of regimes that find favor with supranational trade and monetary bodies. With few exceptions, theocracy has been and remains detested by the military—a symbol of modern nationalism in many developing polities. The powerful Turkish, Pakistani, and Algerian militaries are only three of many examples that come to mind here. The global spread of international human rights norms and watchdog organizations further pressures regimes to implement modernizing reforms and to limit the spread of distinctly antiliberal and antimodernist aspects of theocratic governance. Finally, the prospect of theocratic government has potentially far-reaching power-shifting implications, both symbolic and material.

From this an uneasy alliance of anti- or atheocratic forces emerges that seeks to tame the spread of religious fundamentalism and defuse attempts to establish a full-fledged theocracy. It comprises secularist or moderately religious political leaders and parties; statist bureaucrats; powerful economic stakeholders, corporations, and the managerial classes; judges and jurists; and, at times, the nationalist military. Each of these groups brings to the table its own worldviews, interests, and communities of reference, and at times there is an embedded distrust between two or more of them—for example, between state bureaucrats and free marketeers, or between supporters of political liberalization and the military (think Turkey or Pakistan). But the threat of theocratic governance drives these groups to leave their animosity toward each other for better days and to collaborate tacitly so as to keep their eyes on the religious ball, so to speak. At the same time, as support for religious parties and policies increases, religious talk of some kind—and it had better come across as genuine—becomes ever more essential to maintaining some of these elites' popular legitimacy and political hegemony.

These conflicting pressures, opinions, and interests have led to intense constitutional maneuvering and interpretive innovation in polities that face deep rifts along secular/religious lines. Therefore, constitutional theocracy has emerged, to some extent as a genuine attempt at aspirational constitutionalism committed to a set of pious principles with a strong ideational outlook, but at the same time also driven, at least in part, by strategic, instrumentalist, irreverent constitutionalism aimed at containing the spread of theocratic government and bringing religious institutions under state control. Granting religion formal constitutional status is not only a legitimacy-enhancing move that appeases popular pressures; it also neutralizes religion's revolutionary sting, co-opts its leaders, ensures state input in the translation of religious precepts into guidelines for public life, helps mutate sacred law and manipulate religious discourse to serve powerful interests, and, above all, brings an alternative, even rival order of authority under state control and supervision.

A range of constitutional strategies have been developed by those who wield political power—and represent the groups and policy preferences that defy principles of theocratic governance—to hedge or mitigate the impact of religiosity on politics and public policy. This is done in different ways in different places because of variance in different countries' constitutional legacy, political culture, and power struggles. But taken as a whole, these forms of constitutional ingenuity allow non- or antitheocratic elites and leaders to talk the talk of commitment to religious values without walking much of the actual walk of that commitment. As a result, constitutional law and courts in virtually all such polities have become bastions of relative secularism, pragmatism, and moderation, thereby emerging as effective shields against the spread of religiosity and increased popular support for principles of theocratic governance. In other words, akin to constitutional democracy, where the former element establishes a core set of entrenched limitations on the scope, nature, and range of possible outcomes of the latter element, constitutionalism in predominantly religious settings plays a key role in curbing the spread and impact of theocratic governance, with its alternative worldviews, texts, and hierarchies of authority. Just as in constitutional democracy the "constitutional" keeps in check the "democracy" aspect, so does the "constitutional" in constitutional theocracy limit the spread of theocratic governance in settings prone to such expansion.

Formal establishment of religion may be portrayed as surrender to religion, but in reality it helps limit the potentially radical impact of religion by bringing it under state control. The constitutionalization of religion and the consequent subjection of religious authority to state scrutiny turn legal and political considerations into key determinants in the evolution of religious law. This process makes the state (and its courts) a key player in picking religion's official interpretive authorities and jurists and gives the state a stake in the interpretive game. The pacifying co-optation impulse may explain why, quite counterintuitively, countries facing increasing support for principles of theocratic governance may elect to become constitutional theocracies.

Constitutional law and courts may be a rational secularist endeavor in other respects. Restrictive constitutional provisions have been used to delegitimize and exclude unwelcome religion-based political association. Even if the jurisdiction of constitutional courts is formally religious in some sense, it will inevitably reflect a less militant view of religious identity. In addition, the very logic of constitutionalism, with its very reasoned set of core tenets and prevalent modes of interpretation, makes it an attractive enterprise to those who wish to contain religiosity and assert state or civil society authority over religious texts, worldviews, and interpretive hierarchies. Effective political control over, as well as better access to, the constitutional arena also makes it attractive to secularists, modernists, and statists who seek to keep religious authority in check. Consequently, constitutional law and courts have become the natural companions of these groups and their political representatives in their struggle against the spread of principles of extreme theocratic governance.

Strikingly, current comparative constitutional law scholarship seldom addresses constitutional theocracies. Several works begin to investigate the vast terrain explored in this book. Nathan Brown's illuminating, politically astute studies of constitutions in the Middle East see constitutional institutions in the region as archetypal of those in authoritarian settings.[14] The focus is on the "Arab world" (understood in the area-studies sense of the term) and the lack of democratic tradition in it. If constitutional courts are established and supported by a regime in the region, this is done mainly to enhance state capacity and regime control. Religion and secularism do not play a key role in this matrix. Olivier Roy's and Gilles Kepel's seminal works focus on the main tenets and embedded problems of global jihad, and political Islam more generally, with little attention to constitutional structures or constitutional politics, let alone jurisprudence or the role of courts.[15] Noah Feldman's widely recognized work skillfully debunks the notion of the "clash of civilizations" by pointing to important conceptual and historical overlaps, not just contradictions, between democracy and Islam.[16] But in comparative constitutional law and politics the silence is deafening. Despite the growing scholarly interest in, and burgeoning literature on, comparative constitutional law and the international migration of constitutional ideas, we still know little about constitutional law and politics in countries where the potentially explosive combination of modern constitutionalism and the fundamentals of theocratic governance come together. Like early maps of the world where tracts of emptiness cover much of the non-Western world, the jurisprudential landscape of constitutional theocracies, as well as constitutional and judicial politics in such polities more generally, remains a terra incognita of sorts, almost completely uncharted, let alone theorized.

Aspects of the constitutional law of religion closer to home are frequently addressed by scholars in the West. Debates over the accommodation of religious diversity in Europe are plentiful. Virtually every French, Dutch, or German politician or intellectual sports a learned opinion on this and related predicaments. The debates are outnumbered only by the numerous scholarly and journalistic accounts of the place of religion in the U.S. Constitution and American public life; dozens of books and hundreds of academic articles are published every year on the First Amendment's Free Exercise Clause and Establishment Clause. However, notwithstanding the increasing prevalence of constitutionalism and principles of theocratic governance in the nonsecular world, very few works have explored the intersection among constitutional law, religion, and politics in the new world of constitutional theocracies, with their competing commitments, conflicting worldviews, and rival visions of the "good sociopolitical order."[17] Rich, theoretically sophisticated, innovative works on the ethics, morality, and practice of religious law—most notably canon law, Jewish law, and Islamic law—are plenty. The study of Islamic jurisprudence and legal theory, in particular, has enjoyed a tremendous renaissance in North America over the last two decades.[18] However, with very few exceptions, relevant studies tend to focus either on the theological or internal aspects of religious law, thus catering mainly to specialty scholars of religion (doctrinal studies of Jewish or Islamic law are good examples of this insular tendency), or on constitutional politics in a single country or region, thus reaching only specific country- or area-studies scholars.

In addition to the traditional disciplinary boundaries that often characterize academic discourse, this lacuna is also due in part to the fact that populist academic and media accounts in the West tend to portray the spread of religious fundamentalism in the developing world as a near-monolithic, one-dimensional, and all-encompassing phenomenon, as I stated earlier. In practice, however, the picture in most predominantly religious polities—be they Islamic, Jewish, Roman Catholic, or Hindu—is much more complex and nuanced, reflecting deep divisions and strife along secular/religious lines, as well as widely divergent beliefs, interpretations, and degrees of practice within religious communities. In fact, most countries that have experienced a revival of religious fundamentalism have long been caught between identities, worldviews, and commitments that are at once secular-nationalist and religious, universalist and particularist. In virtually all these countries the very nature of the sociopolitical order has been highly contested. Civic-nationalist ideology, principles of modern economics, relatively cosmopolitan lifestyles, and diverse worldviews and policy preferences all strive to establish or maintain their hegemony vis-à-vis embedded symbols of tradition, religiosity, and exceptionalism.

In short, constitutional theocracies and, by extension, the emerging global encounter of constitutionalism and religion more generally are a Galapagos-like paradise for scholars of comparative constitutional law and politics. They reflect a sociopolitical order under constant duress. We often see striking tensions between the rule of law and the rule of God, cosmopolitanism and parochialism, economic interests and public will, modern government and religious authorities, new constitutions and ancient texts, and judicial and pious interpretation. A unique hybrid of apparently conflicting worldviews, values, and interests, constitutional theocracies thus offer an ideal setting—a living laboratory, as it were—for studying constitutional law as a form of politics by other means.

In this book I combine insights from legal theory, economics, theology, and political sociology with a genuinely comparative analysis of religion-and-state jurisprudence from dozens of countries worldwide to explore the evolving role of constitutional law and courts in a nonsecularist world. Emphasis is put on the largely unexplored universe of constitutional design and jurisprudence in the increasingly large number of polities caught between the popular resurgence of religion and overarching principles of modern constitutionalism—two of the most powerful ideas of our time, an odd couple of sorts, diametrically opposed in many respects, but at the same time sharing strikingly similar characteristics, each with its own sacred texts, interpretive practices, and communities of reference. The numerous examples explored herein know no borders; they stretch from antiquity to the present day, from the banal and familiar to the exotic and spectacular, from the tiniest sects to the most established religions, from remote archipelagoes to the most powerful nations, and from new courts and constitutions to the oldest constitutional orders known.

The discussion focuses on several core questions. How are we to explain the recent resurgence of constitutional enshrinement of religion in so many countries in the developing world, in stark contrast to its confinement to the private sphere and the demise of the theological-political form of governance in much of the West? Why are constitutional courts so appealing to antireligious social forces in polities that face deep divisions along secular/religious lines? What has been the role of constitutional law and courts in co-opting and mutating the interpretation of religious precepts—theoretically derived from sacred sources—to reflect the interests of influential political and economic stakeholders and the modern state? What are the unique characteristics of the emerging theocratic-infused constitutional jurisprudence, and how is the expansion of religious law tempered through it? What are the differences and similarities between the role of constitutional law and courts in theocratic and nontheocratic settings? Are there nonpious (e.g., political and economic) origins to doctrinal change, jurisdictional wars, and intra- and interfaith clashes within and between the religious and the constitutional domains? And how are we to explain the conceptual and sociolegal parallels between constitutional and religious interpretive approaches?

I address these questions through five different lenses. In Chapter 2 I place the rise of constitutional theocracy in the context of other models—from the distant past to the present day; Christian, Muslim, Hindu, and Jewish; and from east, west, north, and south—for arranging religion and state relations. I point to some serious shortcomings of canonical constitutional theory in accounting for the jurisprudential and sociopolitical realities of the secular/theocratic rift in a nonliberal context. Constitutional theocracy is only one of several main templates for addressing religion-and-state relations, but there is a strong echo of religion in each and all of these models. In fact, all constitutions, from France to Iran and anywhere in between, address the issue of religion head-on. Some constitutions despise it, others embrace or even defer to it, and still others are agnostic but are willing to accommodate certain aspects of it, but not a single constitution abstains from, overlooks, or remains otherwise silent with respect to religion. With the exception of the concrete organizing principles and prerogatives of the polity's governing institutions, the only substantive domain addressed by all modern constitutions is religion. What could be a more telling illustration of religion's omnipresence in today's world or a stronger testament to constitutionalism's existential fear of religion?

In Chapter 3 I explore the secularist appeal of constitutional law and courts. I identify six broad rationales—from the most abstract epistemological platform to the most concrete political level—that make these institutions attractive to secularist, modernist, cosmopolitan, and other antireligious social forces in polities that face deep divisions along secular/religious lines: (1) co-optation; (2) jurisdictional advantages; (3) strategic delegation; (4) the very nature and characteristics of constitutional law, its epistemology, and its interpretive logic; (5) constitutional delegitimation of radical religious association; and (6) political control of constitutional courts and judges. Drawing on all these rationales, the state, even in the most theocratic settings let alone in more lax ones, invests tremendous energy in bringing religion under constitutional check.

In Chapter 4 I examine in considerable detail how constitutional courts in seven countries featuring widespread popular support for political religion (Egypt, Kuwait, Pakistan, Malaysia, Nigeria, Israel, and Turkey)—each court within the different constitutional framework and political context in which it operates—advance secular or secularizing solutions to problems of state and religion. To that end, courts in these countries have developed extraordinary interpretive ingenuity, the richness of which makes the vibrant interpretive debates in the United States look rather meager. To press forward with their religion-taming agenda, courts in these countries have been engaged in zealous jurisdictional wars unseen in any liberal constitutional setting. I also show how and why, under certain politically charged circumstances, constitutional courts in these and similarly situated polities may side with religion law and authorities against their own secularist, religion-subjugating tilt.

In Chapter 5 I show how constitutional law and courts in several nontheocratic settings—from the battle over religious attire in Europe to the struggle over reproductive freedoms in Colombia and Mexico, the status of customary law in South Africa, and the erection of boundaries to multicultural accommodation in Canada—essentially display the same secularist sentiment as their counterparts in predominantly religious settings. Courts in these polities, each operating in a different political context and preoccupied with a distinct state-and-religion challenge of their own, have nonetheless positioned themselves at the secularist end of the acceptable continuum in each of their respective polities. Even some of the most accommodating polities—think of South Africa's "rainbow nation" or Canada's "mosaic" conception of citizenship—are open to diversity-as-inclusion claims but resist nonstate-law-as-competition claims that seek to establish "islands of jurisdictions" lying outside the governance of the state and its official agents. Constitutional courts worldwide share a secularist tilt relative to the context within which they operate.

In Chapter 6 I suggest that although constitutional law and religion law seem fundamentally different from each other, they ultimately have much more in common than meets the eye. The conceptual affinity between "originalist" and "living-tree" interpretive approaches in the two domains is only one example, but there are several other core commonalities, conceptual and political, between constitutionalism and religion, and the concrete interests, some quite profane, that drive their respective institutions, epistemic communities, and interpretive practices. These may help us understand why and how these two domains mutate, collaborate, or fight each other to address ideational platforms, economic interests, or political aspirations.

I conclude by stressing the significance of the lessons learned from this comparative inquiry into the intersection of religion, state, and constitutionalism for the study of constitutional law and politics in a nonsecularist world. Ultimately, I argue that however challenging the quandaries and disharmonies of constitutional theocracy may be, they pale compared with the tectonic political pressures created by the increasing popular support for principles of theocratic governance and the corresponding need for some religious talk, or even policies, to maintain political legitimacy and appease religious pressures, when stacked against the bundle of powerful antireligious interests and stakeholders. More than anything else, I argue, constitutional theocracy is a political phenomenon, not a theological or juridical one. It may seem an oxymoronic, even potentially explosive compound, but from an antitheocratic point of view it is ultimately a rational solution to the mounting pressures of political religion with its alternative cultural, political, and distributive agenda. The constitutional incorporation of religious directives, I suggest, is not done for the pure love of religion. It is a response and at times even preemptive move aimed at appropriating religion to counter fundamentalist threats. As support for theocratic governance continues to grow, religious establishment becomes an increasingly attractive, lesser-evil solution for secularists, statists, modernists, and other religion-taming interests that strive to protect or advance their agendas in a nonsecularist world.

At the most abstract level, the rise of constitutional theocracy provides insights into the political construction of constitutional law and courts and the key role of these institutions in taming the spread and limiting the impact of theocratic politics in predominantly religious settings. The rise of constitutional theocracy, much like the process of separation of church and state before it, is merely another stage, a politically driven synthesis that is already becoming the new thesis throughout much of the developing world in the ongoing tug-of-war between two of the most powerful belief systems of our time. Turning to constitutional law and courts to bring religiosity under check or defuse its potentially radical edge is a rational choice of action by secularists and moderates. Despite occasional and inevitable setbacks, it is a prudent, judicious gamble.

At a more concrete level, however, I suggest that the key to understanding why constitutionalism may be effective in taming the impact of religious thought lies in the similarity, not the difference, between constitutionalism and religion. Although constitutionalism and religion are often portrayed as diametrically opposed or at least unrelated domains, they are in fact two analogous symbolic, but also workaday, systems—each with its own constitutive texts, sets of beliefs, high priests, and earthly interests—that vie to establish, maintain, or enhance their hegemony, worldviews, and preferences vis-à-vis each other. Precisely because constitutionalism is a religion-like domain, a civic faith with its high priests, constitutive texts, and interpretive institutions, fostered by the modern state and the international community, it is distinctly better positioned than blunter, ostensibly more forceful means to defuse, mutate, co-opt, or mitigate principles of theocratic governance. As a de facto civic religion, the constitutional scripture may be an effective counterpoint to a religious scripture.

But before I turn to address these big ideas, two preliminary queries ought to be dealt with: What is the place of constitutional theocracy in the broader matrix of religion-and-state relations worldwide? And what exactly is the theocratic challenge to conventional constitutional theory? Let the erudite journey begin.

CHAPTER TWO

Constitutional Theocracy in Context

As every amateur historian acknowledges, religion and politics were closely allied, indeed, often inseparable and unified, throughout much of pre-eighteenth-century human history. The gradual transition from an abstract, omnipresent, and near-communal perception of divine powers to the separate but often-symbiotic existence of the political and the religious appears to have started about 3,500 years ago with the initial emergence of embryonic forms of what may be termed state power.[1] That ancient cultures are often perceived as, well, ancient, medieval Europe, where "it was virtually impossible not to believe in God," is perhaps the most vivid illustration of the close entanglement of religion and politics in the pre-modern world.[2] Religion was embedded in the political and social fabric of the community and was integral to, and inseparable from, everything else. The prevalence of theological politics in medieval Europe was reflected in virtually all aspects of life of the time, from economics and jurisprudence to architecture, culture, and the arts. The spread of monasticism in the early Middle Ages, the rise of Byzantium (Eastern Roman Empire) in the sixth to eighth centuries, the crusades of the eleventh to the thirteenth centuries, and the themes of Raphael's, Botticelli's, and Michelangelo's paintings during the High Renaissance of the early sixteenth century are popular illustrations of the centrality of religion and its governing institutions in premodern Europe's political and public life. Occasional attempts to establish pure theocracies took place in various parts of Europe. Two examples are the Savonarola reign in Florence (1494–1498), and the Anabaptist Kingdom of Münster (1534–1535).

The sixteenth century also brought to the fore the doctrine of royal absolutism, the "divine right of kings," according to which a monarch was the ultimate authority in both political and spiritual matters and was subject to no earthly authority but derived his right to rule directly from the will of God. The king was thus not perceived as subject to the will of his people, the aristocracy, or any other estate of the realm, including the church. This doctrine implied that any attempt to depose the king or to restrict his powers ran contrary to the will of God and could constitute treason. The doctrine reached its zenith in the seventeenth century during the reign of King James I in England and King Louis XIV of France. Meanwhile, religion wars in late medieval Europe, most notably the French Wars of Religion in the second half of the sixteenth century (ending with the Edict of Nantes, 1592) over claims for accommodation and access to wealth and power between Catholics and Huguenots, are said to have cost the lives of hundreds of thousands of people, perhaps as many as two million.

The idea of closely tied but parallel political and religious leadership existed in several early civilizations as well. In most ancient cultures in the Near and Middle East, for example, Egypt, Canaan, and Mesopotamia, the predominant religious model was polytheism, which centered on the cult of regional patron deities. By contrast, the ancient Israelite kings, for example, were not deified and seldom assumed any priestly functions. There are close ties but also a clear distinction between the Israelite kings as state rulers and the pastors *(cohanim)* and prophets *(nevi'im)* as religious authorities. Philosopher judges *(shoftim)* turned political leaders were raised up at critical moments to fight Israel's battles and judge the people.[3] Separation of the political and the religious also characterized the postbiblical period in ancient Israelite history (the Persian period circa 538 B.C.E. to circa 332 B.C.E., and later for the first 160 years of the Hellenistic period, circa 331 B.C.E. to circa 169 B.C.E., with the rise of the Hasmonean dynasty). Upon the return of Israelites from exile in Babylon (following the fall of Babylon and the Koresh Declaration, circa 536 B.C.E.), for example, the leadership was shared between Zerubbabel as the civic authority and Joshua as the high priest. This distinction between religious and political leadership became fuzzier later on, but was re-established after the end of the Second Temple Period in 70 C.E. Likewise, in the Jewish *kehila* (community) in medieval and early modern Europe, religious shepherding and political guidance were theoretically separate but remained closely entwined. Jewish statelessness helped maintain the distinction between intracommunity spiritual guidance and more earthly affairs negotiated with or dictated by the gentile authorities. Except for a few episodes of false prophecy—for example, the seventeenth-century rise and fall of Shabbetai Tsvi, who professed himself to be the long-awaited Jewish Messiah, only to convert to Islam when God refused to collaborate—separation of religious leadership and political leadership has long characterized the Jewish tradition.[4]

The premodern Islamic world had its own experiments with relations of state and religion. The Constitution of Medina—commonly considered to have established the first Islamic state—was drafted by the Prophet Muhammad circa 622 C.E. It formed an alliance among several local tribes (pagan at the time) and Muslim emigrants from Mecca. The community defined in the Constitution of Medina—the *ummah* (nation)—had a distinctly religious outlook. It sought to replace tribal identities as the main binding tie among people with a new-created nation where faith served as the foundational binding concept. At the same time, the Constitution of Medina, while certainly not envisioning any distinction between the religious and the political or featuring any remote resemblance to modern constitutions, did address earthly issues such as taxation and day-to-day governance. It specified the rights and duties of citizens, as well as the relationship between Muslim and non-Muslim communities, most notably Jews. Importantly, it also distinguished between the polity's wars, which were binding on non-Muslim members of the polity, and wars of the Muslims, from which non-Muslims were exempt. Still, the Constitution of Medina was an exercise in theological politics, where the distinction between divine and political authority was vague at best. Innovation, historical contingencies, and struggles within caliphate dynasties from the late 7th century to the demise of the Ottoman Empire, brought about considerable variation in the relations between theocratic and political government.

In the modern era the short-lived Law of the Tunisian State (1861–1864) is considered the first written constitution in the Muslim world.[5] It combined some Islamic elements with reference to nonreligious sources of sovereignty alongside principles for fiscal and administrative organization of the state. At the other end of the continuum, the Mahdiyah (1884–1898) was a short-lived theocratic state in most of the territory of today's Sudan. Driven by the political and military aspirations of Muhammad Ahmad, known as the "Mahdi," the Mahdiyah was a hierarchical state, run like a military operation. It was entangled in an ongoing war with the Anglo-Egyptian army led initially by Charles "Chinese" Gordon and after Gordon's death in Khartoum by Lord Herbert Kitchener. (In 1898 Kitchener defeated the Khalifa, the Mahdi's successor, and reestablished British rule over the Sudan.) The Mahdi modified Islam's five pillars to support the dogma that loyalty to him was essential to true belief. The Mahdi also added the declaration "and Muhammad Ahmad is the Mahdi of God and the representative of His Prophet" to the recitation of the creed, the Shahada. Moreover, service in the jihad replaced the *hajj* (pilgrimage to Mecca) as a duty incumbent on the faithful. *Zakat* (almsgiving) became the tax paid to the state. The Mahdi justified these and other innovations and reforms as responses to instructions conveyed to him by God in visions. Interestingly, the tension between religion and other forces, most notably nationalism, played itself out even in this theocratic setting. Alongside strong Islamism, the Mahdiyah has become known as the first genuine Sudanese nationalist government. The Mahdi maintained that his movement was not a religious order that could be accepted or rejected at will but a universal regime that challenged mankind to join or to be destroyed.

Arguably the most noteworthy pioneering experiment with constitutionalism in the Muslim world took place in Iran in the early twentieth century. The Islamic Republic of Iran is commonly considered a fundamentalist theocracy, with governing principles and practices that bear very little resemblance to prevailing principles of Western constitutionalism. However, its system of government features many elements of modern constitutionalism. In fact, Iran has a long legacy of constitutionalism. Toward the end of the nineteenth century the established feudal-like nobility, religious authorities, and the emerging educated elites began to demand a curb on royal authority and the establishment of the rule of law. In late 1905 a mutiny erupted, led by a coalition of Tehran merchants and supported by the clergy. It ultimately forced the corrupt, extravagant, and at times dysfunctional late reign of the Qajar dynasty to agree to constitutional limits on its power. In August 1906 Mozaffareddin Shah agreed to allow the establishment of a parliament, the Majlis. In the fall of that year the first elections were held. The First Majlis was established in October 1906 and immediately declared itself a constitutional assembly. Because the shah's political clout and influence were on the wane, a new constitution was introduced on December 31, 1906, modeled primarily on European constitutions, mainly the Belgian Constitution. The shah was from then on "under the rule of law," and the crown became a divine gift given to the shah by the people.

The 1906 Imperial Constitution, as it has come to be known, had been in effect for over seven decades when the 1979 Islamic revolution erupted. Much of the institutional nexus it established has been a part of Iranian political life for over a century now. It stipulated that sovereignty came from the people, symbolized in the person of the monarch. It stated that an elected parliament should ensure that this power was represented through the deputies and should be implemented through the laws enacted by them. It also established a bicameral legislature and set up detailed electoral rules and procedures. Articles 1 and 2 of the supplementary fundamental laws of 1907 established Islam as the official religion of Iran and specified that all laws of the nation must be approved by a committee of Shi'a clerics. That the Pahlavi dynasty ignored this directive in the later part of the twentieth century was one of the reasons for the Islamic revolution of 1979, which, among other things, replaced the 1906 constitution with a new one.

Meanwhile, in Europe the Protestant Reformation of the sixteenth and early seventeenth centuries, with its emphasis on breaking down the invidious political structures of the Catholic Church, is often thought of as the birth point of the secular age.[6] However, the big transformation of state-and-religion relations did not occur before the late seventeenth and early eighteenth centuries. In the late seventeenth century Spinoza and other rationalists started to raise persuasive arguments against theology-induced politics. Because of a confluence of more concrete political, economic, societal, and technological factors—all are widely documented by historians of Western civilization—republican ideas and modern nationalism started to gain momentum in Europe and among European settlers in the New World. Consequently, the unified theological-political pact of the Middle Ages began to implode. The theory of divine right was abandoned in England during the Glorious Revolution of 1688–1689, alongside the imposition of certain constitutional limitations on the monarch's power and authority.

The eighteenth century saw the emergence of a doctrine of separation of church and state, advocated by Enlightenment thinkers as a means of confining dangerous and irrational religious passions to the private sphere. Whereas the public sphere was portrayed as the realm of reason, the private sphere began to be regarded as the realm of faith, superstition, and other such nonverifiable beliefs. In creating its characteristic division between secular public space and religious private space, European secularism sought to shuffle religious ritual and discipline into the private realm.[7] This distinction, however reductionist and otherwise problematic, has come to be identified as the secularist state's defining marker. With the American and French revolutions of the late eighteenth century, the form of the absolute monarchy with feudal privileges for the aristocracy and for the Catholic clergy in Europe underwent a radical change based on Enlightenment principles of secularist nationalism, citizenship, inalienable rights, and the strict separation of church and state. Throughout the twentieth century the ideal of separation of religion and state became prevalent in what is termed the West. However, in practice, as Charles Taylor notes, secularism never completely banished religion. The religious has never been lost in Western culture, let alone in other cultures; it has only become one of many stories striving for acceptance.[8]

Extant Models of State and Religion Relations

A taxonomy of contemporary approaches to govern religion and state relations suggests at least nine archetypical models may be identified, ranging from atheism or strict separation to weak establishment, and from models of jurisdictional enclaves to strong establishment, or parallel governance of constitutionalism and religion. I briefly discuss each in turn.

At the antireligious end of the continuum of state-and-religion models we find the position of Communist regimes. At least at the declaratory level, such regimes hold an atheist position that associates religion in both the public and the private spheres with backwardness, colonialism, and false consciousness. The Communist-atheist vision thus advocates, at least at a principled level, a concentrated effort by the state to eliminate religion. The establishment of the People's Republic of China in 1949, for example, was accompanied by a campaign to eradicate religion from Chinese life and culture. China's attitude toward religion was relaxed considerably in the late 1970s with the 1978 constitution's formal guarantee of freedom of religion. In Ethiopia the Ethiopian Orthodox Church was disestablished as the state church in 1974, and its patriarch was executed by the Marxist Derg military junta in 1979. The introduction of strict antireligious laws followed a military junta's ferocious overthrow of Emperor Haile Selassie, believed by some to be descendant of King Solomon and the queen of Sheba, who was a sacred figure for the Rastafarian movement in Jamaica and negotiated the autocephaly of the Ethiopian Orthodox Church. A move in the opposite direction may be seen in the Russian state of the post-Communist era, which, unlike the days of the Soviet Union, is no longer antireligious, has become passively secularist, and even has affirmative relations with the Orthodox Church.[9]

With regard to the formal place of religion in the modern West, the long-standing French policy of *laïcité* is arguably the clearest manifestation of the desire to restrict clerical and religious influence over the state and to establish a uniform, religion-free citizenship and nationhood.[10] It establishes a form of assertive, even militant secularism that goes beyond neutrality toward religion or even a declared areligiosity to advance an explicitly secular civic religion that resents manifestations of religion in all avenues of public life (but not in the relatively narrowly defined private sphere) and views secularism as a core element of the modern nation and its members' collective identity. This form of secularism tied to the polity's collective identity is accompanied by an explicitly assimilationist approach to citizenship and national identity. With the changing demographics of French society, a multicultural challenge to France's secularism has emerged, but the resistance to diversity as inclusion prevails and has led, in France's case, to blunt antireligious statements by government officials (including former President Jacques Chirac), as well as to national legislation that uncompromisingly bans the display in public schools of any "conspicuous religious symbols" (including the Islamic headscarf).[11]

Turkey, which I discuss in detail in Chapter 4, provides another example of such assertive, even militant, secularism. The secularization of predominantly religious Turkey, led by Mustafa Kemal Atatürk, is perhaps the best-known example of separationist reformism in the twentieth century. After the demise of the Ottoman Empire the Kemalist secular-nationalist elite rejected Islamic culture and laws in favor of secularism and modernism. Accordingly, the words "the religion of the Turkish State is Islam" were removed from the constitution in 1928. In 1937 the words "republican, popular, atheist, secular, and reformist" were inserted into the constitution to better reflect modern Turkey's adherence to a strict separation of state and religion. Both the 1961 and the 1982 constitutions established an official state policy of laicism. This official policy has become a linchpin of modern Turkish identity but has been challenged by the moderately religious AKP-led government, as illustrated by the constitutional amendment of February 2008 that effectively lifted the ban on wearing the Islamic headscarf in the public education system. However, in June 2008 the Turkish Constitutional Court declared that amendment unconstitutional and restored the strictly secularist nature of the Turkish Constitution.

In most other countries where formal separation of church and state exists, a third, less assertive, secularism-as-neutrality mode emerged that emphasizes the state's impartial, neutral stance toward religious creeds rather than active advancement of secularism per se. Although religion has always been a core element of American society and culture, the First Amendment to the U.S. Constitution provides that "Congress shall make no law respecting an establishment of religion, or prohibiting the free exercise thereof." The Establishment Clause prohibits the state from adopting, preferring, or endorsing a religion, as well as from preferring religion over nonreligion (the nonestablishment principle); the Free Exercise Clause enjoins the state from interfering with the religious freedom of its citizens (the principle of freedom of religious expression). There is an inherent tension between a command not to establish religion and a command not to inhibit its practice. However, both clauses advance neutrality toward religion by preventing the government from singling out specific religious sects for special benefits or burdens unless the action is necessary to promote a compelling interest.

At the same time, comparative polls often suggest that Americans are among the most likely people in the West to refer to God, depend on divine authority for decision-making guidance, or otherwise draw on religious morality or principles in their everyday lives. "In God We Trust" is on all American currency; each Supreme Court session begins with the invocation "God save the United States and this Honorable Court";[12] and a copy of the Gideon Bible is in virtually every hotel room in America. Given such disharmony, to borrow Gary Jacobsohn's phrase, it is hardly surprising that over its many years of existence the U.S. Supreme Court has issued hundreds of landmark rulings on the scope and nature of each of the two clauses, as well as on their intersection with each other and with other constitutional provisions.[13]

In several other "immigrant-society" democracies, most notably Canada and postapartheid South Africa, a fourth, softer version of the formal separation accompanied by a true commitment to multiculturalism and diversity (a mosaic or accommodationist rather than a melting pot or assimilationist approach) has emerged, whereby state and religion are separated, but the conception of citizenship is not tied to strict secularism or neutrality. The true sense of citizenship, and indeed of liberalism more generally, is perceived here as respect for the common aspects of statehood and nationality while celebrating the difference in citizens' cultural, linguistic, and religious traditions. In that regard, Section 2 of the Canadian Charter of Rights and Freedoms protects freedom of religion; Sections 16–23 of the Charter establish the constitutional status of (French/English) bilingualism in Canada; and Section 27 of the Charter complements these principles by enshrining multiculturalism and diversity as one of the linchpins of Canadian national and constitutional identity. In short, there are important variations within the dominant separationist model deployed throughout the liberal democratic world.

In other parts of the world important variations of the separationist model, and even divergence from and rejection of it, have emerged. Although the separation approach in its several versions is the one most familiar to scholars of constitutional law and politics in the United States, expanding our horizons comparatively reveals several other constitutional-institutional models for delineating the relationship between religion and state; these models are of considerable importance to an analysis of the phenomenon of constitutional theocracy.

A fifth pertinent constitutional model is the *weak form of religious establishment*—for example, establishment through the formal, mainly ceremonial, designation of a certain religion as the "state religion." Several European countries illustrate this model. A case in point is the designation of the Evangelical Lutheran Church as the "state church" in Norway, Denmark, Finland, and Iceland—arguably some of Europe's most liberal and progressive polities. Norway's head of state, for example, is also the leader of the church. Article 2 of the Norwegian Constitution guarantees freedom of religion but also states that Evangelical Lutheranism is the official state religion. Article 12 requires that more than half the members of the Norwegian Council of State be members of the state church. Similarly, Greece and Cyprus formally designate the Greek Orthodox Church as their state church. In England the monarch is the "supreme governor" of the Church of England and "defender of the faith." The Crown has a role in senior ecclesiastical matters, and, by the same token, the church is involved in the coronation of a new monarch, and senior bishops are represented in the House of Lords. A diluted version of this model operates in Germany, where the institutional apparatuses of the Evangelical, Catholic, and Jewish religious communities are designated as public corporations and therefore qualify for state support from the German church tax.

A sixth model, more a de facto scenario than a de jure model, involves countries where formal separation of church and state, as well as religious freedoms more generally, is constitutionally guaranteed, but where longstanding patterns of politically systemized church hegemony and religion-centric morality continue to loom large over the constitutional arena. Ireland provides a good example. Although the special status of Catholicism was removed from the Irish Constitution in 1973, Article 41 of the constitution "recognises the Family as the natural primary and fundamental unit group of Society, and as a moral institution possessing inalienable and imprescriptible rights, antecedent and superior to all positive law." Until 1995 the constitution essentially banned divorce and remarriage and in effect subjected Irish Catholics to concurrent jurisdiction of the church and the state in such matters.[14] Article 44, which continues to be in effect today, reads: "The State acknowledges that the homage of public worship is due to Almighty God. It shall hold His Name in reverence, and shall respect and honour religion." The specter of Catholic morality, despite formal separation of church and state, does not end there. The Eighth Amendment (1983)—the "Pro-Life Amendment" passed by referendum—asserts that the fetus has an explicit right to life equal to that of the pregnant woman and that the Irish state guarantees to vindicate that right. Exceptions are made in cases where there is a threat to the life of the mother, and it may not be used to limit the right to travel to other countries to procure an abortion.[15]

Other predominantly Catholic countries in Europe, most notably Malta and Poland, and to a considerably lesser degree Slovakia, continue to grapple with similar tensions. Portugal (1976), Spain (1978), and Italy (1984) all adopted new constitutions or constitutional amendments that disestablished Catholicism as their state religion. In at least the former two cases the church had been historically entangled with right-wing authoritarianism—close ties that the transition to democracy sought to dismantle. As a result, Roman Catholic morality lost some (but not all) of its grip over public morality even though it continues to be prevalent in the private sphere. The gradual convergence toward judicial review, constitutional rights and liberties, gender-equality standards, and growing social acceptance of homosexuality, stacked against a history of church dominance and legalized religion-centered morality, has also characterized the constitutional jurisprudence of predominantly Catholic countries in the global South. Courts in the Philippines, Chile, and Ecuador, to pick three examples, have been quite adamant in their refusal to liberalize various aspects of women's reproductive freedoms. In other countries—Colombia, Mexico, and Argentina, for example—constitutional courts have been notably more receptive to challenges to systemized religion-centric morality. But any way one looks at it, although religion and state are formally separated in Ireland, as well as in other countries with a similar history of church dominance, they continue to be tied together in some nontrivial ways.

A seventh constitutional response to the tension between secularism and religiosity is the *selective accommodation of religion in certain areas of the law.* Here the general law is secular, but a degree of jurisdictional autonomy is granted to religious communities, primarily in matters of personal status and education. Countries such as Kenya, India, and Israel grant recognized religious or customary communities the jurisdictional autonomy to pursue their own traditions in several areas of law, most notably family law. Kenya, for example, has enacted a set of statutes to recognize the diversity of personal laws pertaining to different groups of citizens. India has long been entangled in a bitter debate concerning the scope and status of Muslim and Hindu religious personal laws versus the individual rights and liberties protected by the Indian Constitution. Each recognized religious community in Israel, including the Jewish community, has autonomous religious courts that hold jurisdiction over its respective members' marriage and divorce affairs.[16] Religious affiliation, conversion, and the provision of religious services are controlled by statutory religious bodies, whose decisions must comply with general principles of administrative and constitutional law. Core features of this arrangement originated from the Ottoman *millet* system of semiautonomous jurisdictional enclaves of religious minorities. In other settings, they resemble elements of the colonial policy of "indirect rule." Ethiopia, Indonesia, Lebanon, Nigeria, the Gambia, Senegal, Ghana, the Philippines, Singapore, Sri Lanka, and Tanzania all follow one form or another of that model with respect to their respective religious-minority populations.

Paradoxically, the status of religious minorities under this model may, in some instances, be better than under the no-establishment arrangement. Whereas Muslim tribunals in Israel or India, for example, are officially recognized and enjoy a certain jurisdictional autonomy, Muslim communities do not enjoy such statutory recognition and jurisdictional autonomy in, say, the United States.[17] In practice, however, religion, ethnicity, and nationality in many of the polities that adhere to this model tend to be closely entangled. Although jurisdictional autonomy in certain areas of law is granted to minority religious groups, foundational national metanarratives, and often the law itself, reflect preferential treatment of members of the majority religious/ethnic group. The political and legal systems of Israel (with respect to Jews), Malaysia (with respect to Muslims), or Sri Lanka (with respect to Buddhists) all feature elements of such religion-based preferential treatment.[18] And although the status of Hindutva (Hinduness) in Indian culture, law, and politics is less overt or formal, it too reflects a notion of religion-based "first-class citizens." In such settings symbiotic relations evolve whereby religion thrives in tandem with nationality. The state has an embedded interest in preserving or promoting a viable "state religion" to the extent that this religion provides meaning to the national metanarratives that constitute the nation as such.

There are other, less formal illustrations of this logic in action. In Ukraine the political affiliation and regional dominance of each of the separate branches of the Ukrainian Orthodox Church correlate neatly with the pro-Russian versus pro-Western political rift in Ukrainian society. In Serbia, another politically turbulent post-Communist country, the ties between Serbian nationalism and the Serbian Orthodox Church are so close that Serbian Orthodox churches in Kosovo have been viewed by the Serbian government as fortresses of Serbian nationality in that seceding territory. As a reaction to the 2008 Kosovo declaration of independence, the Serbian government's minister of religion, Radomir Naumov, decided to pay the salaries of the Serbian Orthodox clergy in Kosovo to signal the strategic significance of the Serbian Orthodox Church to Serbian nationalism and sovereignty.

The close ties between church and nation in Ukraine and Serbia lead us to question the thesis that religion's vitality depends on the capacity of organized religion to serve as a critic of and counterweight to secular political authority.[19] José Casanova, for example, credits the sustained religiosity of Catholic Poland to the church's energetic opposition to the Communist state. In contrast, he argues that because the Catholic Church in Spain collaborated and was associated with the Franco regime, its stature therefore plummeted considerably when that regime was dissolved. Granted, this thesis has some bite in places such as Egypt or Turkey, where religious parties indeed fulfill the role of an effective alternative to the statist establishment. But in other countries, and Serbia is certainly not an exception, close ties between nationalism and religious affiliation are mutually beneficial and reinforcing for both sides.

The model of *religious jurisdictional enclaves* may be based on substantive or subject-matter jurisdictional boundaries or on more conventional spatial/regional boundaries (e.g., federalism). Two vivid illustrations of the latter version are Nigeria and Indonesia. The Constitution of Nigeria (1999) establishes that country as a secular state with constitutionally enshrined freedom of religion. At the same time, the constitution allows subnational units to grant additional jurisdiction to their local courts. Twelve predominantly Muslim northern states have used this provision to expand the substantive jurisdictional boundaries of their Shari'a tribunals. As we will see in Chapter 4, secularist interests have employed principles of federalism and constitutional supremacy, alongside self-restraint by high religious tribunals, to mitigate the impact of Islamization in these twelve Nigerian states.

Indonesia has one of the largest Muslim populations in the world; approximately 90 percent of its roughly 250 million citizens identify as Muslim. One of the five core principles *(pancasila)* established by the Indonesian Constitution (1945, reaffirmed 1959) is that "the state shall be based on the belief in the one and only God." However, the constitution does not establish Islam as the sole state religion; Christianity, Buddhism, Hinduism, and, as of 1998, Confucianism also enjoy equal status as state-recognized religions. In addition, freedom of religion is guaranteed by Chapter 10 of the constitution. In 2001, following the rise of intense secessionist impulses in the state of Aceh, the historical stronghold of Islam in Southeast Asia, the federal government agreed to grant Aceh special autonomy. Federal laws 44/1999 and 18/2001 provided the legal basis for Aceh to apply certain aspects of Shari'a without contested aspects of Islamic criminal law and procedure. Federal authorities, meanwhile, have used the procedure of presidential decrees—essentially executive orders by Jakarta—to limit the codification and implementation of certain controversial aspects of Shari'a law in Aceh.

Another increasingly prevalent but seldom-discussed model is essentially a mirror image of these religious jurisdictional enclaves—what we might call *secular jurisdictional enclaves.* Here most of the law is religious; however, certain areas of the law, such as economic law, are "carved out" and insulated from influence by religious law. An interesting case in point is Saudi Arabia, arguably one of the countries whose legal system comes closest to being fully based on *fiqh* (Islamic jurisprudence). Article 1 of the Saudi Basic Law (1993) reads: "The Kingdom of Saudi Arabia is a sovereign Arab Islamic state with Islam as its religion; God's Book and the Sunnah of His Prophet, God's prayers and peace be upon him, are its constitution." Article 23 establishes the state's duty to advance Islam: "The state protects Islam; it implements its Shari'a; it orders people to do right and shun evil; it fulfills the duty regarding God's call." Shari'a law is often less than attractive for business, however, and the Saudi royal family came to the rescue. Chapter 4 of the Basic Law (titled "Economic Principles") protects private property, guarantees against confiscation of assets, and suggests that "economic and social development is to be achieved according to a just and scientific plan." Moreover, whereas Saudi courts apply Shari'a in all matters of civil, criminal, or personal status, Article 232 of a 1965 royal decree provides for the establishment of a commission for the settlement of all commercial disputes. Although judges of the ordinary courts are usually appointed by the Ministry of Justice from graduates of recognized Shari'a law colleges, members of the commission for the settlement of commercial disputes are appointed by the Ministry of Trade. In other words, Saudi Arabia has effectively exempted the entire finance, banking, and corporate capital sectors from application of Shari'a rules. A modern, business-friendly foreign-investment law was adopted in 2000, and taxes on foreign firms were drastically slashed in 2003. Foreign investors have not protested the move.

Softer examples of this model are common in the Islamic world. Article 1 of Qatar's new constitution (2003) states that "Qatar is an independent Arab state; Islam is the State's religion and the Islamic Shari'a is the main source of its legislations." But this has not proved a major obstacle to Qatar's emergence as a regional economic superpower. Although it has long been endowed with oil and natural gas resources that are among the richest worldwide, it was not until 1995, under the leadership of Emir Hamad bin Khalifa al-Thani, that Qatar begun to experience a notable cultural and economic liberalization, including the endorsement of women's right to vote, a modern constitution, and the launch of Al Jazeera, a leading English and Arabic news source that operates a website and a widely watched satellite television news channel. Qatar's new investment law (Law No. 13, 2000) creates a business-friendly investing environment. It is little wonder that, according to recent statistics by the International Monetary Fund, Qatar is the country with the highest per capita gross domestic product (GDP) worldwide, alongside Luxembourg. It has also become an emerging hot spot for international events, including the Doha Development Round of trade negotiations of the World Trade Organization, the 2006 Asian Games, the 2010 Athletics World Indoor Championship, and a failed but competitive bid to host the 2016 Summer Olympic Games.

Similarly, Islam has been the state religion in the Maldives since the twelfth century. Section 2 of the most recent constitution (2008) reads: "The Maldives is a sovereign, independent, democratic Republic based on the principles of Islam." Section 10 reads: "The religion of the State of the Maldives is Islam. Islam shall be the basis of all the laws of the Maldives; No law contrary to any tenet of Islam shall be enacted in the Maldives." Adherence to Islam is required for citizenship; as Section 9 of the 2008 constitution states, "A non-Muslim may not become a citizen of the Maldives." Furthermore, there is no secular legal system; rather, the local version of Shari'a law, as it is interpreted by state authorities and the Majlis, is the law of the land. But the Maldives continues to boast some of the world's finest hotels, catering to jet-set tourists attracted to the country's world-class coral reefs. Over half a million tourists visit the country every year. A special presidential decree exempts the thriving tourist industry, which accounts for over 20 percent of the country's GDP, from several non-tourist-friendly religious imperatives. Therefore, although most of Malé's (the Maldives' capital city) hotels are alcohol free, drinking is common in luxurious beach resorts (although most still prohibit the sale of alcohol to Maldivian nationals). And while in Malé locals are bathing fully clothed, the swimsuits in most beach resorts leave little to one's imagination.

Another example of the model of secular jurisdictional enclaves—a close relative of constitutional theocracy—is provided by the legal system of the Comoros, which rests on two tenets: Islamic law and an inherited Napoleonic French legal code. Islam has increasingly dominated the political sphere, and the May 2006 elections were won by Ahmed Abdallah Mohamed Sambi, a Sunni Muslim cleric nicknamed the "Ayatollah" for his time spent studying Islam in Iran. The Constitutional Court, the ultimate arbiter of constitutional questions, consists of seven judges who are all well versed in both the French civil law tradition and the Shafi'i school. But the French civil code prevails in most areas of commercial life. In fact, the Comoros is a signatory to the Treaty on the Harmonization of Business Law in Africa, which binds signatories to apply a civil code framework in areas of business law. Furthermore, Article 3 of the constitution provides that international treaties take precedence over local island law.

The jurisdictional-enclaves model is not limited to economic law. In several countries it has been extended, to a varying degree, to other important aspects of the law such as civil procedure, labor law, laws regulating the legal profession itself, and to a lesser extent the contested domain of family and personal-status law. Once officially taken out of the exclusive purview of sacred law, the jurisdictional authority of ordinary courts (whose decisions are subject to scrutiny by the constitutional courts) is expanded to adjudicate these areas of the law at the expense of religious tribunals.

Finally, an increasingly common approach to governing relations of religion and state is a *mixed system of religious law and general legal principles*. Like a few exemplars of the jurisdictional-enclaves model, several manifestations of this model of religion and state relations come close, perhaps even the closest, to the ideal type of constitutional theocracy. It is well known that Afghanistan has long been torn between conflicting values of tradition and modernism. From 1994 to 2001 the country was ruled by the radical Islamist Taliban, but the U.S.-led military campaign removed the Taliban from power and installed a more moderate regime representing an array of groups hitherto in opposition: moderate religious leaders and the country's elites and intellectuals in exile. The new Constitution of Afghanistan came into effect in January 2004. It states that Afghanistan is an Islamic republic (Article 1); that the "sacred religion of Islam is the religion of the Islamic Republic of Afghanistan" (Article 2); and that "[n]o law shall contravene the tenets and provisions of the holy religion of Islam in Afghanistan" (Article 3). Courts are allowed to use Hanafi jurisprudence in situations of constitutional lacunae (Article 130). At the same time, the constitution also enshrines the right to private property (Article 40) and resurrects a woman's right to vote, as well as to run for and serve in office (Article 22). The 2004 constitution also establishes a Supreme Court (Stera Mahkama) composed of nine judges appointed by the president for a term of ten years (Articles 116–117). All members of the court "[s]hall have higher education in legal studies or Islamic jurisprudence" (Article 118).

The newly adopted Iraqi Constitution of 2005 offers another variant of this amalgam. Article 2.1 states that "Islam is the official religion of the state and a basic source of legislation." No law can be passed that contradicts settled Islamic (legal) rules. At the same time, Article 2.1(b) states that "[n]o law can be passed that contradicts the principles of democracy," and Article 5 declares: "The law is sovereign and the people are the sources of power and its legitimacy." The Federal Supreme Court, states Article 92, "shall be made up of a number of judges, experts in Islamic jurisprudence, and legal scholars, whose number, the method of their selection, and the work of the Court shall be determined by a law enacted by a two-thirds majority of the members of the Council of Representatives." Influenced by the circumstances of its adoption, the Iraqi Constitution also emulates Western constitutional catalogues of rights by protecting a host of rights and liberties, such as religious freedoms (Articles 2.2, 41, and 42); formal equality, including antidiscrimination on the basis of religion (Articles 14 and 16); privacy (Article 17); and personal freedom and dignity (Article 37). More important still is that the constitution incorporates into Iraqi law (via Article 44) provisions of international human rights treaties to which Iraq is a signatory, so long as they do not conflict with other elements of the constitution. The commitment to rights and liberties is also affirmed by a declarative umbrella section (Article 2.1(c)), which reads: "No law can be passed that contradicts the rights and basic freedoms outlined in this constitution." To pass comprehensive constitutional scrutiny, then, a law has to conform to the common tenets of Islam, democracy, individual rights and liberties, and international human rights—a difficult task, to put it mildly, even for distinctly more stable polities.

Or consider the Yemenite amalgam of constitutionalism and religiosity. Article 2 of the Constitution of Yemen (adopted in 1994) declares that Islam is the religion of the state. Article 3 provides that Shari'a is the source of all legislation. Non-Muslims are forbidden to run for or hold elected office. The same constitution calls for an independent judiciary and establishes a separate commercial court system and a Supreme Court, where a combination of Shari'a interpretations and principles of modern constitutional law is applied. Unique constitutional amalgamations of religious and modern principles emerge, such as Article 31 of the constitution, which states, "Women are the sisters of men. They have rights and duties, which are guaranteed and assigned by Shari'a *and* stipulated by law," and Article 46, according to which "Criminal liability is personal. No crime or punishment shall be undertaken without a provision in the Shari'a or the law."

The preamble of the 1979 Constitution of the Islamic Republic of Iran enshrines Shari'a as the supreme law—superior even to the constitution itself. Articles 2 and 3 declare that authority for sovereignty and legislation has a divine provenance (from Shari'a) and that the leadership of the clergy is a principle of faith. According to Article 6, the administration of the state is to be conducted by the wider population: the general public participates in the election of the president, the Majlis representatives (members of parliament), and municipality councils. Article 8 further entrenches principles of popular participation in deciding political, economic, and social issues. Most notably, Iran has seen the emergence of the Guardian Council, a de facto constitutional court armed with mandatory constitutional preview powers and composed of six mullahs appointed by *velayate faqih* (the supreme leader) and six jurists proposed by the head of the judicial system of Iran and voted on by the Majlis. The supreme leader has the power to dismiss the religious members of the Guardian Council, but not its jurist members (Article 91). Featuring a combination of religious supremacy, pragmatist institutional innovations (e.g., Ayatollah Khomeini's 1989 introduction of the Regime's Discernment Expediency Council [Majma-e Tashkhis Maslahat Nezam] to serve as the final arbiter between the generally more progressive Consultative Assembly and the distinctly more conservative Guardian Council), and carried-over legacies of the 1906 Imperial Constitution, primarily with respect to the popular source of sovereignty, an elected parliament, and some separation-of-powers principles, Iran's constitutional order is a living exemplar of a strong form of constitutional theocracy.

Despite fundamental differences, a pattern of controlled religious establishment through constitutionalism has taken place in many other predominantly Islamic polities over the last forty years. Three prime examples, despite considerable dissimilarities among them, are Sudan, Pakistan, and Egypt, all of which underwent the constitutionalization of Shari'a during that era. Sudan has a long history of ambivalence with respect to law and religion. Unlike the conventional image of the country, at least one-fifth of Sudan's population is non-Muslim, subscribing to either Christianity or traditional animist religions. Its legal system is an amalgam of British colonial heritage and legal influence, the socialist state-building years led by President Gaafar an-Nimeiry, and Islamic law introduced by Nimeiry in the early 1980s and further expanded by Omar al-Bashir's authoritarian leadership (1989–present). Although Nimeiry was the only Arab leader who maintained close relations with Anwar el-Sadat after the Camp David Accords and attended Sadat's funeral, in 1981, pressured by his Islamic opponents and still president of Sudan, he began a dramatic shift toward Islamist political governance. He allied himself with the Muslim Brotherhood and in 1983 imposed Shari'a law throughout the country, thereby alienating the non-Muslim (predominantly Christian or animist) south. In violation of the Addis Ababa Agreement he dissolved the southern Sudanese government, thereby prompting a renewal of the civil war.[20]

Many aspects of Sudan's less-than-dazzling image are no doubt accurate, but even in this bleak corner of the world of new constitutionalism some interesting constitutional provisions exist. Article 1 of the 1998 constitution, for example, states: "The State of Sudan is a country of racial and cultural harmony and religious tolerance. Islam is the religion of the majority of the population and Christianity and traditional religions have a large following." Article 2 states: "Sudan is a Federal Republic governed at its highest level of authority in accordance with a federal system of government based on the Constitution and at the local level it is governed by local councils acting in accordance with the law." The 1998 constitution also includes an extensive bill of rights (Articles 21–29) with guarantees that, at least on paper, meet the criteria of any modern constitutional state. At the same time, Article 7 states that "[d]efense of the motherland is an honor and Jihad is a duty"; Article 35 holds that it is the duty of every Sudanese citizen "to defend the country and respond to the Jihad call and national service."

Two distinctly softer, albeit equally fascinating, exemplars of the drift toward constitutional theocracy are Pakistan and Egypt. Pakistan has a long-standing tradition of constitutionalism and a British-influenced tradition of legal education and practice. It has been one of the West's closest allies in the fight against radical Islamism in the Middle East and central Asia. Pakistan is also a military superpower and one of the few members of the world's nuclear club. At the same time, Islam has been a major political force in Pakistan at least since the early 1970s, and many would say since the country gained its independence in 1947. The province of Baluchistan has become one of the main frontiers of the "war on terror." Pakistan's North-West Frontier Province (including the Swat valley region) has been governed by the religious-fundamentalist Muttahida Majilis-I-Amal party since 2003. These conflicting trends reflect a complex, if not completely blurred, collective identity, torn between modernity and tradition, universalism and religiosity, that has been rapidly translated at both the institutional and jurisprudential levels of Pakistan's constitutional landscape.

In 1973 Pakistani legislators departed from the country's rich British common-law tradition by enabling the Pakistani judiciary to use Islam as an authoritative source in constitutional interpretation. From 1978 to 1980 President Zia-ul-Haq established a system of Shari'a-based high courts at the provincial level, as well as the Shari'at Appellate Bench at the Supreme Court; each of these would be responsible for ensuring the appropriate implementation of Shari'a law. In 1985 President Zia went on to introduce a set of amendments to the constitution that effectively stipulated that "[a]ll existing laws shall be brought in conformity with the Injunctions of Islam as laid down in the Holy Qur'an and Sunna, in this Part referred to as the Injunctions of Islam, and no law shall be enacted which is repugnant to such Injunctions." In theory, this means that legislation must be in full compliance with principles of Shari'a. How the Supreme

Court of Pakistan has skillfully managed to contain the jurisdictional expansion of Shari'a courts and avoid elevating Islamization into a fundamental norm of the entire Pakistani constitutional order through the development of the "harmonization doctrine" is a fascinating story that I tell in some detail in Chapter 4.

Egypt presents a further telling example of the softer approach, having established a system of judicial review in 1979. The criminal penal code is largely nonreligious, as are numerous economic, property, and investment rules. In 1971 President Sadat passed a new constitution that, on the one hand, preserved Egypt's socialist legacy and, on the other, stated that Shari'a was a primary source of legislation in Egypt. In 1980 Article 2 of the Egyptian Constitution was amended to establish principles of Islamic jurisprudence (Shari'a) as *the* (not *a*) primary source of legislation in Egypt. It now reads: "Islam is the religion of the State, Arabic is its official language, and the principles of Islamic Shari'a are the principal source of legislation." Alongside this amendment, Islamism in Egypt has enjoyed an astounding growth in popularity over the last three decades. Under the guidance of the Muslim Brotherhood, Egyptian Islamism has consistently opposed the modernist-nationalist agenda advocated by the government, the historically powerful National Democratic Party, the pro-statist military, and, above all, Egypt's moderate, economically well-off elites. Of course, with this expansion the familiar challenges of constitutional theocracy emerged. For nearly thirty years now the Egyptian political and constitutional order and, consequently, Egypt's courts have been grappling with the contested status and role of Shari'a as a potentially determinative source of authority in an otherwise strong state with a historically powerful executive branch.

In sum, there is much more diversity in the religion-and-state universe than often meets the popular Western eye. The dichotomous view of separation in the West versus entanglement of religion and state elsewhere is rather unrefined. A taxonomy of contemporary approaches to governing relations of religion and state suggests, as discussed above, several archetypal models: (1) atheism and proactive elimination of religion; (2) an assertive form of secularism or separationist reformism, often established as a modernist reaction to backwardness and religious dominance; (3) separation as state neutrality toward religion, often accompanied by an assimilationist approach to religious or cultural difference; (4) separation with a de facto accommodationist approach to diversity and religious difference; (5) formal separation with de facto preeminence of a given religion and its moral preaching; (6) a weak form of religious establishment, where there is a formal, mainly ceremonial designation of a certain religion as the "state religion" but few or no implications in public life; (7) selective accommodation of religion in certain areas of the law, often with "religious jurisdictional enclaves" in matters of personal status; (8) the model of secular jurisdictional enclaves, where most of the law is religious, but certain areas of the law, such as economic law, are carved out and insulated from influence by religious law; and finally, (9) mixed system of religious law and general legal principles, where the entire legal and constitutional system is based on a dual commitment to religious fundamentals and constitutional principles, or a bipolar system of constitutional and sacred texts and authority. The last two models of relations of religion and state come the closest to the ideal type of constitutional theocracy. However, various degrees of reaction to, accommodation of, deference to, and control over religion are evident in virtually all these models. In fact, there are very few, if any, constitutional orders in today's world, their various outlooks notwithstanding, that are completely separable from religion, conceived as either a friend, a foe, or a bit of both.

The Theocratic Challenge to Conventional Constitutional Theory

The apparently oxymoronic nature of a constitution that features significant theocratic substance does not necessarily mean that such a form of constitutionalism is partial, incomplete, or illegitimate. (A few friends pointed to other compound creations, such as "vegetarian meatballs," "nuit blanche," or *Altneuland*—German for "old new land," the title of Theodor Herzl's utopian novel—to support this point). To begin with, an array of possible interpretations and schools of thought, from the strictest to the most liberal, exists within virtually all major religious traditions. While certain ultraconservative interpretations of religious precepts defy universal values such as tolerance or equality, liberal interpretations of the same precepts suggest that some Venn-diagram-like common ground between religion and democracy or liberalism may be found.[21] As scholars of Islamic jurisprudence have noted, some interpretations of Islam are certainly not conducive to principles of modern constitutionalism, while others are consistent with these principles and perhaps even positively support them.[22] Reform Judaism, to cite another example, is notably easier than Orthodox (let alone Haredi or ultra-Orthodox) Judaism to reconcile with modern ideals of gender equality or freedom of thought. Some might even contest the very idea of a religious state as deriving from genuine reading of pertinent religious teachings.[23]

Like most other constitutional orders, theocratic constitutionalism includes reference to high morality and limits the sorts of policy choices the government can make. As Andrew March lucidly explains, the Islamic conception of religious morality is that "a political order is legitimate to the extent that it approximates an ideal legal order as expressed in the idea of *Shari'a*, just as for a political liberal a political order is legitimate to the extent it approximates the terms of social cooperation as would be endorsed by parties contracting in ideal circumstances."[24] Thus state, law, and religious morality are inseparable; a religion-less political order that seeks to replace divine guidance and God's injunctions with man-made rule of law is viewed by classical Islam as illegitimate and unacceptable.[25] Where the substantive ideational core of a theocratic political order may be nonliberal, this in itself does not make a constitutional order based on it flawed, just nonliberal. Other core aspects of constitutionalism, aspirational and practical, may very well be adhered to by constitutional theocracy. Granted much depends on our understanding of constitutionalism as a hardware-like concept that may accommodate and reflect various contents as opposed to a software-like understanding of it as a bundle of substantive aspirational commitments. Either way, constitutional theocracy is not an illegitimate order. As discussed above, virtually all constitutional theocracies adhere to many software-like (let alone hardware-like) aspects of constitutionalism.

What is more, although constitutional theocracy may be deemed organically incoherent or committed to different sets of values, this in itself is certainly not an unheard-of scenario in the world of modern constitutionalism. Most constitutions, liberal, theocratic, or otherwise, include provisions and statements that may be interpreted as standing at odds with other provisions in the same constitution. One of my favorite examples of this is the Canadian Charter of Rights and Freedoms—arguably one of the most frequently cited constitutional bills of rights currently in existence—which protects formal equality in Section 15(1) and substantive equality and affirmative action in Section 15(2). The same document also commits to bilingualism (English and French) and at the same time to multiculturalism. It also begins with this preamble: "Whereas Canada is founded upon principles that recognize the supremacy of God and the rule of law." Thus an apparently incoherent mix of constitutional sources and provisions is not something over which constitutional theocracy has exclusive monopoly.

It is true that like any other intolerant perception of the good, a constitutional theocracy is not a natural companion of liberalism or liberal constitutionalism. But it is not inherently at odds with a plain and simple definition of constitutional democracy.[26] The demos in most constitutional theocracies has some nontrivial say in the choice of government (e.g., by periodic elections), which is not the case in a pure theocracy. Even in countries where the democratic process fails to meet Western standards, popular legitimacy is not something constitutional theocratic regimes take lightly. The powers of the government are constrained by a constitution in which certain basic rules, norms, rights, entitlements, and limitations are granted entrenched status and are therefore not easily amenable to change. True, constitutional theocracy is incompatible with a radical notion of democracy that sees any limitation on the demos's will—for example, through constitutionally entrenched rules or sources of authority other than the people themselves—as violating the ultimate essence of democracy. By that standard, however, no constitutional democracy is indeed purely democratic.

More subtle is the tension between a constitutional theocracy and the view of constitutional protection of certain classic civil liberties as an integral element of democratic (not merely liberal) constitutionalism. To begin with, most liberal constitutions limit the scope and application of the rights they protect to full members of the polity. Not everyone in such polities enjoys the right to have rights. Whereas some provisions apply to "everyone" or "every individual," others apply selectively to citizens and to a variable degree to permanent lawful aliens, but not to other classes of people. Prevalent birthright citizenship principles, such as jus soli or jus sanguinis, have long been applied in most liberal democracies, thereby excluding millions of people from initial access to the collective good.[27] The existence of de facto two-tier conceptions of citizenship that differentiate between full members and "second-class" citizens is certainly not a practice foreign to the history and, in some cases, the present-day policies of certain Western societies. Black Americans and German-born Turks, not to mention "nonwhite" South Africans, are obvious examples of such historically disenfranchised groups. The exclusion or limitation of certain rights in some theocratic constitutions is therefore not a unique practice, unheard of in other, supposedly liberal settings.

But perhaps more significantly, the obvious tension between theocracy and religious pluralism or religious neutrality (e.g., free expression and disestablishment of religion) is not the same as religion-based differential access to core political rights and access to public goods. This problem is illustrated vividly when a polity uses religious ascriptions to establish an "ethnocracy" (or its more mellow version, "ethnic democracy") where the entire political system and the hegemonic religious or ethnic group's foundational national metanarratives are developed and organized so as to benefit members of that group to the detriment of others, and where few or no members of minority ethnic groups are granted proportional access to wealth, power, and opportunities.

Malaysia, for example, defines itself as an Islamic state despite the fact that over one-third of its population consists of members of other denominations and ethnic origins, mainly Chinese and Indian. Ethnic Malays are Muslim and are granted constitutionally entrenched preferential treatment over members of other ethnic groups. Muslims (and non-Muslims who marry a Muslim) are obliged to follow the decisions of Syariah (Behasa Melayu or Malay for "Shari'a") courts in matters concerning their religion, most notably marriage, inheritance, apostasy, child custody, and conversion. Israel, likewise, defines itself as a Jewish and democratic state. Its citizenship and immigration policy gives preferential treatment to Jews. Its anthem features explicitly Jewish or Zionist themes, despite the fact that approximately 20 percent of its citizenry consists of non-Jews. So while neither Malaysia nor Israel is a pure constitutional theocracy, the formal constitutional status of a foundational ethnoreligious criterion that determines which members of the polity enjoy privileged access to desired public goods illustrates the tension between religion-based ascriptive traits and fundamental democratic governing principles of participation and representation.

More complex still are the challenges that theocracy poses to less idealist notions of constitutionalism. Arguably one of the most admirable functionalist or result-oriented perspectives on constitutions sees them as establishing an institutional framework for democratic deliberation and, by extension, as an effective mechanism for nation building.[28] Unlike Bruce Ackerman's idealist notion of constitution making that is shaped by and reflects the authentic "we the people" will, a pragmatic vision of constitution making sees it as constituting the demos and providing a framework for its establishment and evolution.[29] (It is little wonder that this latter view of constitutionalism has been popular among advocates of a European Union [EU] constitution). Unlike social contract, Rawlsian, or even public choice theories of constitutionalism, an instrumentalist, problem-solving view of constitutionalism has emerged, one which advocates a negotiated, voluntarily accepted or externally imposed constitutional pact as a means for resolving existential tensions in multiethnic settings. A voluminous body of literature on constitutional design and engineering in its more practical guise has evolved. Its canonical tenor suggests that when constitutionalization is seen as a pragmatic, second-order measure—as opposed to instances of constitutionalization involving a more principled, first-order, ideational outlook—it may help institutionalize attempts to mitigate tensions in ethnically divided polities through the adoption of federalism, secured representation, and other trust-building and power-sharing mechanisms.[30] The literature on constitutional design of this kind, often referred to as "consociationalism," emphasizes the significance of joint-governance institutions, mutual veto points, power-sharing mechanisms, and the like.[31] In its more strategic, "integrationist" guise this brand of scholarship advocates the adoption of institutions that would make the political process more attractive to recalcitrant stakeholders, encourage moderation, and defuse the causes of strife by providing incentives to vote across group lines.[32] Surprisingly, however, although there are many examples of discussions of the mitigating potential of constitutional power-sharing mechanisms to ease rifts along national, ethnic, or linguistic lines, scholars of comparative constitutional design have given little attention to the increasing divisions along secular/religious lines per se (i.e., not in association with ethnic divisions). From an analytical standpoint, the secular/religious divide differs in at least four respects from these more obvious and more commonly addressed markers of identity.

First, more than any other divisions along ascriptive or imagined lines, the secular/religious divide cuts across nations otherwise unified by their members' joint ethnic, linguistic, and historical origins. In this sense the secularism/religiosity factor or other closely associated distinctions, such as universalism versus parochialism, are closer in nature to less visible categories such as income deciles, social class, or cultural milieu than they are to other kinds of markers such as race, gender, or ethnicity. Nationalist Catalans, the Flemish, and Quebecers see themselves as autonomous people with a unique cultural heritage, language, and history that are distinct from those of Spaniards, Walloons, or Anglophone Canadians, respectively. By contrast, most cosmopolitan *and* traditionalist Egyptians define themselves as members of the same nation, speak the same language or dialects of it, treasure the pharaoh dynasties, and share the same ancestral ties. However, some Egyptians are close adherents of religious directives, while others follow them more casually.

Second, the territorial boundaries of the secular/religious divide are often blurred. Although residents of certain regions within a given country may be more prone to hold theocratic views than residents of other regions, this divide is not neatly demarcated along territorial lines, as is often the case with ethnic or linguistic boundaries. Proponents of theocratic governance may reside in rural towns or in blue-collar neighborhoods on the outskirts of large urban centers, but they may also reside within a few bus stops from bastions of modernism such as art galleries, universities, posh hotels, shopping malls, and government buildings. Thus the secular/religious divide manifests itself in a wide range of situations in everyday life, from the sidewalk to the market and from schools to workplaces. This is in stark contrast to, say, Sri Lanka, where the vast majority of Tamils live in one region of the island; or, better yet, Cyprus, where the territorial divide between the Greeks and the Turks is clearly demarcated. Territory-based power-sharing mechanisms or any other kind of joint-governance structures that are based on the allocation of powers or goods according to region may not be an efficient means for analyzing, let alone reducing, tensions along secular/religious lines.

Third, accounts of religion and state tend to assume firm identities and fixed group affiliations, although in reality this is not always the case.[33] To begin with, people have multiple identities beyond their faith-based affiliation. Feminist philosopher Judith Butler notes: "I identify, for example, as a Lesbian and as Jewish. But I have additional identities: I am a peculiar philosopher, a short person, and a woman who is getting old. Lesbian and Jewish clearly does not define everything that I am."[34] More important, membership in a group is in some instances voluntary and self-professed, whereas in others it is determined by laws external to the group, and in still other cases it is imposed by intragroup practices and traditions. Religious labels such as "Jewish," "Christian," or "Muslim" do not tell us much because there are a variety of schools, from very moderate to ultraconservative, within each of these categories. At certain times one school may enjoy greater support or become more dominant than others, but as the political kaleidoscope shifts, other voices within each religious community become more prevalent, and different aspects of that religion are emphasized. Thus identity and group affiliation are not primordial. They are to a large extent politically constructed by a dynamic interplay between intragroup politics and the political context within which that group operates. And religiosity as a marker of identity may be brought to the fore or relegated to lesser status as coalitions shift, elites transform, and interests change. The Zionist movement, for example, drew on aspects of Orthodox Judaism to support its cause in the years before and after the establishment of Israel. But as Orthodox Judaism fulfilled its historic role and new challenges of membership in the global community emerged, Orthodox Judaism became more of a burden than an asset for many Israelis. This holds true in smaller-scale, non-theocratic settings as well. In their recent study of the shifting dimensions of ethnicity in the Romanian-Transylvanian city of Cluj-Napoca, Rogers Brubaker and his coauthors show how groups use ethnic or nationalist symbols to announce their presence and promote their interests.[35] When such markers of identity exhaust their effectiveness they are gradually replaced with others.

One might add the numerous intrafaith struggles and interpretive debates that question the validity of such labels as "Jewish," "Christian," or

"Muslim" identity. At least since the immediately pre-Jesus Judea and the days of King Herod the Great, when the Hellenic world faded away and the Roman Empire emerged, intrareligion splits and intense rivalry, theological, political, economic, and otherwise, have come to dominate much of the history of religion. The split between the Western and Eastern churches in the eleventh century, the emergence of the Anglican Church, and the Reformation and the Counter-Reformation are only a few obvious examples. Today the Christian world is divided into several established churches and dozens of smaller sects, some distinctly more conservative than others. Even within established churches—the current rift within the Anglican Church is only one illustration—internal interpretive and political divides are fierce and plentiful.

The Jewish world of the Second Temple was divided into Sadducees, Pharisees, and Essenes (I explore the theological and political differences among these sects in Chapter 6). Today Orthodox Judaism remains hegemonic (although not unchallenged) in Israel, whereas Reform and Conservative branches of Judaism are distinctly more popular in the Diaspora. The Muslim world is divided into two major branches—Sunni and Shi'a—but also draws on several traditional interpretive schools within Islamic law and features a wide variety of sects and subdivisions, from radical Wahhabism to spiritual Sufism. In fact, even relatively stable labels describing modernist communities of faith—"constitutionalists," for example—are increasingly contested ones; the age-old debate between "textual" and "living" interpretive schools or the current deliberation in the United States concerning the constitutional legitimacy of reference to foreign jurisprudence are two immediate examples. Therefore, group identities not only are dynamic and fluid but also are contested from within, because intragroup struggles may emerge over who should speak for the group and on what basis. These problems, one would expect, intensify with formal state recognition of some or all aspects of religion, as intragroup contestation emerges over who officially serves as the community's voice, who represents its "authentic" precepts and traditions, or who "owns" the community's constitutive metanarratives.

Fourth, as I have already argued, the assumption that whole peoples share unified interests is, at best, highly questionable. The spread of religious fundamentalism in the developing world is sometimes wrongfully depicted as a phenomenon that is near monolithic, all-encompassing, or free of fierce internal opposition.[36] More religiosity in the public sphere or in the political domain serves the interests of some at the expense of others. It poses a clear and present danger to the cultural propensities, worldviews, and policy preferences of many, ranging from most of the urban intelligentsia and the majority of the managerial classes to the strong statist bureaucracy and powerful industries and economic stakeholders. The secular/religious divide and the struggle over the nation's aspirational commitments more generally are not free of large-scale distributive-justice aspects and material interests because, more often than not, support for religious parties emanates from occupiers of the polity's periphery, real or imagined. Furthermore, principles of theocratic governance often stem from alternative sources of authority and legitimacy that constitutionalism may regard as exogenous and even threatening to overarching state authority. Moreover, the holistic nature of theocratic governance is not prima facie conducive to constitutional compromise, power-sharing pacts, separation of powers, checks and balances, relative judicial independence, and other essentials of modern constitutionalism. These conflicting pressures and interests have led to intense constitutional maneuvering in predominantly religious polities. I explore the religion-taming nature of this maneuvering in the following chapters.

Conclusion

This chapter points to five main lessons. First, approximately half of the world's population, perhaps more, now lives in polities where religion not only has remained public but also has been playing a key role in political and constitutional life. Of these, approximately a billion people live in polities, national or subnational, that feature key elements of what I have termed constitutional theocracy.

Second, despite the general agreement that the world has witnessed a convergence on principles of constitutional supremacy and international human rights alongside increasing popular support for principles of theocratic governance, we still know precious little about constitutional law and practices in countries that are facing the dilemma of constitutional theocracy. As I hope to show in the following chapters, any attempt to explore the scope and nature of constitutional democracy in the early twenty-first century must include serious contemplation of the scope and nature of a different and increasingly common model—*constitutional theocracy.* The theocratic challenge has become a significant factor in world politics, as well as constitutional law. It stretches well beyond current media hot spots like Iran, Iraq, and Afghanistan, and any attempt to examine the complexities of constitution drafting in postconflict settings without paying close attention to the ever more relevant divide between the secular and universal and the religious and particularist is bound to come up short.

Third, constitutional theocracy shakes up the traditional affinity between liberalism, democracy, and constitutionalism. It questions canonical literature that considers constitutionalism an effective means for mitigating tensions in multiethnic or multilinguistic states and does not adequately address the theocratic challenge. That literature rests on five main presumptions: territorial concentration and demarcation; social and demographic cohesiveness among members of a given group; fixed identities; unified interests, worldviews, and policy preferences among group members; and an underlying vision of constitutionalism as a viable forum of compromise. Although these assumptions may provide a plausible set of working hypotheses with respect to dividing factors such as nationality, ethnicity, or language, they are less relevant in capturing the realities of the secular/religious divide. Of particular significance here are the apparently inherent tensions between principles of modern constitutionalism and the rule of law, on the one hand, and fundamentals of theocratic governance, on the other.

Fourth, although there were several notable premodern and early modern exercises in separating the theological from the political, the major transformation in the relationship between these two realms did not occur until the late eighteenth century, and in many settings much later. What is striking, however, is that unlike the conventional linear, "developmental," or "evolutionist" story, at least half of the world's population now lives in polities that, despite having been through a secularization process for decades, have recently undergone a postsecularist or an antisecularist transformation, with the inevitable cultural, political, and legal clashes this trend brings to the fore. As we have seen, there are several prototypical models for managing religion and state affairs, ranging from strict separation to weak establishment and from models of jurisdictional enclaves to parallel governance.

Obviously, there is considerable variance within, let alone among, these prototypical or ideal models; each comes in different shapes, forms, and sizes, with local nuances and idiosyncrasies abounding. This variance is often rooted in distinctive political legacies, differences in constitutional structures and aspirations, and dissimilarities in historical inheritances and formative experiences, as well as nontrivial differences in value systems and foundational national metanarratives. These differences often feed and shape the specific ways in which the tension between religion and constitutional governance manifests itself. Gary Jacobsohn explains, for example, how different national constitutional understandings of religious freedom are consequences of constitutional efforts to disestablish a previously established religion (India), maintain an established religion (Israel), or prevent any religion from becoming established (United States).[37]

Finally, these differences notwithstanding, a common motif in the non- and postsecularist age, whether in polities that adhere to separation of state and religion or in those where a strong constitutional establishment of religion exists, seems to be the increasing reliance worldwide on constitutional law and courts to mediate the seemingly contradictory aims and commitments of constitutionalism and religion, and, more often than not, to contain, tame, and limit the spread and impact of religion-induced policies.

CHAPTER THREE

The Secularist Appeal of Constitutional Law and Courts

CONSTITUTIONAL LAW and constitutional courts may be an effective place of refuge for secularists under duress. As we will see in the following chapters, the appeal of constitutionalism and the accompanying transfer to the courts of some of the most contentious questions a polity can contemplate are vividly evident in polities that face deep divisions along secular/religious lines. Constitutional law and courts in virtually all such polities have become bastions of relative secularism, pragmatism, and moderation, thereby emerging as effective shields against the spread of religiosity and garnering increased popular support for principles of theocratic governance. In a constitutional democracy the powers of the government are constrained by a constitution, in which certain basic rules, norms, rights, entitlements, and checks are entrenched. These latter elements are therefore not easily amenable to change by the political power holders of the moment. In some respects constitutionalism in predominantly religious settings operates in ways that are not fundamentally different from constitutionalism in constitutional democracies. In constitutional democracies the constitution establishes a core set of entrenched limitations on the scope, nature, and range of possible outcomes of the democratic process. Analogously, while in religious states the constitution is said to be steeped in religious norms and directives, it simultaneously plays a key role in curbing the spread and impact of theocratic governance, with its alternative worldviews, texts, and hierarchies of authority.

Why, however, are constitutional law and constitutional courts so appealing to secularist, modernist, cosmopolitan, and other antireligious social forces in polities that face deep divisions along secular/religious lines? What makes the domain of constitutional law so attractive to such groups, with their well-defined worldviews, cultural propensities, interests, and policy preferences? Several broad rationales come to mind: (1) co-optation; (2) jurisdictional advantages; (3) strategic delegation; (4) the very nature and characteristics of constitutional law, its epistemology, and its interpretive logic; (5) constitutional delegitimation of radical religious association; and (6) political control of constitutional courts and judges. In this chapter I address each of these six rationales in turn.

Co-optation

The formal enshrinement of a specific religion as the sole "state religion" of a given polity not only grants that religion status, prestige, and protection from possible competitors but also subjects certain aspects of religious affairs to monitoring by the state. With state recognition and funding come statutory regulation and monitoring, judicial or otherwise. Like the legalization of otherwise unregulated and unauthorized norms and practices, the constitutionalization of religion may help prevent the development of an "underworld" of religious authority and institutions. Such legalization also entails tighter government influence over appointments to key religious leadership positions. In other words, one of the main strategic impulses that may push antitheocratic stakeholders to endorse constitutionalism is *co-optation.*

The limiting effect of establishment on religious autonomy is evident in a variety of forms. At the most basic level, constitutional enshrinement of a state religion facilitates state interference in, if not control over, the appointment of religious leaders. As the famous circumstances that brought about the creation of the Anglican Church by Henry VIII show, ensuring the loyalty of religious authorities is not something besieged political leaders can take lightly. Israel's Chief Rabbinate, the supreme Jewish religious governing body in Israel and provider of most religious services to Israel's Jewish community, is a statutory body that is funded by the state. Its leaders, Israel's two chief rabbis, are selected and appointed by politicians. Tunisia's 1988 Law on Mosques provides that only personnel appointed by the government may lead activities in mosques and stipulates that mosques must remain closed except during prayer times and other authorized religious ceremonies such as marriages or funerals.[1] An archetypal example from the emerging world of constitutional theocracies is the 1996 appointment by Egypt's president Hosni Mubarak of the moderate Muhammad Sayyid Tantawi as the grand imam of al-Azhar Mosque and grand sheikh of al-Azhar University, one of the (some say *the*) highest spiritual authorities for nearly a billion Sunni Muslims. Until his death in 2010, Tantawi issued numerous moderate fatwas that countered rigid, conservative interpretation of Shari'a precepts. He continuously angered radicals by supporting organ transplants, denouncing female mutilation, and ruling that women should be appointed to senior judicial and administrative positions. In 2009, to pick one recent example, Tantawi issued a fatwa suggesting that female students may not wear the *niqab* (Islamic face veil) in universities, including al-Azhar premises. To reiterate, the head of al-Azhar issues a typically moderate edict on a hotly contested symbolic issue that has been at the core of the struggle between the Egyptian state and Islamic fundamentalism. The benefits of co-optation are quite clear here. The appointment of Tantawi, to be sure, is only one episode in a much longer and deeper institutional and historical process of "nationalizing" al-Azhar by state elites in postcolonial Egypt. After the 1961 formal nationalization of al-Azhar by Gamal Abdel Nasser, the control of al-Azhar by the military was tight until the 1970s when it became somewhat more relaxed.[2]

In Saudi Arabia Wahhabi discourse is channeled through the ulama (learned Muslim high clergy), who are largely state-appointed and historically loyal to the royal family. Rare attempts (most notably in 1992) by groups of conservative ulama to criticize the king or the royal family have resulted in severe sanctions or dismissal of senior clergy members from their official position. The carrot? "Today state ulama travel abroad for medical treatment, live in luxurious villas, receive substantial sums of money for their noble services to political authority . . . The image of the blind, miserable and poor scholar living on a meagre income in return for religious services, has given way to wealthy guardians of the tradition, who are seen on television screens greeting princes and international delegations visiting the country."[3]

Controlling the provision of religious services by co-opting religious leaders may also facilitate state control of unregistered religious organizations, even if such organizations subscribe to the majority or state religion. In many countries—Tajikistan and Uzbekistan are only two examples—Muslim followers of non-state-approved religious organizations are often arrested for holding "unsanctioned gatherings" or are labeled "extremists" by state courts and by leaders of registered religious organizations. In 2007, for example, the Supreme Court of Tajikistan declared a dozen such unregistered organizations, including the Islamic Movement of Turkestan, "extremist." The practice is by no means confined to predominantly Muslim countries. Most Vietnamese, for example, follow Mahayana Buddhism. Vietnamese law requires that religious groups register with the government.[4] Those groups that do not join one of the officially authorized religious organizations, the governing boards of which are under government control, are considered illegal. This has led to effective infringement on religious freedom of various Christian and non-state-controlled Buddhist sects. Meanwhile, the Indonesian Constitutional Court upheld in 2010 the constitutionality of the country's Blasphemy Law (1965), which prohibits "unofficial" religious interpretation and activities that deviate from the basic teachings of Indonesia's six officially acknowledged religions. The law has been used by government to keep the process of religious interpretation under official check at the expense of religious freedom.

There are also more subtle examples. In 2002 tension arose in Singapore concerning the insistence of the parents of four six-year-old girls that their daughters should be allowed to wear headscarves *(tudung)* at their primary school.[5] The school principals and the government were adamant in their refusal to permit this, arguing that a headscarf was not part of the Singapore school uniform, and that the girls must therefore remove their headscarves before entering school premises. The impasse was broken by none other than the mufti of Singapore and the Majlis Ugama Islam Singapore—the state-appointed religion commission—who advanced the view that according to Islam, when one is forced to choose between education for one's children and wearing a headscarf, the former prevails. The pronouncement was couched as an advisory or recommendation, not a rigid ruling. The move proved successful, and the tension was dissolved. Thus politically astute, state-friendly religious interpreters may be an effective tool in taming radicalism.

A different twist on the co-optation logic in a religion-infused setting seems to be at work in Chechnya, one of Russia's federal subject regions in the northern Caucasus. As is well known, the war in Chechnya has taken a significant toll on the Russian army, as well as on the Chechen people, virtually all of whom are devout Muslims. Islam has also made major inroads in neighboring Ingushetia and Dagestan. To contain the spread of Islamic fundamentalism in the region, Moscow threw its support behind Ramzan Kadyrov, a young local Chechen "big man," a former rebel, and the son of assassinated former Chechen president Akhmad Kadyrov. Young Kadyrov's pertinent track record on respect for human rights, along with the legality of some of his other habits, is very much in question, but a co-optation impulse quickly cleared these dark clouds, for only an insider can effectively tame fundamentalism. Because the Islamic impulse in Chechnya is widespread, neither Moscow nor Kadyrov can govern the region effectively without allowing some accommodation of Islamic values and traditions. Therefore, as the president of Chechnya, Kadyrov talks the talk of Islamic values and advances religion-infused views concerning revisions to public moral standards, personal-status laws, and the penal code. At the same time, Kadyrov and his Russian patrons cannot live with fundamentalist Wahhabism. Therefore, a rigid dichotomy has been erected by Kadyrov's administration between Sufism, consistently portrayed as the "right," "proper," and "traditional" form of Islam in Chechnya, and Wahhabism, portrayed as the "wrong" or "evil" form of Islam and often equated with terrorism.[6] This allows the regime to express its commitment to Islam but to reject the less pleasant aspects of it.

The potential disarming of threatening forms of religion by co-opted interpreters makes religious communities ambivalent toward formal state recognition or even suspicious of it. An interesting twist on the conventional separationist vision of the First Amendment is told by Stephen Feldman in *Please Don't Wish Me a Merry Christmas.*[7] In this version the First Amendment's disestablishment element is a product of a certain strand of Protestant theology that saw the state as a potential corrupter of religion. The First Amendment, from this perspective, is not a secularist declaration but, at least in part, a reflection of a religious principle and, perhaps, interests. As Stanford Professor of History and American Studies Jack Rakove explains, American society during the revolutionary era was profoundly Protestant and would become even more so in the nineteenth century. In fact, it would be difficult to identify any American in the revolutionary era who could be classified as a secularist in any robust sense of the term. It is fairly easy to draw a straight line from a Lockean aversion to "priestcraft" to the similar feelings voiced by Jefferson and Madison as indicated in their writings on religion, including Madison's later-life correspondence on the subject and the Detached Memoranda. We need to consider, in this vein, how Madison goes on at great length in his Remonstrance about how establishment is both inconsistent with and subversive of Christianity. Disestablishment, therefore, may be as much a consequence of religious principles or interests as the triumph of the secular over the religious.

Therefore, religious institutions and authorities, not secular elites or the modernist state, may have an interest in maintaining the public/private distinction and in keeping religion within the confines of the private sphere, much like the business sphere, in order to shield it from state interference, manipulation, and co-optation. From religion's standpoint, formal recognition by the state, let alone establishment through state funding, may be seen as a sacrifice of autonomy in exchange for support. An argument of that nature was made by certain religious voices embroiled in the famous *Kiryas Joel* case decided by the U.S. Supreme Court in 1994.[8] The issue at stake was whether a law that created a separate school district for a village populated exclusively by a Satmar Hasidic community violated the Establishment Clause. The stated goal of the law was to provide accommodation for Satmar children with special needs. The majority of the Court struck down the law on the basis that it violated the neutrality principle. Three judges (Scalia, Rehnquist, and Thomas) dissented, holding that the Court's precedent of prohibiting religious accommodation was improper. Within the Hasidic religious community itself a split emerged. While some argued that a separate, state-created school district would indeed cater to the community's special needs, others argued that any such move would only allow the state and its regulatory agencies to cross the public/private line, penetrate the religious community, and, over time, transform its beliefs and worldviews. A similar isolationist impulse guides the relative secrecy of nonstatutory community-based religious tribunals, such as the Hasidic ultra-Orthodox *Beit Din Tsedek* (Hebrew acronym *Badatz*). Much like other unofficial alternative dispute resolution forums, interested parties are expected to keep things behind closed doors and not to challenge decisions of such tribunals (presumably based on religious law) before state courts, in part to maintain the de facto autonomy of these tribunals. This is not a far-fetched concern; the modern state and its regulatory agencies are often driven by this logic. Consider, for example, why legislatures may choose to legalize morally questionable practices; while legalization means formal recognition of less-than-ideal practices, it also allows for close state monitoring and regulation of these practices. Such pragmatic considerations brought Dutch legislators in the early 2000s to legalize certain aspects of euthanasia, to pick one example.

There is, no doubt, a qualitative difference between the effect of constitutionalization on statutory and nonstatutory religious tribunals—the former operate under the direct shadow and control of state law, whereas the latter operate within communities of faith, and although they lack formal extrafaith standing, they maintain their state-free autonomy within the communities in which they operate. Statutory religious tribunals in the liberal and in the theocratic world must pay close attention to external legal influences, most notably administrative and constitutional law norms, if they wish that their rulings not be overturned by the civil court system. They are, therefore, said to be more adaptive and accommodating with respect to state law. Nonstatutory adjudicative bodies, by contrast, are not bound by such external norms and are thus said to be more rigid, reflect intracommunity power relations, and often see themselves as "true to faith" (or, at least, they develop a two-tier system of religious norms where extrafaith laws govern ancillary or earthly aspects of life, whereas sacred law governs matters seen by the community as essential to preserving the faith's "pith and substance").

Another rationale for co-optation echoes Adam Smith's treatment of religions as if they were firms developing products and competing for customers.[9] The official establishment of a religion may turn religious authorities into inefficient and lazy monopolists who try to please government officials and elites interested in theology rather than attract potential customers. Formal establishment, along with government support and privileges, is likely to discourage the monopoly clergy from engaging in any type of dissident social activism. It is here that the pacifying co-optation impulse and the insight that official establishment can promote inefficient complacency within that state religion may come together to explain why, quite counterintuitively, countries facing increasing support for principles of theocratic governance may elect to enshrine such principles constitutionally as their state religion.

By contrast, disestablishment of religion creates a free market in which religions can compete for the attention of particular believers.[10] As Roger Finke and Rodney Stark suggest, sectlike religions, which tend to be populist and demanding of their followers, will generally fare better in unregulated, disestablishment markets than churchlike religions, which tend to be hierarchical and more accommodating of mainstream lifestyles. In their terminology, sects emphasize "salvation," whereas churches specialize in "theology." Most consumers, they argue, prefer salvation.[11] Thus, as several astute observers of American political development—from Alexis de Tocqueville to Seymour M. Lipset—have argued, the elimination of established religion in the United States has helped strengthen religion in that country.[12] An ultra-vibrant market of religion has emerged, with thousands of different types of religious congregations, sects, and splinter groups, many of which are active and zealous. The remarkable development and growth of African American churches from the early nineteenth century forward may be explained by America's free marketplace of religion. Like other upstart sects, these churches competed for adherents and used American norms of religious freedom to construct organizational havens with little outside intervention. Likewise, under monopolistic conditions, the Catholic Church in Latin America lacked an incentive to advance the religious and social needs of the poor, rural communities. But when the Catholic clergy were confronted with the expansion of mainline Protestantism emanating from the United States, they had to fight for support and thus became major institutional promoters of rural indigenous causes, and the church even adjusted its theological teachings and symbolism to reflect this new indigenous rights agenda.[13]

Furthermore, the legalization point has another centralizing aspect to it. Historically, in most places religious law has operated primarily as private law. Its traditional location was in noncentralized religious institutions in which the judgment of individual jurists was autonomous, final, and certainly not subject to appeal.[14] Cases were voluntarily brought to religious tribunals by private parties, not by a public prosecuting authority, and there was no state enforcement mechanism. The whole enterprise was run as an informal but socially and morally binding arbitration system. As Martin Shapiro has noted, drawing on social theorist Max Weber's ideal-type categorization, nonappellate "*kadi* justice" in Islamic jurisprudence (e.g., judgments by individual *mujtahid*s) reflects the absence of central political authority.[15] In fact, it was not until the later days of the Ottoman Empire that appeal courts began to emerge in the Islamic tradition, possibly because judicial appeal procedures require some political and administrative centralization.[16]

By contrast, formal codification of Islamic law transfers the locus of authority to interpret it from *kadi* justice settings to state-appointed judges. More broadly, the change of religious law from an uncodified and locally administered set of legal practices to a codified, state-centered system of laws and tribunals allowed colonial authorities, and later state administration in postcolonial Africa and Asia, to revise and redefine certain aspects of religious law in ways they deemed essential to their interests. The Tanzimat legal reforms and the codification of Islamic law in the late days of the Ottoman Empire transformed Shari'a from being the product of perpetual and dynamic processes of interpretation to a more static and delineated set of rules. Perhaps even more important, it moved authority over the law from the scholars to the state. Scholars were "relegated to the role of the minor religious functionaries," with adjudicative jurisdiction over family law as their only "consolation prize."[17] Instead, judges not rigorously trained as Islamic scholars were appointed by the state to administer the law in all other areas. The fact that law now emanated from the state and not God translated into judges' reluctance to treat organs of the state as subordinate to religious directives.[18]

Likewise, the formal constitutionalization of religion brings religious law to the fore of the public law domain, where the state, with its central political authority, regulatory hierarchies, and appellate procedures, has always been a key stakeholder. The history of constitutionalism in Iran—alas, seldom referred to by scholars of comparative constitutionalism—is a vivid example of precisely these public/private tensions. The 1979 Islamic revolution in Iran was marred from its outset by an internal divide between religious-conservative forces advocating a traditional reading of Shari'a and socially progressive forces who advocated redistributive policies against the backdrop of the tremendous social and economic gaps created and maintained by the shah's regime. Whereas the former camp took a more classical (private-law-oriented) approach to religious law, the second faction within the revolutionary movement adopted a collectivist-egalitarian (social or public) approach to it. The conservative religious cleric-based Guardian Council emerged as the bastion of the traditionalist view, whereas the Majlis (the parliament or consultative assembly) represented a distinctly more progressive view. In fact, the very establishment (in the 1980 minicounterrevolution) of the Guardian Council was aimed at ensuring the conformity of the Majlis's legislation with the constitution and Shari'a, thereby setting up an institutional and ideological war between the Guardian Council, with its classical (private) legal interpretive doctrine, and the Majlis's tilt toward social (public) law and enhanced state power. The clash between the two bodies, therefore, focused on the breadth of private legal rights vis-à-vis state powers, and by extension the very challenge of transforming a historically private law enterprise into a public law one.

In 1987 the clash between individualist-libertarian (classical or private) and collectivist-egalitarian (social or public) factions within the revolutionary movement in Iran grew into a constitutional crisis that eventually brought about the establishment of an overarching judicial-review-like body to protect "state interest" and to promote a more flexible, pragmatic, "public law" form of Shari'a-based law.[19] The post-1979 constitutional arrangement had vested tremendous power in the hands of the Guardian Council's classical jurists with the overwhelming institutional power to veto socially oriented legislation. The effect was dramatic. From 1980 until the unfolding of the crisis in 1987, the Guardian Council vetoed 220 pieces of legislation, over one-third of the overall bills, effectively prioritizing the interests of the wealthiest merchants *(bazaaris)* over those of the peasantry and the urban working class.[20]

Khomeini, the supreme leader, had to resolve the ideological and institutional war. He opted for a two-punch move. In 1988 he dismissed his designated successor, Ayatollah Montazeri, the foremost supporter of the social faction. Khomeini then called for an amendment of the constitution institutionalizing the Regime's Discernment Expediency Council (Majma-e Tashkhis Maslahat Nezam) to serve as the final arbiter between the generally more progressive Majlis and the distinctly more conservative Guardian Council (Shoray-e Negahban).[21] Article 112 of the 1989 amended constitution states that the newly created Expediency Council "shall be convened at the order of the Leader to determine such expedience in cases where the Council of Guardians finds an approval of the Majlis against the principles of Shari'a or the Constitution, and the Majlis in view of the expedience of the System is unable to satisfy the Council of Guardians, as well as for consultation in matters referred to it by the Leader, and for discharging other functions laid down in this law." In other words, the 1989 amendment introduced a local, mutated version of judicial review in Iran. The authority of the Expediency Council was expanded further by Ayatollah Seyed Ali Khamenei. This new body aids the government in asserting its pragmatist approach to public policy making (based on the concept of "national necessity") over the Guardian Council's more doctrinal, rigid interpretive approach to pertinent religious directives.[22] At the same time, the creation of the Expediency Council was also aimed at aiding the national project of transforming the traditional private law enterprise of Shari'a law into a public law enterprise. The Expediency Council is also used as a device to maintain cohesion or coordinate the disparate interests within the ruling class.[23] At any rate, it seems that constitutional law and institutional structures, even in the least favorable settings, disarm the clerical voice of much of its rigid, counterpragmatic tone.

Jurisdictional Advantages

Another reason that constitutional law and courts appeal to antireligionists is state law's *jurisdictional advantages,* both prescriptive and adjudicative, over religious law and tribunals. Jurisdictional struggles and wars of courts are, of course, not exclusive to the secular/religious rift. Law in federal countries or in supranational polities has always been marred by jurisdictional tensions between the center and the units, be they subnational provincial or state authorities or member states in a supranational regime. Jurisdictional competition and coordination, or questions regarding which set of laws applies to various scenarios, are common features in the European Union. In fact, the European Court of Justice's landmark *Van Gend and Loos* and *Costa v. ENEL* (1964) decisions mark a defining moment in the history of the European Union. In these decisions the court declared that European law was paramount over national law, thereby creating an obligation for national courts to enforce EU law over conflicting national laws. Some evidence even suggests that lower courts in member states tend to support EU legislation more than upper courts because the latter view supranational law as a possible threat to their authority, whereas lower courts regard supranational law as a tool to curtail upper courts' hegemony. In other settings courts vie to carve out an autonomous space for their influence and, more generally, attempt to establish, maintain, or extend their authority and ambit of influence vis-à-vis other sources of authority, judicial or political. Civil law systems that have established constitutional courts alongside their systems of ordinary courts have traditionally had difficulty defining the precise jurisdictional dividing line between them.[24]

In the secular/religious context state law and courts, whether religion infused or not, often enjoy the edge over religious law and tribunals. State law is centrally legislated, is standardized, and catches the activities of most or all private and public entities. Ideally, it is uniformly enforced and applied throughout the territory and over members of the polity. As we shall see in the following chapters, the effective jurisdictional dominance of state law and courts has proven instrumental in the secularist bid to tame religion. The Supreme Court of Pakistan, for example, has been successfully protecting its overarching review authority vis-à-vis the proreligious jurisprudence of the Shari'at Appellate Bench. The Federal Court of Malaysia and the Nigerian Supreme Court have applied constitutional principles of federalism to bog down the implementation of far-reaching religious legislation at the state level. A pinnacle of the Supreme Court of Israel's liberalizing jurisprudence in matters of religion and state is its subjection of the religious courts' jurisprudential autonomy in matters of personal status to the general principles of due process and gender equality. The court's reasoning has been that religious tribunals in Israel are statutory entities, created by Israeli state law and funded by the government, and therefore are subject to the state's enabling as well as limiting functions, administrative law norms, and overall constitutional principles. In India (with respect to personal-status laws) and in South Africa (with respect to tribal or customary law) constitutional jurisprudence has advanced legal uniformity and standardized norms against religion-based autonomous jurisdictional enclaves and quests for substantive exemptions.

Ironically, the uniformity and standardization aspect was initially one of the main reasons that the church gained an edge over its nonreligious competitors in medieval Europe. In fact, the initial streamlining and unification of religious law under what is known as canon law and the expansion of its territorial applicability throughout much of medieval Europe planted the seeds of modern law.[25] This is worthy of consideration when one seeks to grasp fully the current jurisdictional advantage of state law over religious law. Canon law is internal ecclesiastical law governing the Roman Catholic Church, the Eastern Orthodox churches, and the Anglican Communion of churches. It deals mainly with matters of faith, morals, and discipline, although these areas have been generously interpreted by church authorities to encompass numerous material aspects of life. The way in which such church law is legislated, interpreted, and at times adjudicated varies widely among these three bodies of churches. In all three traditions, however, a canon was initially a rule adopted by a central council or religious authorities. It was imposed over a vast territory by regional and local agents who were part of a hierarchical structure of authority. Its ontological and epistemological structure, modes of adjudication, and application resembled in many respects our perception of modern law today. Over the years the study of canon law became a major scholarly discipline, and, through a continual process of precedent accumulation, elaboration, and interpretation, canon law was refined into an internally consistent code.[26]

Before this process of codification occurred, and until the eleventh century, most law was customary, and very little of it was in writing. No professional judiciary, no professional class of lawyers, and no distinct "science" of law existed. As Harold Berman notes, there was "no independent, integrated, developing body of legal principles and procedures clearly differentiated from other processes of social organization and consciously articulated by a corps of persons specifically trained for that task."[27] But in the late eleventh and early twelfth centuries a wave of legalism spread throughout Europe. The main driving force behind this sudden transformation was the assertion of papal supremacy over the entire Western church and a push toward the independence of the church from secular control. This has come to be known as the Papal Revolution, marked by the formal declaration to that effect by Pope Gregory VII in 1075. Of course, neither monarch nor civil authorities conceded without a fight. Bloody wars took place throughout Europe between the emperor's party and the papal party, which eventually emerged triumphant toward the end of the twelfth century. Canon law, and with it modern law, was born.

As Berman notes, from that moment on, the "folklaw" of peoples of Europe disappeared almost completely and was replaced by sophisticated legal systems, first for the church and then for the secular political orders—canon law, urban law, royal law, mercantile law, and feudal and manorial law. Studies of concrete legal practices—for example, Marianne Constable's account of the English "mixed-jury" doctrine from the Middle Ages to the nineteenth century—also reveal the disappearance of "law as practice" and a process whereby law rooted in actual practices and customs of communities was replaced by law determined by officials.[28] Eventually a series of great political and economic revolutions further transformed the Western legal tradition and established it in the professional form it has taken over the last century. But its origins may be traced back to the successful papal attempt to establish a uniform church-based legal authority over a vast territory and an array of subject matters and, in so doing, to minimize the impact of competition such as local customary law or secular political orders. Today's state-backed secular law's advantage is merely a mirror image of religious law's edge in the premodern era.

By being more or less universal, internally coherent, and cumulative, the church's canon law, administered by ecclesiastical courts overseen by bishops, enjoyed an organic advantage over its possible competitors. Ecclesiastical courts claimed jurisdiction over a wide array of subject matters, from all matrimonial and testamentary cases to all civil and criminal cases involving clerics and church property, and to cases involving issues the church considered crucial, such as heresy, blasphemy, sorcery, usury, defamation, fornication, homosexuality, adultery, violation of oaths and perjury (effective jurisdiction over much of the contract law of the day), and injury to and assault on clerics or religious places.[29] "As far as canon law was concerned, any case involving any of these matters could be instituted by filing a complaint in the court of the appropriate archdeacon or bishop, and an appeal could be taken by the losing party to the court of the appropriate archbishop and thence to the court of the pope in Rome."[30] As we shall see in Chapter 6, the resemblance to today's secular/religious jurisdictional wars and especially to both parties' "imperialist," expansive conceptualization of subject-matter jurisdiction is striking.

The similarity does not end there. Another clear advantage that canon law had over secular counterparts in premodern Europe, but that it no longer enjoys in today's nation-state, is cheaper enforcement costs. The omnipresence of the church in most avenues of life in Middle Ages Europe made conviction or faith an effective substitute for police forces.[31] The threat of hell or an otherwise doomed afterlife was an effective deterrent. As a result, canon law in medieval Europe was nearly self-enforcing. By contrast, not all secular entities at the time possessed the fiscal means to establish effective deterrence or enforcement mechanisms, and those entities that lacked such mechanisms had to cede authority to the church. In fact, there is some evidence suggesting that secular courts in medieval Europe "free rode" on the effective excommunication mechanisms developed by the church to enhance enforcement of punishments for "secular" offenses.[32] Excommunication became a common punishment for such offenses as failure to appear in court when summoned, civil debts, and property disputes.

To establish its authority despite these tough market conditions, the state resorted to brutal modes of punishment, captured by Michel Foucault in his acclaimed *Discipline and Punish: The Birth of the Prison.*[33] When state authority was not all-encompassing and wide enclaves of resistance persisted (think of Robin Hood's control over Sherwood Forest), the monarch pursued repression of the populace through brutal public displays of executions and torture. By contrast, in the modern era, when state authority became less contested and was gradually extended to the entire territory controlled by the state, the trial stage became more important, while the punishment itself became far less public. The dark dungeon of the embattled premodern state has been replaced with the bright modern prison (for Foucault, a metaphor for modernity) modeled on Jeremy Bentham's Panopticon design for prisons, whereby a single guard can watch over many prisoners while the guard remains unseen. At any rate, the modern state's enforcement edge over religion—a mirror image of religious law's jurisdictional advantage in the premodern era—is one of the reasons, alongside co-optation, that those who are not keen on overreligiosity turn to courts in their fight against theocracy.

The state's jurisdictional advantage over religious authorities is also reflected in a move in countries that enshrine a given religion and its sacred texts and interpretations in their constitutions to enact laws that carve out and insulate certain areas of the law, most notably economic law, from the influence of religious law. Secular jurisdictional enclaves of several sorts exist in many predominantly Muslim countries, ranging from Saudi Arabia to Qatar to the Maldives and from Dubai to the Comoros. Even in the Ras al-Khaimah emirate at the northern tip of the United Arab Emirates—a relative stronghold of Iranian-influenced Shi'ite fundamentalism—new legislation and regulations adopted over the last few years favor big international interests for offshore business purposes and exempt certain aspects of economic law from religious restrictions. Such jurisdictional enclaves allow lucrative industries that require departure from religious directives (e.g., finance, commerce, or tourism) to mitigate many of the non-business-friendly implications of Islamic restrictions on usury, insurance, and nonworkmanship enrichment more generally.

In some instances certain geographic regions are insulated or partly exempted from religious precepts, such as the so-called free-trade zones in Iran. In 1993, the Iranian Majlis approved the Free Zones Act, which established Kish Island, Qeshm Island, and the Port of Chabahar as the Free Zones of Iran. These were introduced in an attempt to alleviate some of the economic hardships following the Iran-Iraq War, as well as in response to the emergence of a supranational trade bloc in the Gulf region. Each of Iran's free-trade zones has a set of bylaws that define and set out all regulations pertaining to import, export, investment, insurance, banking, and employment within these zones. Among the perks offered to the international investor are full exemption from "Islamic banking" hurdles, tourist attractions, guaranteed repatriation of capital and accumulated profit in case of nationalization, and other benefits that are, by any stretch of the imagination, not fully compatible with a straightforward reading of Shari'a.

Jurisdictional reforms are not limited to economic law. Several countries in the Middle East (e.g., Egypt in 2000, Morocco in 2004, and Algeria in 2005) have embarked on family-law reforms that involve the codification of legal amalgams of moderate Islamic sources and secular legal principles such as gender equality and procedural justice.[34] The reform in the Moroccan Personal Status Code (Mudawwana), for example, declares that husband and wife are jointly responsible for the family, and that women are not subject to the "guardianship" of a male family member, can institute a divorce, and have the right to demand a monogamous commitment from their husbands as a condition for the acceptance of a marriage. A National Women's Day was established in 2008 to commemorate the adoption of the family-law reform. In a similar vein, Israel has adopted a system of civil family courts that adjudicate all matters of personal status except marriage and divorce, thereby curtailing the jurisdictional autonomy of religious tribunals. These legal reforms erode the jurisdictional and interpretive stature of religious authorities and make the modernized areas of law justiciable by ordinary courts.

Strategic Delegation

A political quest for legitimacy, or for lowering risks or costs, often drives deference to the judiciary in cases involving hotly contested political issues. To begin with, politicians and policy makers may commission and value expert knowledge as a way of lending authority to their preferences or to signal their capacity to make sound decisions. They likewise may draw selectively on expert knowledge—state bureaucracy, academic research, or judicial authority—to justify or legitimize the policy choices they make or to establish authority in contentious and risky areas of policy.[35] At a bare minimum, a blame-deflection logic may be at work. From the politicians' points of view, the strategic delegation of contentious political questions to the courts may be an effective means of shifting responsibility and thereby reducing the risks to themselves and to the institutional apparatus within which they operate. The calculus of this blame-deflection strategy is intuitive. If a delegation of decision-making power to the courts will increase the credit or reduce the blame attributed to the politician as a result of the policy decision of a delegated body, then a referral of this sort to the courts will benefit the politician.[36] At the very least, the transfer of contested political issues to the courts offers a convenient retreat for politicians who have been unwilling or unable to settle contentious public disputes in the political sphere. It may also offer refuge for politicians seeking to avoid difficult or no-win decisions or the collapse of deadlocked or fragile governing coalitions.[37] Likewise, when politicians are obstructed from fully implementing their own policy agenda, they may favor the active exercise of constitutional review by a sympathetic judiciary in order to overcome those obstructions.[38] In other words, transferring these contested issues to the courts allows secularist leaders to offer up their commitment to religious values without having actually to sign on to the concurrent expectations that are attached.

What I have termed elsewhere the logic of "hegemonic preservation" may also be at work here.[39] In relatively open political settings judicial empowerment may reflect the competitiveness of a polity's electoral market or governing politicians' time horizons. According to the "party-alternation" model, for example, when a ruling party expects to win elections repeatedly, the likelihood of an independent and powerful judiciary is low. When a ruling party has a low expectation of remaining in power, it is more likely to support a powerful judiciary to ensure that the next ruling party cannot use the judiciary to achieve its policy goals. Scholars draw on this "insurance" logic to explain the variance in judicial power between Japan and the United States; between different periods in the late nineteenth-century United States; between three postauthoritarian Asian countries (South Korea, Mongolia, and Taiwan); between several polities in Eastern Europe and between new democracies in southern Europe (Greece, Spain, and Portugal); and between two Argentine provinces.[40]

The same logic may explain deference to the judiciary by increasingly vulnerable elites and influential political power holders. The threat of losing control over pertinent policy-making processes and outcomes may be a significant driving force behind attempts to transfer contentious issues to the courts. Politicians are more likely to divert policy-making responsibility to a relatively supportive judiciary when present or prospective transformations in the political system seem to threaten their own political status and policy preferences. Influential sociopolitical groups fearful of losing their grip on political power may support the judicialization of megapolitics, and the establishment of judicial review and empowerment of constitutional courts more generally, as a hegemony-preserving maneuver. Such groups and their political representatives are more likely to support the judicialization of formative nation-building and collective-identity questions when their hegemony, worldviews, and entitlement to disproportional perks and benefits are being increasingly challenged in majoritarian decision-making arenas. Examples abound.

Having opposed constitutionalism and judicial review throughout most of the twentieth century, white elites in South Africa discovered the virtues of judicial review only when it became clear that the days of apartheid were numbered. The Mexican government, led for more than seventy years by the Partido Revolucionario Institucional (PRI), launched a major expansion of judicial power during the 1990s when it became clear that the PRI's control over Mexican politics was about to end. The historically hegemonic but electorally challenged coalition of monarchists, army generals, and state bureaucracy in Thailand turned to the previously passive judiciary to depose the antiestablishment Prime Minister Thaksin Shinawatra and his Thai Rak Thai Party, to topple Prime Minister Samak Sundaravej (for nothing more than violating the Thai Constitution by accepting payment of $200 for appearing on two cooking shows while in office), and to disband much of the People Power Party (an offshoot of the formerly banned Thai Rak Thai), which had won the 2007 parliamentary election. Conversely, little or no judicial empowerment has taken place in countries such as Japan or Singapore where a single political force has controlled the political system for most of the last half century. The same logic may apply with regard to constitutionalization itself.

Although throughout the 1950s and 1960s Great Britain was unwilling to incorporate the provisions of the European Convention on Human Rights into its own legal system (let alone to enact a constitutional bill of rights of its own), it promoted enthusiastically the entrenchment of convention rights in the "independence constitutions" of newly self-governing African states as a device to protect established interests from the "whims" of independent majoritarian politics.[41] The 1991 constitutionalization of rights in British-ruled Hong Kong took place shortly after the British Parliament had ratified the Joint Declaration on the Question of Hong Kong, whereby Britain was to restore Hong Kong to China in July 1997. Likewise, the contemporaneous emergence of a sense of urgency in adopting an EU constitution and the European Union's eastward expansion could seem to be anything but coincidental. The EU constitution may be viewed as an attempt to increase the credibility of interstate commitments through the introduction of a binding mechanism that would effectively reduce the threat of accession countries (present and future) advocating worldviews and policy preferences that diverge significantly from those favored by core EU member states. In short, it is the potential or actual arrival of credible political competition, or the emergence of new constituencies or constellations of power, that leads threatened elites to discover the charms of constitutional protections and judicial review.

Politicians' drive toward using the courts when it is politically expedient to do so is perhaps best illustrated in countries where growing popular support for principles of theocratic governance threatens the cultural propensities and policy preferences of secular-nationalist elites. The Kemalist elite in Turkey discerned the benefits of a strong constitutional court mainly in the last few decades, when its historical grip on Turkish politics became seriously challenged by Kurdish and later by Islamist parties. Similarly, the newly elected government of Pakistan led by the Pakistan People's Party (PPP) was quick to ratify the International Covenant on Economic, Social, and Cultural Rights in April 2008 and to sign the International Covenant on Civil and Political Rights,[42] having defeated President Pervez Musharraf in the February 2008 elections and in anticipation of a horror-film-character–like rise from the ashes of a military regime.

Support for Hamas, whose emerald green banner bears the Islamic axiom "There is no God but God, and Muhammad is his prophet," is centered in the refugee camps and shantytowns of the Gaza Strip and in the West Bank's smaller towns, while the old Palestinian elite who favor the secular-nationalist Fatah movement are located mainly in the West Bank's business and government centers. Having won the Palestinian Authority parliamentary elections in 2006, Hamas managed a takeover in Gaza in June 2007, while the West Bank continued to be controlled by the Palestinian Authority government. Following the surprise victory by Hamas in the January 2006 parliamentary elections, the historically hegemonic Fatah movement attempted to establish a constitutional court with wide judicial review powers. This move can only be seen as an attempt to constrain Hamas when it took over the Legislative Authority. A new nine-judge court was to be convened with judges appointed by President Mahmoud Abbas of Fatah, which would have the power to rule illegal those laws judged to violate the Palestinian Basic Law. Theoretically, at least, Abbas would have effectively been in a position to veto laws passed by Hamas legislators. In its first legislative move in Parliament, however, Hamas voted to invalidate all legislation passed by the outgoing Fatah following the 2006 election, including the creation of the constitutional court.

In other words, in addition to being a Ulysses and the sirens-like self-binding against a polity's own imperfections, constitutionalization may also be driven by self-interested binding of other rival groups, worldviews, and policy preferences. The main assertions of such a realist position—most notably that the degree of political uncertainty facing governing elites and politicians, either on the decline or insecure in their newly acquired power, is an important predictor of whether or not a constitutional court will be established—have been supported in a variety of studies ranging from formal modeling to large-N statistical analyses. Furthermore, its basic premise that people tend to be risk-averse under conditions of systemic uncertainty has been advanced by a wide array of thinkers in other scholalry domains, from Rawls's "principles of justice" agreed upon behind a veil of ignorance to Marshall Sahlins's paradigm-shifting explanation for the lack of food accummulation or storage among hunter-gatherer societies (a perception of unlimited resources and a pervasive belief in a "giving environment"), and to Tversky and Kahneman's seminal work on the psychology of choice.

Neighboring Israel provides a paradigmatic illustration of the hegemonic-preservation impulse behind judicial empowerment. Israel's Mapai (Labor) Party and its mainly secular Ashkenazi establishment constituencies opposed judicial review for decades but embraced constitutional supremacy once the country's electoral balance shifted against it. From the prestatehood years to the 1970s, the Labor movement's grip over Israel's political arena was almost undisturbed. During the first three decades of Israel's independence, when its control of Israeli politics was virtually unchallenged, Prime Minister David Ben-Gurion's Mapai opposed the adoption of a bill of rights and repeatedly championed the democratic character of parliamentary sovereignty and majority rule. However, for a host of demographic, political, and economic reasons, domestic and international, the last three decades have seen a continuous decline in the political power and representation of the Labor camp and its traditional allies. The Labor Party held 63 Knesset seats in 1968, but shrank to 19 seats in the 2006 elections and to a meager 13 in the 2009 elections, based on approximately 10 percent popular support, an incredible record low for this formerly dominant, all-encompassing movement. Meretz (identified mainly with the Zionist Left, the secular urban intelligentsia, and the kibbutzim), won only 5 seats in 2006 and continued its free fall in 2009 with only 3 seats, the lowest numbers in the party's history.[43] Meanwhile, hitherto-antiestablishment voices have gradually gained popular (and electoral) support. The Shas Party alone (representing mainly religious Mizrahi [mostly Jews of North African and Middle Eastern origin] residents of development towns and poor urban neighborhoods) increased its power impressively from 4 Knesset seats in 1984 (63,600 votes) to 10 seats in 1996 (260,000 votes) and to 17 seats in 1999 (430,000 votes), making it the third-largest party in the 15th Knesset. Although its electoral power has declined somewhat, Shas remains one of the largest parties in the Knesset, and its leader, Eli Yishai, is the deputy prime minister and holds the key office of minister of the interior, which controls Israel's local government, municipalities, and the national population registry.[44] Meanwhile, religious luminaries and "spiritual leaders" gained tremendous authority and popularity among low-income voters associated with Shas or with other religious parties. At the margins of this trend, Israel has seen the rise of what may be termed Jewish fundamentalism, which has manifested itself in vigorous opposition to the peace process and played a key role, as well, in the assassination of Prime Minister Yitzhak Rabin and the murder of Muslims at prayer sites, riots in the mixed cities of Haifa, Nazareth, and Acre, and other incidents.[45]

The expansion of the electorate by the addition of approximately one million newly arrived immigrants from the former Soviet Union and elsewhere (roughly 15 percent of Israel's population) also contributed to destabilizing the Labor movement's historical grip on political power. In the 2009 elections the Israel Beiteinu Party ("Israel is our home" in Hebrew), representing primarily the Russian immigrant population, managed to receive 12 percent of the popular vote, which translated into fifteen Knesset seats. Led by the controversial Avigdor Liberman, the party established itself as a main opponent, alongside religious parties and leaders, of judicial activism and what it sees as the court's "leftist" jurisprudential agenda. Ironically, Israel Beiteinu as well as other political movements representing settled immigrants from the former Soviet Union advance a right-wing nationalist agenda combined with an antireligious stand, primarily in matters of personal status issues (applying strict religious definition for determining "who is a Jew," for example, runs against the interests of some of these parties' voters). These parties are thus anything but natural allies of the Orthodox religious parties.

These changes in the body politic have also been reflected in municipal elections. Candidates representing the policy preferences of religious, Mizrahi, and other previously peripheral voices have become influential political actors in major urban centers traditionally dominated by Labor and the Ashkenazi establishment, as well as in numerous development towns and peripheral local authorities.[46] The decline in Labor's electoral representation has been accompanied by the crumbling of the Histadrut, Israel's main labor union and one of the Labor movement's traditional power bases. In short, the heyday of the historically hegemonic Labor Party and the Ashkenazi establishment is over. As long as these historically hegemonic elites remained virtually unchallenged in their control of core political and economic institutions, they had no reason to undermine their position by delegating power to the judiciary through the entrenchment of rights and the establishment of judicial review. This led to a constitutional stalemate that persisted from the early 1950s until the late 1980s. But as Israel's historically hegemonic elites increasingly lost their grip on Israel's core policy-making forums, their attitude toward judicial review changed. Given the court's record of adjudication and its personal composition, as well as the ideological tilts, educational background, and cultural propensities of its justices, Israel's embattled old elites can safely assume that its worldviews and policy preferences will be less effectively contested by emerging voices in Israeli politics. The "constitutional revolution" of 1992–1995 and the wholesale judicialization of existential political questions followed the Labor Party's decline too closely to discount the relationship between these events.[47]

What helped reduce the short-term risk for those who initiated the transition to juristocracy was a sufficient level of certainty that the judiciary in general, and the Supreme Court in particular, were likely to produce decisions that would serve the interests and reflect the ideological preferences of the politicians who advocated stronger courts. In that respect the Supreme Court has certainly delivered the goods for those who chose to empower it. The court has, in this way, become a bastion of "reason" and "sanity" for Israel's "enlightened public"—a criterion frequently used by the Supreme Court of Israel (SCI) throughout the 1990s to determine the "reasonableness" of specific acts.[48] As we shall see in the next chapter, this court-constructed "enlightened public" closely conforms to the characteristics of the old secular Ashkenazi establishment at the center of the Zionist consensus and shares its worldviews and policy preferences. Unsurprisingly, most political opposition to the court has come primarily from orthodox, traditionalist, or nationalist religious circles who accuse the court of forwarding its own unrepresentative, liberalizing, antireligious, and even anti-Jewish agenda.

The religious resentment toward the court and its jurisprudence is perhaps the best indication of the court's ideological leanings. It is evident in mass demonstrations and acerbic public speeches as well as at the most ordinary lower-court proceedings involving religious litigants. For example, in a recent case concerning a forged signature on a check heard before the Tel-Aviv Municipal Court, the respondent, an Orthodox yeshiva, suggested that the court was an illegitimate forum and referred to its judges as *akum,* a Talmudic acronym made up of the initial letters of the words *ovde kokhabkim u mazzaloth* ("worshippers of stars and planets"; the Talmud refers in that way to the Gentiles, who lacked all knowledge of the true God). Needless to say, the court dismissed these claims out of hand.[49] More aggressive resistance to court rulings perceived as antireligious are not uncommon. In recent years alone, Haredi clashes with police took place following court rulings on work, shopping, or traffic during the Jewish Sabbath; the sale of leavened products during Passover; and the use of forensic pathology to determine the cause of death in suspicious cases.

The serious verbal attacks on the Supreme Court intensified considerably in the late 1990s, following the "constitutional revolution" and later the conviction of former member of the Knesset (MK) Arieh Deri (then the leader of Shas) on charges of bribery, fraud, and breach of fidelity by the Jerusalem District Court. This conviction (which led ultimately to Deri's resignation from the political leadership of Shas) was characterized by Shas's leaders as the outcome of a secular Ashkenazi establishment conspiracy against the whole Mizrahi Orthodox community. Fierce verbal attacks on the judiciary by Orthodox Mizrahi religious leaders resumed in the wake of the Supreme Court's rejection of Deri's appeal in the summer of 2000. In response to this decision, Shas's leadership declared that the closure of the Deri case was "the signal for the start of the Mizrahi Jewry's revolution" and that the Supreme Court's decision was "another twist of the knife that has been stuck in the Mizrahi body for 52 years"[50] (the State of Israel was established in 1948).

In 1999, following a Supreme Court decision expressing dissatisfaction over the delay in convening gender-mixed religious councils, an unprecedented uprising against the secular legal establishment in Israel in general and the Supreme Court in particular erupted in Orthodox circles. The uprising reached its zenith when some 250,000 people attended a mass demonstration against the court in Jerusalem. The demonstration was headed by most of the Orthodox religious leaders in Israel. In his public speech at this event Rabbi Ovadia Yosef, the spiritual leader of the Shas Party and the most important Mizrahi religious leader in Israel, went so far as to declare:

> The justices of the Supreme Court are wicked, stubborn, and rebellious . . . they are empty-headed and reckless . . . they violate Shabbat . . . and they are the cause of all the world's torments . . . The justices are slaves who now rule us . . . they are not worthy of even the lowest court . . . Any seven-year-old boy is better versed in the Torah than they are.[51]

Rabbi Yosef also attacked then Justice Minister Tzahi Ha'Negbi (one of the supporters of the new Basic Laws), calling him an "enemy" who "loves those people and made them judges. Did they hold elections? Who says the nation wants wicked judges like these?" Rabbi Moshe Gafni, an ultra-Orthodox MK, stated that the court's interpretation of the 1992 Basic Laws was "a complete fraud" and vowed that "these are the last Basic Laws that will pass the Knesset." Menachem Porush, a prominent ultra-Orthodox leader, threatened the court by saying that "if after this demonstration the Supreme Court is not convinced to cease involvement in religion-state issues, there will be war . . . The people who were here are ready to invade any space."[52] Little has changed over the last decade. In 2009, following the conviction of yet another Shas leader (former Health Minister Shlomo Benizri), Rabbi Ovadia Yosef went on record saying that "the courts are twisted and the judges don't believe in anything. They are apostates."[53] If such vitriolic statements are any indication, secularists' gamble on constitutional law and courts seems to have delivered the core goods for them.

The Epistemology of Constitutional Law

Co-optation, jurisdictional advantages, and strategic delegation are not all that attract certain polity members to the lure of the constitutional court. Rather, the very logic of modern constitutional law, with its embedded notion of overarching objectives and conceptual supremacy, state-driven legitimacy and authority, separation-of-powers structure, procedural rules of engagement, methods and styles of reasoning, and its often measured approaches to politically charged questions, seems intrinsically appealing to those advocating a moderate approach to matters of religion and state.

By definition, constitutional supremacy means that the constitution is the highest law of the land. The constitution's supremacy entails not only that all constituencies and political institutions must abide by it, but also that all other sources of law or legal authority are placed lower than the constitution in a given country's legal hierarchy. It also means that in principle, all other laws, policies, and practices must conform with, or at least not unjustifiably and disproportionately infringe on, principles enshrined in the constitution. So at the simplest, most obvious level, the overarching and all-encompassing supremacy of the constitution brings together everything that moves under its jurisdiction, thereby making it a potentially effective framework for taming antiestablishment forces, religious or otherwise.

But there is much more to the invisible force of constitutionalism that makes it attractive to antireligious interests. To begin with, constitutionalism shares the core elements of what may be termed the *modernist narra-*

tive. Destiny may be averted and passions controlled, for man has the ability to tame nature and to shape and reshape reality through rational, goal-oriented data gathering, planning, and implementation. While nature is fearsome and possibly chaotic, careful institutional engineering can introduce order, help overcome challenges, solve problems, and ultimately create better opportunities in order to serve the public good. At the most abstract level, constitutionalism suggests that desirable social and political outcomes may be accomplished through optimal institutional planning and implementation. Like most other design sciences—the many disciplines, domains, and activities, from urban planning to space exploration, that rely on design to accomplish big, noble goals—it rests on utterly optimistic (albeit not always empirically substantiated) predispositions toward order over chaos, reason over passion, formal authority over informal custom, collective good over individual whims, and evidence-based planning over improvisation and instincts. These goals may be accomplished through careful institutional design, which is assumed to be capable of changing human behavior by enlightenment and education, deterrence and enforcement, or creating meaningful incentives for people (or groups) to behave in a desirable way. Constitutionalism is said to provide a rational, effective way of organizing public life. This involves balancing common good and individual freedoms; fundamental democratic governing principles with realities of very large numbers of participants and inputs; serious disagreements among participants on values, worldviews, identities, policy goals, and methods; and inevitable gaps between aspirations and realities.

More specifically, most modern constitutions establish a nexus of governing institutions and state organs whose legitimacy and raison d'être do not derive from celestial authority. Constitutions are human-made law, adopted by mere mortals, politicians and legal innovators who often purport to represent the authentic public will. Thus constitutions, in essence, are political and earthly, not divine. Although religious and aspirational statements are common in many constitutions, a practical, pragmatic aura surrounds many or all of the governing structures they create. By its very nature a constitution—an entrenched, special piece of legislation—advances the rule of law, often in lieu of and at times in tandem with the rule of God.

Most modern constitutions, including those of most Middle Eastern, African, and Southeast Asian countries, contain some form of constitutional catalogue of rights, individual freedoms, formal equality, and procedural justice, including basic due-process rights, freedom of expression, freedom of religion, and in some cases the right to privacy. By their very nature these rights and liberties are much closer friends of liberalism and secularism than of theocratic governance. Aggregate data suggest that the most common type of constitutional rights cases worldwide is cases dealing with procedural justice and criminal due-process rights, which account for approximately two-thirds of all constitutional rights cases in the world of new constitutionalism dealing with these types of rights. Also common are rulings involving classic civil liberties, the right to privacy, and formal equality. This ever-expanding body of civil liberties jurisprudence has widened and fortified the boundaries of the constitutionally protected private sphere and has transformed numerous policy areas involving individual freedoms.[54] Granted, not all countries, theocratic or otherwise, take an across-the-board endorsing approach toward such rights. However, no matter how weak or tentative these rights provisions are in practice, they still provide a potentially favorable antitheocratic legal platform for secularists, universalists, reformers, and cosmopolitans alike. Either way, Western-style individual rights fare better under constitutionalism than under most systems that engage with either exclusionary or hierarchical discourses of divine authority.

There seems to be another, deeper aspect to this point, namely, the conceptual affinity between the prevalent conception of rights as essentially protecting the private sphere from state interference and the pervasive small-state social and economic thought. Prevalent rights discourse is far more individualistic in its focus than religious law. It assumes that the individual is the ultimate source of meaning, and that individual autonomy is a sine qua non of any just moral order. Religious (or state) coercion disrespects individuals' dignity and autonomy. Overarching belief or meaning systems (except, of course, the secularist, liberal, constitutionalist faith itself) are often treated by contemporary rights discourse as failing to recognize the elevated moral status ("higher than the universal" as Danish philosopher Søren Kierkegaard put it) of the individual. In fact, no sacred law, association, or religious-group identity can fully capture the "true" autonomous essence of the individual. Thus prevalent rights discourse has an a priori secularist tilt to it.

Although many religious directives are aimed at shaping individual, single-agent behavior, the ultimate goal and spirit of such directives are collective. They are aimed, at least prima facie, at creating a better and more moral, ethical, and just society. Much as in the case of nationalism, communism, and other collective ideologies, individual believers may be asked to sacrifice their immediate well-being and desires in order to advance a larger, morally superior collective goal. The survival and well-being of the religious community itself is perceived as a larger collective goal than the well-being or self-fulfillment of its individual participants. Unlike popular rights discourse in the West, most religions are preoccupied with modest lifestyles, welfare rights, redistribution of wealth, and meaningful contribution to the collective. Solipsism and narcissism, let alone lavish, Fifth Avenue–style expensive taste and conspicuous consumption, are not ranked highly in the preaching of most religions. Self-restraint, contributions to collective property and projects, and care for the poor and needy are. In short, the community, not the individual, is at the center of most major religious social orders.

By contrast, canonical rights discourse tends to have a dyadic view of society and often takes an atomistic and at times even solipsistic form. The prevalent culture of rights often leads people to see in others a limitation of their freedom, thereby promoting a morally questionable conception of human relations in which "my fulfillment, my freedom and my self-realization depend upon my self-assertive capacity to place limits on yours."[55] It also exponentially multiplies the occasions for clashes of rights and impedes mutual understanding and the discovery of common ground, thereby trivializing core democratic values.[56] As Pope Benedict XVI noted, without mincing his words, "We are moving towards a dictatorship of relativism, which has as its highest goal one's own ego and one's own desires."[57] This dominant notion of rights as negative freedoms is based on an atomistic view of society as composed of unencumbered individuals operating within an autonomous and self-sufficient private sphere. While this form of rights discourse emphasizes individual freedoms, it does not prioritize substantive equality or equality of outcome, redistribution of material resources, and access to an adequate standard of living, basic needs, services, protections, and meaningful life opportunities.

The canonical interpretation of rights within the potentially richer framework of the "new-constitutionalism" order has done little to block the widening disparities in fundamental living conditions within and among polities. It has proven virtually futile in mitigating, let alone reversing, wide-ranging social and economic processes of deregulation, privatization, reduced social spending, and the removal of "market rigidities." With a few notable exceptions, it has failed to promote the notion that no man, woman, or child can fully enjoy or exercise the classic civil liberties in a meaningful way if he or she lacks the basic essentials for a healthy and decent life in the first place.[58] In fact, in most post-Communist countries, for example, the constitutionalization of rights has been associated with precisely the opposite ethos, placing private ownership and other economic freedoms beyond the reach of majoritarian politics and state regulation and thereby planting the seeds for more, not less, disparity in essential life conditions.

Many religious directives are based on the experience of simple agrarian societies or otherwise premodern markets. Whereas strict adherence to some religious directives may stifle economic growth, constitutional law and courts are generally beneficial for business. It is well established in the law and development literature that constitutionalization and the establishment of judicial review may increase the international reputation and the economic credibility of regimes vis-à-vis foreign creditors and investors.[59] In several Middle Eastern countries, for example, national high courts have played a role in supporting privatization processes, entrenching property rights, and protecting the rights of investors, landlords, and private business.[60] What is more, authoritarian or quasi-democratic regimes may be selective here, abiding by their constitutional rules and maintaining the property and contract rights necessary to establish the credible commitments that create a healthy climate for foreign investment while employing those same formal constitutional procedures when restricting other, noneconomic freedoms.[61] But there also seems to be a deeper, conceptual resemblance between the prevalent conception of rights as essentially negative liberties and ubiquitous neoliberal social and economic thought. The sanctity of the private sphere, human or economic, is a common element in both. Deregulation and privatization, free markets and commodity flow, and economic efficiency and fiscal responsibility are all fundamentals of economic neoliberal orthodoxy. These objectives are rooted in concepts of antistatism, anticollectivism, and social atomism that inform the current hegemonic discourses of rights.[62]

What is more, constitutional courts' very conception of the rule of (state) law, with its deep-rooted orientation toward the European legal tradition and what Max Weber characterized as formal and rational reasoning, with consistent application leading to certainty and predictability, necessarily weakens the potential accommodation of alternative hierarchies of traditional or religious interpretation, supposedly less rational or formal, in Weber's terminology. Modes and methods of constitutional deliberation and reasoning are more hospitable to adversarial argumentation and counterargumentation than to an unquestioningly obedient "Na'aseh Ve'nishma" (Hebrew for "All that the Lord has spoken we will do, and we will be obedient").[63] They reflect the atheistic (or at least agnostic) predisposition to the power and logic of human-made law over that of an unseen creator-god. At a more abstract level, constitutional discourse is often understood as a relatively value-neutral domain that emphasizes a procedural, justice-as-fairness approach over substantive conceptions of the good.[64] As in its antagonism toward any other intolerant, substantive, or holistic perception of the good, this kind of constitutional discourse is not a natural companion to principles of theocratic governance.

A systemic judicial antipathy toward religion and its pre- and extralegal authority and morality resembles, and perhaps to some extent even stems from, what James Scott describes as the modern state's aversion to "local knowledge" and its drive to "cultivate" and domesticate nomads, register and monitor the movement of people, and assert its authority over the entire polity. More generally, the modern state aspires to control things in a "rational" or "planned" manner, often cleverly disguised as a high modernist ideology, with a firm belief that progress can and will make the world a better place.[65] By its very nature the modern state seeks to establish a centralized, one-rule-fits-all governance schema, with a monopoly over the historic national metanarratives that constitute the body politic as such. The modern state is thus at best agnostic and often hostile toward alternative or competing systems of collective identity. As we shall see in Chapter 5, this very difference between commitment to diversity as inclusion and judicial antipathy toward nonstate law viewed as competition explains much of the religion-and-state jurisprudence in contemporary multicultural jurisdictions, ranging from India to Canada to South Africa. When one comprehensive doctrine collides with another, the challenge for courts is fitting one doctrine within the other.[66]

As long as legal claims for accommodation are not seen by courts as challenging the lexical superiority of the constitutional religion itself ("diversity as inclusion"), they stand a fair chance of success. Contrast that with the unyielding reluctance of legislatures and judiciaries to accept as binding or even cognizable any potentially competing legal order that originates in sacred or customary sources of identity and authority. This pattern of clamping down on and refusing to accept any alternative sources of regulation becomes particularly visible where the legal challenge at issue is interpreted as raising doubts regarding which set of norms and institutions, or what set of high priests, should have the final word in authoritatively resolving legal disputes within a given society ("nonstate law as competition"). This is a challenge that no secular legal order, no matter how tolerant and otherwise open to providing exemptions and accommodations to religious believers, can accept with indifference, for what is perceived to be at stake here is the very authority and source of legitimacy of the accepted civil religion.

As I suggest in Chapter 5, this logic may be demonstrated by focusing on recent jurisprudence from Canada and South Africa, two polities that represent the most difficult cases for this argument; if there is any place where we would expect to find recognition by secular countries of religious or customary sources of law and authority, it would be in these diverse societies that have made an explicit constitutional commitment to promote their citizens' freedom to preserve and enhance their multitude of backgrounds and distinctive cultural, linguistic, and religious heritages as part of their "mosaic" (Canada) or "rainbow nation" (South Africa) conceptions of citizenship. Although they operate in different contexts, the South African Constitutional Court and the Supreme Court of Canada seem to have made every effort to subject traditional legal regimes to general principles of constitutional law. By so doing, they have erected a new wall of separation that places noncompliance with the values of the civil religion beyond the pale of accepted accommodation, offering to those who espouse these alternative legal domains the choice either to bring them under the general rule of constitutional law or to encounter the wrath of state fiat.

Indeed, as Charles Taylor observes, early societies with a holistic, omnipresent religion have often been described as "stateless." No monopoly over interpreting God's will was present. But once something like state power arose—with pharaohs in Egypt, say, or stewards of the God in Mesopotamia—the unlimited presence and diffused, communal nature of religion started to break down. "States concentrate power and exercise control; by nature they cannot be entirely guided by preexisting law or custom . . . The sacred web of order now mutates to hierarchy. There are now people, or strata, that are closer to the invisible order than others. The Steward of the God, or the divine king, is the link by which the higher power of the God makes connection with society."[67]

A constitutional court's reluctance to grant support to radical religious views may also derive from its interest in retaining its status as the one and only legitimate interpreter of laws vis-à-vis the perceived menace of alternative interpretation systems (e.g., religious interpreters and authorities that are well established within the circles of supporters of strict theocratic governance and have been steadily gaining support among new crowds). The legal arena here functions much like Pierre Bourdieu's concept of a *field*—a professional arena in which people maneuver and struggle in pursuit of desirable symbolic resources. (Think of how professional guilds, e.g., lawyers' bar associations, are concerned with monitoring the credentials of their members.) Much like conventional medicine's predispositions against alternative treatment methods (sometimes portrayed as mostly unproven, nonscientific, lacking in supportive empirical evidence, even superstitious, and so on), the judges' *habitus* (Bourdieu's term) reflects embedded predispositions for the rule of law and against alternative interpretive systems. Bourdieu's *doxa*—fundamental, deep-founded beliefs, taken as self-evident universals—inform the judges' actions and thoughts within the legal domain. And as Bourdieu famously noted, the combination of *habitus* and *doxa*—certainly in this context—tends to favor the particular social arrangement of the field, thus privileging the dominant and taking their position of dominance as self-evident and universally favorable. Therefore, the categories of understanding and perception that constitute a *habitus,* being congruous with the objective organization of the field, tend to reproduce the very structures of the field. This process of "reproduction of the modes of production" is made transparent by legal discourse that not only "brings into existence that which it utters" but is also "the divine word, the word of divine right, which, like the *intuitus originarius* which Kant ascribed to God, creates what it states, in contrast to all derived, observational statements, which simply record a pre-existing given."[68] In short, it is little wonder that the deep, near-organic reluctance of constitutional courts to recognize the legitimacy of alternative, primarily religious interpretation systems is one of the main reasons for their near-universal appeal to the urban intelligentsia, the managerial class, and proponents of civic nationalism.

Dominant interpretive methods in constitutional law—the "living-constitution" (or "living-tree") doctrine and the "proportionality" (or balancing) approach are two prime examples of how structures of reasoning tend to reinforce courts' centrality in the process of interpretation and norm creation. They also make constitutional law and courts a very appealing domain to pragmatic worldviews and to relatively moderate or secular elites. According to the living-constitution doctrine, a constitution is organic and must be read in a broad and progressive manner so as to adapt it to changing times. Specifically, it should be regarded and interpreted as continually evolving in accordance with pertinent changes in the value system of the society within which it operates. The pragmatist view of the living-constitution doctrine suggests that interpreting the constitution in accordance with long-outdated views leads to arcane and practically unacceptable policies that will thus be rejected by society. For a constitution to remain relevant and applicable, an evolving interpretation is necessary. What is more, proponents of the living-constitution approach contend that most constitutions were intentionally written in broad and flexible terms so as to accommodate, and indeed encourage, a dynamic, "living" document. Without getting into a detailed account of the virtues and vices of the doctrine, one can say that it certainly lends itself more easily than most other interpretive approaches to an injection of the personal values of those who interpret the constitution, and it is a much more practical and effective, if admittedly less principled, way of introducing constitutional change than, say, the process of constitutional amendment. In any case, secular, modernist views in contested areas such as gender equality, reproductive freedoms, nonorthodox sexual preferences, or even principles of modern economy are likely to fare distinctly better under such a living-constitution interpretive approach than under any originalist or ultraorthodox approach to interpreting religious or constitutional provisions.

The living-tree approach is complemented by the emergence of *proportionality* as the prevalent interpretive method in comparative constitutional jurisprudence. It has become the lingua franca of constitutional jurisprudence virtually anywhere beyond the United States, most notably throughout Europe, as well as in India, Canada, New Zealand, Israel, and South Africa,[69] and it is making its way into the jurisprudence of many higher courts in the developing world, from Latin America to Asia, Africa, and the Middle East. This interpretive method, commonly used throughout the world of new constitutionalism, is based on judicious balancing of competing claims, rights, and policy considerations.[70] What is proportionality? It is a practical solution (although its avid proponents insist that it is principled) to the tension between rigidity and flexibility in interpretation of constitutive texts; a quasi-scientific, ideology-free weighing of competing claims, where the "spirit" or "purpose" of the law matters more than its words, and where no principle is absolute, although some are more important than others. Hence infringement on core principles, say, basic rights and liberties, may be allowed, but only to the extent that it is deemed necessary, serves a worthy or just goal, and represents the least drastic violation required to accomplish that goal. A limitation of rights must not go beyond the minimum required under the circumstances; deviation from basic principles of human dignity during wartime should be proportional to the level of threat or "necessity"; and so on. There is another pseudosophisticated element to proportionality: the degree of infringement on core principles reflects the relative significance, principled or practical, the balancer assigns to a competing value or argument. So the more worthy a claim against a core principle is regarded as being, the more willing an interpreter should be to accommodate it, and the deeper the encroachment on the core principle may be. And vice versa: claims deemed of little worth or of too high a cost will be weighed against core principles, but their accommodation will be minimal, in a way that is reflective of their questionable worth. State-appointed courts and judges are to serve as the forum of ultimate wisdom, determine what constitutes a proportional balance, and decide what is the "worth" or "weight" of a given claim in the overall balancing matrix.

By its very nature proportionality epitomizes moderation and conciliation, and favors middle-of-the-road, balanced, or pragmatic solutions to contested issues. It also allows judges to consider nearly any factor, principled or practical, real or hypothetical, in weighing and balancing competing claims. This is a consequentialist, compromise-oriented interpretive method. Extreme or radical positions are not likely to fare well under proportionality. In that respect the appeal of proportionality resembles the triumph of catchall liberalism over narrower, less flexible ideologies. The more absorbent a sponge is, the more liquid it can contain; and the larger a tent is, the more people can find refuge under it. A high-culture product or a specialty food store is not going to attract nearly as many customers as a mainstream news show or a large shopping mall. Likewise, more accommodating, permissive, eclectic, or elastic worldviews enjoy an inherent advantage over strict doctrinal worldviews. Not only do flexible worldviews require less sacrifice from their followers, but their lax boundaries can also appeal to or contain a wider array of preferences. By contrast, rigid doctrinal ideologies, say, religious fundamentalism or radical Maoism, are distinctly more demanding and less accommodating. Regardless of their substantive message, then, they appeal to far fewer people. Thus, much like the "median-voter" or catchall party logic in electoral politics, proportionality enjoys an a priori broader appeal base than more principled or overtly ideological interpretive approaches.

Constitutional jurisprudence in the early twenty-first century is also quite open to foreign influence. Given other broad economic, technological, and cultural convergence processes, let alone the dramatically improved availability of and access to comparative constitutional jurisprudence, jurisprudential cross-fertilization and the globalization of constitutional law more generally seem almost inevitable.[71] In a transnational age, even bastions of insular parochialism cannot avoid a certain degree of international impact.[72] However idiosyncratic or rooted in local traditions and practices a given polity's constitutional law may be, it is unavoidably open to liberalizing global influences either through the migration of constitutional ideas or the urge of transnational constitutional norms. Constitutional courts worldwide increasingly rely on comparative constitutional law to frame and articulate their own position on a given constitutional question. This trend has been described as "a brisk international traffic in ideas about rights," carried on through advanced information technologies by high-court judges who form an international epistemic community of jurists.[73] Indeed, "constitution interpretation across the globe is taking on an increasingly cosmopolitan character, as comparative jurisprudence comes to assume a central place in constitutional adjudication."[74] In short, "Courts are talking to one another all over the world."[75] This has given rise to what may be termed *generic constitutional law*—a supposedly universal, Esperanto-like discourse of constitutional adjudication and reasoning, primarily visible in the context of core civil rights and liberties.[76] This phenomenon is particularly evident with respect to constitutional rights jurisprudence—a perennial bone of contention in constitutional theocracies.

Within this emerging comparative constitutional law enterprise there is an embedded tilt toward cosmopolitanism. In practice, comparative constitutional law is often used for purposes of self-reflection through analogy, distinction, and contrast. The underlying assumption here is that whereas most relatively open, rule-of-law polities face essentially the same set of constitutional challenges, they may adopt quite different means or approaches for dealing with these challenges. By referring to the constitutional jurisprudence and practices of other presumably similarly situated polities, scholars and jurists might be able to gain a better understanding of the set of constitutional values and structures inherent in their own systems. These references also enrich, and ultimately advance, a more cosmopolitan or universalist view of constitutional discourse. This is aided by the rise of supranational human rights regimes and the spread of their norms and jargon to their respective member states. The European Convention on Human Rights and the European Court of Human Rights, for example, have had a nontrivial impact on limiting the influence of religion in predominantly Catholic Spain, Ireland, and Poland, as well as in predominantly Muslim Turkey.

Finally, constitutions and constitutionalism may become a religion-like domain of their own, thereby counterbalancing or even replacing more traditional religious symbols, interpretive discourses, and sources of authority. As several European social theorists have suggested, it is arguable that modernity, despite its secular pretensions, never really was "disenchanted," and that many of its revered institutions, including the very idea of the constitutional democratic state itself, were themselves sacred forms that few dare to question seriously. The U.S. Constitution (most notably the Bill of Rights) and the U.S. Supreme Court have long enjoyed a near-sacred position in American political and civic culture.[77] This trend has been rapidly spreading beyond the United States, with constitutional jurisprudence acquiring the status of a prevalent, morally elevated mode of public deliberation from the European Union and Latin America to South Africa and Canada. This new "civil religion" enhances the attractiveness of legal and constitutional solutions to blazing political problems.

Constitutional law is a modernist enterprise. The very structure, predisposition, epistemology, and contemporary practice of constitutional law make it a more hospitable domain for secularist worldviews and policy preferences than for religious ideology and social order, or for rule-of-God-based perceptions of the good.

Constitutional Delegitimation of Religious Association

As several shrewd observers note, democracy is beneficial to its participants mainly in cases where political divisions do not cut much deeper than the marginal issues on which the polity's constituents can achieve democratic compromise.[78] But when the stakes are very high, democracy loses much of its appeal, particularly for the projected losers. Constitutional provisions that prohibit political association based on religion are one of the common weapons (their questionable effectiveness notwithstanding) used by regimes to contain the tremendous popular following that religious parties in these polities have gained. Algeria, Tunisia, and Egypt are obvious examples.

A constitutional amendment in 1988 allowed for the establishment of political parties in Algeria other than the historically hegemonic National Liberation Front (Front de Libération Nationale, FLN), commonly credited with obtaining Algeria's independence from France. One of the outcomes was the foundation of the now outlawed Islamic Salvation Front (Front Islamique du Salut, FIS), which advocated a Shari'a-based agenda. A vicious decade-long civil war between the French-backed Algerian army and religious militants erupted in 1992 after FIS gained tremendous support among Algerian voters. The FIS won municipal elections in 1990 and later the first round of the parliamentary elections in December 1991, having won over 75 percent of the seats contested in that round, which was the first multiparty election in Algeria.

The army reacted with a military coup that introduced a state of emergency and suspended all electoral processes. Under the state of emergency, impunity for past wrongdoing against Islamists is guaranteed. In 1996 a revised constitution was introduced that remains in effect today. Article 2 of the Algerian Constitution states that "Islam is the religion of the State." Article 42 allows for the formation of political parties. However, it also states that the right to form political parties "cannot be used to violate the fundamental values and components of the national identity . . . as well as the democratic and Republican nature of the State. Political parties cannot be founded on religious, linguistic, racial, sex, corporatist or regional basis." Furthermore, political parties are prohibited from resorting to partisan propaganda based on any of these grounds. No political party can resort to any form of violence or constraint of any nature. If some threat to the National Liberation Front's hegemony appears on the horizon, the constitution has been amended to address it. In November 2008 Parliament approved without debate, and by a vote of 500 in favor, 21 against, and 8 abstentions, a constitutional amendment ending presidential term limits. This allowed President Abdelaziz Bouteflika of the National Liberation Front to run for (and win) a third five-year term in the spring of 2009.[79]

Similarly, Article 1 of the Tunisian Constitution establishes Islam as the state religion. Article 38 further states that the president of the republic must be a Muslim. Article 8 of the constitution guarantees the right to form political parties but states that "political parties must respect the sovereignty of the people, the values of the republic, human rights, and the principles pertaining to personal status. Political parties pledge to prohibit all forms of violence, fanaticism, racism and discrimination. No political party may take religion, language, race, sex or region as the foundation for its principles, objectives, activity or programs." Accordingly, the Islamist party An-Nahdha is banned. It is prohibited for any party to be dependent upon foreign parties or interests. So although Islam is the official state religion and must be the religion of its leader, no political party may take Islam as the basis of its principles.

In a blatant anti–Muslim Brotherhood move in March 2007, Egypt's president Hosni Mubarak introduced a set of constitutional amendments that effectively give more power to the president, ban the establishment of religious parties, and loosen controls on security forces in Egypt's "war on terror." (Quite ironically, "antiterrorism" post-9/11 measures are often distinctly stricter throughout much of the Islamic world than they are in the West.) Among the reforms introduced is the removal of judicial scrutiny of electoral lists, ballots, and procedures. In addition, the Political Parties Law (Law 40/1977), as amended in 2005, allows a committee headed by the ruling party to suspend an existing party's activities if the ruling party judges the suspension to be "in the national interest."

A more restrained version of such constitutional constraints on political participation exists in other "blurred-identity" polities. Consider, for example, the reoccurring dispute in Israel over disbandment of political parties that question the ideological consensus on which the country is based. In 1985 the Knesset passed a law that allowed the Central Election Committee (CEC, a partisan body headed by a senior judge but consisting mainly of mainstream MKs) to disqualify a party on the grounds of its ideological platform. The ground for banning by the CEC has always been that a party favors either a Jewish or a democratic platform exclusively. The CEC's decisions are subject to review by the Supreme Court, which, aside from upholding the ban on the extreme Jewish-nationalist party led by Rabbi Meir Kahane in 1988, has overruled all the CEC decisions to ban parties.[80] A widely reported example of such judicial overturn was the

2003 approval of Azmi B'Shara's Balad Party.[81] In a more recent case in early 2009 the CEC ordered the disqualification of two Arab parties that call for the establishment of Israel as a country for all its citizens, that is, an Israel that is a fully egalitarian, nonethnocratic polity that does not adhere to the Zionist narrative and does not enshrine Judaism as one of its core values. On appeal the Supreme Court overruled the CEC decision and allowed the two parties to take part in the February 2009 elections. Democracy calls for an array of opinions, said the Court, and without a "clear and present danger" to public order there is no reason to limit political participation in this case. At any rate, the constitutional scrutiny of any serious attempt to question the validity of Israel's two-tenet matrix of a Jewish and democratic state, alongside other consensus-building measures, has effectively rendered such questioning socially marginal and politically unviable.

Granted, banning or dissolution of political parties on the basis of these parties' controversial position vis-à-vis sacred national metanarratives is not limited to countries that officially establish religion in their constitutions. As I discuss in Chapter 4, the Turkish Constitution allows for the closure of political parties deemed by the Turkish Constitutional Court as advocating an antistatist or antisecularist agenda. This has led to the closure of nineteen political parties in Turkey since 1983, and most notably pro-Kurdish or pro-religious parties. Courts in countries as diverse as Belgium, Spain, the Czech Republic, Thailand, and Bangladesh have in recent years restricted the political participation of parties advocating messages regarded as dangerous to national integrity, security, or unity. In 2009, the ECtHR upheld a Spanish constitutional court's ban on the Basque Batasuna party and its proxies for its assumed association with—and failure to condemn—a terrorist organization (the ETA) despite not having acted illegally itself (*Herri Batasuna v. Spain*). Such pro-ETA parties, ruled the ECtHR, "contradicted the concept of a 'democratic society' and presented a major danger to Spain's democracy." However, there seems to be a qualitative difference between these instances and bans of parties on the basis of their pro-religious outlook and policy preferences in polities where the constitution itself enshrines the principles of that very religion as a core normative pillar.

Political Control of Constitutional Courts and Judges

In *Taking Rights Seriously* Ronald Dworkin admits that in order to determine the "enduring values" of their particular societies, judges inevitably have to make value choices. Although they might conscientiously seek to decide on the basis of objective principles or aim to discover the enduring values of society, it is difficult to see how this could be done without bringing personal values and political opinions to bear on the process. Therefore, if judges are bound to make value choices, it would be better, from the perspective of political power holders, if the judges' values were in line with the values of those who appoint them. Political power holders often have some control over the personal composition of national high courts. No matter how the judicial selection process is constructed, it always has an important political dimension.[82] In Canada the Office of the Prime Minister controls appointments to the Supreme Court. In Japan loyalty to the ruling party apparatus has been a crucial factor in judicial appointments.[83] As Robert Dahl observes with regard to the U.S. Supreme Court, "it is unrealistic to suppose that a Court whose members are recruited in the fashion of the Supreme Court justices would long hold to norms of Right or Justice that are substantially at odds with the rest of the political elite."[84]

A fortiori, it does not require a major leap of imagination to understand the scope of political control, direct or indirect, on judicial appointment processes in polities that feature a distinctly lesser degree of judicial autonomy than the United States. In countries with distinctly less established traditions of an apolitical, autonomous civil service and court system, political power holders often handpick individual candidates to serve in key judicial roles. In short, when it comes to judicial appointments, a tight "police-patrol" model of oversight is often employed, as opposed to the more lenient "fire-alarm" model.[85]

Accordingly, it is hardly surprising that Maher Abdel Wahed, the chief justice of Egypt's Supreme Constitutional Court (SCC) from 2006 to 2009, served as Egypt's attorney general before his appointment to the court and was appointed to the top judicial position via a presidential decree. His appointment was supported by members of the ruling National Democratic Party, as well as by the police, military, and prosecutors, who all regarded Abdel Wahed as a tough law-and-order type. Some individuals pass from judgeship to civil service with the same ease. Mamdouh Marei, the chief justice of the SCC in the early 2000s, was appointed minister of justice in August 2006 by President Mubarak. In Egypt and elsewhere, seldom have law and politics been so unified since the days of Carl Schmitt.

In 2006 Egyptian judges took a significant stance when they protested against the state's interference in their work and were joined by a number of opposition blocs in their sit-ins and huge demonstrations. In 2009 Judge Mahmud al-Khudayri, deputy chairman of Egypt's Court of Cassation, submitted his resignation in protest of the state's violation of judicial independence. Al-Khudayri added that the state had interfered in the elections of the judges' club and had penetrated the Supreme Council of Magistracy, which is in charge of the government's accountability.[86] This protest came on the heels of the July 2009 appointment of Farouk Sultan, a distinctly "system-friendly" jurist, as the new chief justice of the Supreme Constitutional Court. But judicial protest notwithstanding, political control of the Egyptian judiciary remains tight.[87]

Consider, for example, the professional biography of Zaki Tun Azmi, who has been the chief justice of Malaysia's Federal Court (the highest court of the country) since October 2008. Zaki's father, Tun Azmi Mohamed, was also chief justice (then lord president) from 1966 to 1974. Like father, like son: Zaki received an elite legal education in both English and Malay. For years he served as legal adviser to the ruling United Malays National Organization party before becoming the first lawyer directly appointed a judge of the Federal Court on September 5, 2007. Three months later, on December 11, Zaki Tun Azmi was appointed president of the Court of Appeal, and on October 21, 2008, following the end of Datuk Abdul Hamid Mohamed's term due to mandatory retirement, Zaki was appointed chief justice. Ascertaining whether Zaki's personal background and close ties to the ruling party are linked to his rapid ascent to positions of judicial power is beyond the scope of this work, but that seems like a reasonable working hypothesis.

In still other countries (Turkey is a good example) the antireligious military is a significant actor in appointments to the constitutional court. As Hootan Shambayati explains, the Turkish military has historically been involved in judicial appointments, with the outcome being rather homogeneous and technocratic, courts composed of like-minded judges who display little diversity of thought.[88] Boualem Bessaih, as of September 2005 the president of Algeria's Constitutional Council, is a distinguished member of the Algerian revolutionary movement of the early 1960s, a former professor of literature, and a prolific author and film director who served as ambassador to several European and Arab capitals, as well as in several ministerial posts. His latest book, *L'Algérie belle et rebelle: De Jugurtha à Novembre,* published on the occasion of the fiftieth anniversary of the revolution, is prefaced by Algeria's president, Abdelaziz Bouteflika.

Less overtly political judicial leaders are at least equally likely to promote secularism. The ideological leanings of Aharon Barak, former chief justice of the Supreme Court of Israel, a prominent constitutional theorist, and an honorary member of the emerging international judicial jet set—the global epistemic community, to be more elegant—are well known.

Idris Legbo Kutigi, now chief justice of the Supreme Court of Nigeria, acquired extensive legal education in Nigeria and in Britain and has been a professional judge since the mid-1970s. Given his educational and professional background, the likelihood of Chief Justice Kutigi siding with the religious agenda put forward by the twelve northern Nigerian states is negligible. César Julio Valencia Copete, the former president of the Supreme Court of Colombia, is a longtime business lawyer who graduated from the Universidad Externado de Colombia in Bogotá with a specialization in commercial law. It is probably safe to say the Colombian Catholic Church would not pick him as its first choice for chief justice. John L. Murray, chief justice of the Supreme Court of Ireland since 2004, had a distinguished career as a commercial and constitutional barrister, served as Ireland's attorney general from 1987 to 1991, and then served as a judge of the European Court of Justice from 1992 to 1999, when he was appointed a judge of the Irish Supreme Court. Such a background surely does not predispose Murray to be an avid parochial. Supreme-court judging seems to run in the family here. Chief Justice Murray is married to Gabrielle Walsh, daughter of former Supreme Court judge Brian Walsh, who is considered to have been one of the more progressive and intellectually notable members of the Irish Supreme Court and a distinctly nonparochial voice in the hotly contested issues of reproductive freedom and same-sex civil unions in Ireland.

In other polities torn between secularism and religiosity—India would be a good example here—prominent supreme court judges have advanced explicitly secularist attitudes, and have gone on record to forcefully state their support of secularism. The struggle between advocates of universal secularism (and, by extension, the adoption of a uniform civil code) and proponents of the status quo, in which religious minorities, most notably Muslims, enjoy a certain jurisdictional autonomy in matters of personal status, has been a perennial bone of contention in India.

Marriage and divorce have been a perennial bone of contention in India. The Supreme Court of India has consistently sided with secularist uniformity even at the cost of occasional clashes with the political sphere.[89] In *Sarla Mugdal v. Union of India* (1995), a case that involved married Hindu men who were converting to Islam in order to practice polygamy, which is legal under Muslim personal law, Justice Kuldip Singh wrote: "Those who preferred to remain in India after the partition, fully knew that the Indian leaders did not believe in two-nation or three-nation theory and that in the Indian Republic there was to be one Nation—Indian nation—and no community could claim to remain a separate entity on the basis of religion . . . The Successive Government till-date have been wholly remiss in their duty of implementing the constitutional mandate under Article 44 of the Constitution of India."[90]

In the *Vallamattom* case (2003; a successful challenge to the constitutionality of Section 118 of the Indian Succession Act, which prohibited bequests to religious or charitable organizations made less than a year before the grantor's death) V. N. Khare, Chief Justice of the Supreme Court of India (2002–2004), stated that "Article 44 [of the Constitution of India] provides that the State shall endeavour to secure for the citizens a uniform civil code throughout the territory of India. The aforesaid provision is based on the premise that there is no necessary connection between religious affiliation and personal law in a civilized society . . . It is a matter of regret that Article 44 of the Constitution has not been given effect to. Parliament is still to take steps for framing a common civil code in the country. A common civil code will help the cause of national integration by removing the contradictions based on ideologies."[91] The same secularist impulse is evident in some the Supreme Court of India's recent freedom-of-religion rulings. In March 2009, for example, the court dismissed the petition of a sixteen-year-old Muslim student who was seeking the right to sport a beard in his Christian convent school in a small Madhya Pradesh town.[92] The student's lawyer argued that the right to keep a beard was a fundamental right under Article 25 of the constitution. The court ruled that fundamental rights lie against the state and its affiliated institutions, not against private citizens or institutions. A private minority school, as was the case here, has the right under Article 30 of the constitution to "establish and administer educational institutions." Since the student voluntarily chose to attend the school and was always free to attend another school if he so wished, he was obliged to abide by the school's rules and regulations as long as he remained enrolled in it. The court also suggested that growing a beard was optional, not mandatory, under Islam, whereas for Sikh students in that school, growing a beard was religiously prescribed and not optional. Even more telling are Justice Markandeya Katju's remarks: "We don't want to have Talibans in the country. Tomorrow, a girl student may come and say that she wants to wear a burqa. Can we allow it?" He then did not mince words when he said: "I am a secularist. We should strike a balance between rights and personal beliefs. We cannot overstretch secularism to accommodate religious whims." It is hard to imagine a blunter, more explicit secularist statement coming from a supreme court judge anywhere.[93]

Political preferences in judicial appointments are equally effective when it comes to supreme-court composition more generally. A key factor that reduced the short-term risk for those who delegated authority to the

Supreme Court of Israel in the 1990s, inter alia in response to the rise of religious parties and leaders, was their general control over the court's personal composition. Compared with the United States, for example, the appointment of judges in Israel is, at least formally, a less overtly political process. Judges (including Supreme Court justices) are selected by a nine-member appointments committee that consists of the president of the Supreme Court and two other justices of that court, two practicing lawyers who are members of the Israeli Bar Association, two members of the Knesset elected in a secret ballot by majority vote, and two ministers, one of whom is the minister of justice (who also chairs the committee and must approve the appointments). Members of the legal profession (three judges and two practicing lawyers) hold the majority on the committee. In addition, as a matter of courtesy to the Supreme Court, few, if any, new Supreme Court judges are selected without the incumbent justices' consent, most notably the chief justice's support.[94] What is more, until 2004 virtually all justice ministers were strong supporters of the constitutional revolution and the expansion of judicial power. These included politicians with a distinctly secularist agenda, such as Yitzhak Modai, Dan Meridor, Yossi Beilin, and Yosef Lapid, as well as prominent law professors David Libai and Amnon Rubinstein. As one would expect, the Supreme Court's composition has been similar in demographic characteristics to that of the country's political elite. Put bluntly, jurists who are operagoers and *Ha'Aretz* subscribers, whose mother knew Yiddish, and who own an apartment or two in an upscale neighborhood are much more likely to be appointed to the Supreme Court than those who celebrate the Mimoona (a North African Jewish feast), wear tefillin (phylacteries) every weekday morning, speak fluent Arabic, were born in the former Soviet Union, or have a close family relative under the poverty line. As it happens, over two-thirds of the Israeli electorate fall into at least one of these historically less politically powerful categories. Juristocracy is certainly not a democracy.

Granted, Aharon Barak's retirement in 2006, coupled with a decline in political support for the court from the populist Kadima-led government, brought about increased public rumblings over judicial activism.[95] As long as Barak, the former proactive chief justice and arguably the most influential, philosopher-king-like figure in Israel's constitutional history, led the court, he and the court were able to block attempts to appoint antiactivist judges. However, Barak reached mandatory retirement age (seventy) in 2006 and was replaced by the arguably less dominant Chief Justice Dorit Beinish. The backlash against the court started to yield some results. In 2007 the rivalry (which some say is personal) between then Minister of Justice Daniel Friedman and the new chief justice triggered the introduction of a law that limits the incumbency of chief justices to seven years. In 2008 a new law was introduced by anti-activist politicians that requires a supermajority of seven votes in the nine-member judicial appointments committee to approve a new appointment to the Supreme Court. Because five members of the committee are incumbent Supreme Court judges (three) or representatives of the bar association (two), the new procedure necessitates support for an appointment from the political component of the committee—the minister of justice, another minister, and two Knesset members. In June 2009 the political backlash against the court reached another peak when two nationalist right-wing MKs critical of the court's "unrepresentative" composition and ideological tilts were elected to the nine-member judicial appointments committee, thereby further threatening the old establishment's grip over the Supreme Court's composition and interpretive direction. At that point a high-noon-like confrontation and possibly a long-term stalemate in judicial appointments seemed inevitable.

Despite all these initiatives, the 2008 appointment to the court of Hanan Meltzer and Yoram Danziger, two well-established mainstream lawyers, certainly does not alter the court's skewed demographics and ideological tilt. And despite the rhetoric to the contrary, the 2009 appointment to the Supreme Court of three new justices, Tel Aviv District Court judge Uzi Fogelman, Haifa District Court judge Yitzhak Amit, and U.S.-born Beersheba District Court judge Neal Hendel, to fill the three vacancies on the fifteen-judge court hardly fits the bill of a true revolution in the court's approach. All three are experienced judges; none is a zealous ideologue. Fogelman, for one, is rumored to have been handpicked by Chief Justice Beinish; she has known him since their days together in the State Attorney's Office.

If we look now at the broader composition of constitutional courts in the Near and Middle East, as well as in North Africa, many judges have received some general legal education and are familiar with some of Western law's basic principles and methods of reasoning. More often than not, the judge's educational background, cultural propensities, and social milieu are closer to those of the urban intelligentsia and top state bureaucrats than to those of any other social group. Constitutional courts are established and funded by the state, and their judges are appointed by state authorities, often with the approval of political leaders. Consequently, a judge's record of adjudication is well known at the time of his or her appointment. In an increasing number of countries in the region, judges are required to attend courses on the role and functions of the judiciary for several years, where they are exposed to international human rights standards and other legal concepts that are not easily compatible with traditional views, pious authority, and sacred texts. Morocco provides an interesting example. Most family-law issues such as marriage, divorce, child support and custody, and inheritance are adjudicated by judges trained in Shari'a law as applied in the country. However, judges trained in recent years are graduates of the National Institute for Judicial Studies, where they undergo three years of study heavily focused on human rights and the rule of law. Over the course of training, seminars and conferences with leading jurists from the Western world are held.

Likewise, government ministries and state bureaucracies have tightened their control over the appointment of judges to religious tribunals and require new appointees to have some formal training or background in general legal principles, in addition to their mastery of religious law. A good illustration is the quiet revolution in the early 2000s that took place during the process of appointing *kadis* to Israel's Shari'a courts. Although historically the process had been controlled by the Ministry of Religious Affairs, the entire Shari'a court portfolio was transferred in 2004 to the Ministry of Justice. This was coupled with the requirement that new appointees to religious tribunals have extensive formal legal education. Simultaneously, the labor-court system, which has initial jurisdiction over much of the employment-conditions and labor-relations domains, has issued several rulings that call on public tenders and employment opportunities in the entire (traditionally male-dominant) religious court system in Israel to comply with general standards of equity, primarily gender equality.[96]

The process of tightening political control over judicial appointments to religious tribunals has symbolic manifestations too. In 2008, for the first time in Israel's history, three new Great Rabbinical Court judges (*dayanim*) were sworn in during a ceremony held at the official residence of the president of Israel, and took the same oath of office that is taken by civil court judges. Prior to that event, appointees to the rabbinical court system had been sworn in at the Chief Rabbinate. The "relocation" to the president's home and the justice minister's dominance in the appointments process itself reflect the transfer of ministerial authority over the religious court system from the Ministry of Religious Affairs to the Ministry of Justice. It also symbolizes the greater significance that the state authorities assign to bringing the religious court system under full, nonsectarian government oversight.

Another telling example is the religious-court reform in Indonesia, with over 200 million of its citizens identifying as Muslims. During the 1980s the hitherto-nonstandardized Islamic court system was integrated into the national judiciary, with all the government supervisory powers that such incorporation entails.[97] The Religious Judicature Act of 1989 established municipal and provincial Shari'a courts' jurisdiction over Muslim litigants in certain civil matters specified by the act, mainly marriage, inheritance, and charitable foundations *(waqf)*, generally subject to ordinary (nonreligious) civil procedure norms. But alongside the formal recognition of Islamic courts' power, educational requirements and judicial appointment procedures were introduced so as to transfer the locus of power from local strongmen to government officials. Whereas in the past judges were recruited locally, under the current system judges are hired through nationwide recruitment and undergo a process of training and socialization in Jakarta before being sent into the field.[98] As a result, judges appointed under the new standards have very different training and backgrounds from their predecessors. The vast majority of judges on Islamic courts—almost 90 percent by one count—have degrees from one of Indonesia's State Islamic Institutes, and many also possess a university degree. What is more, the number of religious-court judges with both university training and graduate training has been consistently increasing because additional education is a major factor in promotions.[99] The reform also increased the number of female judges serving on Islamic courts from roughly 5 percent in the early 1980s to roughly 20 percent today.[100]

State efforts to appoint moderate judges to religious tribunals are evident across the new world of constitutional theocracies. A vivid illustration is the appointment of Justice Ch. Ejaz Yousaf in 1997 as judge of the Federal Shari'at Court of Pakistan and his promotion to chief justice of the Federal Shari'at Court in 2003, a position he occupied until 2006, before he was appointed by President Mushanaf to the Supreme Court of Pakistan in 2007 (Yousaf was dismissed after the reinstatement of C. J. Chaudry in 2009). In addition to his Islamic law credentials, Justice Yousaf has also been president of the chess, baseball, and softball federations of Pakistan. He served as manager of Pakistan's national cricket team in 1996–1997 and captain of Pakistan's national chess team in several high-profile international championships. In the 1990s Yousaf was a member of Pakistan's delegation to the world baseball congress in Lausanne, Switzerland, and to the cricket World Cup in India (1994) and in England (1999). He was also president of the provinces of Baluchistan and Quetta cricket associations. Among his many other eclectic civil service credentials are chairman of the Press Council of Pakistan and member of the board of governors of the Asia-British Law Council and of the British-Pakistan Law Council. To cap his versatile public career, Yousaf was appointed by the president of Pakistan as a member of the Governing Board of the Pakistan Cricket Board (cricket is Pakistan's most popular sport and enjoys immense, cultlike national exposure). In short, Yousaf is not exactly a typical religious cleric. What better person could those who are not keen on turning Pakistan into a full-fledged theocracy have picked to serve as chief justice of the Federal Shari'at Court of Pakistan?

In other countries judicial reform brought about the appointment of women to influential judging positions. An interesting illustration of how such liberalization is pursued is the appointment in 2003 of Tahani al-Gebali to Egypt's Supreme Constitutional Court. Although many luminaries advance the view that nothing in either the Egyptian Constitution or, indeed, in Islam itself prevented qualified and competent women from handling the gavel, there had been a long-standing resistance to the appointment of female justices to Egyptian courts. However, on the basis of the SCC's two-tier hierarchy of Shari'a norms, the grand imam sheikh of al-Azhar himself asserted that there is no categorical text in the Qur'an and Sunna forbidding women to assume the post of judge. The credit for influencing the president's decision to appoint Tahani al-Gebali to the bench is widely given to Suzanne Mubarak, an active campaigner for women's rights, who declared 2003 "the year of Egyptian women." Portraying this appointment as "a glorious victory to Egypt who always played a pioneering role in backing progress and enlightenment,"[101] Suzanne Mubarak asserted that "the issue of [a woman's] right to assume the post of a judge has long been controversial. Some social and cultural concepts that proved inconsistent with the cultural background of the Egyptian collective mind [were] to blame." Minister of Justice Counselor Farouq Seif an-Nasr echoed her statement, noting that "appointing Tahani al-Gebali a judge in the Supreme Constitutional Court is a landmark in the history of [the] Egyptian woman. It is quite reminiscent of the historic moment when the first school for educating girls was established and when the first Egyptian girl entered [the] university."[102] The chief justice of the SCC was likewise quoted as saying, "[T]his is a momentous event in the history of Egypt and Egyptian judiciary; justice and equality are noble values extolled by all Egyptians." In a major follow-up move in 2007 Egypt's Supreme Judicial Council selected thirty-one female judges to serve on courts throughout the country. These candidates were later appointed by a presidential decree, in a move that angered conservatives. In February 2010, the Supreme Judicial Council overturned the Council of State's (an administrative body) vote to bar women from judicial positions. The matter reached Egypt's Supreme Constitutional Court on referral by the government. The court took an inclusive approach and stressed that the law grants both men and women equal rights to assume judicial positions in administrative courts. The pertinent legislation stipulates that members of the Council of State must be "Egyptian," a word which in Arabic is specific to the male gender. However, the Supreme Constitutional Court ruled that in this context the word means "citizen," which includes both genders. Gradual gender equalization reforms are evident in other important domains: a 2009 law requires that beginning with the election scheduled for November 2010, women must hold at least 12 percent of the seats in the lower house of parliament.

These changes to the appointment and training procedures have practical implications for judicial outcomes. To begin with, judges in centralized and overly politicized court systems controlled by a dominant political force are likely to support the government position—especially in politically charged cases—to avoid harsh reaction by influential political power holders.[103] In some cases self-censorship may be exercised by court leaders who push all judges to avoid confrontations with the interests of the executive in order to protect the institutional autonomy of the court.[104] Tightened political control over judicial appointments suggests that an "attitudinal" approach to judicial behavior is likely to manifest itself, with most (or, indeed, all) higher-court judges adhering to ideological preferences, worldviews, and values that are not in line with the fundamental tenets of theocratic governance. Most judges belong to the very same social stratum that, by and large, has the most to lose through the spread of religious radicalism. Likewise, judges seem to care about their reputations within their immediate social milieu, court colleagues, and the legal profession more generally and will therefore likely seek to advance notions of collective identity that are popular among these epistemic communities of reference.[105] It may also be argued that judges' policy preferences grow in part from their training and practice in the law, and that existing legal doctrines and analytic frameworks help shape those preferences.[106]

Supreme Court judges may also be viewed as strategic actors to the extent that they seek to increase their policy-making influence or maintain or augment the court's independence and institutional position vis-à-vis other major national decision-making bodies.[107] They may also wish to enhance the court's symbolic power and international prestige by fostering its alignment with a growing community of liberal democratic nations engaged in judicial review and rights-based discourses. Strategic judges may recognize the changing fates or preferences of influential political actors or gaps in the institutional context within which they operate; such events might allow them to strengthen their own position by extending the ambit of their jurisprudence and fortifying their status as key national policy makers.

What is more, because justices do not have the institutional capacities to enforce their rulings, they must take into account the extent to which pertinent political decision makers will support their rulings.[108] Strategic judges must gauge the prevailing winds that drive political stakeholders and make decisions accordingly. Even in stable democratic settings where formal dimensions of judicial independence are preserved (for instance, the United States, Canada, or Germany), de facto judicial independence has been "bounded"; supreme courts have been shown to have modified their position over time to respond to criticism and opposition. This is certainly so in semidemocratic or authoritarian settings where judicial independence is notably less entrenched. In short, courts and judges may engage in strategic decision making either because of the variety of costs that judges as individuals or courts as institutions may incur as a result of adverse reactions to their unwelcome decisions, or because of the various benefits that they may acquire through the rendering of strategically tailored decisions.[109]

When judicial self-restraint or political pressure, tacit or explicit, on the courts does not achieve the intended objectives of those who appoint and promote judges, these actors may take harsher measures. As the recent history of comparative constitutional politics shows us, the recurrence of unsolicited judicial intervention in the political sphere in general, and unwelcome judgments concerning contentious political issues in particular, has brought about significant political backlashes, targeted at clipping the wings of overactive courts. The most common of these reactions is the executive override of controversial or unwelcome rulings. The infamous Saudi "Qatif Girl" rape case (2007) is a good illustration of such executive override in action. The perpetrators of a brutal gang rape were sentenced to eighty to one thousand lashes and imprisonment of up to ten years. However, the victim and a man with whom she was having an illicit affair were also sentenced for being together in a parked car before the rape. The Appeals Court doubled the victims' sentences in late 2007 because they allegedly attempted to use the media to manipulate the justice system, causing an international media storm about Saudi judicial practices. However, in December 2007 King Abdullah issued an official pardon to the two victims, citing his ultimate authority to revise "discretionary" punishments in accordance with the public good.

Among other more common power-constraining strategies are the following: political tinkering with judicial appointment and tenure procedures to ensure the appointment of compliant judges or to block the appointment of undesirable judges; court-packing attempts by those who hold political power; disciplinary sanctions against "overly independent" judges; impeachment or removal of objectionable or overactive judges; and the introduction of serious jurisdictional restrictions that limit the boundaries and powers of judicial review.[110] In some instances (e.g., Russia in 1993, Kazakhstan in 1995, Zimbabwe in 2001, Thailand in 2006, on three occasions in Ecuador from 2004 to 2007, and most recently in Niger in 2009 and again in 2010) such a backlash has ended in a constitutional crisis, leading to the reconstruction or dissolution of the high courts. To this we may add another political response to unwelcome rulings, more subtle and possibly more lethal to the court's influence: bureaucratic disregard or protracted or reluctant implementation.[111]

A classic illustration of a political override of an unwelcome judicial ruling in the realm of religious freedom is the 1993 enactment by the U.S. Congress of the Religious Freedom Restoration Act (commonly known as RFRA). In American constitutional jurisprudence a religion-based claim seldom exempts a person from the application of a religiously neutral criminal law. In *Employment Division, Dept. of Human Resources v. Smith* (1990) the Supreme Court held that a law banning the use of peyote was constitutional, despite a claim that the Native American Church used peyote for sacramental purposes.[112] The political backlash against this ruling was quite significant. In 1993 Congress adopted the RFRA in an explicit attempt to override the Court decision, reinstate the supremacy of the Free Exercise Clause, and prevent laws from substantially burdening free exercise of religion. But the power game did not stop there. In 1997 the Supreme Court struck down parts of RFRA because it overstepped Congress's power to enforce the Fourteenth Amendment (*City of Boerne v. Flores*, 1997). That said, parts of RFRA continue to stand.[113]

At the other end of the political-reaction continuum stands the outright dismissal of constitutional-court personnel. A glaring example is the widely documented 1993 constitutional crisis in Russia. President Boris Yeltsin reacted to an overactive involvement of the first Constitutional Court in Russia's political sphere by decreeing the Constitutional Court suspended until the adoption of a new constitution. This marked the demise of the first Constitutional Court and the downfall of its controversial chair, Valerii Zorkin, and brought about the establishment of the second Constitutional Court. A controlled comparison of the dockets of the first and second Constitutional Courts reveals that in the era of the first court the docket was dominated by politically charged federalism and separation-of-powers cases, whereas the second court drew on its control of much of its docket and issue agenda to resort to the "safe area" of individual rights jurisprudence and tended to avoid federalism issues or separation-of-powers disputes.[114] In other words, harsh political responses to unwelcome activism or interventions on the part of the courts, or even the credible threat of such a response, can have a chilling effect on judicial decision-making patterns. Constitutional courts, then, are "constrained actors . . . who must be attentive to preferences and likely actions of other relevant players."[115] And that holds true even more in settings where these other relevant players are perceived as possessing an arsenal of potentially effective weapons against overactive or too-independent courts. Variations on the same logic explain prudent or strategic judicial behavior in countries as different as Argentina; Germany; Pakistan; Georgia, Ukraine, and Kyrgyzstan; and Japan.[116] Who says that supreme-court judges are not at times shrewd political animals?

The experience of constitutional politics in predominantly religious polities has not been different. Notable examples that immediately come to mind are the 1988 removal of Lord President Tun Salleh Abas of Malaysia, the 1997 suspension of Chief Justice Sajjad Ali Shah of the Pakistan Supreme Court, the "court packing" of the Egyptian Supreme Constitutional Court with new judges sympathetic to the government, and the "competency" hearings held in 2005 against Egypt's Court of Cassation judges Hisham al-Bastawisi and Mahmoud Makki. A paradigmatic example is the replacement of the Supreme Court's chief justice in Afghanistan. Following more than two years of conservative jurisprudence in religious matters by the newly established Afghan Supreme Court, President Hamid Karzai opted for a shake-up of the court's composition. In 2006 Karzai appointed several new, more moderate members to the court. In addition, the reappointment of Chief Justice Faisal Ahmad Shinwari—a conservative Islamic cleric with questionable educational credentials—did not pass the parliamentary vote. Karzai then chose his legal counsel Abdul Salam Azimi, a former university professor who was educated in the United States, to succeed Shinwari. In August 2006 the new, distinctly more moderate court was sworn in.[117]

In addition to taming religious fundamentalism, political influence over the court has also paid dividends for the Karzai administration in a more direct way. According to the Afghan Constitution, Karzai's term as president should have ended in May 2009. However, presidential elections were set for August 2009, and thus questions arose about who should lead the fragile and violence-hit country in the interim months. Political opponents wanted Karzai to end his term as provided in the constitution and to appoint a caretaker president, saying that their adversary's chances at the polls would be boosted if he held on to the presidency until the vote. Karzai deflected the issue to the Supreme Court, which ruled on March 29, 2009, that it was "in the interest of the country" to extend the term of President Karzai and allow him to stay in power until the election was held.[118]

In neighboring Pakistan past rulers have often tinkered with the court system and the Supreme Court in order to cement their grip on power. The 2007 dismissal and 2009 reinstatement of Chief Justice Iftikhar Chaudhry of the Pakistan Supreme Court is a prime recent example. In March 2007 Pakistan's then President Pervez Musharraf ordered Chief Justice Chaudhry to resign, presumably for being overly independent and therefore "unreliable" from the government's point of view. Chaudhry was reinstated in July 2007. However, in early November 2007 Musharraf declared a state of emergency in Pakistan (which lasted until mid-December 2007), suspended the constitution, dismissed Chief Justice Chaudhry for the second time in eight months, and appointed several loyalist judges to the Pakistan Supreme Court. Musharraf's decision came only days before the Supreme Court was set to rule on whether it was constitutional for him to serve as both the president and the head of Pakistan's military.

The political control of the judiciary in Pakistan did not end with Musharraf's departure. The dispute between the two parties of the ruling coalition over the fate of Chaudhry and about sixty other judges ousted by Musharraf remained fierce well after the February 2008 elections. Whereas former Prime Minister Nawaz Sharif (leader of the Pakistan Muslim League-N [PML-N] party) demanded unconditional reinstatement of all fired judges, Asif Ali Zardari (leader of the Pakistan People's Party [PPP] and president of Pakistan as of September 2008) supported reinstatement, but only as part of a broader constitutional overhaul that would limit judicial power and the chief justice's term. That Zardari and the PPP might face serious corruption charges related to Benazir Bhutto's (Zardari's late wife) era as prime minister clearly did not help create an apolitical court. Before his fall President Musharraf signed an ordinance that granted amnesty in serious corruption cases to Zardari and Bhutto. The possibility of judicial scrutiny of that amnesty ordinance—a scenario that has eventually materialized in January 2010 (see the discussion in Chapter 4) with Chaudhry as chief justice—played into the hands of Nawaz Sharif, the main political rival of Zardari. That Nawaz Sharif's supporters joined the authentic "lawyers for democracy" movement in 2008 to demand Chaudhry's reinstatement therefore might have been driven less by a genuine commitment to civil rights and judicial independence than has been made out to the public. This may also explain why Zardari himself was less than enthusiastic about reinstating Chaudhry unconditionally, as Sharif demanded.

Abdul Hameed Dogar, a well-connected jurist who was appointed to the Supreme Court in 2000 and became Pakistan's chief justice in December

2007, served in that position until the reinstatement of Chief Justice Chaudhry in March 2009.[119] In late 2008 members of the Pakistan Bar Association took to the streets, demanding the reinstatement of Chaudhry and the bolstering of judicial independence in Pakistan more generally. In March 2009 Nawaz Sharif's PML-N party threw its full weight behind this movement only days after both Nawaz and his brother, Shahbaz Sharif, had been banned from elected office by the Supreme Court; this can hardly be seen as merely coincidental.[120] President Zardari then quickly dismissed the government led by Shahbaz Sharif in Punjab Province, the wealthiest province in Pakistan and a vital prize for politicians. That Nawaz Sharif's supporters went out to the streets to demand Chaudhry's reinstatement is hardly surprising, and it paid off.[121] In May 2009, once the deposed judges had been reinstated, the Supreme Court reversed course and lifted the election ban on the Sharif brothers.

Chaudhry himself, it should be noted, sat on the court that rubber-stamped Musharraf's military rule in 2000. However, starting in 2005, when Musharraf's grip on power began to weaken, Chaudhry had a surprising conversion, taking on controversial cases that embarrassed the government and challenged tradition and authority. These cases raised issues ranging from "honor crimes" against women to a controversial privatization deal by former Prime Minister Shaukat Aziz and from environmental protection to the secret detention of terror suspects, some of whom were later released. Chaudhry has become an icon of civil liberties in Pakistan and is certainly not the kind of judge that proponents of more religion in public life would have preferred.

Given all these factors, it is hardly surprising that in a number of Middle Eastern polities that lack established traditions of judicial activism, judicial reform has been instigated in order to create and empower state-controlled courts in an attempt to counterbalance the spread of religious fundamentalism. Saudi Arabia, for example, has recently embarked on a comprehensive modernization of its judicial system. Part of the rationale for the overhaul is the creation of courts that specialize in dealing with criminal, commercial, labor, and family issues to replace the existing general judge-made, Shari'a-based interpretation in these matters that has prevailed for many years. Additionally, the Supreme Judicial Council that used to act as the highest court and was controlled by some of the most reactionary clerics in the kingdom has been relegated to an administrative role. A new ten-member Supreme Court was established in 2009, staffed mostly with royal appointees, not merely with religious clerics, thereby allowing the kingdom to extend a more pragmatic, flexible application of Shari'a to various aspects of public life.[122] This is modeled in part on the experience of neighboring Bahrain, where a two-tier court system exists: civil courts that adjudicate commercial, civil, and criminal law issues (as well as personal-status laws of non-Muslims) and a Shari'a court system that handles personal-status issues of Muslims. More important, the constitution of 2002 established a Higher Judicial Council with full oversight over the entire court system, as well as an appointed constitutional court to rule on the constitutionality of both civil and Shari'a court rulings. In short, even in the least likely settings constitutional courts and tribunals have been established or reformed so as to hedge or mitigate the tension between political interests, modern-day needs, and principles of theocratic governance.

Conclusion

Constitutional law is a form of politics by other means, and constitutional courts are man-made, not God-given institutions. Like any other political institution, they do not operate in an institutional or ideological vacuum. They are steeped in the epistemological communities that surround them. Their establishment and maintenance do not develop and cannot be understood separately from the concrete social, cultural, political, and economic struggles that shape a given political system. At the same time, constitutional courts and practices do more than simply reflect their political surroundings; they also serve as important agents of discursive, conceptual, and at times real, on-the-ground change. Accordingly, there are important epistemological and ideological reasons, alongside more strategic and practical ones, that constitutional law and constitutional courts are so appealing to secularist, modernist, cosmopolitan, and other antireligious social forces in polities that face deep divisions along secular/religious lines.

The very logic of constitutional law, with its reasoned set of core tenets, prevalent modes of interpretation, and embedded emphasis on overarching state authority, makes it an attractive enterprise to those who wish to contain religiosity and assert state or civil society authority over religious texts, worldviews, and interpretive hierarchies. The important role of rights provisions and jurisprudence in contemporary constitutional discourse alongside the ever-increasing cross-jurisdictional fertilization in that area adds to constitutional law's secularist appeal. Many of the jurisdictional and enforcement advantages that gave religious legal regimes an edge in the premodern era are now aiding the modern state and its laws in its effort to contain religion. A political quest for legitimacy, or for lowering risks or costs, is often what drives deference to the judiciary in cases involving hotly contested collective-identity issues. Constitutional provisions have been used to delegitimize and restrict unwelcome religion-based political association, and to impose a downright ban on parties that advocate a strong religion-based platform. Effective political control over, as well as better access to, the constitutional arena also makes it attractive to political power holders who seek to keep religious authority under check.

Of the several key secularist appeals of constitutionalism, co-optation seems a very attractive and effective one. Counterintuitively, the constitutional establishment of religion helps limit the potentially radical impact of religion by bringing it under state control. It makes the state (and its courts) a key player in picking religion's official interpretive authorities and jurists and gives the state a stake in the interpretive game itself. Statutory regulations, selective funding, and promotion incentives (not to mention less overt state activity within potentially fundamentalist religious communities) encourage moderate or state-dependent voices within religion to curtail the impact of extremism. Moreover, the constitutionalization of religion transforms the practice of religious interpretation from a seemingly theological discourse into a more straightforward political act. In the new world of constitutional theocracy, the age-old call for religious authorities to adjust their preaching to changing social and economic circumstances is now giving way to a more pressing force of adaptation—the grand game of constitutional law and politics.

CHAPTER FOUR

Constitutionalism versus Theocracy

Constitutional Courts and the Containment of Sacred Law

ONE OF THE most fascinating but seldom-explored phenomena in comparative constitutional law is the growing reliance on constitutional courts and their jurisprudential ingenuity to block the spread of religiosity or advance a relatively universalist interpretation of sacred texts. It is well established in the literature that constitutionalization and the establishment of judicial review may increase the international reputation and credibility of regimes, thereby promoting investment, development, and economic growth.[1] But this is only part of the picture. In countries struggling with the complex issue of constitutional theocracy, constitutional courts may also be viewed as the guardians of secularism, modernism, and universalism against the increasing popularity of theocratic principles. In order to govern effectively, politicians and ruling elites in predominantly religious polities must confront the challenge of constitutional theocracy while simultaneously maintaining popular support for their regimes. Indeed, an increasingly common strategy by those who wield political power and represent the groups and policy preferences that object to principles of theocratic governance is the transfer of fundamental collective-identity questions of "religion and state" from the political sphere to the courts. Consequently, constitutional courts have been assigned the sensitive task of dealing with contentious political hot potatoes. The result has been an unprecedented judicialization of foundational collective identity, particularly as regards issues of religion and state, and the consequent emergence of constitutional courts as important forums for defining the very nature of the body politic.

In this chapter I explore the scope and nature of this phenomenon. To that end, I look at various modes of interpretive ingenuity (some would say strategic judicial behavior) used by constitutional courts in Egypt, Kuwait, Pakistan, Malaysia, Nigeria, Israel, and Turkey in order to contain, limit, and mitigate the resurgence of sacred law in their respective polities. All these countries have experienced a growth in the influence of religious political movements, with a commensurate increase in the levels of popular support that they receive, but they differ in their formal recognition of, and commitment to, religious values. In Pakistan the law underwent full Islamization in 1973 and again in 1985. Section 2 of the constitution (1973) states that "Islam shall be the State religion of Pakistan." Section 227(1) of the constitution stipulates that "[a]ll existing laws shall be brought in conformity with the Injunctions of Islam as laid down in the Holy Qur'an and Sunna." In theory, these provisions mean that legislation must be in full compliance with the principles of Shari'a. Similarly, Article 2 of the Egyptian Constitution, as amended in 1980, states that principles of Islamic jurisprudence (Shari'a) are *the* primary source of legislation in Egypt. The preamble to the Constitution of Kuwait (1962) states that "Islam is the religion of the state" and Shari'a is "a main source of legislation" (this phrasing was copied into Egypt's 1971 Constitution, and was amended to "the source" from "a source" in 1980). Article 3 of the Malaysian Constitution takes a slightly different form and states that "Islam is the religion of the Federation, but other religions may be practiced in peace and harmony in any part of the Federation." Although freedom of religion is enshrined in the Malaysian Constitution (Article 11), each of the thirteen states "may control or restrict the propagation of any religious doctrine or belief among persons professing the religion of Islam" (Article 11.4). The Constitution of Nigeria establishes it as a secular state with constitutionally enshrined freedom of religion. At the same time, the constitution allows subnational units to grant additional jurisdiction to their local courts. This provision has been used by twelve predominantly Muslim northern states to expand the substantive jurisdictional boundaries of their Shari'a tribunals. Israel's constitutional system is based on two fundamental tenets: that the state is *Jewish* and *democratic*. It is this commitment to the creation of an ideologically plausible and politically feasible synthesis between particularistic (Jewish) and universalistic (democratic) values that has proved to be the major constitutional challenge faced by Israel since its foundation. Modern Turkey, for its part, characterizes itself as secular, and with the exception of the short-lived AKP-initiated constitutional amendment of February 2008 that attempted to allow the wearing of religious attire in the public education system (declared unconstitutional by the Turkish Constitutional Court in June 2008), has adhered to the Western model of strict separation of state and religion. Accordingly, there are considerable differences in the interpretive approaches and practical solutions adopted by the seven countries' respective high courts in dealing with core questions of religion and state.

Despite these dissimilarities, however, there are some striking parallels in the way in which the constitutional courts in these and some other similarly situated countries have positioned themselves as important secularizing forces within their respective societies despite intense scrutiny from the more religious segments of the public. Each of these countries illustrates the remarkably creative interpretive techniques adopted by judges confronted with concrete legal disputes that reflect and encapsulate the greater issues emerging from a constitutional theocracy. I conclude by drawing some general lessons concerning the political construction of judicial review and the secularizing role of constitutional courts in an increasingly religious world.

Egypt (and a Brief Voyage to Kuwait)

Modern Egypt has long been torn between multiple and at times even contradictory identities; tensions between an authoritarian and a democratic spirit, a centralized and a liberal market, a modernist and a traditionalist value system, and, above all, secularism and religiosity have characterized the country for at least forty years.[2] After the 1952 revolution that removed King Farouk I, Egypt entered two decades of industrialization and profound advancement of Arab nationalism, established by an authoritarian government and aided by the military. But in the 1970s a new political force came to the fore. The Muslim Brotherhood (al-Ikhwan al-Muslimin), founded in 1928 by Hassan al-Banna as a radical anti-Western, militarist movement, has emerged as a powerful legal and political reform group. Under the guidance of the Muslim Brotherhood, Islamism has enjoyed an astounding growth in Egypt over the last three decades. Egyptian Islamism has consistently opposed the modernist-nationalist agenda advocated by the government, the historically powerful National Democratic Party (NDP), the pro-statist military, and, above all, Egypt's high-income elites. Islamist groups within the established political and legal order grew in strength during the 1990s and have continued to encourage the development of religious sectarianism in the spheres of education, religion, and the media. Political Islamists have also mobilized certain elements in the al-Azhar center for Islamic higher learning in Cairo. These same actors have likewise been increasingly using the fatwa procedure (a declarative decree issued by religious leaders) to influence the public policy agenda. From 1992 to 1996 al-Azhar's leadership—dominated by the conservative incumbency of Ali Jad al-Haqq as the shaykh al-Azhar, the supreme religious authority in Egypt—intensified its antigovernment stance by advocating an explicitly conservative position on a number of hotly contested issues.[3]

The Islamist agenda began to make electoral inroads in 1987, when Islamic candidates gained thirty-six seats in the People's Assembly and became the primary parliamentary opposition group as the result of a tactical alliance among the New Wafd, Labor, and Liberal parties (liberal-progressive parties opposing the NDP political and electoral hegemony). In the 2005 parliamentary elections, candidates representing the banned Muslim Brotherhood (running as independents) were able to capture approximately 20 percent (87 of 454) of the seats in the National Assembly. The statist establishment responded with constitutional amendments aimed at tightening government control of the political sphere. A 2005 amendment added constitutional permanence to the state-of-emergency law in place since 1981. In March 2007 President Hosni Mubarak introduced another set of constitutional amendments (approved in a referendum) that effectively give more power to the president, ban the establishment of religious parties (a blatant anti–Muslim Brotherhood move), and loosen controls on security forces in its "war on terror."[4]

Corresponding with the resurgence of political Islam in Egypt, the Egyptian Supreme Constitutional Court (SCC) has emerged as an important forum for dealing with the core question of the status of Shari'a rules—arguably the most controversial and fundamental collective-identity issue troubling the Egyptian polity. The SCC was established in 1969 to determine questions pertaining to the constitutionality of laws, rules, and regulations.[5] During its first decade the court exhibited restraint, only seldom commenting on the possible unconstitutionality of laws. In 1979, however, President Anwar al-Sadat responded to the growing popular pressure from religious fundamentalists by granting the SCC a relatively broad judicial authority to review the constitutionality of laws and regulations, settle jurisdictional conflicts between courts, and reconcile conflicting judgments issued by lower courts.[6] In addition, the SCC was authorized to provide the definitive interpretation of a legal text when the meaning of the text was brought into question during the course of a trial.[7]

The constitutional reform of 1979 also ensured the court's formal independence from government, political parties, and other improper influences and interferences. Unlike ordinary Egyptian courts, which are managed through the Supreme Council of Judicial Bodies or the Ministry of Justice, the SCC has control over its members' remuneration and enjoys a separate budget and administrative apparatus. (The informal, de facto judicial independence credentials are far less dazzling and in fact may be said to resemble much of the malaise typical of political control of high courts in other authoritarian regimes.) Appointments to the court are made by presidential decrees based on nominations put forth by the General Assembly for the court (headed by the chief justice and consisting of the member judges). Most SCC judges appointed over the last twenty years are well versed in general principles of modern constitutional law and maintain close ties with constitutional-court judges overseas.[8] Several SCC justices, most notably Deputy Chief Justice Adel Omar Sherif, have delivered lectures in Europe and North American universities. At least until the late 1990s, the SCC emerged as a fairly active, independent court that on a nontrivial number of occasions took an antigovernment position on matters of human rights and economic liberalization.[9] These heydays appear to be over, at least temporarily, because during the last few years the government has tightened its control of the Egyptian judiciary.

Less than a year after judicial review was established in Egypt, and under intense pressure from the religious opposition, Article 2 of the Egyptian Constitution (1971) was amended to make principles of Muslim jurisprudence (Shari'a) the main source of legislation in Egypt. The original text of Article 2 of the 1971 constitution read: "Islam is the religion of the State, Arabic is its official language, and the principles of Islamic Shari'a are a principal source of legislation." On May 22, 1980, the text of Article 2 was changed to read: "Islam is the religion of the State, Arabic is its official language, and the principles of Islamic Shari'a are *the* principal source of legislation" (emphasis mine). The result of this amendment was the effective transformation of Egypt into a constitutional theocracy, where no legislation could contravene Islamic legal principles. The commitment to both constitutional and religious values is reflected in many constitutional provisions, most notably in Section 2, Part I (Social and Moral Constituents). Article 9, for example, states that "the family is the basis of the society founded on religion, morality and patriotism." Article 11 states that "the State shall guarantee the proper coordination between the duties of woman towards the family and her work in the society, considering her equal with man in the fields of political, social, cultural and economic life *without violation of the rules of Islamic jurisprudence*" (emphasis mine).

According to Article 12, "[T]he society shall be committed to safeguarding and protecting morals, promoting the genuine Egyptian traditions and abiding by the high standards of religious education, moral and national values, historical heritage of the people, scientific facts, socialist conduct and public morality within the limits of the law"—yes, religious education, national values, scientific facts, and public morality, among other guiding principles. For nearly thirty years now the SCC has increasingly been called on to determine the constitutionality of legislative and administrative acts on the basis of their adherence to the principles of Shari'a.[10] In light of Article 2's enshrinement of Shari'a as *the* source of legislation, the question before the court in many of these cases has been which principles of Shari'a possess determinative and absolute authority, and which are more flexible and thus may allow for some interpretive variance.

To address this question in a moderate way, the court developed a complex, innovative interpretive matrix of religious directives—the first of its kind by a nonreligious tribunal. It departed from the ancient traditions of the *fiqh* (Islamic jurisprudence or the cumulative knowledge/science of studying Shari'a) schools and has instead developed a new framework for interpreting Shari'a. Specifically, the court has developed a flexible, modernist approach to interpretation that distinguishes between "unalterable and universally binding principles, and malleable applications of those principles."[11] In developing this somewhat elastic interpretive device, the court relied on the fact that the classical Islamic jurists and the different schools of jurisprudence vary in their interpretations and applications of the texts. This wide scope offers the chance to implement Shari'a in different social environments and to allow jurists, including constitutional-court judges who wish to invoke religious law, to choose which school of interpretation they deem applicable in a given instance. In so doing, this interpretive approach provides one of the clearest concrete illustrations currently on offer of the argument that Islamic law is not inherently incompatible with interpretive pluralism or with democracy.[12]

According to the Supreme Constitutional Court, legislation that contravenes a strict, unalterable principle recognized as such by all interpretive schools is declared unconstitutional and void, while at the same time, *ijtihad* (contemplation or external interpretation) is permitted in cases of textual lacunae, or where the pertinent rules are vague or open ended. Furthermore, the government has been given broad legislative discretion in policy areas where Shari'a is found to provide unclear or multiple answers, provided that the legislative outcome does not contravene the general spirit of Shari'a.[13] This interpretive approach has marked a true shift in the paradigm for legitimizing government policies on the basis of a moderate, fairly liberal interpretation *(ijtihad)* of Shari'a. In several landmark judgments concerning the scope of Shari'a in Egypt's public life, the court engaged in a substantive interpretation of both the Qur'an and evidence available in Sunna. It established its own interpretation of *ijtihad* irrespective of the contradictory opinions in Islamic jurisprudence and its traditional methods. This practice stands in stark contrast to the tradition whereby muftis (leading religious jurists) alone are allowed to perform *ijtihad* and advance novel interpretations of Shari'a. It also stands in contrast to the practice in most liberal democracies, where civil courts refrain from determining which side of a religious dispute is "correct" in theological terms and will often defer to religious authorities on such matters.[14]

The first step in the Egyptian Supreme Constitutional Court's positioning as a de facto interpreter of religious norms, and as a major forum for dealing with Egypt's dilemma of constitutional theocracy, was its 1985 decision to limit the retroactive application of the amended Article 2. Traditional Islamic jurisprudence prohibits charging usury or interest *(riba)* in business transactions. Applying this prohibition in a strict fashion would undermine a major foundation of domestic and international trade and commerce, corporate financial governance, and modern banking. In the mid-1970s the Faculty of Medicine at al-Azhar University failed to repay a medical supplies provider on time. The supplier charged the university interest at a rate of 4 percent, starting from the date of the transaction. Although Article 226 of the Civil Code authorized the payment of interest on delayed debts, the rector of al-Azhar claimed that this provision contradicted the Shari'a prohibition of *riba*. The case was brought before the SCC in 1978, two years before the rewording of Article 2 of the constitution. In a lengthy judgment released seven years after the commencement of litigation, the SCC dismissed al-Azhar's argument on the basis of the nonretroactivity of Article 2.[15] The court held that an across-the-board nullification of all existing legislation that contradicted Shari'a was not acceptable, because the constitutional amendment had a prospective purpose; Article 2 could apply only to laws enacted subsequent to the adoption of the amendment (after May 1980). The SCC also stated that a retroactive application of Article 2 to strike down pre-1980 laws that contradicted Shari'a would lead to inconsistency, instability, and confusion in Egypt's judicial system. This meant that all pre-1980 legislation could be aligned with Shari'a rules only through fresh legislation. By establishing the nonretroactivity of Article 2, the court eliminated the possibility of using the article to bring all Egyptian legislation into conformity with Shari'a rules, at least by way of litigation. Although the court's ruling was hailed as a victory by both the government and Egypt's business and banking sectors, it was a devastating blow for revivalist Islamists, who described the SCC's nonretroactive application of Article 2 as politically driven, not as a logical interpretation of the article's applicability.[16]

In the decade that followed, the court went on to suggest that Article 2 did not preclude the government from enacting laws that adopt a nonclassical interpretation of Islamic norms with respect to family-law matters, most notably in the context of women's rights in the areas of child custody, alimony, and maintenance postdivorce payments.[17] Although such laws are not in line with classical Islam, they do not contravene Egypt's overall commitment to Islamic values. As Clark Lombardi has carefully analyzed, the court went on to rule that the government may enact laws that allow a woman to sue for dissolution of her marriage in case her husband takes another wife, and it could allow a court to issue retroactive orders of child support.[18]

In 1996 the court released what is arguably its most significant Article 2 ruling to date, concerning the constitutionality of a governmental decree that permitted parents or legal guardians of female pupils below university level to request from school authorities that the female pupils be permitted to cover their hair in contravention of the school's dress code, provided that the covering did not hide their faces. In other words, the government was prepared to accept the wearing of the *hijab* (head cover), as opposed to the *niqab* (mask or full head and face cover that only leaves the area around the eyes clear). The case arose when the father of two secondary-school girls challenged the decree and invoked, inter alia, Article 2. The court upheld the constitutionality of the government decree and ruled that the relevant Shari'a directives were contestable, flexible, and subject to evolution; the pertinent religious canon was not sacred and could be amended or replaced.[19] Specifically, the SCC determined that as long as a woman wore clothes that were modest and did not show any of her private parts *(aurat)* or her legs, she was abiding by the spirit of the Shari'a prescriptions with respect to *hijab*.[20] The dress code imposed by the contested government decree fell within the boundaries of that general tenet.

From the perspective of constitutional jurisprudence, the significance of the SCC's ruling on the *niqab* issue is multifaceted. First, the SCC reiterated its commitment to a prospective application of Article 2 to laws enacted after 1980. Second, the decision extended the SCC's jurisdiction to include ministerial edicts, thereby expanding the scope of legislation that falls under the purview of Article 2. Third, the SCC emphasized the need to develop an interpretation of Article 2 that would be consistent with other constitutional provisions protecting liberties. Finally, as it did in the

Riba case, the SCC engaged in its own substantive interpretation of both the Qur'an and evidence available on Sunna, irrespective of the contradictory opinions in Islamic jurisprudence. The SCC thereby positioned itself as a de facto and de jure interpreter of religious norms.

Similarly, in 1997 the SCC upheld the constitutionality of a law that stated that a wife's right to alimony was not foreclosed if she left to seek legal employment without her husband's permission. The court rejected the plaintiff's claim that the law infringed on Article 2 of the constitution. Instead, the court reemphasized that Shari'a is not rigid, and that its nonfundamental aspects are subject to evolution.[21] Egypt's Court of Cassation (the country's highest court of appeal) used the same reasoning in a November 2000 ruling that an Interior Ministry decree permitting men the authority to prevent their wives from traveling was unconstitutional by virtue of its infringement on women's equality rights.

The SCC's curbing of Article 2's potential scope was echoed by its counterpart, Egypt's Supreme Administrative Court, in a landmark decision concerning the controversial practice of clitoridectomy. In December 1997 the Supreme Administrative Court upheld the health minister's July 1996 decision to ban government-certified doctors and health workers from performing female circumcisions. The court stated, "With this ruling it has become prohibited for all to perform the operation of female circumcision, even with the consent of the girl or her guardians. Violators will be subjected to criminal, disciplinary and administrative punishment." The court further warned that anyone caught performing the operation risked three years in prison, and that doctors and health workers could lose their licenses. The decision was subsequently decried by fundamentalists who argued that the ruling went against all Islamic principles. In June 2007 the Ministry of Health finally fully criminalized female genital mutilation, eliminating a legal loophole that allowed girls to undergo the procedure for ostensible health reasons.[22]

Despite the significant curtailment these judgments imposed on the 1980 "Islamization" amendment, the rulings were merely a precursor to the SCC's most important judgment on personal-status laws to date: the *Khul* case. Since 1985, when the SCC ruled that the comprehensive overhaul of Egypt's Islamic personal-status laws (the reforms are known collectively as "Jihan's law" after the late President al-Sadat's wife) was unconstitutional and contrary to the fundamental principles of Shari'a, Egyptian feminist activists have intensified their attempts to liberalize the country's religious family-law regime. These efforts finally bore fruit in March 2000, when a new personal-status law was passed by Parliament and signed into law by President Hosni Mubarak. The new law (Law 1 of 2000) reformed the terms and procedures of personal-status cases and included the creation of a family court authorized to facilitate divorce cases, a prospective family insurance plan, the right to file for divorce from unregistered marriages, and other liberalizing revisions.[23] The most significant and hotly contested clause of the new law, however, was Article 20, guaranteeing women's right to file for no-fault divorce. Essentially, Article 20 established a women's right to invoke *khul*—divorce on any grounds, so long as the groom's gifts of jewelry *(shabka)* and dowry payments *(mahr)* are returned, and certain financial rights are relinquished.[24] The new law allowed this divorce by court order (without the husband's consent) if a mandatory mediation and reconciliation process between the couple had failed. The new provisions also effectively outlawed the abusive practice of men divorcing their wives by simply pronouncing "I divorce thee" three times *(talaq al-bid'a),* bypassing any efforts to mediate or reconcile partners *(talaq al-ghyabi).*

The constitutionality of the new law was challenged on Article 2 grounds by an Alexandrian resident whose wife was granted the right of *khul* by Alexandria's Personal Status Court. In December 2002, adhering to its distinction between core, uncontested Shari'a directives and their contested, malleable interpretations, the SCC upheld the constitutionality of the Personal Status Law (2000), including the provisions establishing the practice of *khul.* Delivering the court's judgment, Justice Maher El-Bahri confirmed that the incorporation of *khul* into Egyptian personal-status law did not violate Shari'a or Article 2 of the constitution because there were definitive Qur'anic verses and corresponding *fiqh* supporting the *khul* procedure.[25]

Two sentences from President Mubarak's address to the Parliament on November 21, 2003, illustrate his support for the ruling and encapsulate Egypt's dual commitment to traditional and modern values: "Ladies and Gentlemen, your new legislative session is being held on blessed days of the holy month of Ramadan . . . We should develop innovative solutions to the obstacles impeding enforcement of the provisions of maintenance, by introducing amendments to Law No. 1 of 2000 [the new Personal Status Law], in addition to upgrading policies as may be necessary to achieve justice and complete equality for women."[26]

In February 2008 the Supreme Administrative Court upheld the conversion back to Christianity of twelve Coptic Christians who had converted to Islam. The court ruled that since the twelve were born Christians, their reconversion to Christianity was not considered apostasy by core tenets of Islam. That ruling was appealed to the Supreme Constitutional Court, which was set to rule on it in November 2008, but the ruling was postponed indefinitely. In December 2008 the Alexandria Administrative Court followed the Supreme Administrative Court's ruling by allowing another person who had lived as a Muslim for thirty-one years to reconvert back to Christianity. In March 2009 the Supreme Administrative Court delivered another important liberalizing ruling when it upheld a lower-court ruling that essentially recognizes the Baha'i community by requiring the government to issue identification cards to Baha'i citizen applicants without forcing applicants to mention either Islam, Christianity, or Judaism—the only three faiths recognized in Egypt before the ruling—as their religion. The ruling put an end to a five-year legal battle between the Egyptian government and the followers of Bahaism in Egypt. The lawsuit, filed by the Egyptian Initiative for Personal Rights, a civil rights advocacy nongovernmental organization (NGO), relied on the Supreme Constitutional Court's key rights rulings, as well as its unique liberalization-from-within approach to religion, in its argument on behalf of Baha'i citizens. The court's ruling establishes that all Egyptians must be treated equally before the law regardless of their religious faiths. And as we have seen in Chapter 3, the SCC ruled in March 2010 that despite the objection of conservatives, women may be appointed as judges.

Given the fact that Egypt is a "strong state," where the president and the executive branch enjoy a wide scope of powers, it is somewhat surprising that the SCC has received such a broad grant of judicial review over administrative and presidential legislative authority. Even more surprising is the fact that the SCC has maintained and fortified its relative independence since its establishment. What is more, the Sadat and Mubarak regimes' support of the SCC and its relative independence stands in stark contrast to the numerous pre-1971 incidents of blatant political interference with Egypt's judicial sphere (for example, the 1969 "massacre of the judiciary," in which more than two hundred senior judicial personnel were dismissed on "overindependence" grounds by a presidential decree). However, when understood as an integral part and an important manifestation of the concrete cultural, religious, and political struggles that have shaped Egypt's political system over the last few decades, the scope and timing of the Egyptian constitutional revolution are more readily comprehended.

The court has delivered the goods for this coalition of supporters from secular factions. Its interpretation of Shari'a rules has advanced a moderate, nonfundamentalist interpretation of the laws, thereby establishing a "modernization from within" of traditional *fiqh*. Further, the SCC's engagement in the interpretation of Shari'a rules has contributed to the secular establishment's efforts to contain religious fundamentalist challenges by delegating the safeguarding of Egyptian Islamic law to a predominantly secular institution, the SCC, while at the same time professing commitment to constitutional enshrinement of Shari'a. Mamdouh Marei, then the chief justice of the SCC, acknowledged in 2003: "President Mubarak has supported the judiciary and eliminated difficulties that faced it. The honoring of the late SCC's Chief Justice Fathi Naguib by President Mubarak showed the appreciation of the President for the judiciary. The Supreme Constitutional Court is an independent judicial authority. It does not perform its role within the frame of public opinion, it performs its role according to the law and constitution as well as the interest of Egypt."[27] It is hardly surprising that as such a loyal spokesperson, Marei was appointed minister of justice by President Mubarak in August 2006.

It is little wonder, then, that President Mubarak constantly praises the SCC. In a public address delivered in March 2009 at an event marking the fortieth anniversary of the Supreme Constitutional Court, he said:

> It gives me pleasure to talk to you on this August occasion from the rostrum of the Supreme Constitutional Court, with its elevated status in the conscience of Egypt and the hearts of Egyptians as a lofty edifice of justice and the rule of law and its esteemed judges who undertake their mission in faith and impartiality, upholding the Constitution and championing citizens' rights and freedoms . . . Since its first day, the Egyptian constitutional judiciary made a robust debut, rising on a solid base and well-established principles. The Constitution assigned a separate chapter for the Supreme Constitutional Court. Its provisions laid down the constitutional base of its jurisdiction as a self-standing independent judicial authority, exclusively entrusting it with the responsibility for controlling the constitutionality of laws and regulations and interpretation of legal provisions and deciding on conflict of jurisdiction. They also defined the rules of forming its bodies and the immunities of its judges. The law establishing the court affirmed that its rulings on constitutional actions and its decisions on the interpretation of legislation are binding to legislative, executive and judiciary authorities. We, in Egypt, take full pride in the fact that the State has never, during and before my tenure, refrained from enforcing one single ruling issued by our constitutional judiciary since its initiation forty years ago.[28]

For the strong Egyptian state apparatus, judicial activism is a faute de mieux option: a course pursued because the alternatives are worse. The court's emergence came at the cost of the government losing its previously unlimited grip over public policy making. Over the last decades the court has issued a number of landmark rulings that have fortified the status of political rights, freedom of the press, and legal due process. Before the 2005 constitutional amendment the court had also asserted its authority to oversee the integrity of electoral processes, thereby positioning itself as a possible foe of the military and state apparatus.[29] However, the court has yet to issue a single ruling on the core question of the status of Shari'a rules that would be deemed unacceptable by the executive branch, the military, or the secular intelligentsia. Along with its establishment of private property rights, the court has consistently advanced a moderate, flexible interpretation of pertinent Shari'a directives, thereby allowing the antifundamentalist coalition in Egypt to stem the advance of constitutional theocracy while shielding its core worldviews and policies from unfavorable popular pressures. Finally, although the court's moderate translation of Shari'a rules into practical guidelines for public life is not what the executive and its largely secular, ad hoc allies would have hoped for under conditions of minimal religious opposition, it nevertheless serves as a buffer between this coalition and the strength of Islamic revivalist groups and ideas. Nathan Brown concludes: "Rather than restricting the state, law in Egypt continues to enable the state to shape and guide society. Executive authorities, while often annoyed by the exercise of judicial power, have no quarrel with such a vision of law."[30]

A brief excursion to Kuwait is quite telling here. As Brown argued in the 1990s, there is an interesting similarity between the way in which leaders in Egypt and in the Gulf states constructed judicial review that on paper constrains their authority as part of their efforts to enhance centralized state capacity.[31] It is interesting to see how this impulse has played itself out over the last two decades with respect to containment of religion in both settings. Much like its Egyptian counterpart, Kuwait's Constitutional Court has emerged as an advocate of a moderate, relatively progressive agenda, given the context of an Islamic state and morality, and it has done so within a constitutional framework that resembles that of Egypt. Interestingly, the Egyptian Supreme Constitutional Court is arguably more politically dependent today than it was throughout much of the 1990s, while the opposite may be said about Kuwait's Constitutional Court. At any rate, with respect to the place of Shari'a in public life, the interpretive lines of each of these two courts share some common features. What is more, the migration of constitutional ideas in the Arab world is illustrated nicely here. The Kuwaiti Constitution (1962) states that "Islam is the religion of the state" and that Shari'a is "a main source of legislation." This phrasing is considered the source of the 1971 Egyptian Constitution's definition of the status of Shari'a as "a" source of legislation until the 1980 amendment changed that to "the" source of legislation. And the Egyptian rulings discussed earlier fed recent Kuwaiti Constitutional Court rulings on similar issues.

Let us consider two recent illustrations of this trend, both of which follow the Egyptian trail. In 2005 Kuwait adopted a law that for the first time in its history allowed women to vote and to hold political office. The law also stipulated that women voters and candidates must comply with Shari'a law. On the basis of that law four women were elected to the Kuwaiti parliament in May 2009—a historic breakthrough, no doubt. But a few months later a religious edict was published by the Ministry of Islamic Affairs' fatwa department (upon request by an ultraconservative MP) stating that any woman who wants to take part in politics must dress in accordance with Shari'a law norms—with her head covered and "a long robe that hides all parts of the body and which is not so tight so that it would give prominence to any curves."[32] Conservative opponents of women's rights cited that edict, alongside the requirement for compliance with Shari'a law stipulated in the 2005 law and the preamble to the constitution, to argue that women who refuse to wear the *hijab* may not serve in parliament.

This claim was a direct attack on two of the explicitly modernist women elected to the parliament. Rola Dashti, a noted women's rights activist, holds a doctoral degree in economics from Johns Hopkins University and has held senior economic positions in Kuwait, including a directorship at the Bank of Kuwait, for the last three decades. Aseel al-Awadhi holds a doctorate in political philosophy from the University of Texas and is a member of one of the most affluent families in Kuwait. In May 2009 she was photographed wearing a long white T-shirt and jumping for joy at news of her election. That photograph was later circulated in the opposition newspapers, which explained to their readers why they demanded that female elected representatives dress modestly. A third prominent woman politician, the only woman in the cabinet, Minister of Education Moudhi al-Humoud, is also uncovered. The struggle over women's dress code found its way to Kuwait's Constitutional Court, which had to decide on a much more substantive question than the way women MPs are clothed: what is the meaning of the clause in the 2005 law that requires compliance with Shari'a law? More generally, what is the scope of the provision "Islam is a main source of legislation" in the constitution?

In October 2009 Kuwait's Constitutional Court ruled that women lawmakers do not have to wear the *hijab* while in parliament.[33] The clause in the 2005 legislation was deemed too broad or vague and failed to specify what concrete norms women voters and candidates must comply with. Because the clause was generic, and because Shari'a law is not unified in its approach to the headscarf, one cannot arrive at the conclusion that wearing the *hijab* is the only possible interpretation of the clause in the 2005 law. What is more, wearing the *hijab,* the court ruled, is a matter of personal preference, not of state policy. This ruling came on the heels of another progressive ruling released by the Kuwaiti Constitutional Court only a week earlier. In that ruling the court held that a provision of the Personal Status Law requiring a woman's husband, parents, or male guardian to grant her permission to obtain a passport (and hence denying her the freedom to travel abroad without permission) violated guarantees of personal freedom and gender equality inherent in the Kuwaiti Constitution.[34] Any way one looks at them, these are secularizing rulings, made all the more important when they come from a court that operates within a constitutional framework that designates Islam as the state religion and enshrines its principles as "a main source of legislation."

Pakistan

Pakistan provides another telling illustration of how constitutional courts and jurisprudence have become key actors in containing the spread of sacred law. Islam has been a major political force in Pakistan at least since the early 1970s, when the new capital, Islamabad, home of the immense Faisal Mosque, replaced Karachi as the governmental epicenter of the state. Embattled President Asif Ali Zardari, much like former leaders Pervez Musharraf, Nawaz Sharif, and the late Benazir Bhutto, is often considered one of the West's best allies in the fight against radical Islamism in the Middle East and central Asia. Pakistan is also one of the few members of the world's nuclear club. At the same time, it has experienced tremendous political unrest, having gone through several major regime changes in the last three decades alone. In addition to these constant power struggles among and within its political elites, daily newspaper headlines report on religious insurgency in Pakistan. The Red Mosque incident (May 2007); the assassination of Benazir Bhutto (December 2007); the bombing of the Marriott Hotel in Islamabad, located steps from the president's and the prime minister's house (September 2008); the alleged links of a Pakistani fundamentalist group to the attacks in Mumbai (November 2008); the attack on Sri Lanka's national cricket team (March 2009); the orchestrated attacks in the cities of Lahore, Kohat, and Peshawa (October 2009); and the suicide bombings of army compounds and government buildings in Lahore (March 2010) that have killed hundreds of people as the army continues its assault on the Taliban, are only a few examples. The province of Baluchistan has become one of the main frontiers of the war on terror. Pakistan's North-West Frontier Province has been governed by the religious-fundamentalist Muttahida Majilis-I-Amal party since 2003.

Upon reflection, these developments are hardly surprising. Since gaining its independence in 1947, Pakistan has been grappling with what may be called an identity crisis, reflecting existential uncertainty with respect to its relation to Islam. From a formal standpoint, notes Farzana Shaikh, Pakistan was created as the first self-professed homeland for Muslims. However, neither Pakistanis nor their governments have ever been able to reach a consensus over the precise role and meaning of Islam.[35] Pakistani constitutional politics reflect a complex, if not completely blurred, collective identity that is torn between modernity and tradition, universalism and religiosity, and various degrees of rigidity and pragmatism. This broad spectrum has turned the Pakistani judiciary, and the Supreme Court in particular, into a key arena for clarifying, or at least legitimizing, some of the country's fuzzy identity.

The Supreme Court of Pakistan, made up of a chief justice and sixteen judges, is one of the busiest supreme courts worldwide in terms of its caseload. Each month it deals with numerous appeals from Pakistan's five High Courts (located in Lahore, Karachi, Peshawar, Quetta, and the capital, Islamabad), in addition to its direct jurisdiction powers. In 2005, for example, it dealt with over 27,000 cases (appeals and direct petitions). In December 2008 alone it decided 1,044 cases, whereas 1,701 new cases were instituted. The backlog of cases in the Supreme Court as of January 1, 2009, was 17,754.[36] The court also has a rich history of direct entanglement with high politics. Since 1985 the Supreme Court of Pakistan has played a key role in each of the radical political transitions and regime changes in that country.[37] Each of Pakistan's four prominent leaders during that period—Benazir Bhutto, Nawaz Sharif, Pervez Musharraf, and Asif Ali Zardari—has been at the center of several landmark Supreme Court rulings, with far-reaching implications for that leader's political standing.

A case in point is the Pakistani Supreme Court's appraisal of the very legitimacy of the military coup d'état of 1999. Charging runaway corruption and gross economic mismanagement by the government, General Pervez Musharraf seized power from Prime Minister Nawaz Sharif in a military coup d'état on October 12, 1999. Musharraf declared himself the country's new chief executive, detained Prime Minister Sharif and several of his political allies, and issued a proclamation of emergency that suspended the operation of Sharif's government, Pakistan's National Assembly, and its Senate. In response, political activists opposed to the military coup filed a petition to the Supreme Court in mid-November 1999, challenging the legality of the overthrow of Sharif's government and the proclamation of emergency and demanding that Nawaz Sharif be released and that his elected government be reinstated. In a widely publicized decision released in May 2000, the Pakistani Supreme Court used the doctrine of "state necessity" to validate unanimously the October 1999 coup as having been necessary to spare the country from chaos and bankruptcy.[38] The Court held:

> On 12th October, 1999, a situation arose for which the Constitution provided no solution and the intervention by the Armed Forces through an extra-constitutional measure became inevitable, which is hereby validated on the basis of the doctrine of State necessity and the principle of *salus populi suprema lex* . . . [S]ufficient corroborative and confirmatory material has been produced . . . in support of the intervention by the Armed Forces through extra-constitutional measure.[39]

However, Chief Justice Irshad Hasan Khan added that "prolonged involvement of the Army in civil affairs runs a grave risk of politicizing it, which would not be in [the] national interest; therefore, civilian rule in the country must be restored within the shortest possible time."[40] Accordingly, the court granted General Musharraf three years to accomplish economic and political reforms and to restore democracy. The court announced that General Musharraf (President Musharraf from 2001 to 2008) should choose a date no later than ninety days before the end of the three-year period for the holding of elections to the National Assembly, the provincial assemblies, and the Senate.[41] The events beginning in 1999 are merely the latest chapter in Pakistan's history as a country in near-constant political turmoil. One thing is clear, however—the courtroom battle over the political legitimacy of the Musharraf regime reemphasized the key political role played by the Supreme Court in present-day Pakistan.

A decade later the political scene changed, and so did the Supreme Court of Pakistan's position on state-of-emergency situations. In July 2009 the court ruled, in a rather expected fashion, that the state of emergency imposed by former President Pervez Musharraf in late 2007 was unconstitutional. The court went on to declare invalid the appointments of judges Musharraf made during that period.[42] The ruling was hardly surprising; the fourteen-member bench that delivered the decision was headed by reinstated Chief Justice Iftikhar Mohammed Chaudhry, whose attempted ouster by Musharraf spurred much of the unrest that led to Musharraf's downfall. The ruling is filled with acclaim for judicial independence, democracy, and other such great ideals. "The constitution is supreme, and this decision will strengthen democracy and democratic institutions," Chaudhry wrote in his decision. That the reinstated chief justice presided over the court that decided the legitimacy of his own ouster was not considered an obstacle to rendering an unbiased ruling by the court. The decision questions the legitimacy of former Chief Justice Abdul Hameed Dogar's appointment as chief justice following the attempted ouster of Chief Justice Chaudhry. The court added that rulings made by the judges who were improperly appointed could still stand, and it told Parliament to decide which of the laws that Musharraf pushed through during the unconstitutional emergency could remain on the books. Musharraf (who resided in London at the time) ignored a summons to appear before the court or to send a lawyer that week to explain his actions. At any rate, the ruling may be viewed as a strong judicial statement against future suspension of the constitution by the military, historically a key player in Pakistani politics.

The Supreme Court of Pakistan's entanglement with high politics continued in early 2010, when in a 290-page judgment it invalidated the National Reconciliation Ordinance—essentially a politically motivated amnesty law promulgated in 2007 by Pervez Musharraf to shield Asif Zardari and his wife, the late Benazir Bhutto, as well as other Pakistani politicians from criminal and civil prosecution for alleged corruption, undue charge of "commissions," and other looting of wealth said to be stashed away in Switzerland.[43] The ruling links morality and constitutionality by suggesting that in order to be a member of parliament, a person must be of "good character." It thus questions Zardari's moral standing as a top public figure. The Supreme Court cited at length the successful legal battles fought by the governments of Nigeria and the Philippines with the Swiss authorities in their bids to get back the billions looted by Sani Abacha and Ferdinand Marcos (thus implicitly equating Zardari's conduct to these two leaders' conduct) and ordered the government to apply to the Swiss authorities to reopen the money-laundering case against Zardari and Bhutto.[44] En route, in what is arguably a key obiter dicta, the Court noted that: "The four salient features of the Constitution, identified in the judgments of this Court are: Parliamentary form of Government; Federating character of the State; Independence of Judiciary; and Fundamental Rights of the people along with Islamic provisions. Even the Parliament has no power to alter these salient features of the Constitution."[45] And so, from a politically contentious case, a powerful statement on the fundamental, "meta-constitutional" status of constitutional theocracy in Pakistan was born.

The political role the court has played has manifested itself clearly in the battle over the place of Shari'a in Pakistan's constitutional system. In 1973 Pakistani legislators departed from that country's British common-law tradition by enabling the Pakistani judiciary to use Islam as an authoritative source in constitutional interpretation. In 1974, under severe pressure from clerics, Pakistan's first elected prime minister, Zulfikar Ali Bhutto (father of Benazir Bhutto), introduced a constitutional amendment, known as the Second Amendment, which declared that members of the Ahmadiyya community were non-Muslims. The Ahmadiyya community in Pakistan and elsewhere in the Islamic world has been under political and legal pressure from orthodox Muslim groups. Violent attacks on Ahmadi mosques are quite common, most recently in Lahore (May 2010). At the core of its conflict with mainstream Muslims lies the Ahmadiyya community's belief that the founder of the sect, Mirza Ghulam Ahmed, was a prophet—a belief that most Muslims resent. The Ahmadis insist that Mirza Ghulam Ahmed was not a "lawgiving" prophet and was only propagating the laws enunciated by Islam's Prophet Muhammad, but few in the Muslim mainstream are willing to accept this argument.[46] At any rate, aside from the change in their constitutional status, the Bhutto government placed no other formal restriction on the Ahmadis' activities.

In 1978 President Zia-ul-Haq established the Shari'at Benches at the provincial High Courts, and in 1980 the Federal Shari'at Court, as well as the Shari'at Appellate Bench (SAB) at the Supreme Court; each of these would be responsible for ensuring the appropriate implementation of Shari'a law.[47] The Federal Shari'at Court was vested with the authority to ensure conformity of all legislation to the Qur'an and Sunna and to strike down any law it considered repugnant to either. An appeal against a ruling of the Federal Shari'at Court was possible only to the Shari'at Appellate Bench. In 1984 President Zia introduced the so-called blasphemy laws forbidding "un-Islamic" activities. In 1985 the Eighth Amendment to the constitution was introduced, which validated Islamization changes made by President Zia. Article 203 of the constitution formally establishes a Shari'a court system, which is designed to operate in parallel with the secular "ordinary" judicial system. The Islamization of law continued with the Enforcement of Shari'a Act 1991, which affirms the supremacy of Shari'a (defined in the act as the injunctions of Islam as laid down in the Holy Qur'an and Sunna) as the supreme law of Pakistan. The act states that all statute law is to be interpreted in light of Shari'a, and that all Muslim citizens of Pakistan shall observe Shari'a and act accordingly.[48]

The preamble to the 1973 constitution states, inter alia, "Whereas sovereignty over the entire universe belongs to Allah Almighty alone and the authority which He has delegated to the State of Pakistan through its people for being exercised within the limits prescribed by Him is a sacred trust . . . Wherein the principles of democracy, freedom, equality, tolerance and social justice as enunciated by Islam shall be fully observed; Wherein the Muslims shall be enable to order their lives in the individual and collective spheres in accordance with the teachings and requirements of Islam as set out in the Holy *Qur'an* and the *Sunnah*." Article 1 of the current constitution declares that Pakistan's official name shall be the Islamic Republic of Pakistan, and Article 2 declares Islam the state religion. The

Objectives Resolution (an annex to the constitution) was made a part of its substantive provisions by the insertion of Article 2A in 1985, thereby incorporating into the constitution a requirement that all laws be brought into consonance with the Qur'an and Sunnah.[49] Articles 227–231 (Chapter IX, Islamic Provisions) organize various governing aspects of Islam as the source of legislation and determine the purpose and composition of the Islamic Council. Article 227(1) stipulates that "[a]ll existing laws shall be brought in conformity with the Injunctions of Islam as laid down in the Holy Qur'an and Sunnah, in this Part referred to as the Injunctions of Islam, and no law shall be enacted which is repugnant to such Injunctions."[50] In theory, this construction of constitutional provisions may reasonably mean that legislation must be in full compliance with principles of Shari'a. The Supreme Court of Pakistan, however, has begged to differ.

In response to the possible conclusiveness of Article 227(1), the court developed its "harmonization doctrine," according to which no specific provision of the constitution, including Article 2A and Article 227(1), stands above any other provision. In the landmark case *Hakim Khan v. Government of Pakistan* (1992) the Supreme Court, led by Justice Ajmal Mian (who later served as chief justice from 1997 to 1999), decided what has been arguably one of its most far-reaching rulings since the Zia reforms.[51] The court held that the "Islamization amendment" that was incorporated as part of the constitution through Article 2A shall not prevail over the other articles of the constitution. Instead, the court held that Article 2A possessed the same weight and status as the other articles of the constitution and therefore "could not be placed on a higher pedestal or treated as a *grundnorm*."[52] The court's subsequent judgments of this key issue "have firmly precluded and strongly warned against an interpretation of Article 2A which would raise it to the point of being a litmus test for gauging, evaluating, and potentially justifying the judiciary to strike down any other constitutional provisions."[53] Any reading of Article 2A as an elevated "special clause" would undermine the entire constitution. The constitution as a whole must be interpreted in a harmonious fashion so that specific provisions are read as an integral part of the entire constitution, not as standing above it.[54] In the words of the court: "It may be observed that the principles for interpreting constitutional documents as laid down by this Court are that all provisions should be read together and harmonious construction should be placed on such provisions so that no provision is rendered nugatory."[55]

Although it has shown some secularizing tendencies, the Supreme Court of Pakistan, like its counterparts elsewhere, does not operate in a political or ideological vacuum. In no small part it may be considered an extension of the executive branch rather than a fully autonomous organ. It is hardly surprising that in several rulings it sided with the Islamist face of the constitution. A notable example is the court's approval in 1993 of part of the 1984 blasphemy laws that made members of the Ahmadiyya community liable to prosecution for engaging in activities associated with Islam.[56] In 1984 the government introduced Ordinance XX and inserted Section 298(c) into the Pakistan Penal Code, which made it illegal for an Ahmadi to call himself a Muslim and banned Ahmadis from using Muslim terminology. In July 1993 the court dismissed (by a 4–1 vote) a constitutional challenge brought by a group of Ahmadis who had been arrested under the Penal Code. The court used a quite creative reading of American and British freedom-of-religion jurisprudence to reject the argument that the law violated the fundamental rights of freedom of speech and freedom of religion guaranteed in the constitution, thereby effectively rubber-stamping this blatantly discriminatory legislation. Being politically astute, the court noted that Shi'a or Sunni Muslims, who vastly outnumber the Ahmadis, consider the "movement ideologically offensive." As a national high court in a predominantly Muslim polity, the court is also required to perform interpretive tasks that may seem unusual to observers of constitutionalism in Western democracies. In 1999, for example, the court was asked to decide whether a request by a person for exemption from compulsory deduction of *zakat* (collective charity or almsgiving) from her wealth was justified by her Hanafi school of *fiqh* or by the Zakat Ordinance of 1980.[57]

A telling illustration of the court's delicate balancing act is its personal-status and gender-equality jurisprudence. In general, in the politically charged area of personal-status and family-law matters, the equality provisions of the constitution are seldom invoked by the court even though in the employment-discrimination context they are invoked quite frequently.[58] But the court has nonetheless managed to block calls for major Islamic-based family-law overhaul. The Muslim Family Laws Ordinance (MFLO) 1961 introduced modernization reforms to various aspects of traditional Islamic law in the context of marriage and divorce. Among its various innovations, it introduced registration of marriage and divorce *(talag)*, inheritance rights of orphaned grandchildren, restrictions on polygamy, consideration of every divorce (except the third of three) as single and revocable, formalization of reconciliation procedures in disputes relating to maintenance or dissolution of marriage, and recovery of *mahr,* along with specified penalties for noncompliance. The MFLO has long been regarded by progressive activists as one of the few pieces of legislation that protect women's rights within the family. It is little wonder, then, that it has been frequently challenged by Islamists in the courts.[59]

Originally the Federal Shari'at Court did not have the mandate to adjudicate on family laws, but the previously mentioned Islamization amendment of 1985 that incorporated the Objectives Resolution into the main body of the constitution granted the Federal Shari'at Court some justification to consider personal-status laws as falling under its jurisdiction. The pressure to amend or scrap the modernizing provisions of the MFLO has intensified in recent years. Initially the Shari'at Appellate Bench took a rather minimalist approach to its jurisdiction. However, in 1994, in the *Faisal* case, the SAB overturned its earlier rulings on the subject of its own powers, deciding that as part of a broad process of Islamization of Pakistani laws, Shari'a courts should have jurisdiction to review the relatively progressive MFLO, as well as similar laws, in order to bring their provisions into accordance with the fundamental tenets of Islam.[60] In January 2000 the Federal Shari'at Court held certain of the MFLO's provisions to be repugnant to Islam and directed the president of Pakistan to take steps to amend the MFLO so as to bring those provisions into conformity with the injunctions of Islam.[61]

Amid all that pressure the Supreme Court of Pakistan has continuously refused to accept the Objectives Resolution as a supraconstitutional provision, and it has retained its overarching jurisdictional authority, including its de facto appellate capacity over the Shari'at Appellate Bench at the Supreme Court. This has proved time and again to be a safety valve for secular interests. In 2002, for example, the Supreme Court ordered the Shari'at Appellate Bench to reconsider its 1999 ruling that interest or usury *(riba)* in any form contravened Shari'a principles and was therefore impermissible.[62] The Supreme Court accepted the government's argument that the transition to a *riba*-free economy, as it had been defined by the Shari'at Appellate Bench, was effectively infeasible. It noted concerns about the economic stability of Pakistan should the reforms occur and stated that they were simply impractical. The court also accepted the government's claim that the reasoning employed by the Shari'at Appellate Bench misinterpreted both the Qur'an and Sunna, had invoked only one conception of *riba,* and thus lacked the objectivity needed to render an adequate verdict in the case. The court thus ordered the Shari'at Appellate Bench "to conduct thorough and elaborate research, and comparative study of the financial systems which are prevalent in the contemporary Muslim countries of the world."[63]

In 2003, to give another example, the Pakistani Supreme Court ruled that the Hudood Ordinances (adopted in 1979 to introduce harsh penalties for offenses described in the Qur'an) had been drafted hastily, had many gaps, were defective, and were the source of many challenges to the establishment of human rights in the country. The enforcement of the ordinances, stated the court, "had brought about injustice rather than justice, which should be the main purpose of the enforcement of Islamic law."[64] In November 2004 the Supreme Court went on to curtail the Federal Shari'at Court's competence to overturn any legislation judged to be inconsistent with the tenets of Islam. The Supreme Court held that any Shari'a-related jurisprudence that involves significant constitutional law aspects must take a cohesive view of Pakistan's constitutional law, as well as the supremacy of federal legislation over provincial legislation.[65]

Principles of federalism have also aided the court in its mission. In July 2005 and again in December 2006, for example, Pakistan's Supreme Court blocked attempts to enact laws to enforce Islamic morality in the North-West Frontier Province (NWFP), which has been governed by an alliance of religious parties sympathetic to the Taliban since 2003. Specifically, the NWFP Islamization bill (also known as the Hisba [Accountability] Act, 2005) aimed at implementing greater Islamic regulation in the NWFP by establishing a government agency headed by a special cleric given the title of *mohtasib* (ombudsman). This agency was responsible for overseeing the Islamization of everyday life in the province, including many aspects of private life. To that end, the act created an enforcement force—essentially a religious police squad—that would help ensure the moral and virtuous conduct of Muslims in the province. President Musharraf, whose administration supported an enlightened, moderate form of Islam, denounced the bill as a fundamental breach of human rights that would, accordingly, violate federal legislation and constitutional rights. Upon Musharraf's request and on these grounds, Pakistan's attorney general challenged the constitutionality of the proposed Islamization bill, using the constitutional reference procedure that allows the executive branch to refer constitutional questions to the Supreme Court in its advisory jurisdiction (Section 186 of the constitution). The main question the court was asked to address was "whether the Hisba Bill or any of its provisions would be constitutionally invalid if enacted."[66]

The Supreme Court unanimously agreed and ordered the NWFP governor not to sign the Hisba Bill into law: "The Governor of the North-West Frontier Province may not assent to Hisba Bill in its present form as its various Sections . . . have been declared *ultra vires* the Constitution of the Islamic Republic of Pakistan, 1973."[67] The court ruled that "Islamic jurists are unanimous on the point that except for *sallat* [prayer] and *zakat* [alms] no other religious obligation stipulated by Islam can be enforced by the state."[68] In other words, the court suggested that even within Islamic jurisprudence there is no agreement that state enforcement of religious values is warranted. In so doing, it came close to adopting Egypt's Supreme Constitutional Court's interpretive approach discussed earlier. The decision again contained a conflation of Islamic and secular constitutional law, suggesting that the functions of the *mohtasib* would interfere in the citizens' "personal life, freedom of assembly, liberty, dignity, and privacy which is strictly prohibited in Islam."[69] The bill was sent back to the NWFP Assembly for redrafting and was subsequently passed in a diluted version, which the Supreme Court later struck down again in December 2006.

The use of the reference procedure in this case is quite telling. Clearly, given the increasing support for Islamization in the NWFP and elsewhere in Pakistan, the costs involved in the Musharraf regime's direct intervention in the NWFP to proactively prevent the imposition of the *hisba* (accountability) regime would be highly significant. Referring the issue to the Supreme Court was a less costly, politically expedient way to ensure that there was at least some impediment to the implementation of the bill. The Supreme Court, for its part, estimated that the costs associated with blocking the bill were outweighed by the benefits of establishing a clear judicial rebuke of the imposition of *hisba* boards in Pakistan. But in present-day Pakistan the political and judicial calculus is quite fluid. In 2008 pressure within the NWFP to move forward with Islamization reached new heights. Pro-Taliban militants started to engage in armed conflict with Pakistani forces in the Swat region (part of the NWFP). In an attempt to restore order in the area, the new Zardari-led federal government, in collaboration with the now more moderate NWFP government, agreed to allow the pro-Taliban movement in Swat and six other districts of the NWFP, collectively known as the Malakand Division, to impose Shari'a rule in the region in return for a halt to the armed conflict and the militants laying down their arms. The accord, named Nizam-e-Adal, was signed on February 16, 2009, and was approved by Parliament on April 13 of that year. In essence Nizam-e-Adal establishes Shari'a courts as the ultimate tribunals in the region, and, some suggest, without an appellate option to high courts or the Supreme Court. The Supreme Court came to the rescue. In late April 2009 the constitutionality of the new Islamization deal in Swat was the subject of a petition by the Muttahida Quami movement (a liberal, progressive, and anti-Pashtun movement and political party based in Karachi) to the Supreme Court on the grounds that such Islamization was incompatible with the laws of Pakistan. Interestingly, the petition also claimed that the Islamization package was at odds with fundamental tenets of Islam, thereby raising questions whether the Shari'at Appellate Bench might be implicated in the review of the proposed laws. In any case, given that from a political standpoint the Islamization deal appears to be a fait accompli, the Supreme Court will once again be asked to serve as the last bastion of antireligionist forces in Pakistan and to allow politicians to talk the talk of religion while transferring the costs of not implementing that talk to the courts.

Thus, as on many occasions in the last few decades, the Supreme Court became a main locus for the struggle between moderates and conservatives over the face and direction of Pakistan. Combined with the general ambiguity and potential for contradiction in a country functioning with both Islamic and Western legal practices, a constitution that seems to protect against the type of punishments established by the Hudood Ordinances but also establishes Pakistan as an Islamic state means that Pakistan has effectively been living the complexities of constitutional theocracy for over three decades now. The Supreme Court, while falling short of advancing a truly progressive human rights agenda by Western standards, has nonetheless served as a bastion of relative cosmopolitanism in an otherwise increasingly religious Pakistan.

Malaysia (and a Brief Comparison with Nigeria)

Malaysia provides a distinctly subtler example of the secularizing jurisprudential pattern described in this chapter. It features what is arguably one of the most fascinating and complex settings for studying the dynamic intersection of constitutional and religious law. Malaysia, despite its vast socioeconomic disparity, is one of Asia's economic tigers and a major tourist destination. Its capital, Kuala Lumpur, is one of Asia's most bustling business centers—home of the landmark Petronas Twin Towers, as well as the Menara Kuala Lumpur, currently the world's fifth-tallest telecommunications tower. Putrajaya, Malaysia's new administrative capital next to Kuala Lumpur, features a fully electronic government, matching with its neighboring planned city Cyberjaya, in accordance with former Prime Minister Mahathir bin Mohamad's vision of Malaysia as the "Japan of the Islamic world."[70] But at the same time, the Malaysian political sphere has undergone substantial Islamization over the last two decades, a fact that has brought to the fore the constitutional status of Islam as Malaysia's state religion and as a marker of Malay collective identity. At this stage a bit of background is necessary in order to appreciate fully the role of the courts in mitigating increasing pressures to expand the role of Islamic law in Malaysian public life.

Malaya (known once as British Malaya and then as the Malayan Union) gained its independence from the United Kingdom in 1957. With the addition of Sabah, Sarawak, and Singapore in 1963, Malaysia was formed (Singapore gained its independence from Malaysia in 1965). The independence constitution of Malaya was adopted in August 1957 and was later changed to incorporate the new territories and to form the Constitution of Malaysia in 1963. It establishes Malaysia as a unique form of Islamic state where "Islam is the religion of the Federation; but other religions may be practiced in peace and harmony in any part of the Federation" (Article 3), and where "every person has the right to profess and practice his religion and to propagate it" (Article 11.1). Further, "every religious group has the right to manage its own religious affairs" (Article 11.3), while state law (and, in the Federal Territories of Kuala Lumpur and Labuan, federal law) "may control or restrict the propagation of any religious doctrine or belief among persons professing the religion of Islam" (Article 11.4).

To add further complication, Malaysian law draws on religious ascriptions to establish what has been termed "ethnic democracy," where, despite the existence of some ethnic power-sharing mechanisms and an accompanying façade of interracial harmony, Malay political dominance is ensured. Core elements of the political system are organized so as to benefit members of the Malay ethnic group to the detriment of others, and members of minority ethnic groups are not granted proportional access to power. Although Islam is constitutionally enshrined as Malaysia's state religion, over one-third of Malaysia's population consists of members of other denominations, mainly Buddhists, Hindus, and Christians. However, ethnic Malays (*Bumiputra,* or "sons of the soil"), generally Muslim, are granted constitutionally entrenched preferential treatment in various aspects of public life over members of other ethnic groups (Article 153 of the constitution).[71] Malay citizens who convert out of Islam are no longer considered Malay under the law and hence forfeit the Bumiputra privileges afforded to Malays under Article 153.[72]

Although the aspiration for a greater role for Islamic law in Malaysia's public life has had a place in Malaysia for many years, a strong commitment to the Federal Constitution and constitutionalism on the part of the judiciary and federal authorities had, for a time, helped keep this aspiration in check. However, things have gradually been changing over the last two decades. The Pan-Malaysian Islamic Party (Parti Islam Se-Malaysia, PAS) has been gaining political support and clout continuously since the 1980s. It has positioned itself as a political party that aims to establish Malaysia as a country based on Islamic legal theory derived from the primary sources of Islam, the Qur'an, Sunna, and Hadiths. In contrast, the National Front (Barisan Nasional, BN) coalition adopts the more mainstream Islam Hadhari doctrine (a moderate or "civilizational" Islam), which PAS sees as based on a watered-down, compromised, secularized understanding of Islam.

In 1990 PAS captured electoral victory in the rural northern state of Kelantan and has been ruling it ever since. In 1999 it won the elections in the neighboring state of Terengganu, which PAS governed until 2004. In both instances it followed its victories with the enactment of Shari'a-based, nondiscretionary criminal law *(hudood)* and with formal gender segregation in public places. The pro-Islamist PAS, together with the pro-Malay, social justice, and anticorruption Parti Keadilan Rakyat (PKR) and the secularist, multiracial Democratic Action Party (DAP), formed part of an ideologically mixed, antiestablishment coalition called Pakatan Rakyat (People's Alliance). As of 2010 Pakatan Rakyat controls four states, including Penang, one of Asia's premier industrial and tourist destinations, and the prized state of Selangor, the country's most developed state.[73] It also won elections in Perak in 2008, but lost control over the state government due to defections.

The PAS has also become a major factor in federal politics. It won an impressive number of seats in the 1999 elections, and despite its relatively poor showing in the 2004 federal elections, it continued to be the most viable political alternative to the dominant United Malay National Organization (UNMO) party. In 2004 PAS underwent a transformation, after which a group of younger, relatively more moderate and inclusionist politicians assumed leadership of the party. As a result, it made a major comeback in the March 2008 general elections, when the coalition of PAS and its allies, led by Wan Azizah Wan Ismail (the wife of prominent opposition leader Anwar Ibrahim, head of the PKR, who assumed the position of opposition leader in August 2008 after winning a by-election), won 82 of the 222 seats, while the establishment BN party won only 140 seats. The slim difference in actual votes was even more staggering: approximately 4.1 million votes for the BN coalition (or 50.1 percent) and approximately 3.8 million votes for the Pakatan Rakyat coalition (46.4 percent). This was the best electoral showing of an Islamic party in Malaysian history.

To be sure, political Islam in Malaysia is, for the most part, a far cry from the image of radical fundamentalism often associated in the West with such movements. Things may occasionally take a radical turn at the margins, but Islamic federal politics there are more in the frame of mind of moderate political Islam in Turkey or Morocco (notable differences notwithstanding) than in places such as Egypt or Algeria where radical political Islam has been outlawed. Anwar Ibrahim, for example, who served in several ministerial posts and was deputy prime minister from 1993 to 1998, was initially a protégé of the establishment prime minister Mahathir bin Mohamad before emerging as the most prominent pro-Malay critic of Mahathir's administration. During his tenure as education minister Ibrahim introduced numerous pro-Malay policies in the national school curriculum, most prominently renaming the national language from Bahasa Malaysia to Bahasa Melayu in 1991, thereby implying that Malaysia is first and foremost a Malay country. In 1999 he was sentenced in a highly controversial trial to six years in prison for corruption, and in 2000 to another nine years for alleged homosexual acts. However, in 2004 the federal court reversed the second conviction and he was released. In 2008 Ibrahim was accused again of sexual harassment of a male intern in his party offices. He has gone on trial in February 2010. Many observers believe, however, that the allegations against Ibrahim are politically motivated. Either way, in 2009, *The Economist* declared Ibrahim "South East Asia's most extraordinary politician"—certainly not a title international media outlets would assign to a radical militant.

The rise of political Islam has affected the mainstream moderate establishment. Even politicians affiliated with the BN must now resort to "religious talk" in their appeal to the Islamic vote. In fact, in many respects, Islamization has been a federal project designed to take the wind out of PAS's sails. The former prime minister of Malaysia, Mahathir bin Mohamad of the corporate nationalist UMNO, the largest political party in Malaysia and the pillar of the BN coalition, declared in September 2001 that the country was an Islamic state *(negara Islam)*, not merely a country that had endorsed Islam as its official religion. This broad Islamization of public life is also reflected in an increasing number of ultraconservative rulings by the National Fatwa Council, Malaysia's top clerical Islamic body. Two 2008 examples are an edict that girls who act like boys or women dressing and behaving like men violate the tenets of Islam and the even more ethnically charged ruling that the practice of yoga involves not just physical exercise but also includes Hindu spiritual elements, chanting, and worship and therefore could corrupt Muslims.[74] Prime Minister Abdullah Ahmad Badawi of the UNMO moved to contain the damage, telling the national news agency Bernama that Muslims could continue doing yoga as a type of physical exercise but should refrain from the spiritual chanting.

Consider another telling anecdote. In accordance with Islam's prohibition of the consumption of alcohol, government regulations in Malaysia prohibit concerts from being sponsored by makers of alcoholic beverages. An exception to the rule was made in 2009 for a concert in Kuala Lumpur by the hip-hop group Black Eyed Peas, who were sponsored by the Irish beer company Guinness. The brewery was celebrating its 250th anniversary by sponsoring celebrations around the world; Malaysian authorities apparently thought that the concert would promote tourism. So the concert did go on, albeit without any Muslim Malaysians—approximately 60 percent of the population—because of another recent government regulation prohibiting ethnic Malays (Muslims) from attending events that promote the consumption of alcohol in public. However, non-Malays (i.e., tourists or non-Muslim residents of Malaysia) aged eighteen and over were encouraged by the Ministry of Information, Communication, and Culture to attend the concert and have fun. This is the multilayered Malaysia in the early twenty-first century.

In the face of this growing Islamization, Malaysia's constitutional division of powers between the federal and state governments has been used to effectively block PAS-led governments in the states of Kelantan and Terengganu from instituting Qur'an- and Sunna-based *hudood* and *qisas* (retaliation) law as the basis for their criminal code.[75] That said, some scholars of Islamic law in Malaysia themselves question the internal logic and legitimacy of implementing harsh Islamic law norms in these states.[76] Although the Kelantan State Assembly passed the Syariah (Behasa Melayu or Malay for "Shari'a") Criminal Enactment in 1993, it has yet to be implemented, mainly because criminal law is in federal hands. According to the Federal Constitution, Syariah courts do not have jurisdiction over offenses "except in so far as conferred by federal law"; state authorities can only legislate for Islamic offenses "except in regard to matters included in the Federal List" (e.g., criminal law and procedure). What is more, Article 75 provides: "If any State law is inconsistent with a federal law, the federal law shall prevail and the State law shall, to the extent of the inconsistency, be void." Finally, item 4(k) in the list of matters falling under federal jurisdiction provides that "[a]scertainment of Islamic Law and other personal laws for purposes of federal law" is a *federal* matter.[77]

Although the power to create and punish offenses against the precepts of Islam has been assigned by the constitution to the states, Syariah courts have jurisdiction only over persons professing the religion of Islam. Further, the enactment of *hudood* as state law runs counter to Article 11 (freedom of religion), which has been interpreted to protect individuals against prosecution on the basis of choice of religion. What is more, Article 8 provides that every citizen is equal before the law, hence rendering the blanket application of *hudood* laws arguably unconstitutional because they discriminate against non-Muslims and women. Finally, as the Malaysian Federal Court—the country's supreme court since 1985—has observed on numerous occasions, Malaysian public law is secular, and unless the Federal Constitution is amended to reflect the Syariah law as the supreme or basic law, this remains the case.[78] To date, the Federal Constitution has not been amended to reflect that position. Article 4(1) still declares that the Federal Constitution is the supreme law.

The religious-secular duality embedded in the Malaysian legal system is further reflected in the changing jurisdictional interrelation between the civil and Syariah courts. Muslims (and non-Muslims who marry Muslims) are obliged to follow the decisions of Syariah courts in matters concerning their religion, most notably marriage, inheritance, apostasy, conversion, and custody. Historically the civil and Syariah courts existed side by side in a dual court structure established at the time of Malaysia's independence, with the prevalent understanding that Syariah courts were subordinate to the civil courts and that the common law was superior to other laws. In the landmark case *Che Omar bin Che Soh* (1984) the Federal Court, then known as the Supreme Court of Malaysia, ruled that the common law had not been ousted or otherwise affected by the introduction of the Federal Constitution, and that it would allow secular courts to resolve legal issues even where the parties to the case were Muslims.[79] However, in 1988 an amendment to the constitution, Article 121(1A), was introduced; it provided that civil courts "shall have no jurisdiction in respect of any matter within the jurisdiction of the Syariah Courts."

Even after the 1988 amendment the civil court system continued to view Syariah courts as subordinates and, at any rate, subject to general principles of administrative and constitutional law. The civil courts consistently interpreted the jurisdictional boundaries between the two court systems so as to prevent the expansion of the Syariah court system. Likewise, the Malaysian Bar Council has continued to argue that Article 121(1A) does not exclude the supervisory review power of the Federal Court. However, because Islam has become a major political force in Malaysia, taking an anti-Islamist stand on the question of jurisdictional boundaries is no longer a feasible option for the court.[80] It has opted instead for a strategy of mixed messages and vagueness. Several recent rulings illustrate this trend.

Let us consider first the issue of conversion. Shortly after the 1988 amendment the Federal Court was asked to rule on the legitimacy of a non-Muslim minor's conversion to Islam without parental consent. The minor was older than fifteen—the age of consent for conversions according to Islamic law—but was still under parental legal guardianship under secular federal law. The court sided with secular law, overturned the lower-court decision, and ruled that the legal guardian retains the right to decide the religion of a child until that child reaches the age of maturity under federal law.[81] More recent decisions concerning conversions have taken a different direction. In 1999, for example, the Federal Court held that Syariah courts had sole jurisdiction over the issue of conversion out of Islam.[82] In 2006 the court considered a non-Muslim woman's petition for an injunction against the Islamic Religious Affairs Council from claiming the body of her husband. The woman argued that her husband practiced Hinduism and had not been converted to Islam without the knowledge of his family before his death, as the Islamic authorities claimed.[83] The court delayed the decision on the jurisdictional issue for many months, while the body of Maniam Moorthy (also known as Mohammad Abdullah) was buried in a Muslim ceremony within days of his death.

All this litigation was only a prologue to the real legal showdown regarding conversion—the *Lina Joy* case (2007), which raised the question of Syariah courts' jurisdictional authority over apostasy in a case of conversion out of Islam.[84] Lina Joy, who was born Azalina Jailani, claimed to have converted from Islam to Christianity and argued that conversion was protected by the right to freedom of religion under Article 11 of the Constitution of Malaysia. However, the National Registration Department refused to change her name or her religious status as they appeared on her identity card on the grounds that the Syariah court had not granted permission for her to renounce Islam.[85] Following a long legal battle, the case reached the Federal Court of Malaysia, which ruled (by a 2–1 vote) in May 2007 that approvals of conversions out of Islam do fall under the jurisdiction of the Syariah court system. In other words, the court refused to limit the jurisdictional boundaries of Syariah courts in Malaysia, even at the cost of infringing on general principles of freedom of religion or formal gender equality.[86]

But only two months later the Federal Court sent a somewhat different message in the *Latifa Mat Zin* case (2007), an inheritance dispute that raised the question whether the applicable law was the Islamic law of gifts *(hibah)* or the federal law of banking or contract.[87] Although the court sided with the claimant, holding that Islamic law should apply in the particular situation under dispute, it also stated clearly that "[i]n case an application to the syariah court is resisted on the ground that the syariah court has no jurisdiction in the matter, let me answer that question right now. Interpretation of the Federal Constitution is a matter for this court, not the syariah court. [If] this court says that the syariah court has jurisdiction, [then] it has."[88]

The court's cautious navigation through this politically charged jurisdictional quagmire continued in the *Subashini* case (2007).[89] The originally Hindu husband of a Hindu woman converted to Islam in 2006 and went on to convert their elder son as well. The husband then applied to the Syariah court to dissolve the couple's civil marriage and to obtain custody of both their sons. The Federal Court, in another 2–1 and equivocal ruling, held that the civil court has jurisdiction over marriage and divorce, as well as over custody of children in a civil marriage, even when one spouse has converted to Islam, since the original marriage took place when both parties were Hindus. At the same time, the court held that the consent of only one parent was sufficient for a conversion of the children to be lawful. To support its ruling, as well as to increase the legitimacy of this and several other contested decisions, the court cited several solicited opinions of respected religious scholars. These opinions and their authors' academic credentials (including their postsecondary degrees and the institutions of higher learning they attended, and their main publications), were cited in great detail by the court, presumably in order to signal the court's respect for sacred law. At any rate, the court granted a partial victory to each side of the dispute, compounding the jurisprudential ambiguity. Or, to be more colloquial, it threw each side a chewy bone, while jurisprudential wishy-washiness reigned. What better way to maintain the court's legitimacy while avoiding the possible wrath of influential stakeholders from both sides? The duality continues. In 2010 a similar case involving a child custody dispute between a Hindu woman and her converted-to-Islam husband reached the Federal Court. This time, the court was asked to make a decisive call on the legality of one parent converting a minor to Islam without the other parent's consent, and by extension, on the scope of Syariah Courts' jurisdiction in conversion cases.

The blurred jurisdictional matrix in Malaysia has given rise to a jurisdictional "war of courts." Aided by increased public support, Syariah courts in several states have begun to suggest that they are authorized to interpret relevant aspects of the constitution itself (i.e., to go beyond the interpretation and application of Shari'a law). In its recent judgment in the *Abdul Kahar bin Ahmad* case (2008) the Federal Court dismissed in an atypically decisive tone an argument that the 1988 amendment and, in particular, Article 121(1A) conferred jurisdiction on Syariah courts to interpret the constitution in matters falling under the jurisdiction of such courts. The Federal Court stated: "Before the jurisdiction of this court is excluded it must be shown that the Syariah Court has jurisdiction over the matter first. That is not the case here . . . The constitutionality of any law, whether a law made by Parliament or by the Legislature of a State . . . is a matter for this court to decide, not the Syariah High Court."[90] The Majlis Agam Islam of Selangor—that state's Islamic council—argued that Article 121(1A) granted full and exclusive jurisdiction to the Syariah court to decide whether a practice falls within the precepts of Islam regardless of its constitutionality. In other words, the Syariah court suggested that the matter of jurisdiction itself should be decided under Shari'a law. The Federal Court countered by ruling that "nowhere in the Constitution is there a provision that the determination of Islamic Law for the purpose of interpreting the Federal Constitution is a matter for the State Legislature."[91] The court held that Article 121(1A) was not inserted "to oust the jurisdiction of this court in matters that rightly belong to it."[92] The entire realm of the constitutionality of state law, however Shari'a based it may be, can be decided only by the Federal Court.

As the Federal Court of Malaysia continues to find itself at the center of the religious/secular jurisdictional struggle, it has begun to grow tired of dealing with this political hot potato, especially given the Malaysian Parliament's inability or unwillingness to resolve the matter via legislation. "Everyone looks to the court to solve the problem of the Legislature," stated then Chief Justice Tun Abdul Hamid Mohamed in the *Latifa Mat Zin* ruling,[93] adding:

> Judges too, (including myself), unwittingly, took upon themselves the responsibility to solve the problem of the Legislature because they believe that they have to decide the case before them one way or the other. That, in my view is a mistake. The function of the court is to apply the law, not make or to amend law not made by the Legislature. Knowing the inadequacy of the law, it is for the Legislature to remedy it, by amendment or by making new law. It is not the court's function to try to remedy it.[94]

But the secular/religious courtroom jurisdictional war in Malaysia goes on. In 2009 an ideal opportunity for the Federal Court to shore up its jurisdiction presented itself.[95] A Muslim couple sought to divorce. A dispute emerged between the husband and the wife about the distribution of their assets. What made this rather common scenario unique was that a major asset under dispute was a registered company of which the wife's share was 8 percent. Whereas under Article 121(1A) the Syariah court has full jurisdiction over asset allocation in divorce, this case involved a registered company, whose operation and disintegration are governed by commercial law, not by religious directives. The wife turned to the civil court system to seek an injunction against dilution or dissipation of her company holdings by her husband. The husband claimed that the issue was incidental to the main dispute, which fell squarely under the Syariah court's jurisdiction. In a brief but forceful ruling by Chief Justice Zaki Tun Azmi (with four other justices concurring), the Federal Court held that a minority shareholder in a registered company has a right to take derivative action to protect the interest of the company. Therefore, the wife was acting in an attempt to protect her interest in the company as a shareholder, not as a wife. What is more, Chief Justice Zaki Tun Azmi went on to turn the jurisdictional situation on its head rather brilliantly, so as to favor the wife. He stated that at the conclusion of the proceedings before the Syariah court, the wife might well be entitled to more than her registered 8 percent portion in the company. Therefore, if the court were to limit the civil injunction to only that percentage of the company's value, "in effect this court would already be deciding that the wife is only entitled to that portion of the monies. This court has no such jurisdiction." As to the wife's rights in the Syariah court, Tun Azmi wrote, "I would not like to make any comments. It is left to the relevant forum to decide."[96]

A further indication of the court's position on Shari'a may be seen in a rare lecture at Harvard University in late 2008 by Chief Justice Mohamed, delivered only weeks after his retirement from the court in October 2008.[97] Malaysia's federal courts, Mohamed opined, should not interpret Shari'a law but, when necessary, analyze the "precepts of Islam" within a constitutional context. On such questions, he said, the federal courts ought to welcome affidavits from Islamic scholars in order to clarify questions that range outside constitutional doctrine. Rejecting an originalist reading of Islamic law, Mohamed insisted that there could be "even better and more Islamic laws than existed at the time of the Prophet." If the Prophet had prescribed traffic laws relevant to the technology of the seventh century, he explained, it would be ridiculous to follow them today. Similarly, he said that he could not find any source to justify Shari'a law's codification of slavery. Given these examples, he claimed, the test for interpreting whether a law was Islamic ought to lie not in seeking its original expression, but in evaluating whether it contradicted the religion's broad principles. This articulation represents a distinctly Malaysian living-tree and purposive interpretive approach. Islamic banking and finance, fields that have exploded in recent years, would not be possible without such flexible reasoning, Mohamed concluded. He also went on to express optimism that the number of judges and lawyers in Muslim-majority countries who were adept at blending Shari'a law with common law and general principles of constitutional law would grow.

In short, the Malaysian Federal Court has used constitutionally enshrined principles of federalism to block attempts to expand the ambit of Shari'a law. Operating within an increasingly Islamic political environment, it has been wrestling with the inconsistencies of constitutional and Shari'a law on a case-by-case basis. And while it has been sending mixed messages with regard to the scope and nature of the 1988 constitutional amendment that established the exclusive jurisdiction of Syariah courts in personal-status matters, it has also asserted its authority vis-à-vis the religious establishment as the sole and ultimate interpreter of Malaysia's Federal Constitution.

A brief analogy may be drawn here between Malaysia and Nigeria. Nigeria is the most populous country in Africa, with approximately 140 million inhabitants. Although it is a secular state with no established state religion, Islam and Christianity play a key role in Nigerian collective identity, alongside various indigenous religions. Nigeria's thirty-six states include nineteen states in northern Nigeria and seventeen states in southern Nigeria, with traditional Muslim dominance in the north and Christian dominance in the south. Filling a gap left by the near collapse of local and federal services in the 1980s and 1990s, as well the economic decline throughout most of the country (oil-rich regions being the exception), new Muslim groups stepped into the breach in the predominantly Muslim north, just as Evangelical and Pentecostal churches did in the mainly Christian south—millions of Nigerians have converted to Pentacostalism over the last three decades alone.[98] Shari'a courts existed in Nigeria, a former British colony, but were limited to areas of family and personal law. Even after independence criminal courts continued to function under inherited British common law.[99] In the late 1980s Islamic parties started to garner massive political support in northern Nigeria. Since 1999, twelve northern state governments, led by Zamfara State and its proactive governor at that time, Alhaji Ahmed Sani, have enacted legislation or executive decrees that establish Shari'a criminal law, with an accompanying implicit threat of civil war in opposition to then President Olusegun Obasanjo.[100] Anticipating federalism-based resistance to the Islamization of criminal law in these states, Sani and proponents of the move argued that because Islam is a faith, "only those who believe in that faith will either determine something is wrong or something is right."[101] This has led to the introduction of penalties such as amputation or death by stoning for serious criminal offenses. Granted, the partial introduction of Shari'a is a vote-winner, not merely a reflection of a genuine doctrinal shift. However, it has posed serious challenges to human rights standards in a country that professes secularism.[102]

This in turn led, inter alia, to the dramatic *Safiyatu Hussaini* and *Amina Lawal* cases. In the *Safiyatu Hussaini* case (decided in March 2002) the Shari'a Court of Appeal of Sokoto State relied on procedural grounds to quash the conviction of Safiyatu Hussaini by a lower Shari'a court for the offense of *zina* (adultery) and her sentence to *rajm* (death by stoning) for giving birth to a child as a single woman.[103] In the twin case *Amina Lawal* a divorced woman was accused of bearing a child outside marriage, which was classified as adultery. She was sentenced to death by stoning in March 2002 by lower Islamic Shari'a courts in the northern state of Katsina. In September 2003, under immense pressure from domestic and international human rights organizations and Nigeria's federal government, Katsina's Shari'a Court of Appeals voted (4–1) to quash the case on the basis that the lower Shari'a courts failed to follow rules of procedure laid down by Islamic law itself, Shari'a-based state criminal law, and some of the federal constitution's provisions protecting due process.[104] This self-restraint of top Shari'a courts is not atypical. In fact, despite the new Islamic criminal provisions in subnational units in countries such as Nigeria, Pakistan, and Libya, the higher criminal courts in these countries have never actually allowed the draconian punishment of stoning to be implemented.[105]

But the main counterreligious weapon in Nigeria has been the constitution. As in Malaysia and to some extent Pakistan, Nigerian judicial attempts to contain religious law have been centered on principles of federalism and the ultimate superiority of the constitution over the laws of any subnational unit. Although the 1999 constitution allows states to grant additional jurisdiction to their local courts, the adoption of Shari'a can criminalize actions deemed permissible by the constitution and its bill of rights, and the accompanying penalties almost always violate protections set out in the same document.[106] Furthermore, the constitution establishes Nigeria as a secular state, and Article 10 explicitly forbids governments at any level from adopting an official religion.[107] The constitution also provides for freedom of religion and the right of all citizens to practice their religion. Any law enacted in the country that conflicts with the constitution is void to the extent of its inconsistency. Much as in Malaysia and Pakistan, the general tenet in Nigeria has been that as a *supreme* law, the Nigerian Constitution is endowed with a higher status, over and above any other legal rules in operation in that polity. Shari'a legislation and practice in the northern states, even though claiming to speak in a religious—and "divine"—vernacular, must nevertheless comply with the provisions of the constitution.[108]

Another interesting analogy to Malaysia is the occasional strategic judicial resort to blurriness, deference, or even sheer silence when the courts are torn between their judicial preferences and political realities, or when the stakes are high but courts are not entirely clear which way the political wind is blowing. Caution appears logical under these circumstances. A case in point is the Supreme Court of Nigeria's "nonruling" in the recent *Kano State v. Nigeria* case (2007).[109] As part of the imposition of Shari'a law in the northern states, the state of Kano created a Hisba Board, very similar in nature to the entity that would have been created in Pakistan's North-West Frontier Province had the Islamization bill become law (see the previous discussion of Pakistan). This created a parallel *hisba* police, the aim of which was to enforce Islamic morality in instances where no "official" crime had been committed. In February 2006 the federal government declared the Hisba Board and its "morality police" unacceptable on constitutional grounds. Federal authorities followed suit with arrests of Hisba Board members for national security concerns and alleged links to Iran and Libya. Kano State then petitioned the Supreme Court, asking for a ruling on the constitutionality of the *hisba* law. Specifically, Kano officials sought a declaration that the Hisba Board was "legal, lawful, and constitutional."[110]

Given the very high political stakes, the court chose to avoid the wrath of both Islamists and the federal government by framing the Kano State petition as focusing on the detention of *hisba* corps members, as well as on its jurisdictional competence with respect to the identity of the party, rather than the constitutionality of the Hisba Board itself. Once the petition had been framed as centering on these arrests and not on the principled question of Shari'a morality, the court could declare that it had no original jurisdiction over state claims against the federal inspector of police (who issued the detention writs). The inspector of police, the Supreme Court reasoned, was "unfortunately not a recognized party subject to the original jurisdiction of this court."[111] Whereas in *Subashini* (discussed earlier) the Malaysian Federal Court resorted to the "everyone-gets-something" strategy, in Kano State the Supreme Court of Nigeria chose to avoid a direct engagement with the issue at stake. Shrewd courts and judges, then, are political not only in the sense that they may opt to expand the ambit of their influence when the political sphere appears amenable to such expansion, but also in the sense that they may resort to restraint or deference when the risks or costs of a clear-cut ruling seem particularly high. Strategic accounts of judicial behavior could not have asked for stronger confirmation.

Israel

In 1947 the secular leadership of the Zionist movement in prestate Israel and leaders of the religious Jewish community concluded an informal agreement that created a framework for the establishment of the country. The agreement, known as the "status quo agreement," laid out ground rules for the relationship between state and religion in four major areas: Shabbat, education, Kashrut (Jewish dietary rules), and matrimonial law. In practice, the agreement froze the common practice at the time of agreement with respect to these four realms. But existential tensions and core collective-identity questions remained unresolved.

The 1948 Declaration of Independence of the State of Israel created temporary governmental institutions. A Constituent Assembly was simultaneously formed and invested with the power to draft a constitution that would eventually establish permanent governing institutions. In 1949 the Constituent Assembly changed its name to the Knesset and established itself as the legislative body of the state of Israel. After debating the merits of a constitution for a year, it became apparent that the religious parties were opposed to the idea of an entrenched constitution because it would invest the ultimate source of sovereignty in the citizenry rather than in God or Jewish law. "The Torah is our Constitution!" argued the religious parties. *Mapai*—the primary component of later days' Labor Party and the unchallenged secular ruling party at the time—was also unwilling to proceed with drafting a constitution. This was partly to avoid jeopardizing the tenuous secular/religious coalition government, partly to maintain the Jewish identity aura of the newly established state, and partly because *Mapai* leaders, notably David Ben-Gurion, had no political incentive to transfer policy-making authority to the judiciary and no desire to impose any limitations on their own power. Thus, in 1950 the first Knesset adopted a compromise known as the "Harari Resolution." This act enabled the Knesset to evade its obligation in terms of the Declaration of Independence to compose a written constitution, while at the same time preserving its power to enact one through the adoption of a series of Basic Laws.[112]

Since the establishment of Israel, a fundamental collective-identity issue remaining on the table has been whether the country is a *medinat hok* (a state based on civil or secular law) or a *medinat halakhah* (a state based on Jewish law). Israel's constitutional system is based on two fundamental tenets: that the state is *Jewish* and *democratic.* It is this commitment to the creation of an ideologically plausible and politically feasible synthesis between particularistic (Jewish) and universalistic (democratic) values that has proven to be the major constitutional challenge faced by Israel ever since its foundation. Reaching such a synthesis is especially difficult given that non-Jews—primarily Muslims, Christians, and Druze—constitute approximately one-fifth of Israel's citizenry (excluding the Palestinian residents of the West Bank and Gaza Strip). Even within the Jewish population itself the exact meaning of Israel as a "Jewish" state has been highly contested. Not only do opinions differ bitterly about whether Jews are citizens of a nation, members of a people, participants in a culture, or coreligionists, but even among adherents of the last opinion—arguably the most stable of these constructions—there are widely divergent beliefs and degrees of practice.

Nevertheless, for a host of historical and political reasons, the Orthodox stream of the Jewish religion has long enjoyed the status of being the sole branch of Judaism formally recognized by the state. This exclusive status has enabled the Orthodox community to establish a near monopoly over the supply of public religious services and to impose rigid standards on the process of determining who is a Jew—a question that has crucial symbolic and practical implications because, according to Israel's Law of Return, Jews who immigrate to Israel are entitled to a variety of benefits, including the right to immediate, full citizenship. On a related front, the potentially far-reaching law Hok Yesodot Ha'Mishpat (the foundations of law) was passed in 1980, making Jewish Law (Mishpat Ivri) a formal source of interpretation in instances involving lack of precedent or legal lacunae. All of this has taken place while over two-thirds of the world's Jews, on whom Israel relies for essential symbolic, material, and strategic support, continue to live outside Israel and many do not subscribe to the Orthodox stream of Judaism.

To add further complication, over the last three decades there has been a continuous decline in the political power and representation of Israel's historically hegemonic and largely secular Ashkenazi constituencies (mostly Jews of European descent), with a corresponding rise of the previously marginalized and distinctly more religious groups, some of which are strong advocates of Halakha (the entire body of Jewish law, biblical, rabbinical, and customary) playing a pivotal role and providing the basis for the operation of the state and its identity. As seen in Chapter 3, the impressive growth of the Shas Party (representing Orthodox religious Mizrahi residents of development towns and poor urban neighborhoods) in the last twenty-five years alone shows a marked departure from Israel's previous political culture.[113]

Until the early 1980s the dominance of the Ashkenazi bourgeoisie in the Knesset, and the fact that its ideological and policy preferences enjoyed an uncontested hegemonic position, created a strong disincentive to delegate policy-making authority from the Knesset to the Supreme Court. When this platform began to erode, the incentive structure gradually changed.[114] As the secular Ashkenazi elite's disproportionate influence over the country's core political decision-making arenas has been increasingly challenged, its willingness (if not eagerness) to transfer crucial religion-and-state questions from the political arena to the Supreme Court has likewise increased. Given the court's record of adjudication and its personal composition, as well as the ideologies of its justices, Israel's secular Ashkenazi bourgeoisie could safely assume that its worldviews and policy preferences with regard to constitutive questions of religion and state would be less effectively contested. This has resulted in the transformation of the Supreme Court of Israel (SCI) into a (if not *the*) crucial present-day forum for addressing the country's most fundamental collective-identity quandaries.

Until 1992 Israel's nexus of Basic Laws did not include an entrenched law dealing with civil liberties and human rights. In the absence of a necessary constitutional framework for actively reviewing primary legislation, the Supreme Court was limited before 1992 to judicial review of administrative acts, informed by the doctrine of an "implied bill of rights." The constitutional landscape in Israel was altered in the early 1990s, when the Knesset initiated and carried out an institutional empowerment of the judiciary. This initiative, tacitly supported by Israel's judicial elite, formally began in 1992 with the enactment of two basic rights and liberties laws—Basic Law: Human Dignity and Liberty and Basic Law: Freedom of Occupation. Although these two new human rights basic laws do not constitute an official bill of rights, they are widely understood to fulfill the functions of such a bill. The Supreme Court swiftly endorsed the new possibility to expand the ambit of its influence. First in the *Meatrael* affair (1993), which reached the court several months after the introduction of the two new basic laws, and later in the *United Mizrahi Bank* case (1995)—the "Israeli *Marbury v. Madison,*" as observers of the Israeli legal system have described it—the SCI formally asserted its authority to exercise judicial review over acts of the Knesset.[115] A majority of the justices held that the two new basic laws had indeed ushered in a new era in the historic quest for a comprehensive constitutional catalogue of rights and active judicial review in Israel. It was recognized that these laws had formal constitutional status and were therefore superior to ordinary legislation.

The SCI responded to the increased tension between Israel's dual commitment to universal (democratic) and particularistic (Jewish) values by subjecting the jurisprudence of religious courts to the general principles of administrative and constitutional law. Over the last two decades the SCI has pursued a distinctly liberalizing agenda in core matters of religion and state. This trend is clearly illustrated in the curtailment of the exclusive jurisdiction of the rabbinical courts in matters of personal status, the erosion of the Orthodox monopoly over the provision of religious services, and the inclusion of women and non-Orthodox Jews as members of religious councils, along with the liberalization of rules pertaining to the solemnization of marriage, *kashrut* (kosher) and *shmita* (land sabbatical) laws, and "prayer rights" in Jewish holy sites. Proponents of secular policies have also scored victories with the court's questioning of the constitutionality of the draft-deferment arrangement (an arrangement that had been in place since the establishment of the state whereby Orthodox yeshiva students receive draft deferments—conscription is otherwise compulsory for Jewish citizens of Israel—as long as they maintain their religious studies) and the court's relatively progressive treatment of the issue of non-Orthodox conversion to Judaism and the related question "Who is a Jew?" A pinnacle of the SCI's liberalizing jurisprudence in matters of religion and state is its subjection of the religious courts' jurisprudential autonomy in matters of personal status to the general principles of due process and gender equality.[116] This has had far-reaching implications in areas as diverse as family and personal-status law, representation in statutory religious bodies, and gender equality in the religious labor market. In Israel no unified civil law applies to all citizens in matters of marriage and divorce. Instead, for various political and historical reasons (the roots of contemporary Israeli family law go back as far as the Ottoman Empire's premodern *millet* system), the courts of the different religious communities hold exclusive jurisdiction over marriage, divorce, and directly associated personal-status matters.[117] A number of other personal-status matters may be adjudicated through the rabbinical court system (controlled by Orthodox Judaism) if the involved parties consent to such extended jurisdiction. Muslim, Christian, and Druze courts also have exclusive jurisdiction over the personal-status affairs of their respective communities.[118]

Since the mid-1990s the SCI has gradually been attempting to limit the authority exercised by religious courts. The most important SCI judgment regarding these matters was rendered in 1995 in the *Bavli* case. In several earlier decisions, the SCI ruled that religious tribunals must comply with provisions of concrete laws pertinent to their operational and jurisdictional boundaries.[119] In its ruling in *Bavli* the SCI expanded considerably its overarching review of religious tribunals' jurisprudence by holding that all religious tribunals, including the Great Rabbinical Court, are statutory bodies established by law and funded by the state; in principle, all aspects of their judgments are thus subject to review by the Supreme Court. Although the SCI recognized the special jurisdictional mandate awarded to Jewish, Muslim, Christian, and Druze courts by the legislature, it nevertheless asserted its power to impose constitutional norms on their exercise of authority.[120] Rabbinical court officials have responded by publicly asserting their resistance to the idea that the Supreme Court, as a secular entity, possesses the authority to review their adjudication, which rests on religious law. Some have gone so far as to declare their intention to ignore the court's ruling in *Bavli,* which they perceive as an illegitimate intrusion into their exclusive jurisdictional sphere. The Supreme Court was not impressed. On the basis of its landmark decision in *Bavli* the SCI went on to overturn at least two dozen other rabbinical court and Shari'a court rulings for not conforming with general principles of Israel's constitutional and administrative law, including gender equality, reasonableness, proportionality, natural justice, and procedural fairness.[121]

A fascinating recent illustration of this trend is the Court's ruling in *Plonit ("Jane Doe") v. The Great Rabbinical Court* (2008).[122] Section 5 of the Property Relations between Spouses Law (Hok Yahasei Mammon bein Bnei Zug 1973, amended in 1995) states that in case of divorce the couple's assets will be split evenly between the two spouses regardless of the formal registration status of these assets. However, Section 8 of that law grants courts the authority to determine "special circumstances" in which an uneven split may be justified. A woman who married her husband in 1985 had an extramarital affair in 2003 that eventually brought about the breakup of her marriage. The Great Rabbinical Court ruled that the wife's unfaithful behavior constituted "special circumstances," and that the husband was entitled to more than half of the couple's assets, in this case, pension monies owed to him.

On appeal, the SCI used its reasoning in *Bavli* to overturn the ruling. It accepted the wife's argument that the Great Rabbinical Court ruling did not comply with earlier SCI decisions on the matter, namely, that adulterous behavior may justify neither a departure from the presumption of an even split nor a retroactive negation of the adulterous spouse's rights to accumulated property in the years before his or her extramarital affair. Even more important, the SCI rejected the husband's claim that the law assigned to either the rabbinical court or the general court dealing with the matter the authority to decide what "special circumstances" were in this context. The SCI stated decisively that the two systems are not parallel, but unitary. Rulings of the rabbinical court system, including rulings of the Great Rabbinical Court, are subject to review by the Supreme Court and must comply with pertinent jurisprudential principles established by the SCI over the years. One can hardly think of a greater blow to the rabbinical court system's jurisdictional autonomy. It is little wonder that religious parties led by Shas vow to pass laws that expand the jurisdiction of the rabbinical court system and exempt it from the Supreme Court's scrutiny.

But the struggle continues. In 2010 the SCI further expanded the scope of its review of rabbinical courts' application of the Property Relations between Spouses Law. In deciding the financial terms of split following a divorce, the Great Rabbinical Court had factored in the gains and losses incurred to the pre-marriage assets of each spouse during the time of marriage. Because the husband's pre-marriage assets suffered a loss (but still far exceeded the wife's assets) while the wife's assets generated a moderate gain (but still fell far short of the husband's assets), the Great Rabbinical Court deviated from the even split rule in the husband's favor. On appeal by the wife, the SCI built on its established tradition of substantive review of religious court jurisprudence. It held that the value of an apartment purchased by the husband during the marriage, and jointly and commonly used by the couple throughout the marriage, is to be split evenly between the husband

and the wife, even though the funds used for purchasing the apartment came largely from the husband's pre-marriage assets. Conjugal life in an apartment for a lengthy period of time, held the court, turns it into a joint "nest of the family" regardless of whose funds were used to purchase it.[123]

Arguably the clearest example of the SCI's secularizing agenda is its series of rulings on the question "Who is a Jew?"[124] The Orthodox stream's exclusive status as the sole branch of Judaism recognized by the state has enabled the Orthodox community to impose rigid standards on the process of determining who is a Jew. This question has crucial symbolic and practical implications because, as stated previously, according to Israel's Law of Return, Jews who immigrate to Israel are entitled to a variety of benefits, including the immediate right to full citizenship. Non-Jewish immigrants are not entitled to these benefits. Since being Jewish is sufficient to qualify for citizenship, Israel's self-definition as a Jewish state is inextricably entangled with defining who is a Jew. This has made the question of conversion a core political issue in Israel for decades because the Orthodox rabbinic establishment has been trying to maintain its control over defining who may claim Jewish status under the Law of Return and to prevent the adoption of more lenient approaches to conversion advanced by Diaspora-based Reform and Conservative rabbis and various immigrant groups.

In 1989 the SCI held that for purposes of immigration, any person who converted to Judaism outside Israel, whether under the auspices of an Orthodox, Conservative, or Reform religious institution, was automatically entitled to all the rights of an *oleh* (Jewish immigrant), as stated in the Law of Return and the Citizenship Law.[125] In 1995 the SCI was once again drawn into the muddy waters of identity politics. This time the question before the court was whether a person who underwent non-Orthodox conversion in Israel was entitled to automatic citizenship based on the right of return in the same way in which someone who converted outside Israel would be. The court avoided giving a clear answer while explicitly reaffirming its 1989 ruling validating non-Orthodox conversions made abroad.[126]

Following this ruling, an increasing number of non-Jewish persons residing in Israel (primarily foreign workers and non-Jewish immigrants from the former Soviet Union) went abroad to pursue non-Orthodox conversion in order to claim the benefits awarded by the state to those newcomers recognized as Jews. In response, the Ministry of the Interior (controlled at the time by the religious Shas Party) renewed its refusal to recognize Reform and Conservative conversions to Judaism made abroad, despite the SCI's ruling. In early 2002 the court responded with a historic decision (9–2) recognizing non-Orthodox conversions to Judaism performed abroad.[127] In another landmark ruling on the subject (March 2005) the court agreed (7–4) to recognize non-Orthodox "bypass" conversions to Judaism performed de jure abroad but de facto in Israel.[128] It held that a person who came to Israel as a non-Jew and, during a period of lawful residence there, underwent conversion in a recognized Jewish community abroad would be considered Jewish. In its judgment the court stated: "The Jewish nation is one . . . It is dispersed around the world, in communities. Whoever converted to Judaism in one of these communities overseas has joined the Jewish nation by so doing, and is to be seen as a 'Jew' under the Law of Return. This can encourage immigration to Israel and maintain the unity of the Jewish nation in the Diaspora and in Israel." Few could articulate the Zionist-nationalist (and anti-Orthodox) view of Judaism in present-day Israel more potently. Thus it is hardly surprising that in May 2009 the court (in a decision written by Chief Justice Dorit Beinish) went on to apply equal-opportunity principles and order the government to fund non-Orthodox conversion study programs, just as it has been funding Orthodox conversion programs.

The Orthodox establishment's fury was quite predictable. In 2008 a minirebellion erupted in the rabbinical establishment against the Supreme Court's continuous relaxation of conversion rules and procedures, as well as against the religious-Zionist movement, which views the expansion of the Jewish people as a national mission and therefore tends to be distinctly more lenient with respect to conversion than the Orthodox establishment. An ordinary divorce case that reached the Great Rabbinical Court resulted in the court's ruling that the petitioning couple's marriage had been religiously invalid from the outset because the woman's conversion to Judaism fourteen years earlier was not genuine. The Great Rabbinical Court held that the woman failed to observe Orthodox ritual law once she was declared Jewish, and that she had never actually intended to observe it. Rabbi Avraham Sherman, who wrote the main opinion, used his ruling to deliver a stinging indictment of Rabbi Haim Druckman, who oversaw the woman's conversion (Druckman was head of Israel's Bnei Akiva schools—a Zionist-nationalist religious movement—and led a task force established by former Prime Minister Ariel Sharon to resolve the problem of conversion to Judaism of approximately 300,000 immigrants from the former Soviet Union whose ties to Judaism were said to be questionable).

Lenient conversion rabbis, wrote Sherman, often accepted converts who mostly "remain gentile in their behavior . . . [and] see themselves as belonging to the Jewish people solely in a patriotic, nationalistic way, without any religiously significant feelings of belonging." In approving these conversions, Rabbi Sherman said, Conversion Authority rabbis had become "transgressors" of Halakha. This harsh language has prompted a wave of angry protests from religious Zionist and moderate Orthodox leaders, including unprecedented threats of a rift within Orthodoxy.[129] Ironically, the fierce intrareligious war reached the Supreme Court. In May 2009 the SCI once again sided with the moderate line, issuing a stern warning to the Great Rabbinical Court to recognize the supposedly "lenient" conversions by Rabbi Druckman before the court forced it to do so. Israel Beiteinu ("Israel is our home"), the main political party representing immigrants from the former Soviet Union, whose leaders have been frequently critical of the Supreme Court's supposed "anti-nationalist" tilt, were this time quick to endorse the secularizing aspect of the court's jurisprudence. Its representatives in the Knesset went on to table a proposal to formally recognize non-Orthodox conversions. Unsurprisingly, members of the ultra-Orthodox Yahadut Ha'Torah ("Torah Jewry") party were outraged.

While the SCI has pursued a distinctly liberalizing agenda in core matters of religion and state, it has also sought to protect the Zionist-nationalist version of Israel's "Jewishness" pillar of collective identity. In a landmark ruling in the *Citizenship Law/Family Unification* case (2006) the SCI upheld (in a divided 6–5, 263-page decision) the new Citizenship and Entry to Israel Law, which imposes age restrictions on the granting of Israeli citizenship and residency permits to Arab residents of the Occupied Territories who marry Israeli citizens.[130] Because the practice of marrying Palestinians is far more common among Israel's Arab minority, the law limiting family unification and spousal naturalization effectively singles out Arab citizens while maintaining the demographic balance in favor of members of Israel's Jewish population, who seldom marry Palestinians, and whose noncitizen spouses are often naturalized by way of marriage to an Israeli (Jewish) citizen. The dividing line between the majority and dissenting opinions was between the six justices who favored the first tenet in Israel's self-definition as a Jewish and democratic state and the five justices (including Chief Justice Aharon Barak) who gave priority to the second. Four more recent petitions against the same prohibiting provisions of the Citizenship Law still await the court's decision.[131] Meanwhile, in Egypt a mirror case has been unfolding. In an ironic twist, Cairo's Administrative Court held in May 2009 that citizenship of Egyptians who married Israeli spouses and who live in Israel should be revoked because their children may be targeted by Israel as recruits for its security services and thereby threaten Egypt's national interests.[132]

At any rate, the landmark SCI ruling in the *Citizenship Law/Family Unification* case was certainly not the first time the nature of Israel's Jewish character has been tested in court against other fundamental constitutional values. In the *Meatrael* affair, one of the first post-1992 cases dealing with the normative foundations of Israel, a prima facie contradiction was raised between the constitutional right to freedom of occupation and Israel's primary character as a Jewish state. Meatrael, a private company that intended to import nonkosher meat products into Israel, appealed to the SCI against the refusal of the Ministry of Religious Affairs to license the company to do so. The company argued that the ministry's decision violated its constitutional right to freedom of occupation. The ministry's refusal was based on the claim that Israel's Jewish character was one of the state's supreme constitutional norms and thus had priority over any other norm.[133]

In its first decision on the case the court declared the refusal of the Ministry of Religious Affairs unconstitutional because it contradicted the principles of the new Basic Law by infringing the company's right to engage in any legal economic initiative. Subsequently, under pressure from religious parties, the Basic Law was amended (in the spirit of the Canadian "notwithstanding clause"—Section 33 of the Charter of Rights and Freedoms) to allow for future modifications by ordinary laws endorsed by an absolute majority of Knesset members. An amendment forbidding the import of nonkosher meat was subsequently enacted in 1994. On the basis of the new 1994 Meat Law the government renewed its refusal to license the import of nonkosher meat. In response, Meatrael appealed to the Supreme Court again, arguing for its constitutional right to engage in any legal economic initiative. This time the court ruled against the company on the basis of the reasonableness of the new Meat Law, in light of the amendments made to the Basic Law. Behind this decision, however, lay immense political pressure for the court to prevent any further erosion of the conception of "Israel as a Jewish state" as the highest constitutional norm. In spite of its somewhat anticlimactic ending—the legislature ultimately managed to circumvent judicial scrutiny of its decision—the *Meatrael* affair clearly illustrated the standing of the SCI at the vanguard of attempts to break the religious establishment's monopoly over the definition of Judaism and provision of religious services.

A closely related frontier of secular/religious struggle is the scope of religious authorities' prerogative over the issuance of *kashrut* (kosher; meaning "fit" or "legitimate" for consumption according to Jewish dietary and food-preparation restrictions) certificates by the Chief Rabbinate. Historically the Chief Rabbinate has refused to issue *kashrut* certificates for businesses that either deal with both kosher and nonkosher foods or sell only kosher food but violate other religious norms (e.g., they operate on the Sabbath, engage in "indecent" acts, or deal with businesses that do not keep kosher). This practice draws on a rather expansive reading by the Chief

Rabbinate of its legal mandate to consider "exclusively kosher food norms" when issuing such certificates. In a series of rulings in the last two decades the court came to the rescue and compelled the Chief Rabbinate to issue kosher food certificates to businesses that sell kosher food regardless of their other practices. This line of rulings reached a peak in 2001 when the SCI harshly criticized the Chief Rabbinate for its continuous misuse of authority and irresponsible contempt of court rulings in illegally denying *kashrut* certificates from kosher meat producers trading with merchants of nonkosher foods.[134] Once again the court stressed that the Chief Rabbinate and the entire rabbinical court system were, first and foremost, statutory bodies created through state laws, and therefore, the decrees and verdicts issued by these bodies must conform with state laws and constitutional norms, even when they contradicted religious customs.

More recently (October 2007) the SCI renewed its course of jurisprudential liberalization in matters of religion and state in the seminal *Shmita* case. A long-standing legal fiction called *heiter mechira* (sale permit) has been used for decades to effectively bypass the biblical injunction about the land sabbatical *(shmita),* according to which Jewish land in Israel should be left uncultivated or fallow every seventh year. The permit allows Jewish farmers and businesses to "sell" their land temporarily to non-Jews during *shmita* years, thereby enabling the land to be cultivated and the agricultural produce to be sold as usual. This arrangement has been used since the rebirth of Jewish agriculture in Israel some 130 years ago, much to the resentment of ultra-Orthodox Jews in Israel, who take the biblical injunction literally and refuse to buy or consume produce unless it is grown by non-Jews on land genuinely owned by non-Jews.

With the increased influence of ultra-Orthodox circles, the Chief Rabbinate decided in early 2007 that it would defer to local rabbinical councils with regard to the decision whether to adhere to the *heiter mechira* loophole. As a result, in cities like Jerusalem, where the ultra-Orthodox make up almost one-third of the total population and a much larger proportion of the Jewish population, the legal fiction was deemed invalid. Consequently, prices for kosher produce went up, while Jewish agribusiness suffered considerably. A group of farmers who were economically hurt by the new policy of deference to local Orthodox religious authorities took the case to the courts. The SCI used the familiar proportionality and reasonableness tests to rule that the Chief Rabbinate did not adequately balance the interests involved and gave undue weight to the independence of the municipal rabbis over the economic, national, and legal interests of farmers and the general public. The court ordered the Chief Rabbinate to reassert its authority and sign *kashrut* certificates for businesses selling produce grown on land that was subject to the legal fiction of *heiter mechira*. The court also invoked the farmers' legitimate interest in predictability—a building block of every viable modern economic enterprise.[135]

Another pertinent constitutional frontier is the clash between the right to sectarian autonomy in education and equality rights. Here too the court tends to side with the secularist approach. In an important case decided in August 2009, the court followed the logic it had laid down in *Bavli* to rule that although the right to cultural pluralism in education is recognized by Israeli law, religious affiliation as a basis for autonomous schooling is not an absolute right when it collides with the overarching right to equality.[136] The background may seem quite exotic to those who are not familiar with the Israeli sociopolitical scene. An ultra-Orthodox girls' school in the predominantly religious West Bank settlement town of Emmanuel established what was essentially a two-tier, ethnically segregated school. One path was for girls of European descent (Jews who follow the Hasidic tradition). The other path was for girls of Sephardi (or Mizrahi) descent. "In order to segregate between the two schools, which are located on different floors of the same building (the Ashkenazi school on top, the Sephardi on the bottom), the Ashkenazi school begins its academic year a few days before the Sephardi school. The two schools begin their days at different times, and students go on break at different times as well. They have separate entrances divided by a plaster wall, and the yard has been covered with jute screening to separate the students. Each group has its own uniform, and even the teachers have separate rooms."[137] Pupils were automatically assigned to one of the two paths on the basis of ethnic origin. The thinly disguised subtext was that of Ashkenazi superiority, ethnicity-based separation between elite and "blue-collar" education, and the like.

An NGO committed to fighting discrimination in education took the case to the Supreme Court. The school authorities (strangely, backed by the Education Ministry, which provides partial funding for the school) tried to persuade the court that the separation was legitimate because of the different worldviews, traditions, and lifestyles of the two communities. Although in this case the ethnicity-based segregation was blunt, the school's claim of legitimate religious difference may find some support in other conventions such as the long-standing practice of parallel nomination of both an Ashkenazi chief rabbi and a Sephardi chief rabbi to oversee the provision of religious services to their respective communities. Synagogues for the two communities are often separated because some oral traditions, religious customs, and practices have evolved in different ways over centuries of scattered contact between the two communities. The two groups are also represented by different political parties and follow different spiritual leaders.

But the court did not buy the argument of two religious traditions. It unanimously denounced the school's argument that the segregation was due to religious, not ethnic, considerations, calling it "camouflage for discrimination" cloaked in cultural disparity. The court ordered the school to nullify without delay all discriminatory practices against Sephardi pupils and to abolish all protocols that separated Orthodox Ashkenazi and Sephardic students. It also set hefty fines for noncompliance and ordered the Education Ministry to make use of all the legal means it possesses to rectify the situation, including revoking the school's license and stopping the institution's funding.[138]

In short, the Supreme Court of Israel, the highest judicial body in Israel, has responded to the increased tension between Israel's dual commitment to universal (democratic) and particularistic (Jewish) values by subjecting the jurisprudence of religious courts and tribunals to the general interpretive standards and principles of administrative and constitutional law. In so doing, the court has become a bastion of hope for the "enlightened public" (at least in its own eyes), an interpretive device frequently used by the SCI throughout the 1990s to determine the "reasonableness" of specific acts. This court-constructed public closely conforms to the characteristics of the secular Ashkenazi bourgeoisie and shares its worldviews and policy preferences.

A quote from a Hannah Arendt letter to Karl Jaspers describing her "ethnographic" impression of the atmosphere in and surrounding the courthouse in Jerusalem where the famous Eichmann Trial took place seems to capture it all: "Impression: On the top, the judges, the best of German Jewry. Below them, the prosecutors, Galicians, but still Europeans. Everything is organized by a police force that gives me the creeps, speaks only Hebrew and looks Arabic. Some downright brutal types among them . . . And outside the doors, the oriental mob, as if one were in Istanbul or some other half-Asiatic country."[139] Fifty years later, few descriptions would capture more accurately the existential fear of Israel's old Ashkenazi bourgeoisie from the non-European aspects of everyday life or how it sees the court as a beacon of "reasonableness" operating amid a rather "Levantine" sociopolitical context. Any resemblance to pro-European sentiments among Turkey's secularists is not coincidental.

Turkey

The Turkish Constitutional Court (TCC) provides a prime example of the key role constitutional courts in the Middle East play in curbing popular support for principles of theocratic governance. Like other countries in the region, modern Turkey has long been torn between its secular Western and traditional religious identities. This is hardly surprising, given Turkey's strategic location as a geographic and cultural bridge between Europe and the Middle East, the long Islamic tradition established by the Ottoman Empire, and the fact that over 98 percent of Turkey's population is Muslim. Unlike many other predominantly Muslim polities, however, Turkey is formally a secular state that adheres to a strict separation of religion and government. Indeed, the secularization of predominantly religious Turkey, led by Mustafa Kemal Atatürk, is perhaps the best-known example of separationist reformism in the twentieth century. After the demise of the Ottoman Empire, the Kemalist secular-nationalist elite decided to abandon Islamic culture and laws in favor of secularism and modernism. Accordingly, the 1937, 1961, and 1982 constitutions established an official state policy of *laïcité*. The Kemalist ruling elites swiftly discarded prerevolution symbols and institutions of Muslim rule and replaced Islamic law with legal structures drawn from Swiss, French, and Italian law. These reforms were complemented by changing the alphabet from Arabic to Latin script, expunging Arabic and Persian words from Turkish, and importing French and German terms in their place.[140]

Despite the strong secularist and modernist agenda established by Kemalist reformism and its constitution, Turkey has witnessed a dramatic resurgence of political Islam over the last few decades. Attempts to reconcile the re-emergence of religion as a powerful political force with the strong Kemalist-secularist project in a context of transition to and consolidation of democracy have been quite troubled.[141] The resurgence of religion is reflected, inter alia, by the growing public support for political parties that advocate principles of theocratic governance. In the elections held in July 2007, for example, the proreligious Justice and Development Party (AKP) won an unprecedented 47 percent of the popular vote, gaining a majority of the votes in sixty-eight of Turkey's eighty-one provinces. This translated into 341 seats in the 550-seat parliament (following the 2002 elections, the AKP controlled 363 seats, although its overall support was lower than in 2007). In the nationwide municipal elections held in March 2009, the AKP received approximately 40 percent of the overall popular vote, lower than its 2007 peak, but still notably more than any other national party.

Support for the AKP originates mainly from the periphery, real or imagined. Opinion polls conducted before the July 2007 elections in Turkey, for example, underline the demographic factors behind the AKP's electoral success.[142] Approximately 60 percent of respondents with only an elementary-school education indicated that they would vote for the AKP, compared with 45 percent of those with a high-school education and 31.6 percent of university graduates. In contrast, 40 percent of university graduates indicated that they would vote for the secularist Republican People's Party (Cumhuriyet Halk Partisi, CHP), compared with 22 percent of high-school graduates and 14 percent of those with only an elementary-school education. The disparities were even more striking when voting preferences were analyzed on the basis of income. Approximately 55 percent of those who earned less than $250 a month said that they would vote for the AKP, but only 23 percent of those who earned more than $2,500 a month. The secularist CHP secured the support of just 8 percent of those earning less than $250 a month but of 50 percent of those who earned more than $2,500 a month.

The existential cultural and economic rifts are evident even to the occasional visitor. Anyone who spends a few hours in Istanbul's spectacular old city core cannot ignore the recurrent and vociferous muezzin calls to attend prayers. These calls are occasionally interrupted by third-generation cell-phone or MP3 pop music ringtones. Political Islam has emerged as a major power over the last few decades. At the same time, this is the same Turkey that produced Orhan Pamuk, a prominent member of Turkey's secular intelligentsia and the 2006 winner of the Nobel Prize in Literature. The expanding antisecularist sentiment among the Turkish populace has evolved alongside Turkey's tight economic and military ties with the West, its continuous quest to join the European Union, and its "nostalgia for the modern," as one astute observer put it.[143] What could possibly illustrate these conflicting visions of Turkish identity better than a Turkish reality television show that began airing in September 2009, offering contestants what it claims is the "biggest prize ever"—the chance for atheists to convert to one of the world's major religions.[144] Istanbul, lest we forget, is also the 2010 European Capital of Culture designated by the European Union.

The AKP's Recep Tayyip Erdoğan, prime minister of Turkey since 2003, is a pragmatic leader who navigates skillfully between tradition and cosmopolitanism. While the AKP portrays itself as a moderate pro-Islamic party that remains committed to a liberal market economy and Turkish membership in the European Union, it at the same time strives to reinsert certain religious values into Turkish national identity and public life. This effort has manifested itself in a variety of initiatives, including attempts to amend the constitution to allow the wearing of religious attire in the public school system and calls for less Americanization of popular culture and a return to traditional values, as well as an official chill toward evolution theory[145] and attempts to criminalize adultery.[146] The AKP also displays little empathy toward business and media moguls, historically associated with the Kemalist establishment. That Kemalist elites disfavor the AKP surely is not merely ideological. These elites also resent the fact that huge economic benefits (such as government contracts) may now go to companies based in what were once the country's hinterlands or companies not associated with the Kemalist establishment. We are not talking about small money here. To provide one example, the AKP government refuses to approve massive tax discounts and public tender bids for companies controlled by Turkish billionaire Aydin Dogan, one of the world's five hundred richest people and owner of almost half of Turkey's print and broadcasting media market, including CNN-Turk. It is little wonder that Dogan has turned his entire business empire into a vocal opposition to the AKP and its policies.[147]

In short, despite its pragmatic, toned-down rhetoric, the AKP and its massive electoral constituencies pose a major challenge to the militant-secularist vision of Turkey favored by the Turkish army (a longtime guarantor of Kemalist values), the urban intelligentsia, and powerful economic stakeholders. As political Islam became an important force, the referral of the secular/religious clash to the Turkish judiciary gradually became an attractive solution for antireligious stakeholders (most notably an unlikely coalition of the military and the secular bourgeoisie) who seek to tame the threat of religious fundamentalism while maintaining a façade of legality and Western-style constitutional democracy. The result has been the emergence of the TCC as an important venue for excluding political Islam and its policy preferences from the purview of legitimate political discourse.

Under the 1982 Turkish Constitution, the TCC is vested with the power to order the closure of political parties whose agenda is found to be "in conflict with the indivisible integrity of the State with its territory and nation, human rights, national sovereignty, and the principles of the democratic and secular Republic" or when "the internal functioning and the decisions of political parties [are] contrary to the principles of democracy."[148] Such closure may take place upon the ruling of the TCC in a suit filed by the public prosecutor of the republic. Since 1983 the TCC has ordered the closure of political parties on nineteen occasions (eighteen of those since 1991).[149]

Although some of these closures were based on technical grounds (e.g., parties' failure to comply with certain bureaucratic standards), others were based on ideological grounds, most notably strong statist (read anti-Kurdish) and secularist impulses. In December 2009, for example, the Court voted to shut down the pro-Kurdish Democratic Society Party (DTP) and banned dozens of DTP members from joining other political parties for five years. It also expelled two of the party's prominent figures, including

Ahmet Turk, the DTP leader, from parliament. The court reportedly found the party guilty of cooperating with the Kurdistan Workers Party (PKK), which has been fighting for autonomy in Turkey's southeast.[150]

A few years earlier, the TCC dissolved two major Islamic parties—the Welfare (Refah) Party (1998) and the Virtue (Fazilet) Party (2001).[151] In its decision in the Refah Party case, for example, the TCC relied mainly on the principle of *laïcité* referred to in the preamble to the Turkish Constitution: "A way of life that has destroyed the mediaeval scholastic dogmatism and has become the basis of the vision of democracy that develops with the enlightenment of science, nation, independence, national sovereignty and the ideal of humanity."[152] In modern secular states, religious creed is a private matter, held the TCC, "saved from politicization, taken out of being a tool of administration, and is kept in its real, respectable place which is the conscience of the people."[153] In such countries, modernity has become "the basic building block of transforming the people from an ummah [religious community] to a nation."[154] In its ruling, the TCC also reiterated its view that wearing a headscarf in the public educational system was unconstitutional as it ran contrary to the principle of secularism.

In a similar fashion, the TCC went on in June 2001 to order the dissolution of a new, more moderate Islamist party that had emerged out of the rubble of Refah—the Virtue Party. Despite Virtue's toned-down platform and the fact that in the 1999 general election it managed to garner 103 seats of Turkey's 550-seat parliament, the court accepted the charge that, like its predecessor, the Virtue Party was violating the fundamental secular principles of the Turkish constitution by using religious symbols for political purposes. Moreover, the court ordered the treasury to confiscate the party's funds and property. This ruling followed the expulsion of Virtue Party deputy Merve Kavakci from the swearing-in ceremony that she was attending, and ultimately stripped her of her Turkish citizenship; the action was taken against Ms. Kavakci because she arrived in Parliament wearing a headscarf in direct defiance of a law prohibiting its use in public buildings.[155]

In February 2003, the European Court of Human Rights dismissed an appeal against the TCC's ruling in the *Refah* dissolution case and concurred with the TCC's view of Shari'a norms as incompatible with fundamental principles of democracy.[156] The ECtHR stated that, in its view, "a political party whose actions seem to be aimed at introducing Shari'a in a State party to the Convention can hardly be regarded as an association complying with the democratic ideal that underlies the whole of the Convention."[157] The court continued, "[t]he offending statements, which contain explicit reference to the introduction of the Shari'a, are difficult to reconcile with the fundamental principles of democracy, as conceived in the

Convention . . . It is difficult to declare one's respect for democracy and human rights while at the same time supporting a regime based on Shari'a, which clearly diverges from Convention values, particularly with regard to its criminal law and criminal procedure, its rules on the legal status of women and the way it intervenes in all spheres of private and public life in accordance with religious precepts."[158]

The TCC continues to be a guardian of the secular state against the new specter of religiosity advanced by the AKP-led government. In May 2007 it annulled the parliamentary vote that designated the pro-Islamic AKP party nominee, Foreign Affairs Minister Abdullah Gül, as president. It declared the first round of the presidential election illegal on the somewhat shaky constitutional grounds that less than the necessary two-thirds of all parliamentary deputies were in attendance for the vote. Prime Minister Recep Tayyip Erdoğan immediately responded by proposing new parliamentary elections, which the AKP won by a landslide.[159] In April 2008 the TCC agreed to hear a challenge brought by the chief public prosecutor to the very constitutionality of the AKP. In a widely publicized decision issued in July 2008, the court came very close to banning the AKP but stopped just short of doing so; six of the eleven judges, one vote shy of the necessary seven votes, found the AKP platform unconstitutional by explicitly advocating anti-secular worldviews and activities.[160] In so doing, the judges signaled that no further Islamization will be tolerated by the court and by its secularist and military establishment backers.[161]

In January 2010, the TCC once again protected the interests of the military by declaring unconstitutional a law that allowed for civilian prosecution of military personnel for nonmilitary crimes.[162] The law was promulgated in 2009 to facilitate investigation of military officials and others who were involved in alleged plots to overthrow the ruling AKP and to assassinate the deputy prime minister. Following the TCC ruling—widely perceived as a blow to Erdoğan and the AKP—military personnel suspected of involvement in these plots are to be tried in friendlier military tribunals. Ironically, while Kemalists would consider outrageous the idea of delegating jurisdictional authority to Shari'a tribunals, they fully support the strong autonomy of military tribunals vis-à-vis the general judiciary.

Attempts to block a full investigation into these alleged plots have been made by other statist/secularist–law–related organs; in February 2010 the supreme council of judges and prosecutors—a nonjudicial administrative body known for its Kemalist inclinations and hostility to the AKP—decided to suspend a prosecutor and three lower court judges who had ordered the arrest of other top-ranked prosecutors for alleged contributions to the plot to oust the AKP. But the grand struggle between the AKP government and the self-appointed guardians of Kemalist legacy continues. In an unprecedented move in February 2010, over fifty military commanders, including many senior ex-generals and admirals, were detained by police, accused of conspiring to overthrow the government, blow up mosques, and stage the shooting down of a Turkish air force plane by the Greek army in order to destabilize the political sphere in Turkey and provide an excuse for a military coup. If there is one thing the detained generals can count on, it is the top judicial echelons' support.

A different, yet equally telling example is the TCC's jurisprudence on female dress code in public schools. A perennial bone of contention between secularists and Islamists in Turkey, as in other similarly situated polities, the struggle has centered on the wearing of the Muslim headscarf *(hijab)* by Islamist female students in public universities. As with the fight against Islamist parties, the TCC has been a major supporter and ultimately the guardian of the ban on wearing a *hijab.* Succumbing to mounting pressure by Islamist groups in 1984, Turkey's Council of Higher Education allowed female students to cover their hair with a turban it deemed a modern version of the traditionally larger *hijab.* Following a series of rulings by lower tribunals, the question of the constitutionality of the council's bylaw reached the TCC. Among the arguments put forth by Islamic women was the claim that a ban on wearing the *hijab* would violate their constitutional right to freedom of religious expression (guaranteed by Article 24 of the 1982 constitution), as well as their right to be free from discrimination on the basis of religious creed (guaranteed by Article 10 of the 1982 constitution). Islamist activists argued that the cumulative effect of these constitutional provisions guaranteed the right of female students to wear the *hijab,* thereby rendering unconstitutional any government prohibition on wearing headscarves.

In a widely publicized ruling in March 1989 the TCC held the bylaw unconstitutional because it undermined the secular character of the state and was incompatible with the law requiring civil servants to have their heads unveiled.[163] In dismissing both the religious-freedom-based and equality-based arguments, the TCC stated that wearing a headscarf was not a practice followed by "civilized countries": it flew in the face of Turkey's long-term commitment to, and constitutional entrenchment of, modern secularism. Moreover, the court found it problematic, and indeed ironic, that groups adhering to an explicitly antiliberal worldview based their pro-*hijab* arguments on religious-freedom grounds. In rejecting the equality-based argument, the TCC held that allowing female students to wear a Muslim headscarf would constitute unfair discrimination against students adhering to other religious creeds.[164]

The European Court of Human Rights (ECtHR) sided with the TCC and dismissed a 1993 appeal filed by a female Turkish student who had been refused her degree certificate until she would submit a photograph of herself with her head uncovered, as required by university disciplinary regulations.[165] A 2002 ECtHR decision similarly affirmed rulings by the Turkish Supreme Military Council that approved the dismissal of soldiers in the strictly secular Turkish army who were found to be members of Islamic sects and whose wives wore *hijab* scarves.[166] In late 2005, adopting a deferential position toward the Turkish authorities' discretion and Turkey's unique sociopolitical context, the ECtHR dismissed an appeal by a Turkish medical student who was barred from attending classes in her university because her headscarf violated the official dress code.[167] This triggered the February 2008 constitutional amendment concerning dress codes in the public education system.

The amendment (passed by an overwhelming 411–103 majority in the National Assembly and later approved by President Gül) guaranteed equal access to the public education system, effectively lifting the ban on wearing Islamic headscarves in the public education system. This amendment directly challenged the official state policy of *laïcité*. In response, the Kemalist Republican People's Party (the main opposition party) and another smaller secular party applied to the Constitutional Court, requesting the annulment of the amendments on the grounds that they violated the principle of secularism in Article 2 of the constitution. In other words, this was a challenge to the constitutionality of a constitutional amendment that was passed legally by parliament.

Despite the high stakes, it is hardly surprising that in June 2008 the Constitutional Court declared that amendment unconstitutional because it contradicted the strict separation of religion and state enshrined in the Turkish Constitution.[168] In the full ruling (9–2) released in October 2008, the court underlined that the rules concerning headscarves have political and religious purposes and that changing them would exacerbate public polarization in Turkey. The court warned that relaxing the ban for religious reasons might lead to pressure on believers or nonbelievers, or those who wear the scarves and those who do not, if the headscarves are used as a political symbol. "Some people might feel obliged to wear a headscarf, which violates freedom of conscience," the court added. The ruling tackled head-on the issue of the perceived religious threat to Turkish secularism. "In a state regime where the nation has sovereignty, there can be no room for divine will based on divine orders." The opinion continued, "In modern systems of law, sovereignty is based on human beings. Legislative changes concern worldly matters, not religious affairs. Laws cannot be based on religious foundations . . . Freedoms that are not in line with secularism cannot be defended and protected. Laws meant to protect secularism cannot be ignored. The headscarf is incompatible with the secular structure of knowledge." The TCC went on to assert its authority to review the constitutionality of constitutional amendments. It stated that it had decided the case on the basis of substance, not as a procedural matter. When a law is contrary to the fundamental principles of the republic, the court has the power to hear challenges to such laws only on the basis of substance, the TCC said.

The AKP and Prime Minister Recep Tayyip Erdoğan were quick to suggest that the court had overstepped its authority. Interestingly, that position was supported by the dissenting opinions of Chief Justice Haşim Kılıç and Justice Sacit Adali, which stressed that under the constitution the court can review constitutional amendments only in terms of their form, not their content, adding that the decision had overstepped the court's authority and usurped parliament's power. "When the court conducts constitutional review by going beyond constitutional restrictions on its authority, then it is no different from other institutions under its supervision," they wrote. The decision on the amendment's merits is unprecedented. After it, "parliament will never even propose or even think of proposing or drafting constitutional amendments, fearing that the court might differ in its interpretation." Mission accomplished, Turkish secularists cheer.

Conclusion

Constitutional law and courts have become a secularist shrine in the post-secularist age. Universalists and modernists increasingly turn to constitutional jurisprudence to block, delay, or mitigate the impact of religion in public life, and they know why. A comparative examination of religion-and-state constitutional jurisprudence of the highest courts in Egypt, Pakistan, Malaysia, Israel, and Turkey demonstrates how the courts have become key religion-containing agents, skillfully delivering the goods for moderate or antireligious stakeholders despite intense scrutiny from the more religious segments of the public who are gaining more sway through electoral processes. Each of these examples illustrates the remarkably creative interpretive techniques adopted by judges confronted with concrete legal disputes that reflect and encapsulate the greater issues emerging from constitutional theocracy.

Bound by Article 2 of the Egyptian Constitution, Egypt's Supreme Constitutional Court has developed its own moderate "interpretation from within" of religious rules and norms. The Supreme Court of Pakistan has been able to advance a holistic view of the constitution that emphasizes the interdependence and harmony of its various sections, so that no specific provision (including Sections 227–231) enjoys an elevated status vis-à-vis any other provision. At the same time, the court has been able to counterbalance the proreligious jurisprudence of the Shari'at Appellate Bench. This has proved time and again to be a safety net for secular interests. The Federal Court of Malaysia has used constitutional principles of federalism to block the implementation of religious legislation at the state level, and while making concessions with regard to civil/religious court jurisdictional boundaries, it has effectively asserted its exclusive authority as the ultimate interpreter of the constitution. Similarly, the Supreme Court of Nigeria has relied on principles of federalism and the constitutional supremacy of federal laws over laws of subnational units to limit the spread of religious law in the predominantly Muslim northern states. The Supreme Court of Israel has meanwhile responded to the increased tension between Israel's dual commitment to cosmopolitan and particularistic values by subjecting the jurisprudence of religious courts to the general principles of administrative and constitutional law. Finally, Turkey's adherence to a Western-style separation of religion and state has allowed the Turkish Constitutional Court to exclude religious practices and policies from the purview of Turkey's political sphere.

To remain relevant and to maintain their public legitimacy, national high courts in polities that have witnessed increasing popular support for theocratic governance do occasionally side with religious authorities and tribunals, mainly those formally recognized and funded by the state. The Malaysian Federal Court's controversial ruling in the *Lina Joy* case (2007) is an illustration of this kind of reactive conservatism. And when the political stakes are high, and the costs of an antireligious ruling seem too high—as illustrated in the Pakistani Supreme Court's ruling on the Ahmadiyya apostasy (*Zaheerudin,* 1993), the Malaysian Federal Court's something-for-everyone approach in *Subashini* (2007), or the Supreme Court of Nigeria's nondecision in the *Kano State Hisba Law* case (2007)—the courts find creative ways to minimize the risk for themselves and to avoid swimming against the stream.

However, these more conservative rulings are the exception. Although courts in constitutional theocracies operate within different constitutional traditions, frameworks, and constraints, they have been able to advance secularizing responses to fundamental religion-and-state questions. In so doing, they have been able to impose effective limitations on the manifestation of religious values in public life. And, as we have seen, there are a number of reasons (ideological, structural, and practical) that constitutional law and courts appeal to, and provide an effective refuge for, anti-traditionalist groups and interests. Given this jurisprudential record, it is hardly surprising that against the strictures of an increasingly conservative interpretation of Shari'a, even in Middle Eastern polities that lack established traditions of judicial activism (e.g., Iran, Afghanistan, and Saudi Arabia), judicial reform has been instigated in order to create and empower state-controlled courts in an attempt to counterbalance the spread of religious fundamentalism.

Finally, the fact that constitutional courts and jurisprudence have been pushed to the forefront of the so-called "clash of civilizations," culture wars, and the tension between universalism and particularism suggests that there may be important similarities between the political construction of judicial review in established democracies and in the world of constitutional theocracies.[169] The judicialization of foundational collective identity, particularly religion-and-state questions in both settings, serves a contrareligious impulse in its struggle to maintain secular hegemony, worldviews, and interests against increasingly popular religious creeds and their precepts. In the following chapter I turn to an examination of this resemblance by looking at courts as secularizing agents in the nontheocratic world.

CHAPTER FIVE

Courts as Secularizing Agents in the Nontheocratic World

One of the common distinctions in the field of comparative law and courts is that between the role of courts as fair and relatively independent adjudicators in democratic polities (read North America, Western Europe, Australia, New Zealand, and perhaps Japan) and their markedly different status and role under authoritarian regimes.[1] Constitutional courts and judges in democratic countries, it is often said, are relatively independent to pursue their own jurisprudential agenda, whereas their counterparts in authoritarian regimes are often politically controlled and manipulated so as to legitimize the regime and its policy preferences. But the reality, alas, is more complex and nuanced than that dichotomous distinction suggests. For one, not more than thirty countries worldwide would qualify as stable democracies even under a lenient definition of the term. Likewise, very few countries are purely authoritarian, with no political competition or diversity of interests. Even more important, constitutional courts in the vast majority of countries, democratic, authoritarian, or otherwise, show certain common patterns of behavior and reasoning and share an inclination toward secularism and modernism. These joint trends, of course, vary from one constitutional setting to another in scope and intensity, but they are not qualitatively different. So without entering into Wittgensteinian ontological debates, while apples and oranges may very well be different in some respects, they do share a lot in common: they are popular, rounded, sweet but tart, tree-growing fruits. Likewise, courts in so-called authoritarian and democratic regimes have common features that are ripe for comparison.

Just how different is the secularizing role of constitutional courts and jurisprudence in the nontheocratic, purportedly liberal world from that of constitutional law and courts in predominantly religious settings? In this chapter I examine in detail four illustrations of constitutional entanglement with the question of religion in nontheocratic polities: Western European courts and the question of religious attire in the public sphere; the struggle for women's reproductive freedoms in Catholic Latin America; the restrictive interpretation of customary law in South Africa; and the boundaries to accommodation of religion in Canada.

These four settings are grouped into two categories. In the first two—Western Europe and Latin America—constitutional courts have emerged as advancing secular or secularizing worldviews and policy preferences, each within its different political context and constitutional legacy. In the latter two settings—South Africa and Canada, arguably two of the most diverse, accommodating polities—constitutional jurisprudence has erected a new wall of separation, permitting diversity and requests for accommodation and inclusion of difference while rejecting claims for insulation, if not outright immunization, from the purview of the state's secular ordering that are based on adherence to sacred or customary sources of authority and identity.

These two groups are helpful in understanding the role of constitutional jurisprudence in constitutional theocracy. The first group of examples illustrates the secularizing tendency embedded in constitutional jurisprudence, whether it operates against the backdrop of religion-infused politics or as the guardian of rights and secularist cultural propensities. The second group of examples illustrates an important antireligious impulse embedded in the constitutional jurisprudence of even the most accommodating, multicultural polities. As long as legal claims for accommodation are not seen as directly or indirectly challenging the lexical superiority of the constitutional religion itself ("diversity as inclusion"), they stand a fair chance of success. Contrast that with the unyielding reluctance of legislatures and judiciaries to accept as binding or even cognizable any potentially competing legal order that originates in sacred or customary sources of identity and authority. This pattern of clamping down and refusing to accept any alternative (here, religious or customary) sources of regulation becomes particularly visible where the legal challenge at issue is interpreted as raising doubts regarding which set of norms and institutions or what set of high priests should have the final word in authoritatively resolving legal disputes within a given society ("nonstate law as competition"). This is a challenge that no secular legal order, no matter how tolerant and otherwise open to providing exemptions and accommodations to religious believers it may be, can accept with indifference.

Europe and Religious Attire: The Politics of Judicial Deference

The specter of religiosity is haunting Europe once again. As we saw in Chapter 1, the history of close entanglement and later gradual disentanglement of religion and politics in Europe has been long and tumultuous. Never totally eliminated from European political discourse, religion has regained a central position on that continent in recent times. To begin with, more countries in Europe than anywhere else except the Middle East designate a single religion as their state religion, however a mere formality such designation may be. Great Britain, Norway, Finland, Malta, Greece, and Cyprus all fall into that category. The central place of Catholicism in the political history and collective identity of countries such as Ireland, Poland, Spain, Italy, and Portugal is well documented. Although freedom of religion is constitutionally and practically guaranteed to members of other denominations, the history of Catholic dominance in these countries cannot be easily ignored.

The tension between Europe's Christian legacy and history of religious zealotry pitted against the changing demographics of Europe over the last half century and, in particular, the growing presence of non-Christian (and often nonwhite) immigrants in virtually all major European urban centers brought to the fore fierce public debates concerning the real neutrality of the European state with respect to religion, as well as the boundaries of reasonable accommodation of religious difference in the public sphere. "Islam" in particular has become a challenge to the so-called integration front. Indeed, as several scholars have noted, an analogy may be drawn between what "Spanish" is to the United States and what "Islam" is to Europe.[2] Prominent politicians and national coalitions rise and fall as core questions of naturalization, assimilation, and national identity are closely linked to the question of how neutral European countries really are when it comes to religion. The battle over the right to wear religious attire in the public education system has come to dominate these debates. As elsewhere, courts throughout Europe have been assigned the sensitive task of dealing with these knotty predicaments. In virtually all these cases courts assumed the role of guardians of secularism against the perceived threat to the concept of a religiously neutral public sphere. Let us consider a few leading examples drawn from the recent constitutional jurisprudence of

Germany, Britain, and France, as well as the European Court of Human Rights (ECtHR).

The question whether religious symbols may be displayed in public school classrooms has occupied European constitutional courts for quite some time now. Courts in predominantly Catholic countries have, by and large, been less disturbed than their counterparts in non-Catholic countries by the exhibition of crucifixes in schools. The Polish Constitutional Court and the Italian Constitutional Court have not taken a strong position against the practice. By contrast, the Swiss Federal Court found that it violates state neutrality.[3] Likewise, in the landmark *Classroom Crucifix* case (1995) the German Constitutional Court ruled that the placing of a cross or crucifix in the classrooms of a state (in this case Bavaria) school that is formally designated as nondenominational infringes Article 4(1) of the German Basic Law (*Grundgesetz*).[4] Section I of that article states that "[f]reedom of faith and conscience, and freedom of religious or ideological creed, are inviolable." Section II adds that "[t]he undisturbed practice of religion is guaranteed." Although these guarantees appear absolute, the Constitutional Court held in the *Classroom Crucifix* case that limits on these religious freedoms that flow from the Basic Law and are constitutionally grounded may be justified. The court stated: "The basic right to religious freedom is guaranteed without reservation. This does not, however, mean that it might not be subject to some sort of restrictions. These would, however, have to follow from the constitution itself. The setting up of limits not already laid out in the constitution is not something the legislature can do. Constitutional grounds that might have justified intervention are not however present here." "To this day," added the court, "the presence of a cross in a home or room is understood as an expression of the dwellers' Christian faith . . . [B]ecause of the significance Christianity attributes to the cross, non-Christians and atheists perceive it to be the symbolic expression of certain faith convictions and a symbol of missionary zeal. To see the cross as nothing more than a cultural artifact of the Western tradition without any particular religious meaning would amount to profanation contrary to the self-understanding of Christians and the Christian church."[5] Therefore, the classroom crucifixes had to be removed from nondenominational schools in Bavaria.

With embedded Christian norms in southern Germany pitted against the changing demographics of the German polity, another constitutional challenge to religious expression in the classroom was bound to present itself, and it rapidly did. Fereshta Ludin, a German citizen born in Afghanistan, applied to teach at a state school near Stuttgart in the state of Baden-Württemberg in southwestern Germany. When she informed the school board that she would wear a headscarf while teaching, the board rejected her application. Ludin protested, saying that the wearing of the veil was both a personal and a religious expression, and that she did not wear it as a symbol or to provoke or influence any students. The school board argued that it was not merely a private symbol but an explicitly political symbol that subjected students to undue religious influence.[6] State authorities backed the school board by arguing that "the objective effect of cultural segregation [*Desintegration*] connected with the head scarf could not be squared with the constitutional requirement of state neutrality in questions of religion." Ludin appealed the school board's decision, and her case eventually proceeded to the Constitutional Court of Germany.

Ludin argued that her freedom of religion, protected by Article 4, Sections I and II, of the Basic Law, had been violated by the ban on the headscarf in the classroom. Following the ruling in the *Classroom Crucifix* case, the core legal question in *Ludin* became whether limits on freedom of religion in this context flow from or may be justified under the German Constitution. In a 3–2 decision released in September 2003, the Constitutional Court upheld Ludin's appeal. However, this was based on the primarily technical grounds that the laws of the state of Baden-Württemberg (where the school board in question was based) at the time did not include an explicit ban on wearing the headscarf in the public school system. Had such a law been in effect, the board's decision to reject Ludin's application would have withstood judicial scrutiny. The state was held to have a legitimate interest in protecting religious and ideological neutrality in the classroom to ensure separation of church and state and the encouragement of pluralism and diversity.[7] Parents of the children in school were also held to have a natural right, guaranteed by Article 6 of the Basic Law, to educate and bring up their children free from religious influences that did not accord with the parents' wishes.[8] The students also had a right to be free from the exercise of freedom of religion by others where they might be held captive to the influence of one person's religion.[9] In other words, there were several constitutional grounds for upholding limits to religious expression in this context.

The court also refused to reject the idea that the scarf was a "danger." It maintained that the abstract danger posed by the scarf could only justify the school board's rejection of Ludin's application if the board had been authorized by statute to employ such a policy against religious dress. States were free, according to the Constitutional Court, to enact statutes identifying the appropriate level of religious dress to be displayed in classrooms after taking into account local context and religious and cultural rights. The court held that it was conceivable that a legislature could require strict secularism and neutrality in some contexts in order to address an increasingly diverse religious community. Because no such statute existed in Ludin's case, there was no justification for the school board's decision.

The minority opinion held that because freedom of religion is an explicitly individual or private matter, one's freedom of religion is not engaged when one seeks employment in the public sector. Rights guaranteed by the Basic Law are held against the state, and where a person has sought employment as a state official, that person cannot assert those rights against the body of which he or she is a part, except in very limited circumstances. These government employees are differently situated than the students at the school and their parents, who retain legitimate interests protected under the Basic Law. Further, the majority's apprehension of an "abstract danger" was held by the minority to constitute reason enough for the school board to reject Ludin's application. The mere possibility of the creation of tension or undue influence should be enough to justify the school board's decision, and the minority held that this danger would not have to materialize into real damage before it could be prevented by the board.[10] In the larger European context this ruling was relatively favorable to the headscarf claim. Nonetheless, and consistently with the court's ruling, a majority of German states have announced plans to pass laws prohibiting teachers from wearing certain religious attire. The state of Baden-Württemberg itself passed a law in 2004 that bans the wearing of the headscarf by teachers. Other states followed suit by prohibiting public school teachers from wearing explicitly religious (non-Christian) attire.

As some readers may recall, in 2009 Swiss voters ratified a constitutional amendment backed by nationalist parties that bans the construction of new minarets in that country. But the constitutional struggle over the place of Islamic symbols in Switzerland's public sphere began earlier. A leading pre-*Ludin* European case on religious attire is the ECtHR's decision in *Dahlab* (2001), involving a primary-school teacher in Geneva, Switzerland, who had converted to Islam and began wearing an Islamic headscarf. The practice continued for several years without complaint from the pupils' parents. However, the Geneva cantonal government authorities eventually came to view the teacher's wearing of the *hijab* to be in violation of the Public Education Act (1940, section 6), which provides that the public education system shall ensure that the political and religious beliefs of pupils and parents are respected. After she was formally requested to cease wearing a headscarf when on duty, Dahlab turned to the Swiss courts but failed to have that decision annulled. In its ruling (1997), the Swiss Federal Court emphasized a "captive audience" argument by holding that: "The wearing of a headscarf and loose-fitting clothes consequently indicates allegiance to a particular faith and a desire to behave in accordance with the precepts laid down by that faith. Such garments may even be said to constitute a 'powerful' religious symbol—that is to say, a sign that is immediately visible to others and provides a clear indication that the person concerned belongs to a particular religion. What is in issue, therefore, is the wearing of a powerful religious symbol by a teacher at a State school in the performance of her professional duties."[11] It also ruled that wearing the *hijab* in the classroom while on duty violated the constitutional principle of denominational neutrality stemming from the separation of church and state (Article 27 of the Swiss constitution). Dahlab appealed to the ECtHR.

The ECtHR rejected Dahlab's claim that the order to refrain from wearing the headscarf when on duty unduly infringed her freedom of religion. The interference with the teacher's freedom to manifest her religion (Art. 9(2) ECHR) was held to be justifiable and proportionate as a measure to protect the freedoms of others; namely, the schoolchildren. The court was concerned with "the impact that a powerful external symbol such as the wearing of a headscarf may have on the freedom of conscience and religion of very young children." The court stated that the headscarf "appeared to be imposed on women by religious precept that was hard to reconcile with the principle of gender equality." Therefore the court found it "difficult to reconcile the wearing of an Islamic headscarf with the message of tolerance, respect for others and, above all, equality and non-discrimination."[12]

This politically charged reasoning by the ECtHR gave way to a less polemical but perhaps more effective containment approach based on the legal doctrine known as the "margin of appreciation," through which courts will afford deference to the regulatory powers of local authorities. This doctrine figured powerfully in the ECtHR's landmark ruling in *Leyla Şahin v. Turkey* (2005), which is arguably the most significant European case to date dealing with the issue of religious attire.[13] A bit of background seems necessary to understand the circumstances and complexity of this case. In 1982 the Higher Education Authority of Turkey issued a circular on the wearing of headscarves in institutions of higher education. The Islamic headscarf was banned in lecture theatres, and these regulations were upheld as lawful by the Supreme Administrative Court of Turkey in 1984.[14] Leyla Şahin was a Sunni Muslim who enrolled as a medical student in 1997 at Istanbul University. She wore a headscarf while attending school. In February 1998 the vice-chancellor of Istanbul University issued a circular reaffirming the prohibition of headscarves in lecture theatres. As a result, Şahin was denied entry to a number of exams and lectures. Subsequently she launched an application for an order setting aside the 1998 circular, stating that it infringed her rights as guaranteed by the European Convention on Human Rights (ECHR). The Istanbul Administrative Court dismissed her application in 1999, and the Supreme Administrative Court dismissed her appeal in April 2001.[15] The case reached the European Court of Human Rights, where Şahin lost her appeal in the Chamber and then appealed the Chamber's ruling to the seventeen-member Grand Chamber. The Chamber had concluded that this was unquestionably an interference with Şahin's religious freedoms under Article 9(2) of the ECHR, and the Turkish government did not contest this finding in the appeal to the Grand Chamber.[16] The only question for the Grand Chamber to decide was whether the interference was justified. The court delivered its much-anticipated judgment on November 10, 2005—coincidentally (or ignorantly) the seventy-seventh anniversary of Kemal Atatürk's death.

Şahin argued first that the 1998 regulation had not been prescribed by law.[17] The court, however, decided that the regulation was prescribed legitimately under Turkish legislation and case law and was sufficiently precise in its terms.[18] Şahin had conceded to the court that the regulation had a legitimate aim—protecting the rights and freedoms of others and protecting public order—so the court then considered whether the restriction on Şahin's rights could be considered necessary in a democratic society.[19] This question required the court to elaborate on the nature of Article 9(2) and its limits in a democratic society. Şahin argued that there should be no margin of appreciation with respect to student dress because there had been no sign of tension in institutions of higher education in any other European state that would justify such an approach, and because the wearing of the headscarf posed no threat to secularism.[20] The government of Turkey argued that a wide margin of appreciation should apply because the court was to rule on a matter of national education that was particular to a liberal democracy with a significant Muslim majority.[21] In other words, Turkey suggested that its situation was sufficiently unique to justify a generous application of the margin-of-appreciation doctrine, inviting the court to adopt a deferential approach. The court accepted the invitation with open arms, holding that it is necessary for the governments of democratic societies in which several religions coexist to place restrictions on the freedom to manifest one's religion or belief for the purpose of ensuring the mutual respect of all beliefs. The court attributed this necessity to Article 9(2) and also to the general positive obligation of states under Article 1 to secure everyone within their jurisdiction the rights and freedoms guaranteed by the ECHR. With respect to these potential restrictions, then, the court held that a wide margin of appreciation must be adopted when reviewing the decisions of national decision-making bodies. The specific domestic context of a particular state would determine the extent and form of such regulations and thus must inevitably be left up to the state to decide.[22]

After determining that a wide margin of appreciation applied, the court held that the interference with Şahin's Article 9(2) right was justified because the preservation of secularism for the purpose of ensuring pluralism and equality before the law constituted a legitimate aim, and that the interference was proportional to the aim pursued. The court held that the university authorities engaged in a thoughtful decision-making process in setting the policy, and "by reason of their direct and continuous contact with the education community, the university authorities are in principle better placed than an international court to evaluate local needs and conditions or the requirements of a particular course."[23] Consequently, the court found no breach of Article 9(2) of the ECHR.

The court went on to briefly assess Şahin's claim under Article 2 of Protocol No. 1 regarding the right to education. The court held that the guarantee under Article 2 was applicable to higher education, and that Şahin's right had been impaired. However, in the court's view, because the restriction on her right was foreseeable and pursued a legitimate aim, the interference was proportional to the aim to be served and "did not impair the very essence of the applicant's right to education."[24] In a concurring opinion, two judges held that the case would have been best dealt with only under Article 9, noting that the central issue was the interference of the state with the right to wear a headscarf at a university, and Article 2 of the First Protocol did not raise a separate issue under the convention.[25]

One judge on the seventeen-judge panel, Françoise Tulkens of Belgium, dissented, concluding that no margin of appreciation was owed in this context because no other states had enacted headscarf bans and because freedom of religion was "not merely a 'local' issue." Judge Tulkens further held that the possible effect that wearing the headscarf might have on those who did not wear it did not appear to satisfy the requirement of a pressing social need. Consequently, the ban on the headscarf was not premised on reasons that were relevant and sufficient, and so the interference could not have been necessary in a democratic society. The minority opinion also found a violation of Article 2 of Protocol 1, noting that by refusing Şahin access to her lectures and examinations, the university de facto deprived her of the right of access to education.[26] According to Judge Tulkens, the view that Muslim women lack free will and are forced to wear headscarves or that the headscarf symbolizes oppression or inequality of women was paternalistic and unwarranted.

The ECtHR's generous application of the margin-of-appreciation doctrine in the *Şahin* case set the stage for a similar application of the same logic on a smaller scale by the British Law Lords in the *Shabina Begum* case (2006).[27] Begum was a Muslim student at Denbigh High School, which had a school uniform policy. Because the vast majority of students at the school were Muslim, the policy was drafted to include an option of a uniform based on the traditional Pakistani dress of *shalwar kameez,* with an optional *hijab* or *khimar* (a veil, commonly understood as a lengthy cover from the head, but not face, to below the knee). These options were included after consultation with local mosques and parents of the school's students. Shabina Begum's older sister had worn the *shalwar kameez* at the school for some time before Shabina with no complaint, and Shabina Begum wore the *shalwar kameez* without complaint for two years. After two years at Denbigh, Begum and her family members met with school administrators to tell them that the only garment that met her religious requirements was a *jilbab,* which was said to conceal the contours of the female body to a greater extent. The head teacher of the school decided not to allow Begum to wear the *jilbab* at school, saying that wearing it could promote tensions between different sects of Islam. A committee of the governors of the school met in October 2003 to consider the matter and, after consultation with local Muslim organizations, upheld the head teacher's decision in a lengthy ruling. The governors informed Begum that if she would not attend school without the *jilbab,* the school would assist her in seeking a place at a school that permitted the *jilbab.* Begum then issued a claim for judicial review of the governors' decision, arguing that by not allowing her to attend school in a *jilbab,* the school authorities had violated her rights under the ECHR. In particular, her claim cited Article 9(2) of the ECHR regarding the freedom to manifest one's religion, as well as Article 2 of the First Protocol regarding the right to education. Begum lost her case in the High Court but won in the Court of Appeal. The case then proceeded on appeal to the House of Lords, which released its ruling in August 2006.[28]

Three of the five judges in the House of Lords found that Begum's religious rights under the ECHR had not been violated (Lords Bingham, Scott, and Hoffman), and two found that they had (Lord Nicholls and Baroness Hale). All five agreed, however, that the alleged interference could be justified, meaning that Shabina Begum could not wear her *jilbab* at that school. Lord Bingham cited British jurisprudence for the proposition that what constitutes an interference with this right is entirely dependent on the particularities of the situation, and he noted specifically that "the Strasbourg institutions have not been at all ready to find an interference with the right to manifest religious belief in practice or observance where a person has voluntarily accepted an employment or role which does not accommodate that practice or observance and there are other means open to the person to practice or observe his or her religion without undue hardship or inconvenience."[29]

In this case Lord Bingham held that because (a) the school "went to unusual lengths to inform parents of its uniform policy," (b) Begum and her sister wore the *shalwar kameez* for a number of years without objection, and (c) there were other schools that permitted the *jilbab* that Begum could have attended, there was no interference with Begum's right to manifest her belief in practice or observance.[30] Lords Hoffman and Scott wrote similar judgments, with Scott noting that "'freedom to manifest one's religion' does not mean that one has the right to manifest one's religion at any time and in any place and in any manner that accords with one's beliefs."[31]

In a short judgment Lord Nicholls stated only that he was "not so sure" that Begum's religious freedom had not been violated, and that he preferred in these types of cases that a violation be found, and that the government be required to explain and justify its decision.[32] Baroness Hale also wrote that she was "uneasy" with the decision of the other lords and stated that the fact that Begum had only recently changed her mind about the wearing of the *jilbab* instead of the *shalwar kameez* represented a "part of growing up" and that wearing of the *jilbab* in years previous might not have been an autonomous choice and thus could not be taken as evidence that there was no violation of her religious freedom.[33]

Despite the dissenting opinion, the majority of the House of Lords justified its decision mainly by deferring to the school board. Lord Bingham stated that because the school did not reject Begum's request out of hand and took advice regarding the conformity of its dress code with Islamic dress requirements, the school's decision was justified. The school decided that accession to the request could have created significant adverse repercussions, and Lord Bingham stated that it would be "irresponsible of any court, lacking the experience, background, and detailed knowledge of the head teacher, staff, and governors to overrule their judgment on a matter as sensitive as this."[34] Lord Hoffman echoed Lord Bingham's judgment, stating that while the concept of the margin of appreciation had no application in domestic courts when considering the Human Rights Act of 1998, "the justification must be sought at the local level and it is there that an area of judgment, comparable to the margin of appreciation, must be allowed to the school."[35] In considering the legitimacy of a school's decision, the process that the school employed in dealing with the problem was held to be merely helpful in persuading a judge that its solution fell within the area of judgment accorded to it. In short, deference to local school authorities was maintained.

Lower courts in Britain followed suit. In 2007 the Employment Appeal Tribunal (EAT) upheld a lower-tribunal finding that an instruction to remove a veil that covered all but the eyes of a bilingual support teacher named Mrs. Azmi was neither direct nor indirect discrimination on grounds of religion and belief.[36] Mrs. Azmi had not been treated less favorably than a comparator (a woman who, whether Muslim or not, wore a face covering) would have been in similar circumstances. The school's instruction to Mrs. Azmi to remove her veil while teaching did not "target the veil." The instruction had been issued to achieve a legitimate aim (the provision of the highest quality education), and the instruction to Mrs. Azmi (to remove her veil while teaching) was a proportionate means of achieving that aim. The EAT refused to refer the case to the ECtHR.

Another paradigmatic example is the recent *Purity Ring* case (2007) where the High Court in London (also known as the High Court of England and Wales, or EWHC) was asked to rule on whether the decision of the governing body of a school to prohibit sixteen-year-old Lydia Playfoot from wearing a silver ring as a symbol of her commitment to celibacy until marriage constituted a violation of Articles 9 (freedom of thought, conscience, and religion) and 14 (prohibition of discrimination) of the European Convention on Human Rights.[37] Miss Playfoot was one of a group of eleven girls at her school who joined a movement called the Silver Ring Thing, which originated in America. Members wear a ring engraved with a reference to the biblical verses I Thessalonians 4:3–4, which translate as "God wants you to be holy, so you should keep clear of all sexual sin. Then each of you will control your body and live in holiness and honor." The school argued that Playfoot had voluntarily accepted the school code that mandated no jewelry. There were many other ways, it suggested, for the pupils to express their views and beliefs.

The court accepted the school's judgment that the ring was not an essential part of the Christian faith, and it found the school's action "fully justified." Wearing a ring was not "intimately linked" to the belief in chastity before marriage. Miss Playfoot "was under no obligation, by reason of her belief, to wear the ring, nor does she suggest that she was so obliged," Judge Supperstone said. He rejected the submission that the ring was a "religious artifact" and therefore exempt from the school's uniform policy that banned jewelry. "Whatever the ring is intended to symbolize, it is a piece of jewelry," he said. "[S]he voluntarily accepted the uniform policy of the school and there are other means open to her to practice her belief without undue hardship or inconvenience." The school's uniform policy was prescribed by law in the legitimate pursuit of creating equality and cohesion, minimizing pressure from markings of difference in wealth or status. Any interference with her Article 9 rights was therefore justified; in other words, the court ordered the girls to abstain from symbols of abstinence.

Whereas deference to local school authorities characterized the House of Lord's ruling in *Shabina Begum*, the newly established United Kingdom Supreme Court (UKSC) was notably less deferential when it contemplated *R. (E) v. Governing Body of JFS* (2009), which involved the legality of a North London Jewish school authorities' apparently discriminatory admission policy that favored strict religious definition of community membership over a general, more inclusive one. According to the traditional Orthodox Judaism definition, a person may be recognized as Jewish only if his or her mother was Jewish, or if he or she converted to Judaism via Orthodox conversion practices. That policy has been adopted by the British Office of the Chief Rabbi. A twelve-year-old applicant to the school came from a devout Jewish family, where the father is Jewish by birth and the mother converted to Judaism via a non-Orthodox (and thus supposedly more lenient) conversion process. There was no doubt about the couple's substantive adherence to Jewish traditions. However, the publicly funded school refused to admit the applicant on the basis of his mother's non-Orthodox conversion, and thus questionable Jewishness, at least by the school's Orthodox definition of "who is a Jew." In a move similar in principle to what the Supreme Court of Israel did in its decision in *Bavli* (1995), discussed in detail in Chapter 4, seven of the nine UKSC judges applied extra-religious, general equality norms (most notably the Race Relations Act 1976) to a denominational school's own membership criteria, thereby ruling that the school's admission policy was unjustly discriminatory. In her majority opinion, Baroness Hale wrote: "It is just as unlawful to treat one person more favourably on the ground of his ethnic origin as it is to treat another person less favourably. There can be no doubt that, if an employer were to take exactly the same criterion as that used by the . . . Chief Rabbi and refuse to employ a person because the Chief Rabbi would regard him as halachically Jewish, the employer would be treating that person less favourably on grounds of his ethnic origin."[38]

Across the Channel, the Conseil d'État—France's highest administrative body, which also acts as a high court—has also positioned itself as a key actor in the orchestrated government effort to contain the increasing popularity of religion and religious symbols. The first French case dealing with the wearing of a headscarf in a public forum was decided in 1989. A French school principal had suspended three students for refusing to remove their headscarves in class. The education minister at that time referred the question regarding the legitimacy of the principal's decision to suspend the students to the Conseil d'État, which held that the wearing of religious dress in school was permissible as long as it was passive, did not attempt to intimidate, influence, or provoke others, and was not distracting or diminishing to other students' freedom and dignity.[39]

The issue reemerged in France in 2003, when a number of public inquiries were launched regarding the presence of religious dress in French schools. French ombudsman Bernard Stasi chaired one such commission that recommended the banning of all religious or political expression in public schools.[40] The French government took up the commission's recommendations and banned all overtly apparent religious dress in French schools, including the headscarf.[41] The same sentiments are now echoed in calls in several European countries, most notably Belgium and France, to legally ban or limit the wearing of full-face veils in the public sphere.

Consider the *Faiza M.* (or *Mme M.*) case (June 2008).[42] Faiza Silmi ("Mme M.") was born in Morocco. She married a French citizen of Moroccan origin and in 2000 moved to France, where she had three French-born children. In 2004 she applied for French citizenship under French law, which allowed noncitizen spouses of French citizens to apply for citizenship after two years of marriage. In May 2005 the French government denied her application, reasoning that her religious beliefs were "incompatible with the fundamental values of the French community, and particularly with the principle of equality of the sexes" ("incompatible avec les valeurs essentielles de la communauté française, et notamment avec le principe d'égalité des sexes"), and that she had not sufficiently assimilated into French society. Silmi appealed.

The Conseil d'État rejected the appeal from the outset, confirming that the government's apprehension of the incompatibility of Silmi's religious beliefs and insufficient assimilation into French society was a legitimate basis for rejecting her application for citizenship.[43] The Conseil d'État relied on reasons provided by the central government's Commissariat, according to which Silmi only began wearing the *niqab* when she arrived in France, refused to remove her headscarf and *niqab* in public, rarely left her home without her husband, and had been living in "submission" to men. The government viewed this interpretation of the facts as indicative of Silmi's insufficient assimilation into French society.[44] Although Silmi "has a good mastery of the French language," the Conseil ruled, "she has nonetheless adopted a radical practice of her religion, incompatible with the essential values of the French community, and notably with the principle of equality of the sexes; that thus, she does not fulfill the requirement of assimilation enunciated by Article 21-4 of the Civil Code; consequently, the government could legally rely on this reason to oppose her acquisition of French citizenship by marriage." The Conseil went on to state that the government decision to deny citizenship under such circumstances "ignores neither the constitutional principle of freedom of religious expression, nor the provisions of article 9 of the European Convention for the Protection of Human Rights and Fundamental Freedoms." In short, Silmi had "no basis to demand the cancellation of the order of May 16, 2005, denying her French citizenship."

In the end, we return to where we started our European excursion—crucifixes in the classroom. In November 2009 the ECtHR's seven-judge Chamber decided unanimously in *Lautsi v. Italy* that the presence of crucifixes in Italian classrooms contravened Article 9 (freedom of thought, conscience, and religion) of the ECHR, as well as Protocol 1 of Article 2, which provides that "the State shall respect the right of parents to ensure such education and teaching in conformity with their own religious and philosophical convictions."[45] A request by a Finnish-born, atheist Italian mother whose children attended an Italian school to remove the crucifixes from her children's classrooms was dismissed by Italy's Consiglio di Stato on the ground that the cross had become one of the secular values of the Italian Constitution and represented the values of civil life. In accepting the mother's appeal, the ECtHR advanced clear "disestablishment" reasoning. It held that the state "was required to observe confessional neutrality in the context of public education, where attending classes was compulsory irrespective of religion, and where the aim should be to foster critical thinking in pupils." The court was "unable to grasp how the display, in classrooms in State schools, of a symbol that could reasonably be associated with Catholicism (the majority religion in Italy) could serve the educational pluralism that was essential to the preservation of a 'democratic society' as that was conceived by the Convention, a pluralism that was recognized by the Italian Constitutional Court."

What makes the ECtHR ruling so significant is the long-standing symbolic status of the crucifix in predominantly Roman Catholic Italy. So ingrained is the secularist tilt in today's constitutional thinking that the ECtHR used one complaint from one claimant to tell a nation that has been the center of world Christianity for two thousand years to remove its most revered and cardinal symbol from its classrooms.[46] Italian political leaders have reacted with outrage. One government minister, Roberto Calderoli, noted that "[t]he European court has trodden on our rights, our culture, our history, our traditions and our values." Another minister noted that preventing the crucifix from being displayed was "an act of violence against the deep-seated feelings of the Italian people and all persons of goodwill."[47] Italy's colorful prime minister Silvio Berlusconi, whose own adherence to Christian morality is occasionally questioned, described the ruling as a "nonsensical attempt to deny Europe's Christian roots" and thus "unacceptable for us Italians." An Italian appeal before the ECtHR seventeen-member Grand Chamber (the same forum that decided *Şahin* in 2005) is pending.

In summary, courts in Europe have been grappling with the question of religious expression and establishment amid repeated challenges to state neutrality from the Christian Right and from the expanding non-Christian community. Although they have not adopted a unified line of interpretation, constitutional courts throughout much of Western Europe have advanced, by and large, a secularist or irreligious approach to the matter, adhering to the concepts of state neutrality and the private/public distinction in determining pertinent boundaries of tolerance.

A Gentle Tango: Courts and Women's Reproductive Freedoms in Latin America

The battle over women's reproductive freedoms, most notably the right to have an abortion, has marked the constitutional scene in virtually all predominantly Christian polities worldwide. It has been hotly contested and at times even elevated to a truly existential level in chiefly Catholic polities in the developing world stretching from the Philippines to most countries in Central and South America. The Catholic Church and those who speak for it have maintained close ties with past authoritarian regimes in most of these countries. Because Catholicism in these and other countries has long been a pillar of collective identity and has been omnipresent in public life, even progressive politicians, let alone more conservative ones, refrain from publicly criticizing the church, its leaders, and the policies they advocate. Frontal clashes with the church are often simply too costly.

Although considerable intercountry variance still exists, the battle for formal liberalization of women's reproductive freedoms has, by and large, been settled throughout much of Europe, including countries such as Spain, Italy, and Portugal where Catholicism is prevalent.[48] Poland, Malta, and to a lesser degree Ireland remain some of the last European bastions of formally legalized, restrictive, antiabortion policies.[49] In Latin America, by contrast, the political and constitutional fight between the Catholic Church and pro-choice activists is far from settled. Unlike in disestablishment settings such as North America and much of Europe where formal separation of religion and state is the baseline norm, constitutional courts in Latin America often operate against the backdrop of centuries of church dominance and so are less likely, because of their own ideological preferences, their astute strategic considerations, or some combination of these and other factors, to advance a straightforward secularizing, progressive jurisprudence on women's reproductive freedoms. Public support for the courts is also a challenge. In polities so dominated by religion, a distinctly antireligious jurisprudence is likely to erode public support for the courts, which, in many postauthoritarian countries in Latin America, is not necessarily a given. But even here, where religion is so socially and politically ingrained, several constitutional courts have, by and large, adopted a moderate and at times even a distinctly progressive approach to women's reproductive freedoms.

From a constitutional standpoint, the issue of reproductive freedoms for women is often framed differently in different places. It may be framed mainly as a clash of rights (e.g., in the United States), as a reflection of the status of the historically influential church (e.g., in Central America), or as a conflict between national preferences and supranational norms (e.g., the compatibility of Irish abortion laws with provisions of the European Convention on Human Rights). In several Latin American countries the issue of abortion has taken another twist with the incorporation of international and trans- or supranational legal standards into domestic law. Just as the passage of the Human Rights Act 1998 in Great Britain effectively incorporated the provisions of the European Convention on Human Rights into British constitutional law, so the incorporation of a bundle of international human rights treaties into domestic constitutional law took place in Colombia in 1991, in Argentina in 1994, and in Brazil in 2004. This has had a varied effect on human rights jurisprudence in these countries, although more often than not, it has served as a platform and a catalyst for progressive jurisprudence.

Consider the series of recent landmark abortion decisions of the Colombian Supreme Court and the Colombian Administrative Court. All are "100 percent Colombian" but at the same time universal triumphs for secularists, modernists, and women's rights activists in that country and beyond. Catholicism was the official religion in Colombia from the Spanish colonization until the country's 1991 constitutional revolution, which, among other changes, granted equal status to all religions. However, Catholicism still remains the main religion, with Catholics constituting an estimated three-quarters of the population. The 1991 constitutional revolution in Colombia—arguably the most comprehensive transformation of its kind in the Americas—also transferred the power of judicial review from the Supreme Court of Justice, which had exercised it quite moderately since 1886, to a newly established Constitutional Court. This new body hears challenges to the constitutionality of laws, legislative decrees, laws approving international treaties, referendum or assembly constituency summonses, and appeals of lower judicial decisions related to tutelage actions that engage constitutional rights. The tutelage action *(tutela)* was instituted as a quick and effective mechanism that allows citizens to assert their fundamental rights as stated in Article 8 of the Universal Declaration of Human Rights of 1948. The impact of the *tutela* mechanism on access to the Constitutional Court has been dramatic. In the first decade of its existence the number of direct *tutela* petitions grew from around 8,000 in 1992 to over 130,000 in 2002, a fifteenfold increase. The number of Constitutional Court decisions increased from 235 in 1992 to 1,123 in 2002. Approximately 70 percent (about 750 decisions) were *tutela* decisions.[50] More significant still is the fact that the Colombian Constitutional Court has established itself as a relatively progressive force in Colombian politics, particularly with respect to a longtime hot potato of Latin American constitutional law—the right to have an abortion.

In April 2005 a citizen-launched petition was filed with the Colombian Constitutional Court challenging the constitutionality of Colombia's abortion law, which categorically prohibited abortion.[51] The petition was based, inter alia, on the international human rights obligations that had been incorporated into Colombian constitutional law by the 1991 constitution. It argued that the blanket denial of abortion rights constituted a violation of Colombia's obligations under international treaties ensuring women's rights to life, health, privacy, and dignity. The petition was aided by several supportive amicus briefs by international pro-choice, women's rights, and human rights organizations.

In a historic 5–3 decision released on May 10, 2006, the court held that the grounds for legal abortion must be extended, and that the criminal prohibition of abortion in all circumstances violates women's fundamental rights as they are protected by the 1991 Colombian Constitution and by international human rights law.[52] It determined that abortion should be permitted under the following circumstances: when the continuation of pregnancy presents a risk to the life or physical or mental health of the woman; when there are serious malformations that make the fetus nonviable; and when the pregnancy is the result of a criminal act of rape, incest, unwanted artificial insemination, or unwanted implantation of a fertilized ovule. The court did not deny the fetus status; it recognized its value of life but not its unlimited right to life, holding that one can protect prenatal life only in a way that is compatible with the rights of the woman.

The court's seminal determination was that the former criminal prohibition of abortion in all circumstances violated women's fundamental rights, which are found in the 1991 Colombian Constitution, as well as international human rights law, including the rights to dignity, liberty, and free development of the individual person; health, life, bodily integrity, and reproductive autonomy; and gender equality. In establishing these rights, the 1991 Colombian Constitution was referenced, as well as several human rights documents. First, the 1994 UN International Conference on Population and Development and the 1995 UN Fourth World Conference on Women were used to establish "the basic right of all couples and individuals to decide freely and responsibly the number, spacing and timing of their children and to have the information and means to do so." According to this law, women cannot be treated as a reproductive instrument of the state. Second, the Convention on the Elimination of All Forms of Discrimination against Women (CEDAW) and the International Covenant on Civil and Political Rights both established the right to sexual nondiscrimination. The court found that criminalizing a type of health care that is exclusively applicable to women was a form of sexual discrimination. Third, the Convention on the Rights of the Child was used to uphold the child's right to health, life, bodily integrity, and reproductive autonomy. This meant that a former law punishing the performance of abortion on a woman under the age of fourteen (even with her full consent) was unconstitutional. Fourth, the court cited the Inter-American Convention on the Prevention, Punishment, and Eradication of Violence against Women to establish that sexual violence against women that results in unwanted pregnancy and the subsequent forced continuation of pregnancy are the responsibility of the state. On this view, states have an obligation to mitigate the results of sexual violence.

The court went on to determine that medical practitioners' right of conscientious objection to participation in abortion was protected by the constitution, but it stipulated that this right applied only to individuals and not entities (e.g., a hospital or the state), and that there might be a case where a doctor would have to perform an abortion (these circumstances are unclear, but presumably this would be the case if every medical practitioner conscientiously objected to abortion, thus infringing on women's rights).

The Colombian public remains sharply divided on the issue of abortion. Opinion polls suggest that the majority of Colombians do not see liberalization of abortion laws as necessary. The legacy of the Catholic Church continues to haunt Colombian politics and society. But the Colombian Constitutional Court has emerged as an effective avenue for progressive realization of the rights enshrined in the 1991 Colombian Constitution and the international human rights norms incorporated in it. Secularists and equality-seeking social activists were elated. "This is a momentous decision for the women of Colombia," said Luisa Cabal, director of the International Legal Program at the Center for Reproductive Rights. "The highest court in the land has taken a major step toward protecting women's dignity and basic human rights."[53] "Colombia's abortion law will now come closer to reflecting the realities of women's lives," said Lilian Sepúlveda, legal adviser for Latin America and the Caribbean at the center. "We are hopeful that other countries in the region—and the world—will follow Colombia's lead. In the year 2006, it is simply unacceptable that women continue to die from unsafe abortions."[54]

The court went on to make further moves in this direction. One of the effective ways in which the Catholic establishment in Latin America counters the liberalization of abortion rights is through the conscientious objection of health-care providers to terminating pregnancy, even in cases of pregnancies that are the clear result of rape, incest, or statutory rape (sex with a minor or with a mentally challenged juvenile). Individual rights are often a double-edged sword. Just as, say, a Jehovah's Witness may refuse to undergo a blood transfusion, health-care providers may invoke their individual right to freedom of religion to avoid performing lawful abortions. A case pitting precisely such claims against the right to a lawful abortion reached the Colombian Constitutional Court in 2008.

A thirteen-year-old girl was raped and became pregnant. On the basis of the requirements set by the Constitutional Court in the previously discussed 2006 ruling, she requested the procedure (through her mother) at the governmental health authority responsible for her care.[55] The first hospital declined, and she was referred successively to four further health-care facilities, each of which declined on the ground that none of its gynecologists would undertake abortion. One hospital added that no legal obligation existed because the girl's life was not at risk, even though she had attempted suicide upon the diagnosis of pregnancy and venereal infection. In February 2008 the Constitutional Court found that the young girl's fundamental constitutional rights had been violated by denial of a lawful abortion and ordered the governmental health authority to pay compensation.[56] The right to respect for conscience, the court ruled, is a human right and thus cannot be enjoyed by institutions such as hospitals. The court found that by allowing their gynecologists' conscientious objections to limit their services, hospitals were unlawfully asserting conscientious objections of their own. Hospitals whose physicians object to undertaking procedures on grounds of conscience must have, on staff or by other means, available physicians who are willing and able to provide the necessary care and to whom patients have convenient, timely access. Women denied abortion services on grounds of conscience must be referred to physicians willing and able to provide these services. Even more important, the court ruled that as a matter of principle, conscientious objection cannot be invoked with the effect of violating women's fundamental rights to lawful health care.

In June 2008 Colombia's Administrative High Court (Consejo de Estado) delivered another landmark ruling on the subject.[57] After deliberating (and withholding its ruling) for six years, the court approved the government health agency's authorization of importation and distribution of emergency contraception pills (known in North America as the "morning-after pill"). The agency's decision was challenged in court by pro-life activists who argued that the emergency contraception measures were "abortive" and violated the right to life guaranteed by the Colombian Constitution. The Colombian high court held that emergency contraception is not abortive and does not infringe the right to life. This is in line with World Health Organization guidelines, which unequivocally state that "Levonorgestrel emergency contraceptive pills have been shown to prevent ovulation and they did not have any detectable effect on the endometrium (uterine lining) or progesterone levels when given after ovulation. Emergency contraception pills are not effective once the process of implantation has begun, and will not cause abortion."[58] The decision is historic in the Latin American context because it recognizes women's rights and international state obligations, as well as the scientific advances that prove the nonabortive nature of the pill.

Similar developments have been unfolding in Mexico. In August 2008 the Supreme Court of Mexico upheld the constitutionality of one of the most lenient abortion laws in Latin America in a landmark decision that has added significance because Mexico is the second-largest Catholic country in the world. Although the Mexican Supreme Court has not been as active as its Colombian counterpart in pursuing a progressive agenda, its influence has become distinctly more significant than in the past. This is part of a broader change in the Mexican constitutional landscape that reflects the remarkable political transformation the country has undergone over the last two decades. The Mexican Constitution of 1917 is still in force. However, the far-reaching electoral reforms of the 1980s and 1990s, the 1987 and 1994 constitutional amendments that bolstered the independence of the Suprema Corte de Justicia de la Nación (Mexico's Supreme Court) and established its role as the ultimate interpreter of the Mexican Constitution, and the historic election of President Vicente Fox in 2000 after seventy-one years of Partido Revolucionario Institucional (PRI) rule have marked the demise of Mexico's authoritarian regime, or *presidencialismo,* and ushered in a new constitutional order in that country. The political liberalization prompted a more vibrant federalism and separation-of-powers modus operandi. The Mexican Supreme Court now plays a more prominent role in Mexican public and political life than it has ever played in the past.[59] And that translates, inter alia, into questioning the constitutionality of certain deeply rooted Catholic norms and values.

In April 2007 the left-leaning Legislative Assembly of Mexico City (Federal District) passed a groundbreaking law allowing doctors to terminate pregnancy through the twelfth week of pregnancy. Physicians who are morally opposed to abortion may be excused from performing the procedure. Previously, abortion was legal only in cases of rape and fetal anomaly or to preserve the health and life of the mother. The new law also requires the Ministry of Health to provide legal abortion services, free of charge, to any woman who requests them.[60] Since the law went into effect, the Ministry of Health has reported a dramatic increase in the number of women who have undergone safe, legal abortions and a clear decline in mortality due to clandestine, unsafe abortions.

The new law has sparked outcry in the predominantly Catholic country. Its constitutionality was challenged in courts by Christian and pro-life groups. Conservative Mexican president Felipe Calderón was not directly involved in the case, but his government, via the nation's Attorney General's Office and the national human rights ombudsman, challenged the Mexico City decision, arguing that health laws should not be the domain of the local assembly. The Supreme Court begged to differ. In August 2008 it upheld the law in an 8–3 ruling. "To affirm that there is an absolute constitutional protection of life in gestation would lead to the violation of the fundamental rights of women," wrote Justice Sergio Valls. In defending the Capital District's legislation, human rights such as life, safe and voluntary motherhood, and the freedom and right to decide "in a free, responsible and informed manner the number and spacing of children" (Article 4 of the Mexican Constitution) were referenced. The decision "recognizes the right of any woman to make reproductive decisions she believes are best for her. It reaffirms the responsibility the state and its institutions have to guarantee women's rights to health and life." The court cited the testimony of noted activists and professionals that had been provided to substantiate the human rights claims. Currently, in the rest of Mexico abortions in the first trimester are permitted only in certain cases, including rape or if the mother's life is in danger. Although the ruling is relevant only to the Capital District—in the full reasoning released in March 2009, the Supreme Court was clear in confining the ruling to the concrete challenged legislation and deliberately avoided any *Roe v. Wade*–like grand statements concerning the right to choose—other Mexican states could follow suit. In January 2009 the court agreed to hear a pro-abortion challenge to an amendment to the state constitution of Baja California that grants legal protection to unborn children from the moment of conception.

Unsurprisingly, the archbishop of Mexico City, Cardinal Norberto Rivera, did not endorse the ruling. In his view the nation's struggle against gang violence, kidnappers, and drug cartels is inconsistent with the court's ruling on abortion. "To me, it is a contradiction to sign an accord against violence with great fanfare while at the same time we are threatened with the violence against the most innocent, those in the wombs of their mothers, being declared constitutional," he said.[61] Human rights activists counter by arguing that the law is intended to equalize the status of women in Mexican society. Women who have resources, they argue, have the option to have abortions. Women who are poor do not. Accordingly, legalizing abortion is not a contest between pro-choice or pro-life stances but is, rather, a social justice issue. On the ground, something of a pro-life backlash seems to have taken place; many Mexican states responded to the 2008 ruling by adopting constitutional amendments stating that the right to life begins at conception. In any case the Mexican Supreme Court, however cautious and minimalist its approach to legalizing abortion has been, has positioned itself as a relative bastion of modernism amid the historic grip of Catholic norms and values in the area of women's reproductive freedoms.

Elsewhere in Latin America a similar alliance between constitutional courts and a (relatively) modernizing agenda is identifiable. The Argentine Supreme Court ruled in 2001 that inducing premature birth of an anencephalic fetus, suffering from a birth defect and doomed quickly to die, did not offend the abortion law. The fetus had no interest in prolonged gestation and would die on delivery because of its pathology, not because of any lethal act.[62] In May 2008 the Supreme Court of Brazil dismissed (6–5) a challenge to the constitutionality of Article 5 of the Law of Biosecurity, which permits stem-cell research. The court set certain conditions for stem-cell research but unanimously upheld its constitutionality.[63] The Supreme Court of Bolivia, that country's high court, issued an order in October 2008 to all lower-court judges obligating them to implement Article 266 of the Penal Code, which allows abortion to protect the life and health of women and in cases of rape and incest.[64] Furthermore, several complaints before international tribunals such as the UN Human Rights Committee have prompted attempts to introduce less restrictive abortion laws in neighboring Peru.

Granted, in several other predominantly Catholic countries the pro-life consensus is so ingrained politically that no credible constitutional challenges to antiabortion policies have been made. It is also true that not all constitutional courts in other parts of the Catholic world have been keen on supporting reproductive-freedom claims. Courts in Chile and Ecuador, to pick two examples, have been quite adamant in their refusal to liberalize various aspects of women's reproductive freedoms. The Chilean Constitutional Court—long known for its deferential, conservative standing—ruled in a recent 5–4 decision that the free distribution by the government of the so-called morning-after pill amounted to abortive medicine.[65] However, even this most conservative ruling struck down only one aspect of a government family-planning initiative that called for the free distribution of emergency contraception by government health centers to all girls and women over the age of fourteen who requested it. The court left intact sales of emergency contraception in pharmacies, which means that women who can afford the pill still have access to it.

But judged against the backdrop of pervasive conservative values and historic church dominance, moral and political, several constitutional courts in Latin America have become one of the key arenas for progressive change in this area. Because of the political context within which such constitutional struggles have been taking place, this has been a distinctly more subtle process than the European courts' strong secularist position on the issue of religious attire in the public education system.

Curbing Traditional Law in South Africa

South Africa poses a difficult test for the jurisprudential pattern described in this chapter. In regard to cultural diversity, it is one of the most accommodating jurisdictions in the world. If there is any jurisdiction in the liberal democratic universe that would accept alternative narratives of law and interpretation, it would be South Africa. Yet here we must think again. Although the South African Constitutional Court has been more sympathetic to claims of difference than most of its counterparts worldwide, even such a generous and accommodating regime can reach its limits of toleration when it encounters a challenge to its overarching reign over law's empire.

One of the main reasons that constitutional law and courts have become secularist darlings in predominantly religious polities is the embedded resentment the modern state and its laws share toward alternative sources of authority or competing systems of collective identity. Any polity bent on acting as a legitimate and representative body of its members must establish a minimal level of "ties that bind" a diverse citizenry, often through inculcating in them the basic values (however defined) that are seen as necessary for a sufficient level of communication and participation in an open, democratic polity. Thus even the most accommodating constitutional systems, those that are committed to a version of "differentiated" citizenship within the boundaries of reasonable or permissible accommodation of collective identities, are not keen on autonomous, rival adjudicative systems that derive their authority and morality from sources external and prior to, and in some cases insulated from, secular law. The writings of Max Weber, James Scott, and Pierre Bourdieu all point to different aspects of this almost organic antagonism of the modern state and its laws toward alternative schemata of meaning and authority.

In societies committed to a multicultural or differentiated conception of citizenship, accommodating religious difference under the umbrella of the rule of law and the overarching monitoring of the courts established by it—the diversity-as-inclusion category—may be acceptable or even desirable as a public measure of facilitating equal citizenship. It permits religious and other minorities, if they so wish, to "express their cultural particularity and pride without it hampering their success in the economic and political institutions of the dominant society."[66] The nonstate-law-as-competition family of claims, by contrast, is not merely about a desire not to erase previous identities or particular religious or cultural heritages, nor is it designed to ensure greater inclusion in the dominant society's institutions. Instead, religious or customary leaders relying on sacred texts or oral traditions are offering an alternative to these institutions. It is in response to this pattern of demand that a statist reaction that is often hostile and imposing is found, especially in regard to faith-based or customary orders of rules, norms, and enforcement systems that are perceived as challenging or defying the state law's ultimate authority over a given territory and its citizenry.[67]

It follows from this that we can assume that the reluctance expressed by guardians of the civil religion to grant support to alternative interpretation systems is driven, at least in part, by their interest in retaining the secular court as the primary and commanding legitimate interpreter of laws, as well as the ultimate arbiter in a legal system. Although the legal system may face difficulty digesting or "translating" calls for accommodation that fall even within the scope of diversity-as-inclusion claims (especially those that require a great degree of visibility for nonmainstream practices and beliefs in the public sphere), law is equipped with the tools to address such claims and, at times, to recognize and accept them. But when Martin Luther King Jr.'s "change-from-within" approach is replaced by a Malcolm X–like "by-all-means-necessary" threat, the legal system resists with all its force. "Surrender and comply or risk elimination" is often its answer to nonstate-law-as-competition challenges, real or manufactured.

Consider, for example, the uneasy relationship between the civil religion of constitutionalism and customary sources of law in South Africa. The challenge of customary law has haunted the new South Africa for years. Described as the "rainbow nation," it prides itself on being multiracial, diverse, and open minded, and in many respects this is true. It features one of the most progressive bodies of constitutional jurisprudence in the world in the areas of gay and lesbian rights (even involving non–South African spouses), workers' rights, and socioeconomic rights. But even here, in this haven or even heaven of (formal) constitutional inclusiveness, the boundaries of accommodation are firmly drawn and enforced on the issue of customary law. The South African Constitutional Court has consistently limited the scope and application of this once-unrecognized system of legal meaning creation. In a series of key rulings over the last decade it has emphasized that individual rights, including the right to gender equality, effectively trump African customary law under the constitution. This is not a foregone conclusion. The South African Constitution requires courts to respect cultural and religious communities and, where relevant, to apply customary law, although such law is applicable only to the degree that it is consistent with the constitution itself.[68] This delicate balancing act has been reserved primarily for the "high priests" of the civil religion in Johannesburg, although the chiefs and headmen of various customary and tribal groups, especially those in rural areas, see themselves as the authoritative voices in determining (or "revealing") the content of customary rules and practices. This combination of legal recognition of customary law and the competition over who has the final word to interpret it has provided a crucible in which tensions can brew. Add to this the fact that many of South Africa's customary traditions impose severe encumbrances on women's rights, and the rumbles of legal disputes over the limits of toleration and accommodation were soon to be heard. Several recent landmark rulings of the South African Constitutional Court provide a vivid illustration.

In a country where roughly half the black population resides in rural areas, African customary rules and practices maintain a significant degree of multiplicity and diversity.[69] They vary among the traditional groups and the different regions of the country. Despite these important distinctions, it is impossible not to notice that many customary rules and traditions are infused with gender inequality and, therefore, potentially stand in tension with the equality guarantees encoded in the Bill of Rights. As the Constitutional Court predicted in its landmark 1996 decision *Certification of the Constitution of the Republic of South Africa,* these tensions were bound to emerge. As the court put it, "[P]atriarchal principles which underlie much of indigenous law would be outlawed by the Bill of Rights, thereby undermining the core of indigenous law."[70] This is particularly true in the realms of marriage, property succession, and access to political power. Women are frequently prohibited from owning or inheriting property, and they are barred from holding traditional leadership positions. The South African Constitution, as part of its commitment to overcoming past racial hierarchies, specifically requires courts to enforce customary law wherever applicable. At the same time, the constitution enshrines individual rights and principles of equality (including gender equality) and dignity, and it declares, more generally, in its founding provisions that "the Republic of South Africa is one, sovereign, democratic state founded on the . . . values [of] non-racialism and non-sexism."[71] How to reconcile these commitments is an obvious and inevitable challenge. A woman's rights to inherit property and to own jointly accumulated property during and upon the breakdown of marriage are two major issues where these frictions have manifested themselves.

In 1998, soon after the transition to democracy, a genuine attempt was made to employ deliberative processes of law reform to generate an agreed-upon compromise between promoting gender equality and recognizing, for the first time in South African's history, customary marriages as binding in the eyes of the state.[72] This effort culminated in the passage of the Recognition of Customary Marriages Act by Parliament. Based on a model developed by the South African Law Commission, the act provides legal recognition to customary marriages that were never before recognized as lawful and attributes to them certain binding obligations. In this respect the Recognition of Customary Marriages Act pays major tribute to traditional and tribal sources of regulating the family. At the same time, the act heavily regulates the content and structure of the recognized customary marriages, injecting "the state bureaucracy into the regulation of customary marriages, first by requiring that all marriages be registered with a government agency and second by permitting divorce only when it is granted by a family court judge."[73] The act also changed significantly the balance of power between the spouses in a customary marriage. For instance, the act declares that women and men are formal equals within the marriage relationship and allows women in customary marriages the power to acquire and dispose of assets, to enter into contracts, and to litigate in their own name; these are powers and rights that they did not possess under traditional customary-family rules. The recognition of customary marriages has thus involved not only acceptance of customary marriages but also a major transformation of these institutions and the traditions they reflect. It replaced, as one scholar concisely notes, "a patriarchal view of marriage with a partnership view."[74] Although many urban dwellers and women's rights advocates celebrated this legislative reform, not everyone was pleased with it. Some saw it as suppressing minority cultures precisely by bringing them into the fold of formal state-centered legalism, in the process taking away the most precious currency that traditional leaders held under the old order: their authority as lawgivers.

The recognition of customary marriage was part of a larger reform that was envisioned by the South African Law Commission, an advisory body associated with the mandarins of the civil religion.[75] The traditional leaders initially had more success, however, in protecting their turf on another front: a bill proposed in 1998 to reform the customary laws of succession by allowing women to inherit property on the same terms as men.[76] This legal reform would have radically changed the economic, social, and gendered status quo in relation to property holding, particularly in light of the fact that most customary laws on succession in South Africa entailed a system of primogeniture that prohibited females from inheriting. The traditional leaders mobilized against the bill, arguing that it would amount to the Westernizing of African customary laws, that laws of succession were critical to the integrity of customary traditions, and that they were "fundamentally opposed to the Eurocentric approach which is prevalent in [our] country."[77] Legislators acquiesced, deciding not to introduce "drastic changes to the customary system" without considering whether "a more gradual approach might be preferable."[78] This compromise did not make the tensions encapsulated in these succession laws—between the grand constitutional commitments to respecting customary rules and at the same time promoting gender equality—wither away. Rather, they were merely postponed.

From 1997 to 2000 the *Mthembu v. Letsela* trilogy of decisions rocked the country. These early cases played out the drama surrounding customary succession laws and women's (and children's) rights.[79] The legal dispute was based on an inheritance claim made by Mthembu on behalf of her daughter, Tembi, against the estate of the deceased, Letsela. In the first *Mthembu* case the court did not directly rule on the question whether the customary rule of primogeniture was valid, instead referring the case for a ruling on whether there was a valid marriage between Mthembu and the deceased, because illegitimate children are barred from inheriting under customary law. The subsequent judgment, which was upheld in the end by the Supreme Court of Appeal, found that Mthembu's case had to fail on the ground of illegitimacy, with a judgment from the Supreme Court of Appeal calling the question of the validity of the rule of primogeniture "academic."[80] In its ruling the Supreme Court of Appeal noted that "in terms of this system of succession, whether or not Tembi is the deceased's legitimate child, being female, she does not qualify as heir to the deceased's estate. Women generally do not inherit in customary law."[81] The Supreme Court of Appeal expressed reluctance, however, to change or reform customary law, saying that this was a task best left to the legislature.

In the face of the *Mthembu* decisions, the South African Law Commission revisited the issue. The result of its investigation was a discussion paper, issued in 2000, outlining the concern that primogeniture discriminated against women and children born out of wedlock and making recommendations to amend the Intestate Succession Act that governed civil law marriages to extend its coverage to customary marriages as well. Out-of-wedlock children would also be recognized as legitimate heirs. These changes would have the advantage of complying with the requirements of the constitution and of being administratively convenient, although they did not directly confront the constitutionality of the practice of primogeniture. That issue was not fully settled until roughly a decade later, when the Constitutional Court weighed in on these charged matters.

Other branches of government did not sit idle, however. Parliament enacted the Promotion of Equality and Prevention of Unfair Discrimination Act in 2000. This act unequivocally prohibits gender discrimination in line with the constitution and South Africa's international obligations, such as CEDAW. As several commentators noted at the time, it is hard to understand this legislative intervention without accounting for the apparent ineffectiveness of court officials in "reining in" or bringing customary succession in line with the equality provisions of the Bill of Rights, as was evident in the consideration of the issue in the *Mthembu* decisions. Seen from this angle, the act is a victory for the side of secular constitutionalism in its battle against a rigid and discriminatory customary law. Others have tried to challenge the very terms of this debate, and their theoretical interventions are important in understanding how this drama unfolded. Instead of conceptualizing customary succession and gender equality in terms of a zero-sum clash, representing traditional versus Western values, authors such as Gardiol van Niekerk held that the reliance on traditional narratives in *Mthembu* and in customary-law litigation in general was itself projecting a partial view of customary traditions: it disregarded traditionally marginalized voices within these communities and imposed an artificial certainty on fluid understandings of customary rules. Thus the view from academia was that written and rule-centered customary law was itself already "Westernized."[82] It followed from this approach that the tension between customary laws and the rights of women and children could be overcome, or at least significantly mitigated, if the stories and perspectives of women and children were actually heard. This attempt to broaden the scope of what should be considered "customary law" proved significant in the eventual jurisprudence of the South African Constitutional

Court in its persistent attempt to domesticate the potential competition and disruption that customary sources of law and identity might otherwise raise in a country committed to both diversity and equality.

More specifically, scholars draw a distinction between two sources of customary law. The first consists of sources such as texts, legislation, and case law, and it is referred to as official customary law. The second is found through the stories and examples of how people actually live and is referred to as living customary law.[83] Advocates of the living tradition argue that official customary law is not, and may never have been, truly representative of the actual workings of the community. Some further argue that these interpretive debates themselves reflect intracultural struggles, as suggested in the South African context by Victoria Bronstein. Although she does not look directly at the issue of succession, Bronstein suggests that clashes between customary laws and women's rights ought not to be characterized as traditional versus Western cultural disputes but should instead be interpreted as intracultural struggles of women confronting traditionally male-dominated power structures within their own cultures and communities.[84] The appeal of this approach is that, in a struggle against paternalism in customary law, it denies the paternalism implicit in "Westernizing" solutions. Moreover, the intracultural-conflict approach characterizes customary law as living and thus makes room for adaptation to the values enshrined in the new South African Constitution.[85] This permits response to the nonstate-law-as-competition claim by effectively disarming its alternative claim for authority and authenticity, bringing it instead within the diversity-as-inclusion fold.

With this background in mind, let us now consider the position taken by the country's highest court. In *Bhe* the South African Constitutional Court heard a constitutional challenge to the rule of male primogeniture as it applies in the customary law of succession.[86] The two minor daughters of Ms. Nontupheko Bhe and her deceased partner argued that the customary-law rule of male primogeniture unfairly discriminated against them in that it prevented the children from inheriting the estate of their late father. Not mincing words, Deputy Chief Justice Langa, writing the majority decision, held that the African customary-law rule of male primogeniture discriminated unfairly against women and illegitimate children and was, therefore, unconstitutional and invalid. Although ordinarily it would be desirable for courts to develop new rules of African customary succession to reflect the living customary law (as opposed to ossified, official customary law) and bring customary law in line with the constitution, that remedy was not seen as feasible in this matter, given that the rule of male primogeniture is fundamental to customary law and ostensibly irreplaceable on a case-by-case basis. The South African Constitutional Court in *Bhe,* therefore, issued a call for Parliament to reconcile through legislation the role of customary law under the new constitution, with its emphasis on fairness, justice, dignity, and equity. The fate of the "competitor" worldview, namely, customary law (as interpreted by traditional leaders), was now placed squarely in the hands of the different branches of the state. This time around, the legislature acted swiftly, passing a law that unified the administration of estates.[87]

This development did not conclude the saga of forcefully responding to the nonstate-law-as-competition challenge; it only set the stage for the next battle, which erupted in the sphere of succession to traditional offices, most prominently chieftainship. In 2008 the Constitutional Court dealt another blow to official customary law by declaring the patrilineal custom of chieftainship unjustifiably discriminatory and therefore unconstitutional.[88] This fascinating case concerned a dispute between Ms. Shilubana and Mr. Nwamitwa over the right to succeed Mr. Nwamitwa's father, Richard Nwamitwa, as hosi (chief) of the Valoyi traditional community in Limpopo. In 1968 Ms. Shilubana's father, Hosi Fofoza Nwamitwa, died without a male heir. Because customary law at the time did not permit a woman to become hosi, Ms. Shilubana did not succeed him as hosi although she was his eldest child. Hosi Fofoza Nwamitwa was instead succeeded by his brother, Richard Nwamitwa. During 1996 and 1997 the traditional authorities of the Valoyi community passed resolutions deciding that Ms. Shilubana would succeed Hosi Richard because, in the new constitutional era, women were equal to men. Her succession was approved by the provincial government. However, following the death of Hosi Richard in 2001, Mr. Nwamitwa interdicted Ms. Shilubana's installation and challenged her succession, claiming that the tribal authorities had acted unlawfully and that he, as Hosi Richard's eldest son, was entitled to succeed his father. Two lower-court rulings supported his claim before the case ultimately reached the Constitutional Court.

Justice Van der Westhuizen, writing for a unanimous court, held that the High Court and the Supreme Court of Appeal failed to acknowledge the power of the traditional authorities to develop and reform customary law, here drawing on the living-customary-law approach. Although courts must consider the past practice of the community, they are also required to respect the right of traditional communities to develop their own law. Courts must also balance the need for flexibility and the imperative to facilitate development against the value of legal certainty and respect for vested rights. As the Constitutional Court stated, "Past practice will . . . not be decisive where the *Constitution* requires the development of the customary law in line with constitutional values."[89] Relevant factors for this balancing test include the nature of the law in question, in particular the implications of the change on constitutional and other legal rights, the process by which the alleged change occurred or is occurring, and the vulnerability of parties affected by the law. Applying this test, the court found that succession to the leadership of the Valoyi had operated in the past according to the principle of male primogeniture. However, the traditional authorities had the authority to develop customary law, and they had done so in furtherance of the constitutional right to equality. The value of recognizing the development by a traditional community of its own law in accordance with the constitution was not outweighed by the need for legal certainty.

On balance, a living-customary-law approach (here understood as customary law that agrees to comply with the constitution) trumps the patrilineal-succession custom, and such a "change from within" of customary law is, from the civil religion's perspective, to be applauded. So, forty years after Ms. Shilubana's father died without a male heir, his daughter was declared eligible to succeed him as hosi. In reaching this decision, the justices of the Constitutional Court were clearly aided by the fact that change had already occurred within and by act of the relevant community (or part thereof). This led the court to pronounce that

> customary law is living and will in the future inevitably be interpreted, applied and, when necessary, amended or developed by the community itself or by the courts. This will be done in view of existing customs and traditions . . . and of course, the demands of the *Constitution* as the supreme law.[90]

With this vision of partnership in interpretation, the specter of nonstate-law-as-competition as challenging the authority of the civil religion was mitigated, if not altogether eliminated. It should come as no surprise that not all were equally satisfied with this result. In response to the press applauding the court's decision, members of Parliament supporting the "official" interpretation of customary law declared that African political leaders were protecting their "own traditions and customs and [were] opposed to their suppression by Westernized norms such as equality."[91] In any case, having provided endorsement of those interpretations of customary law that incorporate general principles of constitutional law with respect to succession of property and succession of tribal leadership, the court swiftly moved on to tackle a third head of customary law: the division of property jointly accumulated during marriage upon its dissolution.

Elizabeth Gumede entered into a customary marriage in 1968. The marriage broke down irretrievably, and in January 2003 her husband instituted formal divorce proceedings. Mrs. Gumede was not employed during the marriage and instead maintained the family household, as well as the four children. The family acquired two pieces of immovable property during the course of the marriage. The Customary Marriage Recognition Act provides that a customary marriage concluded after the commencement of that act (in 2000) is automatically viewed as splitting any jointly acquired property between spouses. The act does not, however, provide for this property regime in respect of customary marriages concluded before the commencement of the act, and those marriages are consequently governed by customary law. Customary law in KwaZulu Natal has been codified in the KwaZulu Act and the Natal Code, both of which provide that the husband is the family head and owner of all family property. The result of the KwaZulu Act, the Natal Code, and the lack of provision in the Recognition Act is therefore that a wife in a customary marriage concluded before the commencement of the act will, in effect, be entitled to nothing upon dissolution of the marriage. Mrs. Gumede challenged the constitutionality of these arrangements in *Gumede v. President of the Republic of South Africa.*[92]

Deputy Chief Justice Moseneke, writing for a unanimous court, found these impugned provisions to be self-evidently discriminatory on at least one listed ground—that of gender.[93] Only women in a customary marriage are subject to these unequal proprietary consequences. Because this is discrimination on a listed ground, it is presumed to be unfair, and the burden fell on the respondents to justify the limitation on the equality right of women engaged in marriages concluded under customary law before the act. Moseneke found that the respondents had failed to provide adequate justification for this unfair discrimination. He held that a section of the Recognition Act that gives a court granting a decree of divorce of a customary marriage the power to order how the assets of the customary marriage should be divided between the parties is no answer to or justification for the unfair discrimination based on the listed ground of gender. That section, the court argued, does not cure the discrimination that a spouse in a customary marriage has to endure during the course of the marriage. The patrimonial proprietary system of customary law during the subsistence of a marriage, as codified in the Natal Code and the KwaZulu Act, "patently limits the equality dictates of our Constitution and of the Recognition Act."

The unanimous court thus confirmed the order of constitutional invalidity issued by the High Court and held that all discriminatory federal and provincial laws that maintain unequal ownership of property between married spouses, during or upon termination of marriage, must be struck down, regardless of whether the couple entered customary marriage before or after the adoption of the Recognition Act. With that decision the whole concept of "family head" was put to rest. In the clash here between customary law as male privileging and the equality rights of women and children, the court has clearly sided with the latter. The triumph of general state law, most notably constitutional law, over the legacy of customary law as a competing normative order with values that stand in tension with those encoded in the civil religion has been completed. The result is not that customary law no longer exists or is derecognized; rather, it has been made palatable to the statist order, transformed, as it were, into a more moderate diversity-as-inclusion mechanism of governing difference by disarming a potential challenge to both the supremacy of the secular legal authority and the clout held by the high priests of constitutionalism.

Canada: Emerging Boundaries of Religious Accommodation

A few words are warranted about equivalent developments in Canada, considered one of the most accommodating national jurisdictions on earth in the areas of religion and, indeed, cultural diversity more broadly. Unlike the French understanding of secular citizenship *(laïcité)* or the United States' "melting-pot" approach, Canada adheres to a multicultural or differentiated citizenship model (or the "mosaic" metaphor), whereby ethnic, religious, or linguistic differences are, in principle, not seen as a threat to citizenship or nationhood. (Quebec adheres to a more explicitly secularist model.) This is reflected in Canadian public discourse and in Canada's official policy of multiculturalism, as well as in the Charter of Rights and Freedoms, adopted in 1982.[94] Section 2 of the Charter protects freedom of religion, Sections 16 to 23 protect language and minority language education rights, and Section 27 states that the Charter "shall be interpreted in a manner consistent with the preservation and enhancement of the multicultural heritage of Canadians."

Over the years the Supreme Court of Canada has developed a rich jurisprudence in support of state-endorsed multiculturalism and generous accommodation of cultural and religious difference in the public sphere.[95] It issued landmark free-exercise rulings concerning Sunday closing (e.g., *R. v. Big M Drug Mart,* 1985; *R. v. Edwards,* 1986) alongside controversial rulings concerning continuation of public funding for Roman Catholic schools in Ontario (e.g., *Adler v. Ontario,* 1996). In two rulings over the last few years, for example, the court went out of its way to generously address faith-based claims falling squarely within the parameters of multicultural citizenship as advancing a vision of diversity as inclusion. In *Amselem*, a case involving Orthodox Montreal Jews who erected sukkahs on their balconies in a residential condominium, partly in contravention of a boilerplate tenancy contract, the majority advocated tolerating a practice where the individual sincerely feels that it is connected to religion, regardless of whether the practice is required by a religious authority.[96] In *Multani* the court used a Section 1 analysis to overturn a Quebec school board's decision not to allow a Sikh student to carry the *kirpan* (a ceremonial dagger) because of potential safety hazards and an apparent conflict with the school's prohibition on weapons and dangerous objects.[97] Indeed, the very categorization of the *kirpan*—as either a prohibited weapon in a schoolyard (as the school board claimed) or as an important religious symbol (the position of the student, his parents, and the interveners on behalf of the Sikh community)—was at the heart of this legal dispute. A decision to ban the kirpan universally, the court ruled, was not the least drastic means to address the rather limited potential of harm, especially when one weighed the sincerity of the student's religious beliefs and the fact that the interference (the ban on the kirpan) was not trivial. The court thus held in favor of Gurjab Singh Multani, providing a resounding statement of the diversity-as-inclusion theme of differentiated citizenship:

> The argument that the wearing of kirpans should be prohibited because the kirpan is a symbol of violence and because it sends the message that using force is necessary to assert rights and resolve conflict must fail. Not only is this assertion contradicted by the evidence regarding the symbolic nature of the kirpan, it is also disrespectful to believers in the Sikh religion and does not take into account Canadian values based on multiculturalism.[98]

But even Canada's multicultural policy, arguably the most accommodating constitutional regime presently on offer, has been obliged to set boundaries. In clashes of religion and culture, arguments that move beyond requests for accommodation (or specific exemption from general laws) to attempts to advance alternative, extrajudicial moral or adjudicative orders appear to fall beyond the limits of tolerance. This is the dividing line where diversity as inclusion ends and nonstate law as competition emerges, the latter often bringing with it the wrath of the state. Unlike the many diversity-as-inclusion cases requesting reasonable accommodation under the rule of law (as these terms are interpreted by the courts or legislatures of the secular state), arguments that pursue the claim that faith-based sources of authority and obligation are, or ought to be, completely unregulated and parallel or superior to the general rule of law are typically answered with ironclad resistance.

Early in the charter era the Supreme Court ruled in *R. v. Jones* that an Alberta pastor in a fundamentalist church could not educate his three children in a church's basement without having any accreditation or approved home-schooling curriculum, as required by the relevant secular legislation.[99] In this case the Alberta Schools Act required all parents to send their children to a public school unless the parent could show that the children were going to an accredited private school or the government had approved the home-school curriculum. Jones was charged with truancy under the Schools Act. In response, he challenged the very authority of general law over the matter, arguing that the rule requiring government approval to educate his children involved "his acknowledging that the government, rather than God, has the final authority over the education of his children" and so contravened his right to freedom of religion under Section 2(a) and his right to have control over how his children were educated, which was protected under Section 7 ("life, liberty and security of the person"). Writing for the majority, Justice La Forest dismissed the religion-based challenge to state authority and held that there was a compelling state interest in requiring accreditation. The certification procedure was in no way manifestly unfair or contrary to any principles of fundamental justice. While the province must reasonably accommodate religious belief in accordance with charter principles, no extraconstitutional source of authority of the kind Jones argued for existed (in the eyes of the state). The court therefore bluntly rejected Jones's assertion that he should not be forced to apply for exemption or certification from the government because, as he saw it, the authority to attend to his children's education came from God, making it sinful for him to request the state's permission to do God's will. Thus the jurisprudential tone was set at the outset of the charter era to accept claims for accommodation that fit the diversity-as-inclusion mold but reject claims for alternative authority or inapplicability of the constitutional law or state regulatory powers, or those falling in the nonstate-law-as-competition category.

In its recent decision in *Alberta v. Hutterian Brethren of Wilson Colony,*[100] the Supreme Court of Canada maintained its antiexemption approach when it upheld the constitutionality of an Alberta provincial regulation requiring that anyone with a provincial driver's license hold a license containing the driver's photograph. The Wilson Colony of Hutterian Brethren maintains a rural, communal lifestyle. Its members sincerely believe that the Second Commandment prohibits them from having their photograph willingly taken and thus objected to having their photographs taken on religious grounds. In a 4–3 decision the court accepted the province's claim and upheld the photograph requirement. The regulation's stated objective of enhancing the security or integrity of the driver's licensing scheme by requiring that an individual photograph appear on the license card and be kept in a provincial government data bank was deemed more important by the majority than the faith-based quest for exemption. Justice Abella's detailed dissenting opinion questioned the potential harm of the requested exemption to the integrity of Alberta's driver's license system. However, a cynic might argue that the shadow of a potential request by face-covering niqab or burka wearers to be exempt from full-face photographs on identification documents played a role in the court's ruling.

In American constitutional jurisprudence *Wisconsin v. Yoder* (1972) stands out as a landmark case of expansive accommodation that exempted members of the Old Amish community who reached the age of fourteen from two additional years of schooling that would have otherwise been mandated by the state's compulsory-education law.[101] As Austin Sarat and Roger Berkowitz observe, the Burger Court's proaccommodation ruling in this case can be partly explained by the fact that the Amish were not perceived as "disorderly" or threatening the social order.[102] If anything, the Court's ruling evokes a nostalgic vision of an agrarian, self-sufficient community that preserves American values of the early Republic that have long since been lost in mainstream society. In this chapter's terminology, the Court stretched the diversity-as-inclusion category to fit the facts of this case, thus rescuing it from the nonstate-law-as-competition framework.

With this background in mind, consider the acrimonious controversy that erupted in 2003 in Ontario following a proposal emanating from some members of the province's large and diverse Muslim community to use the provincial Arbitration Act of 1991 to establish Shari'a-based arbitration tribunals in personal-status matters.[103] This proposal did not come to the fore in the usual legislative process, nor did it originate from a governmental initiative or law-reform process. Instead, a small and relatively conservative nongovernmental organization, the Canadian Society of Muslims, declared in a series of press releases its intention to establish a "private Islamic Court of Justice," or Shari'a tribunal, as this proposal came to be known in the ensuing debate.[104] The envisioned tribunal, according to its proponents, would have permitted consenting parties to rely on the then-existing Arbitration Act not only to enter a less adversarial, out-of-court dispute-resolution process but also to use the act's choice-of-law provisions to apply religious norms to the resolution of family disputes, according to the "laws *(fiqh)* of any [Islamic] school, e.g. Shiah or Sunni (Hanafi, Shafi'i, Hambali, or Maliki)."[105] The tribunal's advocates further argued that once the possibility to turn to binding Shari'a arbitration became readily available, it should represent a clear choice for Muslim Canadians: governance of oneself by the personal law of religion or governance by secular Canadian family law. This construction of the proposal had the effect of presenting it as a frontal nonstate-law-as-competition challenge that even tolerant, multicultural Ontario (the most populous Canadian province and arguably the country's most influential common-law jurisdiction) could not accept with indifference.

A major controversy soon erupted. Opponents argued that a religious tribunal of this kind would set a dangerous precedent by allowing different communities to carve out certain aspects of the law and to insulate themselves from the purview of charter provisions and other basic norms of statutory and administrative law. Establishing such enclaves of unregulated "islands of privatized jurisdiction" would be detrimental to the universality of the rule of law in Canada. Feminist activists and grassroots organizations, such as the Canadian Council of Muslim Women, further emphasized that such tribunals would put an undue burden on Muslim women who, for fear of being ostracized or otherwise sanctioned, would be coerced by the community to consent to such Shari'a-based arbitration processes. Others expressed the concern that these tribunals would fall prey to intracommunity politics or would be dominated by community "big men." As tensions mounted, the debate over the proposed faith-based tribunal became highly politicized and polarized. It was in this climate that Ontario premier Dalton McGuinty decided to terminate the debate by publicly announcing that no religious or faith-based arbitration in Ontario was to be based on the province's Arbitration Act. The concept of alternative dispute resolution (ADR) was thus deemed potentially effective in reducing the burden on the court system. However, it was not meant to carve out enclaves of religious jurisdiction operating outside the purview of the general rule of law.

The clearest statement of this governmental position was expressed by the attorney general, the highest civil official in Ontario authorized to develop and enforce the tenets of the civil religion. Upon revealing the proposed legislation that amended the Arbitration Act, the attorney general stated that "[a]ll family law arbitrations in Ontario will be conducted using only *Canadian* law." The answer to the nonstate-law-as-competition challenge, then, was to declare officially and legislate accordingly that "resolutions based on other laws and principles—including religious principles—would have no legal effect and would amount to advice only." This change took effect in 2006 and was further elaborated with regulations issued in 2007. Bringing the point home, the attorney general reaffirmed that only those charged with securing the implementation of the civil religion have a claim to speak authoritatively on behalf of the governed, stating forcefully that "[t]here is one family law for all Ontarians and that is Canadian law."[106] Any other sources of normativity and authority, including religious principles, are relegated to the realm of "unofficial," "unrecognized," and, indeed, "nonlaw" status.

Arguably, the debate provoked by the tribunal proposal was whether this ought to remain the status quo or whether alternative, nonstatist (in this example, religious) principles should gain a degree of authority in regulating certain aspects of family-law disputes among voluntarily consenting adults. Without a doubt, concerns about potential coercion and duress, as well as deeply ingrained gendered power inequities, were well considered in this context.[107] However, it is difficult to explain the austere and unequivocal response of the government to the Shari'a tribunal proposal solely in terms of a commitment to promoting women's rights, especially given that Canadian (federal and provincial) family laws still permit a great degree of flexibility to spouses who wish to opt out of the statutory default rules of equitable division, potentially leaving women with far less than an equitable division.[108] The specter of witnessing the creation of a reality in which not all law is state law or is administered exclusively by its approved members of the bar or the judiciary seemed to have played a major role, too, in this clampdown.

The government, in short, decided to respond to the Shari'a tribunal challenge by ultimately barring the operation of any faith-based family arbitration process. Such a universal ban ensures that Islam is not singled out as being more (or less) friendly to women's interests than any other religious or customary tradition. It further aims to realign the regulation of the family exclusively within the state, leaving no room (except for informal religious mediation, which has no legal effect in the eyes of civil courts or legislatures) for communities' own institutions and authorities to exercise any formal role in defining the parties' marriage and divorce status. In effect, this resolution draws a high and formidable wall of separation between state and religion. It also reasserts in unambiguous terms the lexical priority of the former over the latter.

Another example of the renewed emphasis on enforcing secular provisions against expressions of pious resistance to the ground rules established by the civil religion is found in the landmark decision in *Bruker v. Marcovitz,* in which the high priests of constitutionalism rejected the idea that noncompliance with a contractual obligation becomes immune to judicial review or intervention merely by virtue of claiming religious freedom as the motivation for such noncompliance.[109] In the *Marcovitz* case a Jewish husband made a contractual commitment to remove barriers to religious remarriage in a negotiated settlement reached with the consent of the parties and after consultation with independent legal counsel. That agreement was incorporated into the final divorce decree between the parties *(decree nisi);* indeed, its provisions became part of the terms that enabled the civil divorce to be finalized by the relevant state authority.[110] Once the husband had the secular divorce in hand, however, he failed to honor the agreement, claiming that he had undertaken a moral rather than legal obligation.

The Supreme Court of Canada, unlike its counterpart in South Africa in the *Gumede* case, refused to enter the fray of exploring competing interpretations of the religious obligation at issue. What remained undisputed between the parties was that unless the husband granted a Jewish divorce decree *(get)* to his wife, she could not be released from that religious marriage because the secular divorce did not terminate or affect that relationship. Mr. Marcovitz's refusal to remove the religious barriers to remarriage thus left Ms. Bruker in the situation known as the *agunah* or "chained wife"; despite being civilly divorced, the woman is unable to remarry or have children who are recognized as members of the faith community. The Supreme Court recognized the gendered harms caused to Ms. Bruker by Mr. Marcovitz's refusal to deliver the *get,* but it was not in a position to order specific performance (e.g., directing the husband to turn to a Jewish *beth din*, a religious law tribunal). Instead, the judgment imposed monetary damages on the husband for the breach of the contractual promise in ways that harmed the wife personally and affected the public interest generally. This decision was made despite the ex-husband's claims that no secular authority had the power or right to enforce damages for breach of contract in this context because his promise to remove the religious barriers was moral, not legal, and, as such, was a protected religious freedom. The court, in a majority opinion penned by Madam Justice Rosalie Abella, rejected this claim. It held, instead, that it was fully within the court's jurisdiction to "[r]ecognize the enforceability by *civil* courts of agreements to discourage *religious* barriers to remarriage, addressing the gender discrimination those barriers may represent and alleviate the effects they may have on extracting unfair concessions in a civil divorce."[111] The key to understanding this decision is found in its opening paragraphs, which conform squarely to the distinction between accepting diversity as inclusion and treating nonstate law as competition as a potential threat that must be curtailed, contained, and regulated. Justice Abella wrote:

> Canada rightly prides itself on its evolutionary tolerance for diversity and pluralism. This journey has included a growing appreciation for multiculturalism, including the recognition that ethnic, religious or cultural differences will be acknowledged and respected. Endorsed in legal instruments ranging from the statutory protections found in human rights codes to their constitutional enshrinement in the *Canadian Charter of Rights and Freedoms,* the right to *integrate into* Canada's mainstream based on and notwithstanding these differences has become a defining part of our national character.[112]

This is a classic manifestation of Canada's now-canonical policy favoring diversity as inclusion, which is more religion-accommodating than most of its European counterparts. Immediately following this declaration, in the subsequent paragraph, the court quickly set limits to its celebrated commitment to tolerance. These restrictions were erected precisely in response to challenges in which differences were seen as failing to accept or submit to the overarching authority of the secular state and the core values enshrined in its civil religion:

> The right to have differences protected, however, does not mean that those differences are always hegemonic. Not all differences are compatible with Canada's fundamental values and, accordingly, not all barriers to their expression are arbitrary. Determining when the assertion of a right based on difference must yield to a more pressing public interest is a complex, nuanced, fact-specific exercise that defies bright-line application. It is, at the same time, a delicate necessity for protecting the evolutionary integrity of both multiculturalism and public confidence in its importance.[113]

The final decision, then, on how to articulate this "delicate necessity" is not reserved for those claiming exemption or immunity from general laws through raising the nonstate-law-as-competition challenge. Instead, the state's high priests retain the crucial designation as the ultimate arbiters in conflicts between the tenets of the civil religion and its competitors. "In this manner, the issue was decided," as Raymond Carver piercingly observed in the closing line of his short story "Popular Mechanics," referring there to a more blatantly violent confrontation.

So the bottom line is this. Although the law is not necessarily as "jurispathic" as Robert Cover assumed many years ago[114]—we have seen throughout this chapter that courts and legislatures prefer to extend olive branches of various kinds to nonstate, alternative, and potentially competing systems of orthodoxy—the high priests of constitutionalism have not hesitated, when encountering what they have perceived as unruly challenges to their own standing as supreme and ultimate lawgivers, to expel their competitors to the no-man's-land of legal exile. Those who do not comply with the constitutional religion's metanarrative come to encounter the outer limits of law's accommodation—and it is a cold place to reside on this side of the new wall of separation.

Conclusion

In a manner similar to its resurgence in Asia, Africa, and the Middle East, religion has made a comeback in North America, Europe, and the Indian subcontinent and continues to be a major force in Latin America. But whereas the vast and elaborate body of disestablishment jurisprudence in the United States is widely documented, relatively little attention has been given to the secularizing role of courts in these other parts of the world.

Much like their counterparts in countries where there is no formal separation of religion and state, constitutional courts in these regions have been grappling with the challenge of secularist and modernist aspirations versus considerable popular support for religion and religious values.

European courts have dealt with the challenge of religious attire in the public education system either by deferring to local authorities' judgments (which often favor a restrictive, uniform approach to dress code in public schools), or by subjecting religious practices to overarching constitutional norms. Whereas manifestations of religious difference in the open public sphere may be accommodated, the public education system is funded by the state and is filled with captive-audience situations. Manifestations of religious difference are thus better kept out of it. In accordance with France's historic *laïcité,* French courts have gone even further to conclude that for the purposes of determining entitlement to naturalization, consistent wearing of religious attire in the open public sphere may serve as an indicator of dissimilation and "non-Frenchness." Courts in several Latin American countries and in Mexico, meanwhile, have used rights-granting provisions, domestic and international, to introduce new norms of women's reproductive freedoms in a continent that has long been a major stronghold of the Catholic Church, and where the long shadow of religious morality still lingers over many privacy and personal-status aspects of the law.

In the last two parts of this chapter I identified two different interpretations of what tolerance and accommodation require in grappling with the challenges of diversity: "diversity as inclusion" and "nonstate law as competition." The focus in these parts has been on courts and legislatures in accommodation-friendly societies that now find themselves embroiled in the search for responses to the postsecularist spread of alternative (here, religious and customary) sources of law and meaning. While accepting the mantra of diversity as inclusion, the high priests of constitutionalism appear to vehemently oppose the nonstate-law-as-competition narrative, at least in part because it challenges the very authority and superiority they hold on account of the secular order. Although they operate in different contexts, the South African Constitutional Court and the Supreme Court of Canada seem to have made every effort to subject traditional law to general principles of constitutional law. By so doing, they have erected a new wall of separation that places noncompliance with the values of the civil religion beyond the pale of accepted accommodation, offering to those who espouse alternative legal domains the potential either to bring them under the general rule of (constitutional) law or to encounter the wrath of state fiat.

The reason for judicial antipathy toward alternative sources of law or interpretive hierarchies is as simple as it is powerful: what is perceived to be at stake here is nothing less than the very authority and source of legitimacy of the accepted civil religion. When courts and legislatures in secular societies are faced with nonstate-law-as-competition claims, they may loudly manifest their commitment to respecting tolerance, balancing rights, protecting the vulnerable, ensuring proportionality, and other important values. However, they may nevertheless interpret the situation as reflecting a more fundamental power struggle between competing systems of knowledge and interpretation: the earthly, human-enacted constitution and the claim to speak in a vernacular of a revealed or divine authority. When faced with this kind of challenge, even the most generous and evenhanded officials of the state are structurally not in a position to rule from a "point of view from nowhere." Instead, as stakeholders in the civil religion, they may feel obliged to take action to restore the superiority of its sources of legitimacy, rules of engagement, methods, and style of reasoning that are state driven and entrenched in the secular constitution precisely when the very foundations of the legal and social order they protect and adhere to are (or are perceived to be) at stake. This is a narrower claim than stating that any type of engagement between law and religion in the West is inevitably tainted by the cultural dominance of liberalism and secularism.

What all the examples discussed here, drawn from recent constitutional jurisprudence of "developed" or "developing" world countries—be they democratic, authoritarian, or anywhere in between—seem to share is embedded judicial sympathy for modernist, religion-light visions of society over traditional, customary, or religion-driven visions. Their considerable differences notwithstanding, constitutional courts in Europe, parts of Latin America, South Africa, and Canada all sense a need to limit the spread and impact of traditional law or religious practices and to keep it in constitutional check. The courts are all committed to their constitutions' modernist tilt, uniform application, individual rights and formal equality provisions, and, above all, overarching authority. As we saw in Chapter 4, this impulse is shared with courts in polities where religion has become a major political force.

This surprisingly unified constitutional front raises a particular irony. Given the dominant conceptualization of rights as mainly negative liberties, the capacity of constitutional rights jurisprudence to advance progressive notions of distributive justice into arenas that require collective action or wider state intervention and redistribution of resources (e.g., basic housing, health care, education, employment, and welfare) is quite limited. But that very conceptualization of rights appears to serve as an effective tool in support of secularist efforts to contain and limit the impact of religiosity. In fact, the same aspect of canonical rights discourse that has limited it when it comes to introducing real change in areas that require larger government and organized collective action makes it a major asset in limiting religion. So whereas the prevalent conceptualization of rights as negative liberties, and more generally the vision of constitutional law as limiting government, may not be appealing to Keynesians, Marxists, or those concerned with issues of distributive or global justice, it has been a rather effective tool for advancing a secularist agenda and secularizing solutions against the backdrop of anti- or nonsecularism.

CHAPTER SIX

Yin and Yang?

Constitutional Law and Religion Law

CONSTITUTIONALISM and religion are often depicted as diametrically opposed to each other, the former reflecting the people's rule, the latter, the rule of God. Whereas constitutions are said to be part of a modernist, secularist narrative, religion is portrayed as premodern, often irrational, and based on beliefs, not facts. And while constitutionalism is said to be a power-defusing and freedom-enhancing enterprise, religion is often hierarchical and restricting. Commonly hailed as an all-out good thing, which in many respects it truly is, constitutionalism has become a natural companion of democracy and of the modern state, whereas religion throughout much of the West has been "relegated" or "confined" to the private sphere. The emergence of constitutional theocracy provides a unique setting for engaging in a closer inspection of the many similarities, not differences, between constitutional law and religion law, each with its own sacred texts, interpretive hierarchies, apolitical self-portrayal, and, yes, earthly interests.

In this chapter I explore some of the conceptual parallels and affinities between constitutional law and religion law. The discussion centers on four main axes of similarity: (1) constitutions and sacred texts as apolitical symbols; (2) the trade-off between interpretation and amendment in constitutional and religious law; (3) the conceptual affinity and sociopolitical parallels between support for "originalist," "purposive," and "living-tree" interpretive schools in constitutional and in sacred law; and (4) the political economy of interpretive change in both domains. This last aspect provides a platform for identifying possible less-than-reverent interests involved in intra- and interfaith rifts, as well as in the secularism-versus-religiosity strife more generally. The combination of constitutionalism and theocracy is clearly not an organic, natural love match. However, the similarities between constitutional law and religion law may suggest that constitutionalism and religion often fail to get along well with each other not because they are so different—although in many respects they no doubt are—but because they are so similar, each with its own constitutive texts, elevated moral aspirations, interpretive institutions, and, at times, less-than-reverent motivations.

Constitution and Religion as Apolitical Symbols

One of the striking parallels between constitutional law and religion law is the apolitical image they share. With remarkable similarity to the perception of law as an autonomous, apolitical, morality-driven, principled domain—the idea of natural law is only one example—religion, religious institutions, and religious interpretation have by and large managed to escape the dictum "everything is political" that drives political science inquiries. Likewise, these institutions have also generally been spared the scrutiny of "economic analysis" theories that view individuals and institutions as predominantly self-interested actors who seek to extend the ambit of their influence or enhance their relative position, material or symbolic, and who are capable of making profit-maximizing or risk-averse cost-benefit judgments toward those ends. In fact, we would be hard pressed to find another domain so central to many aspects of our lives that has been as sheltered from political or economic questioning of its motives as religion. Just as the enterprise of constitutional law thrives on the distinction between law and politics, so does the enterprise of religion.

As we have seen in earlier chapters, constitutional law and courts have emerged as important secularizing agents in predominantly religious polities. In virtually all these settings the jurisprudential domain has been infused with worldviews and interests from the larger political context within which constitutional courts operate. Religion, by contrast, is often portrayed as a sphere of dedicated learning and worship that reflects true faith, deep convictions, and an elevated moral calling that differ from everyday life's hardships, profanity, and calculated behavior. Studies of religion are all too often caught up in that view of religion as a predominantly principled or spiritual domain, largely insulated from concrete strategic political or economic considerations. Such studies tend to focus on either the demand side of religion (e.g., the anthropology or psychology of faith and worshipping) or the theological or moral aspects of religious doctrine and teachings. Such types of scholarship capture key aspects of faith and spirituality per se, but they seldom address the political and economic motivators that have influenced the religious domain and its actors. Established religions are arguably among the most influential and wealthiest organizations on earth, with complex institutional structures and motives. They are embroiled in internal and external power struggles, have vested interests, and strive to maintain their status and standing vis-à-vis the state, as well as their worshippers' loyalty in a competitive marketplace of religious ideas and institutions.

As is the case with religion, there has been a persistent resistance within legal academia and in popular culture more generally to the notion that law operates not only as a semiautonomous professional universe with its own rules and rationales but also as a site of social struggle and political strife. As the seminal works of Robert McCloskey, Robert Dahl, and Martin Shapiro (among others) established, constitutional courts and their jurisprudence—to pick only one aspect of the constitutional order—are integral elements of a larger political setting and cannot be understood in isolation.[1] Taking the notion of courts as political institutions even further, recent social science scholarship suggests that judicial review is often politically constructed, and that elected officials may have political and policy reasons for pursuing constitutionalization and judicial empowerment. This emerging body of literature attempts to go beyond the traditional focus on constitutionalization as emanating from polities' commitment to a "thick" notion of democracy to identify broad demand-side pressures to establish judicial review (e.g., the prevalence of rights ideology and discourse), alongside specific supply-side factors that are conducive to the establishment and maintenance of constitutional review, most notably the changing interests and incentives of pertinent political stakeholders. Unlike most social scientists, however, popular accounts of constitutional law and courts continue to resist the notion that law is a species of politics and that courts are a part of the political system, not a thing apart. This doctrinal separation of law and politics, or at least the sense that there is distinctly more law than politics in constitutional law (perhaps the most observably political branch of law), continues to hold among many scholars of constitutional law. Even those who are critical of judicial "hyperactivism," whether on the right or on the left, focus their criticism on judicial imperialism and how courts single-handedly extend their powers, usurp authority, and so on. Few have given due consideration to the actual political conditions and incentives that are conducive to the expansion of judicial power.

Despite the legacy of legal realists and critical legal scholars, there is still an embedded reluctance to treat law as a dependent variable that often reflects powerful ideologies, hegemonic interests, and strategic choices. With a few notable exceptions, too many constitutional law professors continue to ignore pertinent political science literature that points to political, not juridical, sources of judicial entanglement with pure politics. While legal analyses of court rulings are countless, only a small handful of articles published in America's leading law reviews every year pay attention to the critical institutional and political conditions within which constitutional courts operate and judicial review is exercised. In fact, political sociology and economy, power relations, and strategic choices have always been a rather peripheral component of mainstream constitutional law studies, comparative or not.

The closer law gets to acquiring a sacred status—the idea of natural law and the near-numinous status of the Constitution as America's "civic religion" are only two examples—the more apolitical it apparently gets. Although natural law is not a religious doctrine in the sense that it does not adhere to any deity or text, it does advocate a notion of law that stems from elevated moral commitments toward humans qua humans, whether those commitments are prescribed by formal law or not. Whereas for the natural-law advocate, ordinary laws may be "political" or driven by profane considerations, natural law is an elevated, godly-like set of guidelines for moral behavior. Who or what is to determine what norms belong to that set of elevated guidelines is not entirely clear. Consequently, the idea of natural law has been embraced by certain religions, most notably the Catholic Church. In 1993 Pope John Paul II, for example, suggested that salvation to nonbelievers may be open through conformity with the moral requirements of natural law.[2]

The apoliticization, indeed, the near sanctity, of religion-like law does not stop here. The constitutions of many nations carry important symbolic weight. Broad aspirations, moral obligations, and foundational principles—for example, Iran's commitment to Islamism and Turkey's commitment to secularism—are often stated in dramatic fashion in a preamble or opening declaration. In other constitutions—Germany's Basic Law is a good example—principles of human dignity serve as an inviolable *Grundnorm*. In still other countries—think of the postapartheid South African Constitution—the entire constitutional order and the new institutions it created are celebrated as the new face of the nation. The debate over the possible inclusion of Europe's Christian heritage in the preamble of the European constitution as opposed to a more universalist outlook has marred the constitutionalization process for years. It is hard not to see the strong symbolic, foundational religion-like motifs embedded in such constitutional visions.

Arguably the clearest illustration of the near-sacred status of the constitution is evident in the United States. In an article published over half a century ago, Max Lerner pointed to the high symbolic status of constitutions and courts, not their output, as a main pillar of their existence.[3] Lerner further described the Constitution as America's "totem and its fetish." "In fact," wrote Lerner, "the very habits of mind begotten by an authoritarian Bible and a religion of submission to higher power have been carried over to an authoritarian Constitution and a philosophy of submission to 'higher law'; and a country like America, in which its early tradition had prohibited a state church, ends by getting a state church after all, although in a secular form."[4] Noted scholar of Christian thought Jaroslav Pelikan suggests that "with the reduction in the private authority of the Christian Scripture, and especially in its public authority, American Scripture has been called upon to fill some of the gap."[5]

As Sanford Levinson astutely observes, the American Constitution is the nation's most revered text and has evolved into a pillar of American "civil religion."[6] This civil religion enjoys a near-sacred position, just like divine religions at their zenith. It has its own rituals, symbols, interpretive discourses, sources of authority, and even a shrine (the Supreme Court) and a rank of "high priests" (the Supreme Court justices). The status of the American Constitution has given a near-numinous appearance to the American act of foundation itself.[7] In fact, "for the past two hundred years," notes another incisive observer, "the Constitution has been as central to American political culture as the New Testament was to medieval Europe. Just as Milton believed that 'all wisdom is enfolded' within the pages of the Bible, all good Americans, from the National Rifle Association to the ACLU, have believed no less of this singular document."[8] An accompanying "myth of rights" has evolved that contrasts the openness of judicial proceedings with the secret bargaining of interest groups in the political sphere so as to underscore the integrity and incorruptibility of the judicial process.[9]

Judgments such as *Brown v. Board of Education* (1954) have been widely celebrated as having had a profound impact on American politics and society and, indeed, as true revelations of poetic justice and high morality. No matter how politically motivated or ideologically tilted less dazzling U.S. Supreme Court rulings have been, the Court and its judges continue to enjoy levels of legitimacy and trust that are second only to those of high priests. Less than a year after its controversial ruling in *Bush v. Gore* (2000), to pick one example, public support for the Supreme Court as a forum of principle in American politics soared back to roughly the same high level as before the ruling. Biographies of judges or media analyses of Supreme Court rulings are a common genre and popular read. Lawyers and legal academia, aided by popular culture's depiction of the Constitution and the Court as near-priestly institutions, complement an overblown and idolizing interpretive community. And the public, like believers anywhere else, often follows and buys into the spectacle.

The combination of parochialism and religion-like apoliticism is equally problematic in the comparative study of religion itself, which for many years has been preoccupied either with the theological aspects of religion, the taxonomy or the genealogy of world religions, or with the social functions of religion and the psychology of faith. Like the somewhat anachronistic classifications in comparative law of different "legal traditions," "family trees for legal systems," and the like, early taxonomies of religion classified religions as "Abrahamic religions" (Christianity, Judaism, Islam) and "other religions" (e.g., pagan, polytheist, heathens). In the late nineteenth and early twentieth centuries a new, apparently more inclusive or pluralistic classification of "world religions" took shape. It included Buddhism, Hinduism, Confucianism, Taoism, and Shinto and often Zoroastrianism, Jainism, and Sikhism. Some scholars suggest that this transformation presents a transition from nineteenth-century Christian supremacy to present-day liberal theology.[10]

In any case, nondoctrinal factors (e.g., politics or economics) have been left largely outside the purview of canonical comparative religion investigations, just as they have been left out of most comparative constitutional law accounts. Although each sphere may have its distinct language, institutions, constitutive texts, and symbolic authorities, ultimately, constitutional law and religion do not belong to distinct, apolitical domains.

The Trade-off between Amendment and Interpretation

The similarity between these two major symbol systems goes well beyond their apolitical image. Interpretation matters a great deal in constitutional law, and examples of this are plentiful. Consider the following illustration, not commonly known but effective. Section 7 of the Canadian Charter of Rights and Freedoms reads: "Everyone has the right to life, liberty and security of the person and the right not to be deprived thereof except in accordance with the principles of fundamental justice." Section 21 of the Constitution of India reads: "No person shall be deprived of his life or personal liberty except according to procedure established by law." Despite the nearly identical wording of these provisions, interpretations of them have taken two very different paths with respect to the constitutional protection of subsistence rights. Such rights are appreciated in Canadian public discourse but have consistently been considered beyond the purview of Section 7 by the Supreme Court of Canada.[11] India, by contrast, features vast socioeconomic gaps, but its Supreme Court has consistently declared claims for subsistence social rights justiciable and enforceable through constitutional litigation that draws on Section 21.[12]

The significance of interpretation intensifies as the ability to change constitutional texts via amendment decreases. Unlike nature, where Darwinism seems to reign, Lamarckism often makes for a better constitutional design.[13] Whereas Darwin's theory of evolution emphasizes the value of natural selection and random mutations in overcoming exogenous shocks (species that lack these beneficial features become extinct), Lamarck's theory of the inheritance of acquired characteristics suggests that learned experience may be incorporated and transformed into organic features. Flexible and reflexive designs with effective, built-in self-adjustment and auto-learning mechanisms work better and tend to have a longer lifespan than rigid designs that lack such adaptation mechanisms. Most constitutions address the issue of change without replacing the constitutional order itself. This is achieved by including self-adjustment mechanisms such as amending formulas and, at times, designated residual powers to fill newly created lacunae, or a "living-constitution" interpretive approach. The amending procedures of some constitutions (e.g., that of the United States) are distinctly rigid and thus quite ineffective in allowing for self-adjustment. Amending formulas elsewhere (e.g., Germany) are more flexible, thereby allowing for adjustments while still entrenching the basic rules of the political game. As the example of the United States illustrates, the overrigidity of constitutions may lead to fierce debates concerning interpretive approaches and practice as interpretation, not amendment, becomes the main constitutional adjustment mechanism.

While constitutions are written to last, they vary considerably in terms of their endurance. Some constitutions are relatively long lived. In addition to the U.S. Constitution, Norway's constitution was adopted in 1814; it is the second oldest constitution currently in existence. Sweden's 1809 constitution was replaced in 1974 at the age of 165. The 1874 constitution of Switzerland was replaced by a new one in 1999, at the age of 125. The life expectancy of other constitutions is quite short. In their empirical study of the lifespan of constitutions worldwide, Elkins, Ginsburg, and Melton report that only half of all constitutions last more than nine years, with an overall average of below twenty years.[14] Thus, the average citizen outside of North America, they report, should expect to see his or her country cycle through four constitutions in one's lifetime. Even an above average endurance of a given constitutional order may not necessarily reflect a nirvana-like ideational harmony as much as it may reflect path-dependence factors as well as the constellations of power that are conducive to its endurance and able to block calls for change.

However difficult it is to amend a venerable constitution that has acquired a "larger than life" status, sacred texts, such as the Bible, are obviously much harder, indeed impossible, to amend once they have acquired their sacred status. (Replacing sacred texts with others and adding new sources to the corpus of sacred texts are options that are seldom used.) Therefore, doctrinal adjustments via interpretation seem even more crucial to religion than they are to constitutional law. It is hardly surprising that fierce interpretive struggles have come to dominate the translation of sacred directives into practical guidelines for private and public life. In fact, one could argue that a main reason that the domain of religion has seen so many internal interpretive wars over the centuries is precisely that sacred texts may be relatively easy to interpret or distort but are impossible to amend.

Taken as a whole, sacred texts are often more complex and thus more difficult to interpret than most constitutional texts. But when one looks to these texts for guidance on a concrete predicament, both types of texts pose serious challenges to their interpreters.[15] Interpretive problems include whether the text dictates absolute or flexible contemporary community standards; whether interpretation could or should be based on textual analysis and the text's intrinsic logic, or perhaps on primary sources and extratextual supplements; whether it should prioritize the original meanings or the current social consensus on what the words mean; whether interpreters should follow doctrinal precedents, opt for consequentialist pragmatism, or perhaps follow some other value judgment concerning justice or social policy; and the question of which interpretive entity possesses the authority to provide the definitive interpretation of the text. The conclusive answers to the above predicaments are only a few examples of the recurrent challenges in the interpretation of constitutional or sacred texts. At the most basic level, interpretation of each of these texts, religious or constitutional, shares adherence to that text's ultimate "*grundnorm*"—its supremacy, conceptual, moral, and political—over any other source of authority. The Constitution for avid constitutionalists is what the Bible is for Judeo-Christian religionists. The two domains thus are filled with existential struggles concerning extratextual interpretive methods, drawn from philosophy, probability, or the social sciences.

Reliance on favorable interpretive methods and approaches to advance certain worldviews, ideologies, or interests has certainly not been confined to constitutionalists in their battle to confine religion. Religious interpreters throughout history, much like some of today's philosopher-king judges, often relied on discerning, result-driven readings of sacred texts to advance their worldviews and preferences, principled or strategic. The entire domain of religious law, one could argue, is the most spectacular example of the living-tree approach to interpretation. In any case, there are striking parallels, largely, alas, underexplored and undertheorized, between the theory and practice of interpretation of sacred and constitutional texts.

Like most constitutional provisions, the wording of religious imperatives is almost always open ended and subject to various interpretations. Driven by a survival instinct to remain relevant and to increase their base, or at least avoid losing followers, as well as by the genuine need to find plausible solutions to widening gaps between traditional interpretations and changing realities, framers and interpreters of religious law have long taken into account social and economic factors, not merely principled theological discourse. The history of religious interpretation is filled with examples of such internal adjustment and adaptation to exogenous changes.

Jewish law, in particular, has been conducive to ingenuity and change driven by social and economic need. In fact, it has evolved mainly through a living-tree—"a tree of life," as the Book of Proverbs puts it—approach to interpretation. The best interpretive minds throughout the last two thousand years—Maimonides is only one pertinent example—spent most of their intellectual energies debating possible changes to the law in response to variance among communities in geographic conditions or to changing social and economic conditions. The Talmud, Mishnah, and other Halakhic literature feature rich legal casuistry aimed at demonstrating how given interpretations and practices that reflect social change or economic necessity are not, in fact, in opposition to pertinent laws, despite appearances to the contrary.

As noted Jewish law scholar Menachem Elon observes, there is interdependence between Halakha's ritual commandments and its civil aspects. As Halakha has crystallized, it has recognized the "essential and fundamental distinction between *issura* [ritual law] and *mamona* [civil or 'nonreligious' law], the latter generally corresponding to most of what is included in the *corpus juris* of contemporary legal systems. This basic distinction offered greater flexibility and an extraordinary potential for development to the civil part of Halakha, that part which is most affected by, and subject to, changes in economic and social life."[16] Another distinction was added by the Talmud between biblical commandments or Halakhic requirements that are biblically mandated (*mitzvot d'oraita,* Aramaic for "directives by an ultimate authority" or "commandments of the Law") and rabbinic injunctions (*mitzvot d'rabbanan,* Aramaic for "directives by our rabbis"). An enormous mass of materials, hundreds of thousands of legal opinions and responses covering all areas of Jewish law, came into being "against the background of, and as a result of, the application of Jewish law to practical, day-to-day life."[17] Furthermore, the areas of law that preoccupied the Jewish community and its leadership were those in which significant social and economic change occurred. "The Halakhic authorities and the lay leadership were required to respond to these changes and supply new solutions."[18]

Although domestic circumstances are far from a Montesquieu-like all-encompassing explanation of variance among legal systems as deriving from various environmental and material factors, they do seem to play a role here. Even though it is normally forbidden for a Jew to instruct a non-Jew to work on the Sabbath, Jewish communities in very cold climates (e.g., Poland and Russia) permitted the practice of asking a non-Jew to heat their homes on the Sabbath. Likewise, the daily afternoon prayer and the evening prayer were combined into one afternoon praying session in Jewish communities in northern Germany because during wintertime darkness fell in the early afternoon hours, and attendance at separate evening prayer was minimal. And while Maimonides, who lived in Muslim Spain, ruled that a married woman who failed to carry out her wifely duties might be physically chastised by a Jewish court, Jewish communities in Christian Europe were horrified at the thought.[19]

Countless other interpretive innovations came into being in the same way. One of the International Monetary Fund's mantras is that a precondition for economic development is the existence of predictable laws governing the marketplace and a legal regime that protects capital formation and ensures property rights. Some two thousand years ago Hillel the Elder, a famous Jewish religious leader and scholar who lived in Jerusalem during the politically tumultuous time of King Herod the Great, introduced the revolutionary *pruzbul,* an institution that, in spite of the Jewish law concerning cancellation of debts in the sabbatical year, ensured the repayment of loans. The motive for this institution was the "repair of the world" *(tikun olam)*; that is, of the social and economic order, because this legal innovation protected both the creditor against the loss of his property and the needy against being refused loans of money for fear of loss. In a similar fashion more ingenuity ensued: the ceremonial sale to a non-Jew of *chametz* (bread, grains, and other leavened products) before Passover; the legal fiction of *eruv chatzerot*—"mixed ownership of courtyards/domains"—which applies on the Jewish

Sabbath only and designates an entire area as its residents' common "home" so that Jews who observe the traditional rules concerning Shabbat may carry children and belongings anywhere within the jointly held property without transgressing the prohibition against carrying a burden across a property line on the Jewish Sabbath; or, in modern times, the invention of the Shabbat elevator *(ma'alit shel Shabbat)*—an elevator that is programmed to go up and down and stop at all the floors by itself so that it can be used without violating the rules of the Jewish Sabbath.[20]

Jewish law is by no means unique here. Shari'a, for example, renders impermissible the idea and practice of usury or charging interest *(riba)*. This is based on a moral objection to "unjust enrichment" or moneymaking without actual work. It is also meant to discourage borrowing, which is feared to be addictive and irresponsible. The classical approach to *riba* involves a definition of it as any increase over the nominal value of the sum lent. In the religious schools of interpretation this view is the most popular and, as such, acts as a considerable force on governments attempting to Islamize their state, or at least to bring their banking practices into accordance with the tenets of Islam. An Islamic government that followed the classical approach would have to rid its banking practices of interest in any form. However, economic exchange without interest-yielding credit is quite limited. In premodern times this gave birth to the "double sell"—a practice whereby a loan is awarded alongside the transfer of another object to the borrower, with the agreement that the nominal value of the loan plus a grossly inflated price for the accompanying object (de facto interest) will be paid back to the lender.

In modern times a flexible, pragmatic, form-over-substance approach to Islamic banking has been developed, with countless innovations to formally circumvent the prohibition on *riba*.[21] Several major banks in the Muslim world have even developed an array of Islamic banking products and employ clerics whose job it is to approve the compliance of such products with pertinent religious directives. Some modern interpreters have suggested that whereas interest would be prohibited in an ideal world, the use of it as a temporary measure promotes the greater good and may be justified on necessity grounds. Some even argue that money and interest are modern concepts outside the scope of the *riba* prohibition, and that interest on moneylending is therefore permissible.

In any case, a survey of current banking laws and practices in the Islamic world reveals that there is significant variance in adherence to, and implementation of, classical Islam-based restrictions on banking and financing practices.[22] Some of the variance may be explained by historical contingencies or differences in religious doctrine and interpretation, but some of it may also emanate from differences in the political significance of various industries or powerful economic and political stakeholders. One could speculate that the greater the significance of oil and other mineral production to a given country's economy, the greater the likelihood that a more lenient approach to Islamic banking will be adopted. This is because international trade in such natural resources relies on financing and is characterized by a significant time lag between sale and the actual provision of commodities. It is little wonder, then, that in countries such as Saudi Arabia, Iran, and Dubai the approach to *riba* and *gharar* (sale of probable commodities whose provision or even existence is not certain) is distinctly more pragmatic than in Sudan, which is not a major player in the global natural resources market.

While interpretive "adjustments" of that kind are quite common, textual "amendments" in religion law are rare. Intentional changes do exist in what we now know as the New Testament. For fifteen hundred years Jesus' words and Saint Paul's writings were hand-copied by scribes who were deeply influenced by the cultural, theological, and political controversies of their day.[23] Jewish prayers in seventeenth-century Europe were changed to include reference to the self-proclaimed Messiah, Shabbetai Tsvi ("Bless our Lord and King, the holy and righteous Shabbetai Tsvi, the Messiah of the God of Jacob").[24] Tsvi's picture was printed together with that of King David in most of the prayer books, as were his kabbalistic formulas and penances. As mentioned earlier in Chapter 2, Muhammad Ahmad (the Mahdi) modified Islam's five pillars to support the dogma that loyalty to him was essential to true belief, and added the declaration "and Muhammad Ahmad is the Mahdi of God and the representative of His Prophet" to the recitation of the creed (*shahada*). The establishment of the Anglican Church as a direct result of Henry VIII's personal circumstances is an extreme example of a seismic shift. However, these inventions are not only exotic but also rare exceptions to the rule. Interpretation, not de- or reconstruction, has dominated religion law throughout the ages.

The bottom line seems to be this: because amendment is a near impossibility, interpretation is an essential element of religion law, just as it has been a key element of viable constitutional law. In both domains there seems to be a trade-off between amendment procedures and interpretation; the more rigid the former are, the greater the significance of the latter, and vice versa. Because the Constitution of the United States is very difficult to amend, constitutional interpretation has become a highly charged arena. This is all the more true with respect to sacred texts that may not be amended and so may remain relevant only through interpretation. It is partly for this reason that the history of religion law is filled with fierce interpretive wars alongside incredible interpretive ingenuity aimed at mitigating the gap between ancient verses and present-day realities.

"Originalism" and "Living Tree" in Constitutional and Religion Law

Another important but often-overlooked similarity between constitutional and religious interpretation is the conceptual affinity between "originalist" interpretive approaches in the two domains. "Originalists" in both religious and constitutional enterprises take the text to reflect the authentic and inerrant word of the pertinent authority and thereby ignore the inevitable fluidity of interpretive practice. The text, they argue, has the ultimate authority by virtue of being original—the actual words of the source that brought it into being. It should be read as a reference to the views of those who drafted it, not as an invitation to subsequent interpreters to make their own judgments about the ideals reflected in the text. The original-intent interpretive principle is seemingly more purist and authentic than any other interpretive practice; the interpreter is regarded as a guardian of faith whose task is to convey the original textual meaning to future generations. Manifestations of originalism in the Judaic tradition of interpreting religious directives are rare—two exceptions are the ancient Sadducees and the "textualist" or "literalist" Kara'ites (a small religious movement that emerged in the ninth century whose adherents resent rabbinic Judaism's emphasis on oral law and tradition and enshrine the written Hebrew Bible [Torah, Nevi'im, K'tuvim, Hebrew acronym *Tanach*] alone as the constitutive religious authority). After the destruction of the Second Temple in Jerusalem (70 C.E.), Rabbinic Judaism turned almost exclusively to normative, evolving, living-tree Judaism based on the Torah and its many written and oral interpretations throughout the centuries.

A possible explanation for the thin originalist tradition in Jewish law as opposed to other major religions may be the "Diaspora thesis" which postulates that because Jews were stateless for two millennia and spread across Europe and northern Africa, adaptive law and flexible interpretation were necessary to sustain religion. Flexible interpretation emerged triumphant over more rigid schools of interpretation in the centuries immediately after the Roman destruction of the Second Temple and the end of the last formal independent Jewish political entity until 1948. Interestingly, emphasis on flexible or "purposive" interpretation has emerged in the theology of several other historically stateless and at times persecuted religious groups whose members were spread across many countries, such as the Ismaili Muslims.

In contrast, fundamentalist approaches to interpreting the New Testament are quite common in North American Christianity. Likewise, the Salafist (or Wahhabist) movement in Islam insists that only the Prophet himself and the two generations that followed should be relied on for spiritual guidance. Other somewhat less rigid but distinctly orthodox interpretive schools exist within virtually all of the world's religions. Unlike the religious domain, originalism or textualism in constitutional interpretation does exist but is distinctly less common beyond the United States. At any rate, all these manifestations of originalist voices take a doctrinal position that genuinely differentiates them from other interpretive approaches. At the same time, these differences are steeped in politics and may not be fully understood in isolation from it.

To begin with, virtually all these originalist voices, whether of the textualist or original intent camp, claim to have a monopoly over the authentic reading of the original text, the meaning of it, and the original intentions of its framers; "nonoriginalist" interpretive schools, they argue, have drifted away from the authentic meaning of that text, thereby inevitably reflecting extratextual influences (how a contemporary interpretation of an old text may be free of such exogenous influences remains unclear, and is a contested issue). Fundamentalist sects in various contexts (e.g., "Torah-true" Naturei Karta Jews, hard-core Christian Reconstructionists, or the Shining Path radical Maoist guerillas in Peru) believe that their cause has grave, even near-cosmic importance. Fundamentalists in all these contexts, some admittedly more than others, see themselves as protecting not only a distinctive doctrine but also a vital principle and a way of life and of salvation. Some prefer to remain insular in their purist beliefs. Other see their raison d'être in proactively advancing their cause against the grain of a hostile, loosely defined "system" or "outer world." They are, by and large, critical of the moral "contamination" in the wider culture. They tend to dismiss relativism and advance instead a rigid set of worldviews and beliefs based on unbending dichotomies of good and bad, pure and corrupt, right and wrong, and just and unjust, which are simplistic by definition. Alternative interpretations of the constitutive texts are viewed as unauthentic, theologically diluted, interest driven, and often overinfused with considerations that are external to the faith's sovereign virtue.

Textualists often claim that doctrines said to be orally revealed and passed on are likely "to be invented by the priests, rabbis, *qadis*, or judges who claim to be transmitting them; to admit oral tradition as a separate source is to grant additional power to its institutional guardians and transmitters."[25]

Fundamentalist schools therefore erect a conceptual "wall of virtue" that protects their identity not only against other religions but also against what they deem irrelevant, nominal, contaminated, and even threatening versions of their own faith or cause. All share common ground in their sharp inward-outward distinction, whereby a limited number of texts, interpreters, and interpretive methods are sacred, as opposed to all other possible sources or interpretations that are external, acontextual, misguided, and interest driven rather than principled. Reference to such sources borders on the sinful.

More important, the divide along interpretive lines is often closely tied to struggles along core-versus-periphery sociopolitical lines. In these prototypical rifts between strict and flexible interpretations, one camp occupies the center—political, cultural, and often geographic—whereas proponents of the rival camp occupy the periphery, physically and symbolically, and use doctrinal disagreements to challenge the other camp's canonical position. In virtually all interpretive contexts originalist (either literalist/textualist or original-intent) approaches emerged as an alternative or an opposition to what its advocates perceive as an inauthentic but all-too-common interpretation. Although the debate is disguised as being purely interpretive, it reflects a struggle for political and cultural hegemony.

A fascinating but seldom-discussed illustration is the political context of the fierce interpretive war between the priestly Sadducees, who adhered to the written Torah as the only binding source, and the Pharisees, contenders in and later winners of this class struggle, who advanced a more flexible mix of primary texts and secondary texts, as well as an oral tradition.[26] It took place in the politically charged context of the Hasmonean Kingdom (Hebrew: Hashmonayim) (circa 164 B.C.E. to circa 63 B.C.E.) that formed an autonomous Jewish state in ancient Israel, the last such state until 1948. The Hasmonean dynasty originated from a successful revolt against Antiochus IV Epiphanes of the Hellenistic Seleucid Empire (which stretched over much of the Near East or Greek Syria) by the Maccabees (Hebrew: Makabim), a Jewish national liberation movement led by a rural Jewish priest from Modi'in, Mattathias the Hasmonean. The weakening of the Seleucid Empire led Antiochus to adopt an aggressive Hellenizing (or de-Judaizing), "back-to-our-roots"-like campaign. A decree forbidding Jewish religious practice sparked the revolt, with Mattathias refusing to worship the Greek gods. When the edict for his arrest was issued, he took refuge in the wilderness of Judea with his five sons and called on all Jews to follow him. "Everyone who has zeal for the law and maintains the testament, let him follow me!" was Mattathias's famous call, and many followed. The revolt resulted in Jewish independence in

Judea, four hundred years after the destruction of the First Temple. The Jewish holiday of Chanukah celebrates these events.

For the first few decades of its existence, the Hasmonean state was governed skillfully by John Hyrcanus (Hebrew: Yochanan Horcanus), with lively theological debates but few political splits emerging among the Second Temple priests. When Hyrcanus died in 104 B.C.E., political divisions emerged. Hyrcanus's elder son, Aristobulus I, and later his younger son, Alexander Jannaeus, began to draw on the Sadducees to justify their claim to power. During the pre-Hasmonean period having a Zadokite lineage became a requirement for priesthood. (Zadok was one of the two priests in King David's court who had the authority to anoint Solomon, son of David, as king). Since the Hasmoneans did not themselves belong to the Zadokite priestly line they were not, strictly speaking, entitled to hold the pontificate or high priest office. A search for a priestly pedigree was thus in the Hasmoneans' political interest, at least until their legitimate claim for the high priest office could be established. To address this need, they instituted a new priestly line (the Sadducees) and promoted stories about the Sadducees' ancestral ties to the high priest Zadok. This brought about the good life for the Sadducees. They lived in splendor, which was justified by their belief that there was neither an afterlife nor a resurrection of the dead. The Pharisees, who believed in an afterlife, were looked down on as people who led a hard life on earth and yet would have nothing in the world to come. The Pharisees' belief in the resurrection of the dead led to their following of a moral call for hard work during real life so as to secure a better afterlife. The Sadducees' dismissal of the idea of a future world stemmed from their belief that one need not serve his master for the sake of compensation but for the sake true commitment and call of duty. This socioeconomic stratification galvanized the Pharisees, whose more lenient interpretive approach now became associated with the less noble priestly families. When they came to power, the Hasmoneans ousted the pre-Hasmonean high priestly leadership, who some scholars believe were the real descendants of the "legitimate" Zadokite lineage. These ousted priests are believed to have formed their own sect (the Essenes), and were possibly related to the Qumran Dead Sea Scrolls community.[27] The Essenes bitterly opposed the newly established Sadducee-led lineage of high priests of the Temple.

When Jannaeus died (76 B.C.E.), his widow Salome Alexandra (Hebrew: Shelomtzion) rose to power, now supported by the Pharisees, who had previously opposed the Hasmonean rulers. Alexandra, who was keenly religious and led a "farewell to wars, back to the Torah" campaign, managed to secure assent to a Hasmonean monarchy from the Pharisees, who in return now became not only a tolerated section of the community but actually the ruling class. According to Josephus Flavius's *The Jewish War*, the Pharisees became quite powerful during Alexandra's reign and managed to manipulate her to bolster their status. "Although she [Alexandra] governed others, the Pharisees actually governed her."[28] Thus the Alexandra-Pharisee pact was a strategic win-win one. Alexandra installed as high priest her eldest son, Hyrcanus II, a strong Pharisee ally. The Sanhedrin, the institution responsible for the administration of justice and religious matters in the kingdom, was reorganized according to Pharisee wishes. Up to that point this body had been a house of lords, the members of which belonged to the Sadducee aristocracy. Its reorganization turned the Sanhedrin into a more demographically representative body, the guidance of which was placed in the hands of the Pharisees. But when Salome Alexandra died in 67 B.C.E., Aristobulus II, the son of the pro-Sadducean Alexander Jannaeus, began to contest Hyrcanus II's claim to the throne. To do so more forcefully, Aristobulus II adopted his father's Sadducean stance and received the old priestly nobility's assent to repel Hyrcanus II, whom he eventually managed to oust. "What does theology have to do with it?" one might ask. Not much. Greed and politics, by contrast, were clearly the main culprits of these ostensibly doctrinal splits.

The sociopolitical context of the Sadducee/Pharisee rivalry was also reflected in some of the interpretive positions taken by these groups with respect to concrete biblical injunctions. One telling example is highlighted by Aharon Shemesh, a noted scholar of Second Temple Judaism.[29] The "law of the fourth year fruits" (Leviticus 19: 23-25) warrants that the fruits of any newly planted trees may not be eaten by the tree owner for the first three years, and that the fourth year fruits "shall be holy for giving praise unto the Lord." From the fifth year onward the owner may eat the fruits. An interpretive dispute arose as to the exact meaning of the holy use of fourth year fruits. It is hardly surprising that the priestly sect adopted the interpretation that fourth year fruits should be assigned exclusively to the priests, whereas the Pharisees adhered to the view that the fourth year fruits belong to their owners, as long as some of the fruits' monetary value is designated for sacramental purposes or is to be spent in Jerusalem (where the Second Temple was located). In a largely agrarian society, the question of whether the fruits belong to the priests or may be enjoyed by the farmers as long as some sacramental use is maintained had very significant material implications. Only a few decades later, toward the end of the Second Temple era, when the Mishna, the core of the Jewish oral tradition, was written, it was the interpretive debate between the strict Shammai and the more lenient Hillel—two prominent rabbis, each with a large school of followers—that formed the basis of much Jewish theological discussion. Over the years the term "House of Shammai" has become associated with convoluted or strict interpretation of the Torah directives, whereas the "House of Hillel" has come to represent care for the simple or more relaxed interpretation of these directives, emphasizing substantive essence and true meaning over forms and rules. Most famously, their debate is remembered through Hillel's immortal words in response to a non-Jew's request to be taught the entire Torah while the teacher was standing on one foot: "That which is hateful to you, do not do to your fellow. That is the entire Torah; the rest is commentary. Go and learn." Nicely said.

Although much philosophical and theological weight has been attributed to this and other deep moral teachings of Hillel, and more generally to the interpretive debate between the lenient and more humanist Hillel and the stricter and more formalist Shammai, it could very well be the case that the political sociology of the time, and to some extent a quest for greater following, played a role in this supposedly purely theological debate. Both schools of interpretation accepted the basic interpretive tenets of the Pharisee school. However, there were also considerable differences between the schools. Whereas the Shammai school was followed mainly by the patrician party (the upper class), the Hillel school represented mainly the plebeians (the lower classes, outsiders, and the less educated), displeased by the exclusionary, elitist tone of the patrician circles. All this came on the heels of the political and interpretive clash discussed earlier between the aristocratic, originalist Sadducees and the more flexible Pharisees. This also took place in the politically charged context of the Hasmonean Kingdom, the dwindling of Hellenic dominance in the region, and later the struggle between the Hasmonean dynasty and King Herod the Great, a Roman client-ruler who advanced a mishmash of Judaic and Roman culture. As part of this struggle, Herod tried his second wife Mariamne I, a woman born of the rival Hasmonean dynasty, for adultery and then executed her. He later laid charges of high treason before a Roman court in Berytos (Beirut) against his own children Alexandros and Aristobulos IV. They were found guilty; the Roman emperor Augustus approved the verdicts, and the two were executed. Herod later executed his eldest son (Antipater, his only child by his first wife Doris), who was accused of conspiring against the ailing Herod and his influential sister Salome. Lest we forget, Christianity was born at that very same time, commonly associated with the birth and tumultuous life of Jesus of Nazareth, who is said to have opposed much of the Pharisee theology of his time, and who is believed to have revolted against the Roman-influenced, Caiaphas-led Second Temple. Could it be the case that the interpretive debate between the

House of Hillel and the House of Shammai was purely doctrinal and completely insulated from all this political turmoil, captured so vividly by Josephus's *The Jewish War?* I doubt it.

Two millennia later, intrachurch rifts and debates over "original" meaning and "tainted" interpretations remain as political as ever. In 1948 the Coptic and Ethiopian churches reached an agreement, negotiated with the active participation of Emperor Haile Selassie, that led to autocephaly for the Ethiopian Church. In 1959 Pope Cyril VI of Alexandria crowned Abune Basilios as the first patriarch of Ethiopia. With the fall of Emperor Haile Selassie in 1974, the Ethiopian Orthodox Tewahedo Church was disestablished as the state church, and its patriarch was later executed by the new Marxist government. Two government-friendly patriarchs were enthroned in 1979 and in 1988. After the fall of the Derg regime in 1991, the church elected a new patriarch, Abune Paulos, who, unlike his two predecessors, was recognized by the Coptic Orthodox pope of Alexandria. The former patriarch, Abune Merkorios, whose main support base is in the city of Gondar, then fled abroad and announced from exile that his abdication had been made under duress and that he was thus still the legitimate patriarch of Ethiopia. Several bishops also went into exile and formed a breakaway alternate synod. This exiled synod is recognized by some Ethiopian churches in North America and Europe that recognize Patriarch Abune Merkorios, in part because of Gondar-based local patriotism, while the synod inside Ethiopia continues to uphold the legitimacy of Patriarch Abune Paulos. To add another twist to this less-than-heavenly political story, after Eritrea fought for and won its independence from Ethiopia, the Coptic Orthodox Church granted autocephaly to the Eritrean Orthodox Tewahedo Church with the reluctant approval of its mother synod, the Ethiopian Orthodox Tewahedo Church. Indeed, everything is political, certainly with regard to the Ethiopian Orthodox Church of the last three decades.

A similarly political split is evident in Ukraine, where three doctrinal camps purport to represent the Ukrainian Orthodox Church: The Ukrainian Autocephalous Orthodox Church established in the 1920s, following Ukraine's independence; the Ukrainian Orthodox Church-Moscow Patriarchate (followed mainly by pro-Russia Ukrainians centered in eastern Ukraine); and the Ukrainian Orthodox Church-Kyiv Patriarchate, a 1989 splinter from the Moscow Patriarchate that is followed mainly in western Ukraine where pro-West and anti-Russian impulses are prevalent. The latter church remains unrecognized by other canonical Eastern Orthodox churches, and its head of church was excommunicated by the Council of Bishops of the Russian Orthodox Church in 1997. The political affiliation of each of these streams correlates neatly with the pro-Russian versus pro-West political rift in Ukrainian society.

Another vivid illustration of such intrareligious rifts and their surprising similarity to interpretive debates in modern constitutionalism is provided by the current division within the Anglican Church. Although the foundational issues in this split concern the role of gays in the church, a division between strict versus liberal interpretation of the Bible also informs this conflict and provides new battlegrounds. In addition, the split has been characterized as one between the global South and the global North, with the leadership traditionally coming from the latter camp, although the majority of church followers now come from the former. The leader of the global South in this debate is Peter Akinola, the Anglican primate of the Church of Nigeria since 2000. Although Akinola uses ideology (a literal interpretation of the Bible) to support his position, he also characterizes the Church of England as attempting to maintain its colonial-era powers over worshippers worldwide. With the majority of worshippers of the Anglican faith residing in the global South, Akinola seeks to upset this dominance of the Church of England, as well as that of the Episcopal Church in the United States and the Anglican Church in Canada. His most frequent tactic is to question the "liberal" practices of those churches he criticizes. Since 2004 the split between the conservative and liberal branches of the Anglican Church worldwide has widened. The tension between the conservatives and liberals has been displayed in a variety of statements issued by both sides. The conservatives, for instance, issued a statement to the Archbishop of Canterbury in 2005, criticizing Dr. Rowan Williams for his "moral laxity" on issues like homosexuality. A few months later the Church of Nigeria's canon law was revised to reflect a shift from communion with the Archbishop of Canterbury to communion based on the authority of the scripture and historic doctrinal statements.[30]

A variant of these culture wars also manifests itself in the current debate in the U.S. Supreme Court and in American legal academia more generally about reference to foreign constitutional case law and principles. Constitutional courts worldwide increasingly rely on comparative constitutional law to frame and articulate their own position on a given constitutional question. This phenomenon has been termed "borrowing" or, more elegantly, "the migration of constitutional ideas." It is particularly evident with respect to constitutional rights jurisprudence. Even the U.S. Supreme Court, perhaps the last bastion of parochialism among the world's leading constitutional courts, has hesitantly joined the comparative reference trend. In two notable cases, *Lawrence v. Texas* (2003) and *Roper v. Simmons* (2005), the Court's majority opinion cited foreign judgments in support of its decision.[31] This has led to a vigorous debate between proponents and critics of the practice over the appropriateness and legitimacy of the U.S. Supreme Court's reliance on the constitutional jurisprudence of other nations' courts.[32]

Of the several arguments advanced by those opposed to constitutional borrowing, of whom Justice Antonin Scalia is the best known, the one that carries the most weight in America's debate is "social progressiveness by stealth." Because the rights jurisprudence of most other leading democracies is more progressive than that of the United States, reference to these countries' rulings advances, almost by definition, a more progressive line of interpretation that in the context of the current culture wars in American society tends to favor views favored by, say, the Kennedy family over those of the Bush family.[33] All pertinent arguments against borrowing reflect a view of American constitutionalism as unique, exceptional, and particular, whereas the main arguments for the practice are neatly aligned with a universal and cosmopolitan view of constitutionalism and human experience more generally. Republicans and right-wingers tend to resent borrowing; Democrats, liberals, and progressives tend to support it. Moreover, the political split in the U.S. Supreme Court is closely aligned with the justices' positions on foreign reference. Most or all of the five judges who voted against a recount in the *Bush v. Gore* (2000) courtroom battle over the fate of the American presidency (thereby paving George W. Bush's way to the White House) reject reference to foreign judgments. Most or all of the justices who voted for a recount (i.e., those who sided with Al Gore's argument) tend to support, either tacitly or explicitly, reference to foreign judgments. Much like other ostensibly principled interpretive debates discussed here, the debate over reference to foreign law in the United States is portrayed as analytical but is also deeply political. It cannot be understood separately from the culture wars that have characterized the American polity for decades and are omnipresent in the American public sphere, from Michelle Obama to Laura Bush, from Harvard Law School to Wyoming's ranches, and from PBS to Fox News.

The Political Economy of Change in Constitutional and Religious Law

Like constitutionalization and the establishment of judicial review, or indeed legal institutions and traditions more generally, religion and religious beliefs are among the determinants of economic organization and performance. Max Weber's *The Protestant Ethic and the Spirit of Capitalism*

(1905) and *Economy and Society* (1914) famously attempt to explain the origins of European capitalism and modernism in terms of Europe's unique religious formation and the ethic of Calvinist Protestantism.[34] The Protestant ethic in Europe, Weber argues, was conducive to economic growth because of its emphasis on the rational pursuit of economic gain. It highlighted values such as workmanship, economic initiative, development of individual or private enterprises, and engagement in trade and the accumulation of wealth for investment. God's love was understood as being reflected in individual believers' worldly success. To obtain the former, one had to work hard to increase the latter. From a legal standpoint, the West had a key advantage in the early development in European societies of formal-rational legal systems juxtaposed with rational systems of political authority. Such a constellation of formal and rational structures and norms provided fertile ground for the development of capitalism. Why is that? As Weber notes, the fundamental building block of every successful capitalist market is a secure "predictability interest" based on formal, unambiguous rules and a rational legal system (as opposed to arbitrary, ad hoc norms), as well as on rational (as opposed to traditional or charismatic) political authority. More recent empirical studies confirm several of Weber's arguments concerning the important consequences that religious practices and beliefs have for economic development. Religious beliefs influence the individual traits that enhance economic performance.[35] Sociological research also confirms the role of religion as a determinant of wealth accumulation via religious affiliation's impact on low educational attainment, early fertility, large family size, or limited female labor-force participation.[36]

In a similar fashion, Douglass North and Robert Thomas argue in *The Rise of the Western World* that efficient economic organization is the key to growth; the development of a rational economic organization in Western Europe accounts for the rise of the West.[37] "Efficient organization entails the establishment of institutional arrangements and property rights that create an incentive to channel individual economic effort into activities that bring the private rate of return close to the social rate of return . . . [I]f a society does not grow, it is because no incentives are provided for economic initiative."[38] The rationality and efficiency has led to emphasis on the adoption of legal mechanisms that enhance investors' trust, most often exemplified by the constitutional protection of property rights, legal mechanisms that have in turn led to economic growth in various historical contexts. Douglass North, for example, has illustrated how legal limitations on rulers' arbitrary power in early capitalist Europe increased legal security and predictability of external lenders who were protected by law from the seizure of their capital.[39] This allowed polities where such limitations existed to borrow capital and to better their position vis-à-vis their rival polities where the arbitrary power of the ruler ("irrational systems," in Weber's terminology) had not been restricted by law. More recent empirical studies that have examined what is often referred to as the "legal-origins" thesis have suggested that common law is better than civil law for economic development because, inter alia, there may be a positive correlation between the existence of institutional limitations on government action (constitutional provisions and judicial review, for example) and economic growth.[40]

Much like constitutions' mitigation of enforcement and credible-commitments problems, religion-based "private-order contract-enforcement institutions" within close-knit communities have been shown to have enabled these communities to overcome systemic problems of economic coordination and enforcement. A significant obstacle to trade development in medieval and early modern times was merchants' difficulties in monitoring and rewarding agents operating in distant locations (consider the Silk Route and similar examples). As Avner Greif illustrates, the trading practices of the eleventh-century Jewish Maghribi community, for example, where any agent accused of dishonesty was shunned by the entire community, could allow agents to be hired for lower rewards and reduce systemic monitoring costs.[41] Aspects of the diamond trade provide a similar example, where Jewish predominance spans several centuries and continents. Activity in the modern-day industry is concentrated in Jewish communities populated by the ultra-Orthodox. This dominance is attributable to Jewish merchants' ability to implement diamond credit sales reliably, using reputational mechanisms supported by a distinctive set of industry, family, and community institutions.[42] In a different context, ethnographic studies of hunter-gatherer societies also support the view that belief systems and "cosmology" affect economic behavior.[43] In short, like constitutions and the institutions they create, religious and cultural belief systems affect economic behavior and performance, from patterns of individual consumption to broad patterns of economic growth and accumulation of wealth.

But the reversal of this causal link—how interests, economic or political, act as catalysts of innovation or transformation in these two domains—also points to some similarity between constitutionalism and religion. Doctrinal changes in religious practice are often believed to stem from theological, moral, or otherwise nonmaterial considerations. But economic interests or self-interested strategic behavior may occasionally play a role in initiating or promoting such changes. Variance in the organization and implementation of *waqf* endowments (property devoted to collective religious or charitable purposes) between two communities in Greater Syria (Tripoli in Lebanon and Nablus in Palestine) during the late Ottoman period may be explained by the differences in the political economy of inheritance patterns in the two communities.[44] Whereas in Nablus religious practice was dominated by a small male elite concerned mostly with using *waqf* as a funding source for projects that asserted its authority, the Tripoli community was less stratified, and this led to a more diverse usage of *waqf* funds directed at targeting communal goals.[45]

The incredible commercialization of Evangelical, born-again Christianity in the United States, with its scores of pastors, churches, and televised salvation ceremonies, is a vivid example of a lucrative marketplace of religion that is not driven solely by the purest theological motives.[46] Along the same lines, some studies suggest that a nontrivial part of the church's behavior at the height of its power in the Middle Ages was driven by economic considerations.[47] Monte di Pietà, a Catholic Church establishment for low-interest lending to the needy that began in fifteenth-century Italy, was sold to the public as a mercy- or compassion-based enterprise but was actually driven in no small part by an urge to prevent Jews from engaging in the lucrative lending business in late medieval Europe. At some point, to pick another illustration, the church and its agents began to sell pardons and indulgences rather than grant them. From the Third Crusade (1187) to the mid-sixteenth century, this lucrative practice became increasingly common.[48]

In the same spirit, the doctrine of purgatory—a provisional third state between heaven and hell where sinful but remediable souls may stay until cleared of wrongdoing—was introduced by usurers into medieval Catholic theology as a means to ensure the repayment of loans by families of deceased debtors. Purgatory was later expanded to encompass payable redemptions for other sins. Before the invention of purgatory, sins could be paid for only during a sinner's earthly lifetime. The invention of purgatory essentially introduced a means of "deferred payment" that allowed penance to be postponed beyond one's earthly life. It also allowed third parties to make payments on behalf of the deceased.[49] Such innovations were reflected in the literary world of that era; Geoffrey Chaucer's fourteenth-century *Canterbury Tales,* especially "The Pardoner's Tale," discussed the practice of designated individuals selling "pardons" to people for their sins. Ultimately, however, the cumulative costs that the faithful were asked to bear priced the Roman Catholic Church out of the market, paving the way for Protestant reformers like Martin Luther. As is well known, Luther's famous Ninety-five Theses (1517) was largely devoted to an attack on the commodification of church services.

Much as in constitutional politics, interest groups can affect modifications to religious doctrine. One illustration is the alteration to rules governing eating meat on Friday introduced by Pope Paul VI in 1966.[50] The apostolic decree to allow meat consumption on Friday overturned a long-standing Roman Catholic policy of mandatory abstinence introduced by Pope Nicholas I in 851. For over eleven hundred years it stood unchanged. But as of February 1966, and with the exception of several Fridays in Lent, Roman Catholics were no longer required to abstain from eating meat on at least forty-six Fridays of the year. The economic effects of this doctrinal change on the global markets of fish and meat were dramatic. With approximately one billion people worldwide now allowed to eat meat on Friday, production, consumption, and pricing of fish dropped sharply, while meat production, consumption, and pricing soared.

As Robert Ekelund and colleagues suggest, economic interests might have played a key role in this doctrinal change. The size and structure of the College of Cardinals, which elects the new pope and serves as the core consultation body for the sitting pope, had not been changed from the twelfth century to the 1950s. But from 1951 to 1966 it was expanded from fifty-two members to ninety-nine members, an increase of approximately 90 percent. Twenty-two of the forty-seven new appointments to the college were made in 1965–1966 alone. This massive expansion was introduced to increase representation of developing-world cardinals in the college. As a result, membership from developing-world countries, mainly in Latin America and Africa, tripled from 1951 to 1966. The decision made by Paul VI was perfectly compatible with world fish- and beef-production patterns between 1951 and 1966. In other words, as the representation of heavy meat- and leather-producing countries in the College of Cardinals increased, the economic interests of these countries and industries were distinctly better represented. The removal of the ban of meat consumption on Friday quickly followed. The pope's seemingly doctrinal decision was also excellent economics for the countries now represented in the expanded College of Cardinals.

Sometimes the formation of an entire religious movement, not merely the initiation of doctrinal change, may be aided by economic interests. The Mahdist movement in late nineteenth-century Sudan is often portrayed as an authentic Muslim uprising against a Christian crusade to curb Arab social dominance in Sudan. In many respects it no doubt was. Initially, however, Muhammad Ahmad (the Mahdi) was brought to the central stage of Sudanese politics and was supported by affluent slave traders who resisted British governor General Charles George Gordon's effective antislavery policies in Sudan. Before Gordon's arrival in 1877, the slave trade was a lucrative business. The large majority of Sudan's population at the time was black; many of whom were enslaved by the small Arab minority. Gordon's fight against the slave trade, combined with increased European financial imperialism, added impetus to the fight of the Arab slave trader minority in the Sudan to maintain its privileged economic position.[51] Partly in support of these interests, the first Shi'ite Wahhabist state in the modern era was born.

The political economy logic of religious authorities' behavior is also vivid in many contemporary, religion-infused settings. At the most basic level, religious authorities, much like constitutional courts, are not free of extradoctrinal, strategic considerations. They strive to maintain or expand their support base (and, as a bonus, diminish their competitors' support base). In the wake of the rift within the Anglican Church discussed earlier, for example, the Vatican launched an extraordinary bid to lure traditionalist Anglicans en masse to re-embrace Catholicism. In October 2009 Pope Benedict XVI announced that the Catholic Church would make it easier for Anglicans uncomfortable with their church's acceptance of female priests and openly gay bishops to join the Roman Catholic Church while retaining many of their traditions. The papal decree, made in the form of a so-called apostolic constitution (the highest form of pontifical ordinance), creates a new entity that transcends diocesan boundaries by creating special enclaves for Anglicans who join the church. In charge of each will be a former Anglican prelate.[52] Australian Bishop John Hepworth, a main splinter Anglican leader, declared himself "profoundly moved by the generosity" of Pope Benedict. But Rowan Williams, the leader of the Anglican mother church, seemed caught by surprise.[53] As George Bernard Shaw, the famous Irish playwright, once said, "I'd rather be a Christian in a den of lions than a lion in a den of Christians." In any case, nearly five centuries of Roman Catholic animosity toward the Anglican Church (and vice versa) have given way to a policy change that few business strategists would have framed more skillfully.

Political economy plays a role in interfaith collaboration, as well as strife. When purportedly rival groups face situations where collaboration seems more beneficial, doctrinal differences may give way to partnership. In al-Andalus, the parts of the Iberian Peninsula governed by the Muslim Moors from the eighth century to the fifteenth century, various dynasties of caliphs and emirs competed for political and military control. Islam was a key marker of collective identity. However, over prolonged periods of time a so-called Muslim-Jewish *convivencia* (coexistence) is said to have existed in al-Andalus. For much of its history al-Andalus existed in conflict with Christian kingdoms to the north, but within al-Andalus, Muslims and Jews collaborated relatively peacefully for centuries (by medieval European standards, at least). How so? Unlike Jews in Christian Europe, who were mostly isolated from the rest of the population in deplored professions such as moneylending, the Islamic marketplace was marked by a substantial degree of interdenominational cooperation.[54] The Jews lived as

Dhimmis (protected non-Muslims living in a land governed by Muslims) and were granted limited religious and cultural autonomy, as well as jurisdictional autonomy in matters pertaining to their faith. This brought about an unprecedented cultural revival within the Jewish community alongside increased cross-fertilization between Jewish and Muslim poets, commentators, and philosophers. In return, the Jews paid a special annual poll tax (*jizya*) to their protective rulers. This tax, higher than the tax Muslims had to pay, was at times one of the most important sources of income for the kingdom. At the same time, in several city-kingdoms (e.g., Córdoba and Toledo) translation programs were established, using Jews as interpreters to translate Arabic books into Romanic languages, mainly Latin, as well as Greek and Hebrew texts into Arabic. In that way many major works of Greek science and philosophy were translated into Arabic, and many accomplishments of the Moorish Empire in mathematics, medicine, botany, geography, astronomy, poetry, and philosophy were disseminated in the Christian world.[55]

Interfaith cooperation may also emanate from the existence of a joint rival (e.g., interfaith collaboration in Southern Sudan against the hegemonic North). Likewise, joint suprareligious affiliation may support collaboration; Christianity and Islam have both thrived simultaneously among the Yoruba in Nigeria without splitting the community because joint ethnic identity has been perceived as stronger than religious affiliation.[56] Or it may be the case that intrafaith class stratification is stronger than interfaith tensions; Hindu nationalists in India may attempt to incite animosity against Muslims, but they rarely succeed in the southern states of Kerala and Tamil Nadu, where caste affiliations among Hindus have more resonance than the Hindu-Muslim polarity.[57] The calculus of interfaith cooperation may be even more straightforwardly economic. Electoral politics may lead certain parties to emphasize religious or ethnic differences to maximize voter support. However, interfaith or sectarian violence has been shown to be reduced significantly in situations where the joint economic interests of otherwise rival parties lead them to work together for their mutual benefit (e.g., mutual dependence in a profitable production process whereby each group controls at least one key aspect of the production process).[58] In regions of India where the cooperation of Hindus and Muslims has been essential for sustaining a mutually beneficial economic enterprise or industry, sectarian violence has been distinctly lower than in regions where the marketplace is less interrelated.

The political economy logic, writ small or large, extends to legal transformation in contemporary, religion-infused settings. Consider, for example, the gap between the modernization of economic law and the slow pace of progress in the sphere of family law in predominantly Islamic polities. In a manner much like the interpretive flexibility within constitutional law, pragmatists within today's religious polities have found innovative ways to advance powerful economic interests amid the increased popular support for religiosity. Nearly all predominantly Muslim polities have found ways to exempt entire economic sectors from the purview of pertinent restrictive Shari'a directives. Qatar, Saudi Arabia, and the United Arab Emirates, for example, have established modern economies while being less flexible with respect to other aspects of religious law. In addition, a rather lax, form-over-substance approach to Islamic banking has been developed throughout most of the Islamic world. In several countries—Dubai is a good example—Islamic banking has been turned into a lucrative industry in itself, catering to rich Muslims worldwide who wish to invest their money in Islam-proof bonds and products.[59]

In contrast to economic law, which even some of the most doctrinal regimes have exempted from the purview of religious law, pressure to modernize the official, and often legally endorsed, religious view of families and gender roles is often viewed with great suspicion.[60] Full modernization of family law and promotion of gender equality more generally have not been achieved in even the most modernized constitutional theocracies. Legal advocacy groups in Algeria, Egypt, India, Jordan, Malaysia, Morocco, Nigeria, and Pakistan have launched campaigns, some more effective than others, targeting polygamy, religion-based divorce practices, unequal inheritance, and adultery laws.[61] The most successful of these campaigns led to the overhaul of family law in Morocco in 2004.

But ingenuity is often much more limited in family law than with respect to economic law.[62] In recent years Egypt has adopted an entirely modern nonreligious set of economic laws, including the new Investment Law, the Anti–Money Laundering Law, the Intellectual Property Rights Law, the Competition Law, the Consumer Protection Law, the Electronic Signatures Law, the Banking Law, and the Taxation Law. Although some significant modernization of Egypt's family law has been made, it does not even come close to the modernization and liberalization Egypt's nexus of economic laws has seen over the last decade. Israel's economic market is among the most advanced in the world, but it has not found a way to institutionalize civil marriage. Furthermore, although Ireland sports one the European Union's most successful economies, religious morality continues to hover over certain aspects of its personal-status laws (let alone reproductive freedoms). Similar contradictions manifest themselves in other mostly Catholic jurisdictions ranging from Chile to the Philippines. India is one of the world's new technological tigers, but it has not been able to adopt a uniform personal-status code. Neighboring Pakistan, likewise, has emerged as a regional nuclear superpower while much of its family law is still governed by religious norms. In virtually all these countries gender equality enjoys a distinctly better jurisprudential status in the context of the workplace than in the context of the family. Much like supporters of any other agendas, religious authorities' approach to legal change or stalemate reflects principled or ideational aspirations alongside strategic, self-interested considerations. Alongside the genuine doctrinal divide, a possible explanation of the adamant objection of the Orthodox establishment in Israel to the recognition of other branches of Judaism (e.g., Conservative or Reform) and to the formal establishment of civil marriage is that the monopoly over the provision of religious services to Israel's Jewish population from birth to death is a crucial source of both status and livelihood for a community that lacks many alternative sources of income. Younger-generation Orthodox Jews who wish to benefit from a richer Israeli economy often lack skills or modern education (e.g., advanced math, sciences, English) and thus are forced into a jobless life of Torah learning in a yeshiva (which for many is supplemented by state welfare benefits) or to take a position in the formal apparatus of religious services provision. The state-recognized institutions of the Orthodox establishment, such as the Chief Rabbinate, have turned their monopoly over the provision of religious services into a lucrative economic business. Brit milah (the Jewish ritual of circumcision performed on the eighth day of the boy's life unless health reasons force a delay); bar mitzvah (performed when Jewish boys reach the age of maturity, generally thirteen years);[63] preparation for and performance of weddings; preparation for and oversight of conversions to Judaism; burials and commemoration; operation and maintenance of synagogues, religious sites, and holy places; and the highly profitable kosher certificates industry where compliance with Jewish dietary-restriction and food-hygiene requirements is assessed and enforced by *kashrut* supervisors (kosher certificates are essential to the entire food and beverage, restaurant, and hotel industries) are some examples. Throughout Israel a nexus of national, regional, and local statutory religious bodies oversees and actually provides this array of religious services. Few would voluntarily share such a gold mine with others without a fight.

Similar logic, applied on a larger scale, may suggest that the secular/theocratic rift itself is often not merely about worldviews, beliefs, or sources of authority but also about distribution of material resources, access to government funding, and employment opportunities. An analogy to intrafaith splits may be drawn here. Such splits within churches are often said to reflect principled doctrinal or theological disagreements or irreconcilable differences in worldviews and ideologies. In many instances this is indeed the case. But such struggles may also mask less noble or principled quests for worldly goods, power, and influence. Interpretive rifts within communities, religious or otherwise, often reflect battles over the community's foundational metanarrative, who is designated as the community's official voice and who is to serve as the interpreter of its constitutive texts. Whoever occupies that position gets to define the community's history and collective identity and, by extension, the community's public face and canonical worldviews as well as its boundaries of reference, belonging, and entitlement. Interpretive wars over constitutive texts or directives are political, not merely doctrinal, theological, or moralistic. They may not be understood in isolation from the pertinent political economy or political sociology of their time.

Much as in the case of religion, proponents of secularism are also driven by interests alongside sincere beliefs in modernism, reason and empiricism, and visions of the good and just social order. As in intrafaith rifts, the secular/theocratic clash is thus not merely about worldviews and ideologies. It is also about concrete distributive policies: allocation of and access to precious goods, both material and symbolic. The political economy aspects of this rift began to manifest themselves in early medieval Europe when conflicts arose between monarchs and the church over the vast amounts of land owned by the church.[64] These assets not only reduced the access of the monarch to revenues but also prevented national consolidation. Further, much like today's economic mismatch of religious directives and economic growth, merchants in medieval Europe, and the capitalist impulse more broadly, were less than keen on religion-based restrictions on income from interest and usury. The jurisdictional struggles discussed in Chapter 3 between church-based canon law and monarch or state law also had crucial implications when it came to appointing officers to lucrative administrative and judicial positions.[65]

Despite the notable differences, some parallels to the political economy of the present-day clash between secularists and religionists are striking. To begin with, the potential of desecularized laws is in many respects bad for business. As we have seen earlier, religious directives are generally not very conducive to a modern market economy. But the political economy of the secular/religious divide stretches well beyond challenges of implementing or circumventing modern or non-business-friendly religious directives. The possibility of theocratic government carries with it nontrivial potential redistributive implications. On the one hand, in most countries torn along secularist/religious lines an important center-versus-periphery economic-distribution dimension has been involved. Support for religious parties in these countries is often closely associated with the relative have-nots or with other protesters of the socioeconomic status quo. It is distinctly more prevalent among occupiers of the sidelines, economic and cultural. Secularism, cosmopolitanism, or moderate religiosity, on the other hand, are often associated with the metaphorical center, the relatively better educated, better connected old elites, the urban intelligentsia, and the managerial classes.

Likewise, those who for generations have had better access to white-collar, relatively high-paying public service jobs tend, by and large, to favor "institutional," moderate, or religion-light policies. And why not? A change of the guard, political and ideological, would allow those at the periphery and their "new elite" representatives to compete for these jobs and contest the historic hegemony of the established oligarchies of wealth and power. It would transform the civil service, the government contracts market, the judiciary, the diplomatic squad, the academic and media scene, and, by extension, much of the existing socioeconomic stratification. The Iranian revolution of 1979, despite all its well-recorded shortcomings, brought with it a complete demographic transformation in the composition of Iran's civil service and public sector more generally. Many beneficiaries of the old regime were either forced to leave the country or did so voluntarily. Gone were the shah administration's sleek suits and fancy cars; in their place came a whole new class of civil servants loyal to the religious cause but also to the professed anticorruption and proclaimed redistributive agenda that redefined core-periphery boundaries in Iran after the shah.

Religious parties often advocate distinctly more generous welfare-state policies with closer attention to the geographic and economic hinterlands, or to previously neglected issues such as provision of health care, child-care benefits, housing, basic income, and so on. Grassroots, independent provision of welfare and community services at the local level and often at the neighborhood level is prevalent among such religious movements. This redistributive platform may emanate from strategic, support-maximizing objectives. It may also emanate from state failure or real consumer need. Religious movements such as Hamas, the Taliban, Hezbollah, the Jewish Underground, and, for that matter, Muslim sects in North American inner cities may emerge as a response to a government's failure to provide local public goods.[66] Nevertheless, genuine belief in redistributive values, or some combination of such genuine belief and other considerations, still does not change the fact that material redistribution or breaking the center's monopoly over access to and enjoyment of valuable social and economic goods is often higher on religious parties' agenda than it is on that of their most secularist competitors. And whereas religion-based charity and community aid are often endorsed by the state—for sincere or service-devolution reasons—powerful economic stakeholders are usually not fond of a truly transformative resource-allocation matrix. This duality is perhaps best captured by Brazilian priest Hélder Câmara, who famously noted, "When I give food to the poor they call me a saint. When I ask why the poor have no food they call me a communist."

Support for religious parties seldom comes from the center. Support for Hamas is found in the refugee camps and shantytowns of the Gaza Strip and in the West Bank's smaller towns, while the old Palestinian elite who favor the historically hegemonic Fatah movement are located mainly in the West Bank's business and government centers. Support for the now outlawed Islamic Salvation Front in Algeria of the late 1980s and early 1990s did not come from the "haves" and other members of the Algerian political and economic establishment. The same pattern exists in Lebanon, where support for Hezbollah has emanated almost exclusively from the predominantly Shi'ite, war-ridden, largely rural south, as well as from various refugee camps at the outskirts of cities. The relevance of economics does not end there. While Hezbollah leaders often professes to be true supporters of religion-based social justice, the organization's voice is seldom heard with regard to long-standing legislated restrictions on employment for the hundreds of thousands of Palestinian refugees in Lebanon. Why this silence? Probably because opening the Lebanese job market to Palestinian refugees would directly harm Hezbollah's Shi'ite supporters, most of whom compete for the same jobs.

As discussed in Chapter 4, support for the Shas party in Israel, the AKP in Turkey, and, despite all the notable differences, for the Muslim Brotherhood in Egypt has been framed by party leaders and supporters as direct opposition to the old establishment at the economic or political center of these polities. A periphery versus center, anti-Ashkenazi establishment sentiment has been a major thread of the Shas' agenda. The main electoral constituencies supporting Shas and its counterparts have traditionally emanated from "development towns" in Israel's economic and geographic periphery, and from relatively underprivileged neighborhoods in Jerusalem, the poorest of Israel's big cities. The party has established its own educational stream, which alongside religious education provides low-cost daycare and schooling solutions to families below the national poverty line. Furthermore, the average educational attainment or annual income of an AKP supporter in Turkey is distinctly lower than that of a secularist CHP voter. The AKP is less than keen on the economic elites who historically have been part of the Kemalist establishment or who have benefited from close ties with it. That these elites disfavor the AKP surely is not purely ideological. Likewise, the Egyptian statist establishment may very well resent the Islamization vision for Egypt advocated by the Muslim Brotherhood, but it surely also dislikes the redistributive implications of a Muslim Brotherhood–led regime. With the threat of a "new sheriff" in town new resource allocation and distribution criteria may be applied, and new hiring criteria for the large civil service may be implemented. One merely has to look at the near-existential concern that the National Democratic Party establishment (which has governed Egypt uninterruptedly for decades) has developed over the potential presidential candidacy of newcomer and pro-liberalization supporter Mohamed ElBaradei (winner of the Nobel Peace Prize and retired head of the International Atomic Energy Agency) to appreciate the party apparatus' strategic, not merely ideological, fear of any alternative power structure or set of policy preferences—liberal, Islamist, or otherwise.

Granted, there are a few exceptions to this trend, as support for religion-infused political agendas has not been confined to lower socioeconomic groups. And while advocating considerable change to the status quo, not all, or even most, religious parties endorse a radical transformation. The AKP in Turkey, the PAS and the PKR in Malaysia, or the PJD in Morocco are merely a few examples.[67]

In Israel, the Shas Party and its counterparts cannot afford a radically antiestablishment line since the economic viability of many of these parties' voters depends on public funding (from welfare to Torah learning institutions). In fact, the very participation of a political party in formal electoral processes entails some self-imposed pacification and implicit acceptance of the rules. An attempt to appeal to the "median voter" or to a wider political spectrum by toning down religious rhetoric may be at play in some settings. Further, the anti-center inclinations may shift once an opposition movement becomes a ruling party. That said, an antiestablishment sentiment is a common denominator of many of these parties. Whether those who support such parties do so for their pro-religious agenda, for their antiestablishment stand, or for some combination of these and other factors is difficult to ascertain.[68] But it is safe to assume that, other variables being equal, those whose interests are well protected by an existing set of institutions, worldviews, and public policies, or those who are set to gain from its continued existence, are not likely to seek a major change to that status quo. Likewise, it makes sense to assume that pressure for change comes from those who are not pleased with an existing institutional setting and its outcomes, or those who are seriously concerned by what it might yield for them in the future.

In short, the clash between secularism and religion may not be explained solely by differences in worldviews or value systems. Institutions, whether secular or religious, produce internal and external differential distributive effects: they privilege some groups and individuals over others. Other variables being equal, influential stakeholders are unlikely voluntarily to accept ideological shifts that would result in institutional or legal transformations that are not beneficial to them. The secular/religious rift not only has significant core-versus-periphery aspects but also stems from and reflects struggles over distributive politics and access to resources and opportunities. Granted, the face of the nation is often at stake as modernity, universalism, and the rule of law fight against tradition, particularism, and the rule of divine authority. But there are other, less idealistic factors to consider as secularists and religionists vie to maintain or expand the ambit of their influence, both material and symbolic. That secular idealists or religious zealots may deny such realist impulses is quite predictable. As American author and social critic Upton Sinclair once noted, "It is difficult to get a man to understand something when his salary depends upon his not understanding it."

Conclusion

Constitutional law and religion law have much more in common than meets the eye. Both domains are revered symbol systems that reflect ideals, aspirations, and principles larger than ordinary life. In both domains there appears to have been a trade-off between interpretation and amendment whereby the harder it is to alter the text, the greater is the likelihood of interpretive wars concerning the text's true meaning. A conceptual affinity and sociopolitical parallels between support for originalist, purposive, and living-tree interpretive schools is evident in both spheres. And neither domain is a purely reverent one. Constitutionalism and religion may both be forums of principle, but they are also domains of political and economic strife, where various stakeholders and interests fight for recognition, influence, and other profane gains. They operate within particular social, political, and economic contexts and cannot be fully understood in separation from these perspectives.

The numerous examples discussed here provide an insight into the often-striking similarities between constitutional law and religious law. They may help us understand why and how religious law and constitutional law mutate to address social needs, economic interests, or political aspirations. Jurisdictional struggles, doctrinal changes, and adaptive interpretation of revered directives, either constitutional or religious, have significant political origins and distributive effects. And we have not even begun to explore broader, more radical ideas suggesting that a significant political vector behind the idea of separating state and religion was the rise of new urban elites and emerging capitalists in late medieval Europe who fought the economic hegemony of the church, or that some religious voices may be fighting modernity not only because they believe it to be morally corrupt but also because it threatens to eradicate the very backwardness upon which the livelihood of these voices depends. As B. R. Ambedkar, noted Indian politician and founder of the Indian Constitution, once said: "[H]istory shows that where ethics and economics come in conflict, victory is always with economics. Vested interests have never been known to have willingly divested themselves unless there was sufficient force to compel them."

As discussed, selective interpretation, whether of constitutional or of sacred texts, is not limited to one of these domains. Reliance on favorable interpretive methods and approaches to advance certain worldviews, ideologies, or interests is common to both constitutional and religion law. Religious interpreters throughout history, much like today's philosopher-king judges, have at times relied on discerning, result-driven readings of sacred texts to advance their worldviews and preferences, principled or strategic. Moreover, risk aversion, profit maximization, competitor elimination, economically and politically astute doctrinal adjustments, and a host of other forms of instrumental or otherwise self-interested behavior are not foreign to religious bodies (just as they are integral to nonreligious bodies' behavior) and cannot be excluded from any serious analysis of their preaching, let alone their deeds. Given the billions of worshippers worldwide, the tremendous size of the religious and the constitutional spheres, and the incomprehensible levels of affluence and power religious and constitutional authorities possess, it would be naïve to assume that all, or even most, of what drives these institutions and their leaders, supporters, and symbol systems may be understood through a purely principled, apolitical, economics-free, theological analysis.

CONCLUSION

"Glocalization"?

Constitutional Law and Politics in a Nonsecularist World

Since the time of Henry Maine, the anthropologists and sociologists have done a great deal in the field of comparative social studies, but the jurists have not been so fertile in the field of comparative legal ideas.

JOHN WIGMORE, AUTHOR OF THE SEMINAL *PANORAMA OF THE WORLD'S LEGAL SYSTEMS*, 1928

AT THE INTERSECTION of two of the most important phenomena in late twentieth- and early twenty-first-century politics—the triumph of constitutionalism as the prevalent form of governance and the return of religion to the world political stage—a new, seemingly improbable but increasingly common legal order has emerged. I call it *constitutional theocracy.* Countless books and articles are devoted each year to the study of religion in the West, most notably with an eye to American constitutional law of religion or the accommodation of religious difference in the supposedly religion-neutral European public sphere. Despite its increasing prevalence and the fact that approximately one billion people now live in polities where one variant or another of constitutional theocracy is in place (not including dozens of other polities where separation of religion and state is formally established but is practically fuzzy and constantly contested), little is known about constitutional theocracy—the other model of governing state and religion relations. With few exceptions, it has remained a black hole of sorts, the dark side of the comparative constitutional law universe, seldom explored or theorized. This book attempts to leap beyond the countless accounts of law and religion in North America or Europe to take a close, genuinely comparative look at the sociopolitical context within which constitutional theocracy emerges and functions, its institutional architecture, and the role of constitutional law and courts in mediating its embedded tensions.

What may be said with some confidence about constitutional theocracy, despite its many past and present variations, is that it defies the Western ideal of separating religion and state along private/public lines. An ideal-type constitutional theocracy formally enshrines a single religion as the state religion; designates that religion's sacred texts as "a" or "the" source of legislation, meaning that legislation must comply with principles of that religion; and grants religious tribunals jurisdiction over important aspects of life, public and private, in addition to the tremendous symbolic weight religious edicts often carry. At the same time, religion and its institutions and interpretive hierarchy are expected to comply with overarching constitutional norms and are subject to review by constitutional courts and judges.

Regimes throughout the new world of constitutional theocracies, as well as in countries where religion-centered morality has been dominating law and politics for generations, have been struggling with questions of a profoundly foundational nature and have been forced to navigate between cosmopolitanism and parochialism, modern and traditional metanarratives, constitutional principles and religious injunctions, contemporary governance and ancient texts, and judicial and pious interpretation. Constitutional courts find themselves at the forefront of this struggle as they attempt to address constitutional theocracy and translate its uneasy bundle of seemingly contradictory aims and commitments into practical guidelines for public life. In dozens of religion-laden settings, even in those that lack an established tradition of constitutionalism and judicial review, constitutional courts have emerged as key mediators between apparently contradictory constitutional and religious commitments. Consequently, throughout the world of constitutional theocracies—be they soft or rigid, formal or informal—fascinating, largely unexplored jurisprudential landscapes form, reflecting uneasy amalgams of universal aspirations and domestic realities and of constitutional principles and religious directives.

Each of this book's chapters addresses a main theme concerning the rise of constitutional theocracy and the place of constitutional law and courts in a nonsecularist world. Each of the chapters concludes with a clear statement of its main arguments, findings, and take-home messages. These need not be replicated here in great detail. In Chapter 1 I defined constitutional theocracy and described its basic tenets, functioning, and intrinsic existential tensions. These embedded disharmonies pose serious challenges to modern constitutional courts operating in such settings. In Chapter 2 I placed constitutional theocracy in the broader matrix of religion-and-state relations worldwide, and examined the theocratic challenge to conventional constitutional theory. In Chapter 3 I explored the secularist appeal—instrumentalist, epistemological, and juridical—of constitutional law and courts as counterreligious instruments; that is, what makes the constitutional domain so attractive to secularist, modernist, cosmopolitan, and other antireligious social forces in polities that face deep divisions along secular/religious lines. In Chapter 4 I addressed the jurisprudential aspects of constitutionalism versus theocracy, the strategic interplay between civil courts and religious tribunals, interpretive and jurisprudential ingenuity, and the role of constitutional law and courts in "containing" sacred law in seven polities steeped in religion-related politics—Egypt, Kuwait, Pakistan, Malaysia, Nigeria, Israel, and Turkey. In Chapter 5 I explored the role of courts as secularizing agents in the nontheocratic world, from the battle over religious attire in Europe to the struggle over reproductive freedoms in Colombia and Mexico, to the status of customary law in South Africa, and to the erection of boundaries to multicultural accommodation in Canada. To wrap up, in Chapter 6, I pointed to a conceptual affinity, indeed a near-equivalence, among the sociology and cosmology of interpretive debates in the constitutional and religious domains, the tension between interpretation and amendment in constitutional and sacred texts, the striking parallels between "originalist" and "purposive" interpretive approaches in constitutional and sacred law, and the political economy, ancient and contemporary, of intrareligious and secular/religious rifts.

From all these ideas, examples, and arguments, several broad messages emerge. First, this book raises the question how truly comparative the study of comparative constitutional law in general, and comparative constitutional law of religion in particular, is. The past decade has witnessed a sharp comparative turn in legal scholarship. "We are all comparativists now" has become the motto of many jurists worldwide. The ever-increasing interest among scholars, practitioners, and policy makers in the laws and legal institutions of other countries is remarkable. This new interest is particularly striking in comparative constitutional law and the transnational migration of constitutional ideas. From a relatively obscure and exotic subject studied by the devoted few, comparative constitutionalism has emerged as one of the more fashionable subjects in contemporary legal scholarship. However, despite the many scholarly advances in the field, works in comparative constitutional law continue to draw heavily on the constitutional experience of half a dozen, mostly liberal democratic countries but seldom refer to the constitutional experience, law, and institutions elsewhere. A quest for universal insights must be based on universal inquiry. As we have seen in this book, there is nothing particularly American, French, or German in the charged intersection of constitutional law and religion law. Just as the animal kingdom does not consist exclusively of mammals (or crustaceans, for that matter), and the periodic table lists many more elements than gold, iron, or copper, so the current religion-and-state world is not confined to the separation of church and state model. The variety and ingenuity in the handling of religion law by the constitutional courts whose jurisprudence is explored here are intellectually intriguing.

An oft-cited hurdle in advancing general theory in comparative constitutional law, and the comparative constitutional law of religion in particular, is the potential neglect of the specific institutional, political, and doctrinal context within which the intersection of law and religion evolves or functions.[1] Surely, details and context matter a great deal. However, the contextualist concern seems to provide an all-too-easy excuse for not turning our gaze overseas. Details and context are important, and that is why many realist accounts of judicial empowerment were written by scholars who are as familiar with the constitutional history, law, and politics of the polities that are the subject of their research as the authors of contextualist accounts are with theirs. In fact, meticulous attention to detail is a necessary feature of any serious strategic account of constitutional law and politics, for without such attention the realist approach is unable to separate the strategic matrix at play from the formalist or ideational sugarcoating that often covers constitutional jargon.

More important, even social anthropology—arguably the most contextual and hermeneutic discipline in the social sciences—attempts to produce generalizable insights regarding human development and behavior that are based on, but ultimately go beyond, detailed ethnographies.[2] Besides, there seems to be a notable difference between the significance of context when one studies the transition from childhood to adolescence in early twentieth-century New Guinea (Margaret Mead), patterns of reciprocity in remote Melanesian islands (Bronislaw Malinowski) or magic rituals among the Nuer of southern Sudan (E. E. Evans-Pritchard), to name but three ethnographic classics, and the much more modest significance of context when one studies popular phenomena such as the mass media, air traffic, professional sports, scientific discoveries, or modern constitutionalism. In other words, the more universal and widespread certain challenges become—the extraordinary resurgence of religion and the astounding convergence worldwide toward constitutional supremacy are good examples here—the less effective or significant the contextualist concern is. So although each language or dialect is surely unique or idiosyncratic in many respects, it is the development and substantiation of a core common element or a general linguistic principle that can be applied to many or all of these languages (e.g., Noam Chomsky's theory of generative grammar) that make for a great theoretical development.

In the area of constitutional law, the world grows increasingly smaller, but the domestic and particular persist. Constitutional theocracy stands at the intersection of the general and the contextual, the universal and the particular. In that respect, constitutional theocracy may very well be constitutional law's version of what has been termed *glocalization*—the process whereby the global and the local merge to form a new, extraordinary yet perfectly authentic synthesis.

Second, constitutionalism in the abstract, with its "virtues" or "vices," has been a fertile topic for countless normative debates in legal and political theory. But for those interested in the political foundations of constitutional orders and institutions, it has always been about who gains and who loses. The rise of constitutional theocracy, despite the important normative quandaries it poses, is no different. It cannot be understood in purely ideational terms or in isolation from the concrete social, economic, and cultural rifts from which it emerges and that it attempts to maintain, contain, or defuse. In other words, constitutional theocracy is more an artifact of political sociology than it is a by-product of either constitutionalism or theocracy.

Religion is commonly regarded as one of the purest, most apolitical symbolic systems. Just as liberal constitutionalism is canonically treated as stemming from genuinely normative commitments (e.g., checks and balances, protection of individual freedoms or minority rights), the constitutional establishment of religion as a pillar of collective identity and governance thus inevitably prompts thoughts of ideational, purist constitutionalism. However, even in post–world War II liberal constitutionalism, rights ideology alone simply cannot explain the tremendous variance in the institutional design, forms of constitutional review, scope of judicial activism, and above all the precise timing of constitutionalization. Such rights-based explanations often tell a broad, at times vague, demand-side causal story that is very difficult to operationalize and which tends to be based on an overly idealist, Ackermanian notion of constitutionalization as reflecting massive political mobilization and genuine popular will. The reality, however, is that the vast majority of the constitutional revolutions of the last few decades do not fit this story. Instead, they were either negotiated among rival parties during times of political transition (even the constitutional revolution in South Africa—a poster child of democratic constitutionalism—has been the product of a long negotiation process steeped with power relations, political interests, and strategic calculations); promoted by external actors (e.g., the new constitutions of Afghanistan in 2004 or Iraq in 2005); or were initiated by political elites whose interests did not exactly reflect popular will at the time. Consider here the continuous attempt by "Eurocentric" politicians, bureaucrats, and jurists to create an "ever closer union" in Europe by the adoption of an EU constitution.

It is therefore hardly surprising that a realist approach to constitutionalization has emerged. This emerging body of scholarship attempts to go beyond the traditional focus on constitutionalization as emanating from polities' commitment to a thick notion of democracy to identify broad demand-side pressures to establish judicial review, alongside specific supply-side factors that are conducive to the establishment and maintenance of constitutional review.

As I have argued elsewhere, the threat of losing control over pertinent policy-making processes and outcomes may be a significant driving force behind attempts to transfer contentious issues to courts.[3] Embattled elites and their political representatives are more likely to divert policy-making responsibility to a relatively supportive judiciary when present or prospective transformations in the political system threaten their own political status, worldviews, and policy preferences. Occupiers of a polity's symbolic "center"—these could be either old-timers on their way down or emerging hegemons who fear a comeback of their sociopolitical rivals—may favor the constitutionalization of rights as a hegemony-preserving maneuver when their grip over politics, cultural dominance, or the allocation of core perks and benefits are, or are likely to be, challenged in majoritarian decision-making arenas.

The realist approach to constitutional politics further suggests that once established, constitutional courts and judges themselves may speak the language of legal doctrine, but their actual decision-making patterns reflect ideological preferences and attitudinal tilts, as well as strategic considerations vis-à-vis their political surroundings. This can be explained by reference to the costs that judges as individuals or courts as institutions may incur as a result of adverse reactions to their unwelcome decisions, or through the various benefits that they may acquire through the rendering of strategically tailored decisions. The strategic interplay does not end there. Once a system of constitutional review is put in place, powerful political stakeholders continue their quest to control the composition of courts and to ensure jurisprudential support for their agendas. Occasionally, courts may side with noncanonical worldviews or actors. This is done either on the merits of the arguments, as a court legitimacy-building measure, or simply because courts assess that the political tide has shifted or is likely to shift. However, when courts issue rulings that threaten to seriously alter the political power relations in which they are embedded, the political sphere generally responds to quell unfavorable judgments or to hinder their implementation.[4] More often than not overactive courts and judges do learn the lesson. The boundaries of judicial independence or activism are thus captured by "relative autonomy."

On this account, a set of concrete political vectors, interests, and incentives affect the interplay between political and constitutional actors and institutions. A quest for legitimacy, or for lowering risks or costs, is a major determinant of both judicial empowerment and corresponding judicial behavior. This, in a nutshell, is the take-home message of the realist turn in comparative constitutional and judicial politics. While this approach to judicial empowerment may not provide a complete explanation of all or even most instances of constitutionalization, it marks an important departure from both normative constitutional theory accounts and from political science's early emphasis on functionalist needs and ideational aspirations as the core motivating factors. Constitutional theocracy is a living laboratory—a rare combination of past formations and future creations, of ideological aspirations and strategic considerations—for studying each of these phenomena. All are cardinal for understanding comparative constitutional law and politics.

On the one hand, religious principles are constitutionally enshrined as "a" or "the" source of legislation in many countries. It is thus hard not to assign at least some genuine ideational, principled, or aspirational motives to constitutional theocracy. On the other hand, constitutional theocracies' actual adherance to and implementation of these principles is often selective, instrumentalist, and self-serving. Every effort is made by moderate, pragmatic regimes, even those that claim to be zealous guardians of tradition, to circumvent or ignore aspects of religion that are deemed nonbeneficial while preserving aspects of religion that are mainly symbolic or that are too costly to modernize. A comparison between the light, "form over substance" approach to many religious economic and redistrbutive directives, as opposed to the notably more solemn approach to family and personal-status aspects of religion law, provides a simple yet effective illustration of the non-ideational, earthly tone of constitutional theocracy.

Third, all things considered, the advancement of constitutional law and courts is a rational, prudent strategy that allows opponents of theocratic governance to talk the religious talk without walking most of what they regard as theocracy's unappealing, costly walk. Constitutional law and courts, as symbols of state sovereignty and authority, owe their existence to the body politic, not to a divine authority. Many of the jurisdictional, enforcement, co-optation, and access-to-power advantages that gave religious legal regimes an edge in the premodern era are now aiding the modern state and its laws in its effort to contain religion. The "constitutional" in a constitutional theocracy thus fulfills the same restricting function it carries out in a constitutional democracy. Like constitutional constraints on democracy, it brings theocratic governance under check and assigns to constitutional law and courts the task of protecting certain worldviews, ideologies, and policy preferences from the threat of radical religion. It comes close to being an exercise in "changing everything so that everything may remain the same."[5]

The formal establishment of religion and the granting of limited jurisdiction to its tribunals may be portrayed as surrender to religion, but in reality it helps limit the potentially radical impact of religion by bringing it under state control. More important, this process makes the state (and its courts) a key player in picking religion's official interpretive authorities and jurists and gives the state a stake in the interpretive game. Although establishment of religion does not come without some compromise on universal outlooks, the jurisdiction of constitutional courts in such settings, even if formally religious in some sense, will almost inevitably reflect a less militant view of religious identity.

Fourth, scholars of comparative constitutional law and courts often talk about differences in the political functions of courts in democratic and authoritarian regimes. The working hypothesis is that constitutional law and courts in the former category are at least semiautonomous, if not purely principled, forums, whereas in the latter type of regimes constitutional law and courts are little more than a regime-serving political tool. At least in the case of constitutional law and religion, the validity of this binary view is very much in doubt. Although there is a kernel of truth to this distinction in the context of this book, to a large extent the differences are of degree or style, not qualitative or of kind. Religion poses existential challenges to constitutional orders in the United States and in China. When all is said and done, there is not much qualitative difference between how courts in France (with its assertive form of secularism) and in Morocco (where Islam is a pillar of the state) view symbols of theocratic governance as a threat to the modern state and its overarching constitutional supremacy.

The judicialization of megapolitics—the reliance on courts and judicial means to address core political controversies that often define and divide whole polities—knows no democratic/authoritarian borders. As the problem of state and religion returns to the fore of world politics, courts in both settings are increasingly called on to articulate and resolve existential collective identity quandaries. The *Bush v. Gore* courtroom struggle over the fate of the American presidency, the constitutional-certification saga in South Africa, and the Supreme Court of Canada's landmark ruling in *Reference re Secession of Quebec*—the first time a democratic country had ever tested in advance the legal terms of its own dissolution—are all illustrations of judicialized megapolitics. Similarly dramatic, perhaps even deeper examples of judicialization of that existential caliber are evident throughout the constitutional theocratic world. Indeed, one can hardly think of a more vivid illustration of judicialized megapolitics than the Israeli Supreme Court's continuous grappling with Israel's self-definition as Jewish and democratic, the Turkish Constitutional Court's guardianship of Turkey's secular nature, or the Egyptian Supreme Constitutional Court's contemplation of the place of Shari'a as the main source of legislation in that country. Much like clash-of-civilizations views of the "West" and the "rest," when it comes to constitutional politics of religion, the validity of the binary distinction between courts in democratic and authoritarian settings is questionable.

In conclusion, the rise of constitutional theocracy points to an intriguing conceptual affinity between constitutional law and religion law, each with its own constitutive texts, interpretive hierarchies, and righteous morality alongside earthly interests. Western secularism, a few scholars have recently argued, has never eradicated religion, is in fact inseparable from religion, and may not be fully understood without appreciating that at root, it grew out of religion.[6] Enter constitutionalism. The assumption that constitutionalism and religion are diametrically opposed domains, or at best unrelated to each other, is often unquestioned. But these two domains are in many respects analogous symbolic systems that vie to establish, maintain, or enhance their hegemony, worldviews, and preferences vis-à-vis each other. Very few, if any, constitutional orders in today's world, their various outlooks notwithstanding, are outright separable from religion. In many countries constitutional law and religion law do coexist in an admittedly tense relationship, but one that is not more overwrought than that of constitutionalism and democracy. Precisely because constitutionalism has certain religion-like aspects to it, all fostered by the modern state and by the post-Westphalian international community, it may be better positioned than blunter, more forceful means to control and pacify principles of theocratic governance effectively. The religion-like nature of the constitutional scripture—its overarching, larger-than-life, and omnipresent character—may just turn it into an effective counterpoint to a religious scripture. In that respect constitutionalism might very well emerge, or perhaps has already emerged, as tomorrow's "opiate of the masses."

APPENDIX

Cases and Laws Cited

Afghanistan

Constitution of Afghanistan (2004), §§ 1, 2, 3, 22, 40, 116, 117, 118, 130

Algeria

Constitution of Algeria (1996), §§ 2, 42
Constitutional Amendment Ending Presidential Term Limits (November 2008)

Argentina

Corte Suprema de Justicia [CSJN] 11/01/2001 *Gobierno de la Ciudad de Buenos Aires,* s/amparo, Fallos 324:05 (Distribution of Contraceptives case)

Bangladesh

Jesmin Sultana v. Mohammad Elias (1997) 17 B.L.D. 4
Md. Hefzur Rahman v. Shamsun Nahar Begum (1995) 15 B.L.D. 34

Bolivia

Supreme Court of Bolivia, Ruling of Oct. 17, 2008 (Abortion case)

Brazil

Supreme Court of Brazil, Ruling of May 29, 2008 (Law of Biosecurity case)

Britain

Azmi v. Kirklees Metropolitan Borough Council (EAT) (Apr. 2, 2007)
R. (E) v. Governing Body of JFS [2009] UKSC 15
R. (on the application of Playfoot) v. Millais School Governing Body [2007] EWHC 1698 (Admin)
R. (on the Application of Shabina Begum) v. Headteacher and Governors of Denbigh High School (Shabina Begum) [2006] UKHL 15
Human Rights Act 1998
Race Relations Act 1976

Canada

Adler v. Ontario, [1996] 3 S.C.R. 609
Alberta v. Hutterian Brethren of Wilson Colony, [2009] 2 S.C.R. 567
Auton (Guardian ad litem of) v. British Columbia (A.G.), [2004] 3 S.C.R. 657
British Columbia (A.G.) v. Christie, [2007] 1 S.C.R. 873
Bruker v. Marcovitz, [2007] 3 S.C.R. 607
Gosselin v. Quebec (A.G.), [2002] 4 S.C.R. 429
Hartshorne v. Hartshorne, [2004] 1 S.C.R. 550
Hofer v. Hofer, [1970] S.C.R. 958
Multani v. Commission scolaire Marguerite-Bourgeoys, [2006] 1 S.C.R. 256
R. v. Big M Drug Mart Ltd., [1985] 1 S.C.R. 295
R. v. Edwards Book and Art Ltd., [1986] 2 S.C.R. 713
R. v. Jones, [1986] 2 S.C.R. 284
R. v. Prosper, [1994] 3 S.C.R. 236
Reference re Secession of Quebec, [1998] 2 S.C.R. 217
Syndicat Northcrest v. Amselem, [2004] 2 S.C.R. 551
Canadian Charter of Rights and Freedoms, Part I of the Constitution Act, 1982, §§ 1, 2, 7, 15(1), 15(2), 23, 27
Divorce Act, R.S.C. 1985, c. 3 (2nd Supp.), § 21.1
Multiculturalism Act, R.S.C. 1985
Ontario Arbitration Act, 1991 (amended 2006)

Chile

Constitutional Court of Chile, ruling of Apr. 4, 2008 (Distribution of the "Morning-After Pill" case).

Colombia

Case No. C-355/2006 (May 10, 2006) (Abortion case)
Case No. T-209/2008 (Feb. 15, 2008) (Denial of Lawful Abortion case)

Colombian State Council, Administrative Chamber, Decision 2002 00251 01 (June 5, 2008) ("Morning-After Pill" case)

The Comoros

Constitution of the Comoros (2001), § 3

Egypt

Decision on Conversion to Christianity [Alexandria Administrative Court] (Dec. 4, 2008)
Decision on Conversion to Christianity [Supreme Administrative Court] (Feb. 9, 2008)
Decision on Revocation of Citizenship [Cairo Administrative Court] (May 19, 2009)
Decision on Status of Baha'i Community [Supreme Administrative Court] (Mar. 12, 2009)
Khul Law case, Case No. 201, 23rd Judicial Year (Dec. 26, 2002)
Moustafa v. President of the Republic, Case No. 18 of the 14th Judicial Year (May 3, 1997)
Riba [usury or interest] *Case,* Case No. 20, 1st Judicial Year, and Decision 28, 2nd Judicial Year (May 4, 1985).
Wassel v. Minister of Education (the *niqab* [veil] case), Case No. 8 of the 17th Judicial Year (May 18, 1996).
Women Judges Case (March 15, 2010)
Constitution of Egypt (1971), §§ 2, 8, 9, 11, 12
Constitutional Amendment re: Islam as the Source of Legislation, 1980
Constitutional Amendment re: Presidential Elections, 2005
Constitutional Amendment re: "War on Terror," 2007
Civil Code of Egypt, § 226
Family Law Reform, Law No. 1 (2000), Law No. 10 (2004), and Law No. 11 (2004)
Political Parties Law, Law No. 40 (1977)
Statute of the Supreme Constitutional Court, Law No. 48 (1979)

European Court of Human Rights

Baspinar v. Turkey, ECtHR, Oct. 3, 2002, Application No. 45631/99
Dahlab v. Switzerland, ECtHR, Feb. 15, 2001, Application No. 42393/98
Dal and Ozen v. Turkey, ECtHR, Oct. 3, 2002, Application No. 45379/99
Herri Batasuna and Batasuna v. Spain, ECtHR, June 30, 2009, Application No. 25803/04, 25817/04
Johnson v. Ireland, 112 ECtHR (ser. A) (1986) 9 EHRR 203
Karaduman v. Turkey, ECtHR, May 3, 1993, Application No. 16278/90
Kokkinakis v. Greece, ECtHR, May 25, 1993, Application No. 14307/88
Lautsi v. Italy, ECtHR, Nov. 3, 2009, Application No. 30814/06
Leyla Şahin v. Turkey, ECtHR, Nov. 10, 2005, Application No. 44774/98

Refah Partisi (The Welfare Party) and Others v. Turkey, ECtHR, Feb. 13, 2003, Application Nos. 41340/98; 41342/98; 41343/98; 41344/98
European Convention on Human Rights (1950), § 9(2); Protocol 1, § 2

European Court of Justice

Case 6/64, *Flaminio Costa v. ENEL* [1964] ECR 585
Case 26/62, *Van Gend en Loos v. Nederlandse Administratie der Belastingen* [1963] ECR 1

France

Décision du Conseil d'État N° 286798, June 28, 2008 (*Faiza M.* (or *Mme M.*) case)
Décision 92-308 DC of Apr. 9, 1992, "Maastricht I," Recueil des Décisions du Conseil Constitutionnel 55, [1992] RJC I-496, [1993] 3 CMLR 345
Civil Code, § 21-4
Law No. 2004-228 (Mar. 15, 2004)

Germany

BVerfG, 1 BvR 1087/91 [1995] (Classroom Crucifix case)
BVerfG, 2 BvR 1436/02 [2003] (*Ludin* case)
BVerfG, 2 BvR 2134/92, and 2 BvR 2159/92 [1994] (Maastricht case)
BVerfG, 2 BvE 2/08 [2009] (Lisbon Treaty case)
German Basic Law, §§ 4(1), 4(2)

India

Danial Latifi v. Union of India, A.I.R. 2001 S.C. 3958
John Vallamattom v. Union of India, A.I.R. 2003 S.C. 384
Mohammed Ahmed Khan v. Shah Bano Begum, A.I.R. 1985 S.C. 985
Olga Tellis v. Bombay Municipal Corporation, A.I.R. 1986 S.C. 180
Sarla Mugdal v. Union of India, A.I.R. 1995 S.C. 1531
Unni Krishnan, JP v. State of Andhra Pradesh, A.I.R. 1993 S.C. 2178
Special Leave Petition (Civil) 5939/2009 *Mohammad Salim v. Nirmala Convent Higher Secondary School* (Supreme Court ruling of Mar. 30, 2009; September 11, 2009)
Constitution of India (1950), Preamble; §§ 14, 15, 21, 21A, 25, 30, 44, 48, 51A, 356
Constitutional Amendment No. 42 (1976)
Code of Criminal Procedure, §§ 125, 127
Guardianship Act (1956)
Hindu Minority and Guardianship Act (1956)
Muslim Women's (Protection of Rights of Divorce) Act (1986)
Penal Code, § 377
Representation of the People Act (1951)
Succession Act (1925)

Indonesia

Blasphemy Law Case (April 19, 2010)
Constitution of Indonesia (1945), Preamble, Chapter X
Law 44/1999, Status of Aceh State (Special Region)
Law 18/2001, Status of Aceh State (Special Autonomy)
Religious Judicature Act (1989)

Iran

Constitution of Iran (1979), Preamble, §§ 1, 2, 3, 6, 8, 91
Constitution of Iran (Amended, 1989), § 112

Iraq

Constitution of Iraq (2005), §§ 2.1, 2.1(b), 2.1(c), 2.2, 5, 14, 16, 17, 37, 41, 42, 44, 92

Ireland

A. G. v. X [1992] IESC 1; [1992] 1 IR 1 (Mar. 5, 1992) (*X* case)
Constitution of Ireland (1937), §§ 41, 44
Constitutional Amendments No. 5 (1973), No. 8 (1983), No. 15 (1995)

Israel

C 16023/08 *Eskimo Trade Inc. v. Vidislavsky et al.*, Tel-Aviv Municipal Court (2008)
HCJ 7052/03 *Adalah v. Minister of Interior,* [2006] 2 TakEi 1754
HCJ 7203/00 *Aviv Osoblanski Ltd. v. The Council of the Chief Rabbinate of Israel,* 56(2) P.D. 196 (2001)
HCJ 1000/92 *Bavli v. The Great Rabbinical Court,* 48(2) P.D. 6 (1995)
HCJ 5070/95 *Conservative Movement v. Minister of Religious Affairs,* 1 TakEl 634 (2002)
HCJ 5227/97 *David v. Great Rabbinical Court,* 55(1) P.D. 453 (1998)
HCJ 2222/99 *Gabai v. Great Rabbinical Court,* 54(5) P.D. 401 (2000)
HCJ 3269/95 *Katz v. Jerusalem Reg'l Rabbinical Court,* 50(4) P.D. 590 (2000)
HCJ 3872/93 *Meatrael Ltd. v. Prime Minister and Minister of Religious Affairs,* 47(5) P.D. 485 (1993)
HCJ 5009/94 *Meatrael Ltd. v. The Council of the Chief Rabbinate of Israel,* 48(5) P.D. 617 (1994)
HCJ 4676/94, *Meatrael Ltd. v. The Knesset,* 50(5) P.D. 15 (1996)
EA 1/88 *Neiman v. Chairman of the Central Elections Committee for the Twelfth Knesset,* 42(4) P.D. 177 (1988)
HCJ 1067/08 *Noar Ke'Halacha v. Ministry of Education* (Aug. 6, 2009)
HCJ 1031/93 *Pessaro (Goldstein) et al. v. Ministry of Interior,* 49(4) P.D. 661 (1995)
HCJ 8928/06 *Plonit ("Jane Doe") v. Great Rabbinical Court* (Oct. 8, 2008)

HCJ 293/00 *Plonit ("Jane Doe") v. Great Rabbinical Court,* 55(3) P.D. 318 (2001)
HCJ5416/09 *Plonit ("Jane Doe") v. Ploni ("John Roe")*
CA 3077/90 *Plonit ("Jane Doe") v. Ploni ("John Doe"),* 49(2) P.D. 578 (1996)
HCJ 72/62 *Rufeisen v. Minister of the Interior,* 16 P.D. 2428 (1962)
HCJ 264/87 *Sepharadi Torah Guardians, Shas Movement v. Population Registrar,* 43(2) P.D. 723 (1989)
HCJ 2274/99 *Shafir v. Regional Rabbinical Court,* 56(1) P.D. 673 (2002)
HCJ 58/68 *Shalit v. Minister of Interior,* 23(2) P.D. 477 (1969)
State of Israel v. Terminal 21 et al., Jerusalem Municipal Affairs Court (Apr. 3, 2008)
HCJ 2597/99 *Thais-Rodriguez Tushbaim v. Minister of Interior,* [2005] IsrSC 59(6)
HCJ 232/81 *Vilozni v. Great Rabbinical Court* 36(2) P.D. 733 (1982)
CA 6821/93 *United Mizrahi Bank v. Migdal Cooperative Village,* 49(4) P.D. 221 (1995)
HCJ 9734/03 *Yemini v. Great Rabbinical Court* 59(2) P.D. 295 (2004)
Basic Law: Freedom of Occupation, 1992 (amended 1994)
Basic Law: Human Dignity and Liberty, 1992, §§ 2, 4
Family Courts Law, 1995
Foundation of Law Act (Hok Yesodot Ha'Mishpat), 1980
Property Relations between Spouses Law (Hok Yahasei Mammon bein Bnei Zug) 1973 (amended 1995)

Kuwait

Constitution of Kuwait (1962), Preamble, §§ 29, 36
Constitutional Court of Kuwait, Decision of Oct. 20, 2009 (women's right to apply for a passport without male guardian permission)
Constitutional Court of Kuwait, Decision of Oct. 28, 2009 (women's duty to wear Islamic attire in order to vote or serve in parliament)
Election Law 2005

Malaysia

Abdul Kahar bin Ahmad v. Kerajaan Negeri Selangor Darul Ehsan (May 22, 2008)
Azizah Bte Shaik Ismail & Anor v. Fatimah Bte Shaik Ismail et al. [2004] 2 MLJ 529
Che Omar bin Che Soh v. Public Prosecutor [1984] 1 MLJ 113
Ismail bin Mohamad v. Wan Khariani binti Wan Mahmood (June 9, 2009)
Kaliammal Sinnasamy v. Pengarah Jabatan Agama Islam Wilayah Persekutuan et al. [2006] 1 MLJ 685
Latifa Mat Zin v. Rosmawati Binti Sharibun et al. [2007] 5 MLJ 101
Lina Joy v. Majlis Agama Islam Wilayah Persekutuan [2007] 4 MLJ 585
Soon Singh a/l Bikar Singh v. Pertubuhan Kebajikan Islam Malaysia (PERKIM) Kedah et al. [1999] 1 MLJ 489
Subashini v. Saravanan and Other [2008] 2 MLJ 147
Sukma Darmawan Sasmitaat Madja v. Ketua Pengarah Penjara Malaysia [1999] 2 MLJ 241

Teoh Eng Huat v. Kadhi Pasir Mas et al. [1990] 2 MLJ 300
Use of "Allah" by Non-Muslims case, High Court of Malaya, Kuala Lumpur (Dec. 31, 2009)
Yong Fuat Meng v. Vhin Yoon Kew, High Court of Sabah and Sarawak (June 25, 2008)
Constitution of Malaysia (1957), §§ 3, 4.1, 11, 11.1, 11.3, 11.4, 75, 121(1A), 153
Central Bank of Malaysia Act 1958 (Act 519)

Maldives

Constitution of Maldives (2008), §§ 2, 9, 10

Mexico

Supreme Court of Mexico, Ruling of Aug. 29, 2008 (Mexico City Abortion Law case)
Constitution of Mexico (1917), § 4

Morocco

Moroccan Personal Status Code (Mudawwana) 2004

Nepal

Achyut Kharel v. Government of Nepal, Lakshmi Dhikta v. Government of Nepal, Supreme Court of Nepal ruling of Aug. 4, 2008 (Abortion Law case)

Nigeria

Amina Lawal v. The State, Case No. KTS/SCA/FT/86/2002 (Shari'a Court of Appeal of Katsina State; Sept. 25, 2003)
S.C. 26/2006 *Attorney-General of Kano State v. Attorney-General of the Federation* (2007) 3 NILR 23 (Mar. 2, 2007)
Safiyatu Hussaini Tungar Tudu v. Attorney-General Sokoto State, Appeal No. SCA/GW/28/2001 (Shari'a Court of Appeal of Sokoto State, Mar. 25, 2002)
Constitution of Nigeria (1999), §§ 10, 36(6), 118, 232(1)

Norway

Constitution of Norway (1814), §§ 2, 12

Pakistan

Begum Nusrat Bhutto v. Chief of Army Staff, P.L.D. 1977 S.C. 657
Benazir Bhutto v. President of Pakistan, P.L.D. 1998 S.C. 388
Dr. M. Aslam Khaki and Others v. Syed Muhammad Hashim and Others, P.L.D. 2000 S.C. 225

Dr. Mahmood-ur-Rahman Faisal v. Govt of Pakistan, P.L.D. 1994 S.C. 607 (SAB)
Federation of Pakistan v. Farishta, P.L.D. 1981 S.C. 120 (SAB)
Federation of Pakistan v. Ms. Farzana Asar, P.L.D. 1999 S.C. 476
Hakim Khan v. Government of Pakistan, P.L.D. 1992 S.C. 595
Muhammad Nawaz Sharif v. President of Pakistan, P.L.D. 1993 S.C. 473
Pakistan Lawyers Forum v. Federation of Pakistan, P.L.D. 2005 S.C. 719
Qazi Hussain Ahmed, Ameer Jamaat-e-Islami Pakistan v. General Pervez Musharraf, Chief Executive & Another, P.L.D. 2002 S.C. 853
United Bank Ltd. v. M/S Farooq Brothers et al.; Muhammad Iqbal Zahid v. M/S Farooq Brothers & Others, P.L.D. 2002 S.C. 800
Zafar Ali Shah v. Pervez Musharraf, Chief Executive of Pakistan, P.L.D. 2000 S.C. 869
Zaheerudin v. State, 26 S.C.M.R. 1718 (S.Ct. 1993)
Civil Review Petition 45-48, 5-52, 58-62 (2009) *Federation of Pakistan v. Nawaz Sharif et al.* (May 26, 2009)
Civil Review Petition 778–779 (2008) *Federation of Pakistan v. Nawaz Sharif et al.* (Feb. 25, 2009)
Civil Review Petition 878 (2008) *Federation of Pakistan v. Shahbaz Sharif et al.* (Feb. 25, 2009)
Civil Review Petition 1512 (2008) *Commodore Shamshad v. Federal Board of Intermediate & Secondary Education et al.* (Dec. 19, 2008)
Civil Shari'at Review Petition 1/2000, *United Bank Ltd. v. M/S Farooq Brothers & Others*
Civil Shari'at Review Petition 1/2001, *Muhammad Iqbal Zahid v. M/S Farooq Brothers & Others* (June 22, 2002) P.L.D. 2002 S.C. 800
Constitution of Pakistan (1973), §§ 1, 2, 2A, 20, 176, 177, 186, 203, 227–231, Annex (Objective Resolution, 1985)
Constitution Petition 23/1999 & 21/2004 *Ch. Muhammad Siddique et al. v. Government of Pakistan* (Nov. 5, 2004)
Constitution Petition 8/2009 *Nadim Ahmed, Advocate v. Federation of Pakistan* (July 31, 2009)
Constitution Petition 9/2009 *Sindh High Court Bar Association v. Federation of Pakistan* (July 31, 2009)
Constitution Petition Nos. 76-80/2007 & 59/2009, *Dr. Mobashir Hassan and Others v. Federation of Pakistan* (January 19, 2010) [NRO case]
Reference No. 2/2005 *In Re: NWFP Hisba Bill,* P.L.D. 2005 S.C. 873

Philippines

Estrada v. Escritor, 408 SCRA 1 (2006)

Qatar

Constitution of Qatar (2003), § 1
New Investment Law (Law No. 13, 2000)

Saudi Arabia

"Qatif Girl" rape case (Nov. 13, 2007; royal pardon granted Dec. 17, 2007)
Basic Law of Saudi Arabia (1993), § 23, Chap. 4
Royal Decree 1965 (settlement of commercial disputes), § 232

Slovakia

Constitution of Slovakia (1992), § 15
Slovakia Constitutional Court Ruling on Abortion (Dec. 5, 2007)

South Africa

Bhe & Others v. Magistrate, Khayelitsha, & Others 2005 (1) SA 580 (CC)
Certification of the Amended Text of the Constitution of the Republic of S. Afr. 1997 (2) SA 97 (CC)
Ex Parte Chairperson of the Constitutional Assembly: In re Certification of the Constitution of the Republic of South Africa 1996 (4) SA 744 (CC).
Gumede v. Pres. of the Rep. of S. Afr. & Others 2009 (3) BCLR 243 (CC)
Moseneke & Others v. Master of the High Court 2001 (2) SA 18 (CC)
Mthembu v. Letsela 1997 (2) SA 936 (TPD)
Mthembu v. Letsela & Another 1998 (2) SA 675 (T)
Mthembu v. Letsela & Another 2000 (3) SA 867 (SCA)
Shilubana & Others v. Nwamitwa 2009 (2) SA 66 (CC)
Constitution of South Africa (1996), §§ 1, 9, 10, 15, 30, 31, 39(3), 211 (3)
Repeal of the Black Administration Act (2005)

Spain

S.T.C. 53/1985 (Abortion/Conscientious Objection case), judgment of Aug. 26, 1988
S.T.C. 120/1990 (Euthanasia case), judgment of June 27, 1990

Sri Lanka

Constitution of Sri Lanka (1978), § 9

Sudan

Constitution of Sudan (1998), §§ 1, 2, 7, 21–29, 35

Switzerland

Former Federal Constitution of Switzerland (1874), § 27.3
Geneva Cantonal Public Education Act (1940)

Tunisia

Constitution of Tunisia (1958), §§ 1, 8, 38
Law on Mosques (1988)

Turkey

TCC Decision 652/1989 (*Hijab* Bylaw case), Mar. 7, 1989
TCC Decision 1/1998 (Welfare [Refah] Party Dissolution case), Jan. 16, 1998
TCC Decision 57/2001 (Virtue [Fazilet] Party Dissolution case), June 21, 2001
TCC Decision 116/2008 (Constitutionality of Constitutional Amendment case), June 5, 2008; legal reasoning released on Oct. 22, 2008
TCC Decision 4/2009 (DTP Party Dissolution case), Dec. 11, 2009
TCC Decision 52/2009 (Civilian Prosecution of Military Personnel case), Jan. 21, 2010
Constitution of Turkey (1982), §§ 2, 10, 24, 143, 145, 149

United States

Atkins v. Virginia, 536 U.S. 304 (2002)
Board of Education of Kiryas Joel Village School District v. Grumet, 512 U.S. 687 (1994)
Brown v. Board of Education of Topeka, 347 U.S. 483 (1954)
Bush v. Gore, 531 U.S. 98 (2000)
City of Boerne v. Flores, 521 U.S. 507 (1997)
Employment Division, Dept. of Human Resources v. Smith, 494 U.S. 872 (1990)
Gonzales v. O Centro Espirita Beneficente Uniao do Vegetal, 546 U.S. 418 (2006)
Gonzalez v. Roman Catholic Archbishop of Manila, 280 U.S. 1 (1929)
Lawrence v. Texas, 539 U.S. 558 (2003)
Presbyterian Church v. Mary Elizabeth Blue Hull Memorial Presbyterian Church, 393 U.S. 440 (1970)
Roper v. Simmons, 543 U.S. 551 (2005)
Texas Monthly, Inc. v. Bullock, 489 U.S. 1 (1989)
Wisconsin v. Yoder, 406 U.S. 205 (1972)
U.S. Constitution, First Amendment

Vatican State (Holy See)

The Lateran Pacts (1929)
Law No. 1/2009 (new Law of the Sources of the Law)

Yemen

Constitution of Yemen (1994), §§ 2, 3, 31, 46

Notes

1. The Rise of Constitutional Theocracy

1. On the resurgence of religion in world politics, see, e.g., John Micklethwait and Adrian Wooldridge, *God Is Back* (New York: Penguin Books, 2009); Gabriel Almond et al., *Strong Religion: The Rise of Fundamentalisms around the World* (Chicago: University of Chicago Press, 2003); Peter Berger, ed., *The Desecularization of the World: Resurgent Religion and World Politics* (Grand Rapids, Mich.: Eerdmans, 1999); Philip Jenkins, *The Next Christendom: The Coming of Global Christianity* (New York: Oxford University Press, 2002); and Hent de Vries and Lawrence Sullivan, eds., *Political Theologies: Public Religions in a Post-secular World* (New York: Fordham University Press, 2006). See also Charles Taylor, *A Secular Age* (Cambridge, Mass.: Belknap Press of Harvard University Press, 2007), 1–22.
2. Jennifer S. Butler, *Born Again: The Christian Right Globalized* (London: Pluto Press, 2006); and Jenkins, *Next Christendom.*
3. This growth has provided support for social conservative dominance within the church because over 40 percent of cardinals now eligible to vote in papal elections are from the developing world. See Butler, *Born Again*, 28; Jenkins, *Next Christendom*, 195.
4. The 1979 Islamic revolution in Iran established what may be considered a paradigmatic example of constitutional theocracy. See Olivier Roy, "Une théocratie constitutionnelle: Les institutions de la République islamique d'Iran," *Politique étrangère* 52 (1987): 327–338.
5. Said A. Arjomand, "Islamic Constitutionalism," *Annual Review of Law and Social Science* 3 (2007): 115–140, 123.

6. See, e.g., Hannibal Travis, "Freedom or Theocracy? Constitutionalism in Afghanistan and Iraq," *Northwestern University Journal of International Human Rights* 3 (2005): 1-52; Intisar A. Rabb, "'We the Jurists': Islamic Constitutionalism in Iraq," *University of Pennsylvania Journal of Constitutional Law* 10 (2008): 527–579.
7. For an oft-cited illustration, see Samuel Huntington, *The Clash of Civilizations and the Remaking of World Order* (New York: Simon and Schuster, 1996). See also Bernard Lewis, *What Went Wrong? The Clash between Islam and Modernity in the Middle East* (New York: Oxford University Press, 2002).
8. See, e.g., Talal Asad, *Genealogies of Religion* (Baltimore: Johns Hopkins University Press, 1993), 27–29.
9. For a debunking of this dichotomy, see Roxanne Euben, *Journeys to the Other Shore: Muslim and Western Travelers in Search of Knowledge* (Princeton, N.J.: Princeton University Press, 2006).
10. See, e.g., Joseph H. H. Weiler, *Un'Europa Cristiana: Un saggio esploratioc* (Milan, Italy: BUR Saggi, 2003); Joseph H.H. Weiler, "A Christian Europe? Europe and Christianity: Rules of Commitment," *European View* 6 (2007): 143–150.
11. Reported by BBC News, Jan. 2, 2009. If Italy were to legalize same-sex marriages or euthanasia, for example, the Vatican would now be able to refuse to recognize such laws.
12. Ernest Gellner, *Nations and Nationalism* (Ithaca, N.Y.: Cornell University Press, 1983).
13. See Haider Ala Hamoudi, "The Muezzin's Call and the Dow Jones Bell: On the Necessity of Realism in the Study of Islamic Law," *American Journal of Comparative Law* 56 (2008): 423–470.
14. See, e.g., Nathan Brown, *The Rule of Law in the Arab World: Courts in Egypt and the Gulf* (New York: Cambridge University Press, 1997); Nathan Brown, *Constitutions in a Nonconstitutional World: Arab Basic Laws and the Prospects for Accountable Government* (Albany: SUNY Press, 2002); Nathan Brown, "Judicial Review and the Arab World," *Journal of Democracy* 9 (1998): 85–99.
15. See, e.g., Olivier Roy, *The Failure of Political Islam* (Cambridge, Mass.: Harvard University Press, 1994); Gilles Kepel, *Jihad: The Trail of Political Islam* (London: I. B. Tauris, 2004).
16. See, e.g., Noah Feldman, *After Jihad: America and the Struggle for Islamic Democracy* (New York: Farrar, Straus and Giroux, 2003); Noah Feldman, *The Fall and Rise of the Islamic State* (Princeton, N.J.: Princeton University Press, 2008). See also Andrew March, *Islamic and Liberal Citizenship: The Search for an Overlapping Consensus* (New York: Oxford University Press, 2009).
17. See, e.g., Anver Emon, "The Limits of Constitutionalism in the Muslim World: History and Identity in Islamic Law," in Sujit Choudhry, ed., *Constitutional Design for Divided Societies* (New York: Oxford University Press, 2008), 258–285; Arjomand, "Islamic Constitutionalism."
18. The pertinent literature is too vast to cite. Among the prominent contributors to this intellectual renaissance are scholars such as Abdullahi An-Na'im, Baber Johansen, and Wael Hallaq.

2. Constitutional Theocracy in Context

1. This is often told as a story of progressive change as supposed rationality and quest for modernity trump irrationality, superstition, and backwardness, but it may also be understood as a story of a gradual breakdown or disintegration of religion. See Marcel Gauchet, *The Disenchantment of the World: A Political History of Religion* (Princeton, N.J.: Princeton University Press, 1997).
2. Charles Taylor, *A Secular Age* (Cambridge, Mass.: Belknap Press of Harvard University Press, 2007).
3. See Michael Waltzer et al., eds., *The Jewish Political Tradition,* vol. 1, *Authority* (New Haven, Conn.: Yale University Press, 2000), 108–165.
4. See generally Gershom Scholem, *Sabbatai Sevi: The Mystical Messiah, 1626–1676* (Princeton, N.J.: Princeton University Press, 1973).
5. See Nathan Brown, *Constitutions in a Nonconstitutional World: Arab Basic Laws and the Prospects for Accountable Government* (Albany: SUNY Press, 2002), 16.
6. For a thorough account of the decline of religion and the rise of secularism in Western culture from the Protestant Reformation onward, see Taylor, *Secular Age.*
7. See Talal Asad, *Genealogies of Religion: Discipline and Reasons of Power in Christianity and Islam* (Baltimore: Johns Hopkins University Press, 1993); and David Scott and Charles Hirschkind, eds., *Powers of the Secular Modern: Talal Asad and His Interlocutors* (Stanford, Calif.: Stanford University Press, 2006).
8. See Taylor, *Secular Age.* See also Graeme Smith, *A Short History of Secularism* (London: I. B. Tauris, 2008).
9. See Ahmet T. Kuru, *Secularism and State Policies toward Religion: The United States, France, and Turkey* (New York: Cambridge University Press, 2009), 11.
10. See Rex Ahdar and Ian Leigh, *Religious Freedom in the Liberal State* (Oxford: Oxford University Press, 2005), 73. On the development of the secularist French national narrative, see Patrick Weil, *How to Be French: Nationality in the Making since 1789* (Durham, N.C.: Duke University Press, 2008).
11. See Law No. 2004-228 of Mar. 15, 2004, *Journal Officiel de la République Française [J.O.]* [Official Gazette of France], Mar. 17, 2004, 5190. See also Jacques Chirac, President, Republic of France, "Statement on France/Secularism" (Jan. 28, 2004).
12. See, e.g., Scott Schieman, "Socioeconomic Status and Beliefs about God's Influence in Everyday Life," *Sociology of Religion* 71 (2010): 25–51; Misty Harris, "Majority of Americans Believe in Divine Will," *The National Post* (March 13, 2010); Kuru, *Secularism and State Policies toward Religion.*
13. Gary J. Jacobsohn, *Wheel of Law: India's Secularism in Comparative Constitutional Context* (Princeton, N.J.: Princeton University Press, 2003). Comprehensive and resourceful analyses of these Supreme Court cases are provided in Kent Greenawalt, *Religion and the Constitution,* vol. 1, *Free Exercise and Fairness* (Princeton, N.J.: Princeton University Press, 2009); and Kent Greenawalt, *Religion and the Constitution,* vol. 2, *Establishment and Fairness* (Princeton, N.J.: Princeton University Press, 2009).

14. Although the church had opposed divorce that allowed remarriage in civil law, its canon law allowed for a law of nullity, effectively a form of marital separation that allowed for remarriage. This duality was the subject of litigation before the ECtHR, e.g., in *Johnson v. Ireland,* 112 ECtHR (ser. A) (1986) 9 EHRR 203. The uncertain boundaries between constitutional and canon law before 1995 have been the subject of several Supreme Court of Ireland rulings over the last fifteen years.
15. See, e.g., *A. G. v. X* [1992] IESC 1; [1992] 1 IR 1 (Mar. 5, 1992) (commonly known as the "*X* case").
16. Jewish rabbinical courts, Islamic Shari'a courts, Druze religious courts, and the courts of the Christian communities.
17. Jacobsohn, *Wheel of Law*, 81–82.
18. I examine the pertinent constitutional landscape in Israel and Malaysia in detail in Chapter 4. The Constitution of Sri Lanka designates Buddha Sasana as "the foremost" religion in that country and calls on the state to protect and foster it (art. 9).
19. See, e.g., José Casanova, *Public Religions in the Modern World* (Chicago: University oOf Chicago Press, 1994).
20. Omar al-Bashir, Sudan's president for nearly two decades now, is considered one of the major culprits in the Darfur conflict. In July 2008 the prosecutor of the International Criminal Court accused al-Bashir of genocide, crimes against humanity, and war crimes in Darfur and requested that the court issue a warrant for his arrest. The international warrant was issued in February 2009.
21. See, e.g., Noah Feldman, *After Jihad: America and the Struggle for Islamic Democracy* (New York: Farrar, Straus and Giroux, 2003).
22. See, e.g., Abdullahi Ahmed An-Na'im, *African Constitutionalism and the Role of Islam* (Philadelphia: University of Pennsylvania Press, 2006), 9.
23. See, e.g., Abdullahi Ahmed An-Na'im, *Islam and the Secular State: Negotiating the Future of Shari'a* (Cambridge, Mass.: Harvard University Press, 2008).
24. Andrew March, "Theocrats Living under Secular Law: An External Engagement with Islamic Legal Theory," *Journal of Political Philosophy* (forthcoming).
25. *Id.*.
26. See, e.g., Walter Murphy, *Constitutional Democracy* (Baltimore: Johns Hopkins University Press, 2007).
27. Ayelet Shachar and Ran Hirschl, "Citizenship as Inherited Property," *Political Theory* 35 (2007): 253–287; Ayelet Shachar, *The Birthright Lottery: Citizenship and Global Inequality* (Cambridge, Mass.: Harvard University Press, 2009).
28. See, e.g., Jürgen Habermas, *Between Facts and Norms* (Cambridge, Mass.: MIT Press, 1998).
29. See, e.g., Bruce Ackerman, *We the People, Volume 1: Foundation* (Cambridge, Mass.: Harvard University Press, 1992); and *We the People, Volume 2: Transformations* (Cambridge, Mass.: Harvard University Press, 1998).
30. The works that propose various versions of this consociational approach are too numerous to cite. A prominent exponent of this line of thought is Arend

Lijphart. See Arend Lijphart, *Democracy in Plural Societies: A Comparative Exploration* (New Haven, Conn.: Yale University Press, 1977).

31. Arend Lijphart, "Constitutional Design for Divided Societies," *Journal of Democracy* 15 (2004): 96–109.
32. See Donald Horowitz, *Ethnic Groups in Conflict* (Berkeley: University of California Press, 2000).
33. See Rogers Brubaker, *Ethnicity without Groups* (Cambridge, Mass.: Harvard University Press, 2004); Rogers Brubaker and Frederick Cooper, "Beyond 'Identity,'" *Theory and Society* 29 (2000): 1–47.
34. Judith Butler, interview in *Ha'Aretz*, Jan. 6, 2004.
35. See Rogers Brubaker et al., *Nationalist Politics and Everyday Ethnicity in a Transylvanian Town* (Princeton, N.J.: Princeton University Press, 2008).
36. See Samuel Huntington, *The Clash of Civilizations and the Remaking of World Order* (New York: Simon and Schuster, 1996).
37. See Jacobsohn, *Wheel of Law*, 49–50.

3. The Secularist Appeal of Constitutional Law and Courts

1. See "Tunisia," U.S. Department of State, International Religious Freedom Report, 2009.
2. See generally Malika C. Zeghal, *Gardiens de l'Islam: Les oulémas d'al Azhar dans l'Egypte contemporaine* (Paris: Presses de Sciences Po, 1996); and Malika C. Zeghal, "Religion and Politics in Egypt: The Ulema of al-Azhar, Radical Islam, and the State (1952–1994)," *International Journal of Middle East Studies* 31 (1999): 371–399.
3. Madawi Al-Rasheed, *Contesting the Saudi State: Islamic Voices from a New Generation* (Cambridge: Cambridge University Press, 2007), 55.
4. The origins of this practice relate to the bloody war with the United States. The Vietnamese socialist regime has developed a strong state grip on society to minimize what it regards as foreign attempts to destabilize the regime.
5. C. van Dijk, "Religious Authority, Politics, and Fatwas in Contemporary Southeast Asia," in R. M. Feener and Mark E. Cammack, eds., *Islamic Law in Contemporary Indonesia* (Cambridge, Mass.: Harvard University Press, 2007), 63.
6. Ieva Raubisko, "Proper 'Traditional' versus Dangerous 'New': Religious Ideology and Idiosyncratic Islamic Practices in Post-Soviet Chechnya," *Journal of the Anthropological Society of Oxford* (online) 1 (2009): 70–93.
7. Stephen Feldman, *Please Don't Wish Me a Merry Christmas: A Critical History of the Separation of Church and State* (New York: New York University Press, 1997).
8. *Board of Education of Kiryas Joel Village School District v. Grumet*, 512 U.S. 687 (1994).
9. See Adam Smith, *The Wealth of Nations* (New York: Random House, 1994 [1776]).
10. See, e.g., Roger Finke and Rodney Stark, *The Churching of America, 1776–2005: Winners and Losers in Our Religious Economy* (New Brunswick, N.J.: Rutgers University Press, 2005).

11. *Id.*, 75–86; discussed in Christopher Eisgruber and Mariah Zeisberg, "Religious Freedom in Canada and the United States," *International Journal of Constitutional Law* 4 (2006): 247–248.
12. See, e.g., Seymour M. Lipset, *Continental Divide: The Values and Institutions of the United States and Canada* (London: Routledge, 1990), 80; discussed in Eisgruber and Zeisberg, "Religious Freedom in Canada and the United States," 247.
13. See, e.g., Guillermo Trejo, "Religious Competition and Ethnic Mobilization in Latin America: Why the Catholic Church Promotes Indigenous Movements in Mexico," *American Political Science Review* 103 (2009): 323–342.
14. See Martin Shapiro, *Courts: A Comparative and Political Analysis* (Chicago: University of Chicago Press, 1981), 194–222. Abdulahi an-Na'im, *Toward an Islamic Reformation: Civil Liberties, Human Rights, and International Law* (Syracuse, N.Y.: University of Syracuse Press, 1990), 100. See also Bassam Tibi, "The Return of the Sacred to Politics as a Constitutional Law," *Theoria* 55 (2008): 91–119.
15. *Id.,* 195–196. See also Sami Zubaida, *Law and Power in the Islamic World* (London: I. B. Tauris, 2003), 202.
16. David Laitin, *Hegemony and Culture: Politics and Change among the Yoruba* (Chicago: University of Chicago Press, 1986), 3.
17. Noah Feldman, *The Fall and Rise of the Islamic State* (Princeton, N.J.: Princeton University Press, 2008), 8; cited in Shadi Mokhtari, "Review of Noah Feldman's The Fall and Rise of the Islamic State," *Law and Politics Book Review* 18 (2008): 1016–1019.
18. Feldman, *Fall and Rise of the Islamic State,* 69.
19. See Kambiz Behi, "Structure and Process of Legal Change in Post-revolutionary Iran: The Emergence of the Third Globalization" (unpublished manuscript; on file with author).
20. As Kambiz Behi reports (*Id.*), the Guardian Council vetoed 118 out of 316 acts during the first parliament (1980–1984) and 102 out of 370 during the second parliament (1984–1988). See Mehdi Moslem, *Factional Politics in Post-Khomeini Iran* (Syracuse, N.Y.: Syracuse University Press, 2002), 62. See also Bahman Baktiari, *Parliamentary Politics in Revolutionary Iran: The Institutionalization of Factional Politics* (Gainesville: University Press of Florida, 1996).
21. Behi, "Structure and Process of Legal Change in Post-revolutionary Iran." See also Said A. Arjomand, *After Khomeini: Iran and Under His Successors* (New York: Oxford University Press, 2009), 36–55.
22. In October 2005 the supreme leader delegated some of his authority to the Expediency Council to supervise, and in some case adjudicate, all branches of the government.
23. This explanation echoes Robert Barros's study of the Chilean Constitutional Court under Augusto Pinochet. See Robert Barros, *Constitutionalism and Dictatorship: Pinochet, the Junta, and the 1980 Constitution* (Cambridge: Cambridge University Press, 2002).
24. See, e.g., Alexei Trochev, *Judging Russia: Constitutional Courts in Russian Politics* (New York: Cambridge University Press, 2008), 265–282; and Wil-

liam Burnham and Alexei Trochev, "Russia's War between the Courts: The Struggle over the Jurisdictional Boundary between the Constitutional Court and Regular Courts," *American Journal of Comparative Law* 55 (2007): 381–452.

25. See Harold J. Berman, *Law and Revolution: The Formation of the Western Legal Tradition* (Cambridge, Mass.: Harvard University Press, 1983). Other medievalists point to the structure of the medieval church and the medieval state (e.g., tensions between central and local government), which they believed influenced the development of modern constitutional thought and institutions. See Brian Tierney, *Religion, Law, and the Growth of Constitutional Thought, 1150–1650* (Cambridge: Cambridge University Press, 1982).
26. Robert B. Ekelund et al., *Sacred Trust: The Medieval Church as an Economic Firm* (New York: Oxford University Press, 1996), 63; John T. Gilchrist, *The Church and Economic Activity in the Middle Ages* (New York: St. Martin's Press, 1969), 12–13.
27. Berman, *Law and Revolution,* 50.
28. Marianne Constable, *The Law of the Other: The Mixed Jury and Changing Conceptions of Citizenship, Law, and Knowledge* (Chicago: University of Chicago Press, 1994).
29. Berman, *Law and Revolution,* 261.
30. *Id.*
31. Ekelund et al., *Sacred Trust,* 64.
32. Berman, *Law and Revolution,* 266.
33. Michel Foucault, *Discipline and Punish: The Birth of the Prison* (New York: Pantheon Books, 1977).
34. See, e.g., Lama Abu-Odeh, "Modernizing Muslim Family Law: The Case of Egypt," *Vanderbilt Journal of Transnational Law* 37 (2004): 1043–1146; Leon Buskens, "Recent Debates on Family Law Reforms in Morocco: Islamic Law as Politics in an Emerging Public Sphere," *Islamic Law and Society* 10 (2003): 70–132; Laura Weingartner, "Family Law and Reform in Morocco—The Mudawwana: Modernist Islam and Women's Rights in the Code of Personal Status," *University of Detroit Mercy Law Review* 82 (2004): 687–713; and Lezzar Nasr-Eddine, "La femme et les droits de l'homme en droit algérien," *Revue NAQD—Femmes et Citoyenneté,* nos. 22/23 (Fall/Winter 2006): 234.
35. Christina Boswell, *The Political Usages of Expert Knowledge* (Cambridge: Cambridge University Press, 2009).
36. Stefan Voigt and Eli Salzberger, "Choosing Not to Choose: When Politicians Choose to Delegate Powers," *Kyklos* 55 (2002): 289–310, 294.
37. See generally Mark Graber, "The Non-majoritarian Difficulty: Legislative Deference to the Judiciary," *Studies in American Political Development* 7 (1993): 35–73.
38. See Ran Hirschl, "Constitutional Courts vs. Religious Fundamentalism: Three Middle Eastern Tales," *Texas Law Review* 82 (2004): 1819–1862; and Keith Whittington, "'Interpose Your Friendly Hand': Political Supports for the Exercise of Judicial Review by the United States Supreme Court," *American Political Science Review* 99 (2005): 583–596.

39. See Ran Hirschl, *Towards Juristocracy: The Origins and Consequences of the New Constitutionalism* (Cambridge, Mass.: Harvard University Press, 2004).
40. See J. Mark Ramseyer, "The Puzzling (In)Dependence of Courts: A Comparative Approach," *Journal of Legal Studies* 23 (1994): 721–748; Howard Gillman, "How Political Parties Can Use the Courts to Advance Their Agendas: Federal Courts in the United States, 1875–1891," *American Political Science Review* 96 (2002): 511–524; Tom Ginsburg, *Judicial Review in New Democracies: Constitutional Courts in Asian Cases* (Cambridge: Cambridge University Press, 2003); Pedro Magalhães, "The Politics of Judicial Reform in Eastern Europe," *Comparative Politics* 32 (1999): 43–62; and Rebecca B. Chavez, "The Construction of Rule of Law in Argentina: A Tale of Two Provinces," *Comparative Politics* 35 (2003): 417–437.
41. Some scholars of British constitutional history argue that the events known as the Glorious Revolution (1688–1689), most notably the establishment of a constitutional monarchy and the adoption of the English Bill of Rights, were aimed at protecting the interests of the propertied classes against Dutch invasion and the ensuing political instability.
42. For earlier examples of such strategic incorporation of international standards into domestic law, see Andrew Moravcsik, "The Origins of Human Rights Regimes," *International Organization* 54 (2000): 217–252.
43. In the late 1980s the three parties that made up Meretz—Ratz, Mapam, and Shinui—combined for 10 to 12 Knesset seats. The unified Meretz won 12 Knesset seats in the 1992 elections.
44. In the 2006 election Shas received 300,000 votes, which translated into 12 seats, and in the 2009 election the party received 280,000 votes, which translated into 11 seats.
45. Israel Shahak and Norton Mezvinsky, *Jewish Fundamentalism in Israel* (London: Pluto Press, 1999).
46. A prime example is Jerusalem. Having been governed for nearly three decades (1965–1993) by Mayor Teddy Kollek, a quintessential Labor politician, Jerusalem was governed from June 2003 until November 2008 by Mayor Uri Lupolianski, an Orthodox Jew who comes from a family of rabbis.
47. To advance their attempt at hegemonic preservation further, those who supported judicial empowerment also instigated a change to the electoral system that saw the 1996 election of the prime minister separated from the general parliamentary elections. This has since been repealed, and the former unified proportional representation system has been reenacted.
48. These terms and phrases, particularly "enlightened public" (Ha'tsibur Ha'naor), were coined and used repeatedly by Aharon Barak, former chief justice of the Israeli Supreme Court.
49. See C 16023/08 *Eskimo Trade Inc. v. Vidislavsky et al.,* Tel-Aviv Municipal Court (May 5, 2008).
50. Cited in *Ha'Aretz* (English edition), Feb. 11, 1999, www.haaretz.co.il/eng.
51. *Id.*
52. *Id.*
53. "Yosef: Supreme Court Judges–Apostates," *Jerusalem Post* (August 31, 2009).

54. See Hirschl, *Towards Juristocracy.* See also Terence Halliday et al., "The Legal Complex in Struggles for Political Liberalisms," in Terence Halliday et al., eds., *Fighting for Political Freedom: Comparative Studies of the Legal Complex and Political Liberalism* (Oxford: Hart Publishing, 2007), 1–42.
55. Jeremy Waldron, *Nonsense upon Stilts: Bentham, Burke, and Marx on the Rights of Man* (London: Methuen, 1987), 196. See also Ronald Beiner, *What's the Matter with Liberalism?* (Berkeley: University of California Press, 1992); Mary Ann Glendon, *Rights Talk: The Impoverishment of Political Discourse* (New York: Free Press, 1991); and Mark Tushnet, "An Essay on Rights," *Texas Law Review* 62 (1984): 1363–1403.
56. Glendon, *Rights Talk,* xi. See also Robert Kagan, *Adversarial Legalism: The American Way of Law* (Cambridge, Mass.: Harvard University Press, 2001).
57. Cited in George Monbiot, "My Heroes Are Driven by God, but I'm Glad My Society Isn't," *Guardian,* Oct. 11, 2005, 31. "We must trust of course," wittily adds Monbiot, "that a man who has spent his life campaigning to become God's go-between, and who now believes he is infallible, is immune to such impulses."
58. This notion is based on Amartya Sen's "capabilities" or "basic-needs" approach to human development. It has been adopted by the United Nations Development Programme and numerous other international human development agencies. See Amartya Sen, "Equality of What?" in S. McMurrin, ed., *Tanner Lectures on Human Values* (Cambridge: Cambridge University Press, 1980); and Amartya Sen, *Inequality Reexamined* (Cambridge, Mass.: Harvard University Press, 1992).
59. The literature on this point is vast. See, e.g., Douglass North and Barry Weingast, "Constitutions and Commitment: The Evolution of Institutions Governing Public Choice in Seventeenth Century England," *Journal of Economic History* 49 (1989): 803–833; and Barry Weingast, "Constitutions as Governance Structures: The Political Foundations of Secure Markets," *Journal of Institutional and Theoretical Economics* 149 (1993): 286–311.
60. See Tamir Moustafa, "Law versus the State: The Judicialization of Politics in Egypt," *Law and Social Inquiry* 28 (2003): 883–930; and Tamir Moustafa, *The Struggle for Constitutional Power: Law, Politics, and Economic Development in Egypt* (New York: Cambridge University Press, 2007).
61. Gordon Silverstein, "Singapore: The Exception That Proves Rules Matter," in Tom Ginsburg and Tamir Moustafa, eds., *Rule by Law: The Politics of Courts in Authoritarian Regimes* (New York: Cambridge University Press, 2008), 73–101.
62. See Joel Bakan, *Just Words: Constitutional Rights and Social Wrongs* (Toronto: University of Toronto Press, 1997), chs. 3–5.
63. The Israelites' (Bnai Yisrael) response to Moses' (Moshe's) presentation of the Divine Covenant, according to the Torah (Exodus 24:7), has become a symbol for a rule-following, "first we obey and perform, and then we ask questions" approach.
64. A canonical version of this view is provided in John Rawls, *A Theory of Justice* (Cambridge, Mass.: Harvard University Press, 1971).

65. James C. Scott, *Seeing like a State* (New Haven, Conn.: Yale University Press, 1999).
66. See, e.g., Beverly McLachlin (Chief Justice of Canada), "Freedom of Religion and the Rule of Law: A Canadian Perspective," in Douglas Farrow, ed., *Recognizing Religion in a Secular Society: Essays in Pluralism, Religion, and Public Policy* (Montreal: McGill–Queen's University Press, 2004), 12–34. Chief Justice McLachlin argues that Canadian courts have struggled to find a place for religious expression within the rule of law and points to some cases that she sees as successes in this regard (notably *Hofer v. Hofer,* [1970] S.C.R. 958, contrasting general norms of Canadian law with Hutterite Church and colony rules). The challenge for courts, in her view, is fitting one comprehensive doctrine within another and determining the limits of religious expression.
67. Charles Taylor, "Foreword," in Marcel Gauchet, *The Disenchantment of the World: A Political History of Religion* (Princeton, N.J.: Princeton University Press, 1997), xi–xii.
68. Pierre Bourdieu, *Language and Symbolic Power* (Cambridge, Mass.: Harvard University Press, 1991), 42.
69. See Alec Stone Sweet and Jud Mathews, "Proportionality Balancing and Global Constitutionalism," *Columbia Journal of Transnational Law* 47 (2008): 73–165.
70. David Beatty, *The Ultimate Rule of Law* (New York: Oxford University Press, 2004).
71. See Mark Tushnet, "The Inevitable Globalization of Constitutional Law," *Virginia Journal of International Law* 49 (2009): 985–1006.
72. See, generally, Vicki Jackson, *Constitutional Engagement in a Transnational Era* (New York: Oxford University Press, 2010).
73. Glendon, *Rights Talk,* 158.
74. Sujit Choudhry, "Globalization in Search of Justification: Toward a Theory of Comparative Constitutional Interpretation," *Indiana Law Review* 74 (1999): 819–948.
75. Anne-Marie Slaughter, "A Typology of Transjudicial Communities," *University of Richmond Law Review* 29 (1994): 99–134.
76. David Law, "Generic Constitutional Law," *Minnesota Law Review* 89 (2005): 652–742; Jiunn-Rong Yeh and Wen-Chen Chang, "The Emergence of Transnational Constitutionalism: Its Features, Challenges and Solutions," *Pennsylvania State International Law Review* 27 (2008): 89–124.
77. Sanford Levinson, *Constitutional Faith* (Princeton, N.J.: Princeton University Press, 1988).
78. See, e.g., Russell Hardin, *Liberalism, Constitutionalism, and Democracy* (Oxford and New York: Oxford University Press, 1999).
79. See *Human Rights Watch World Report 2009,* 444.
80. EA 1/88, *Neiman v. Chairman of the Central Elections Committee for the Twelfth Knesset,* 42(4) P. D. 177 (1988).
81. The Balad Party's agenda has been deemed controversial because it advocates a vision of Israel as a country of all its citizens (i.e., fully inclusive of its Arab citizens), a true commitment to Hebrew-Arab bilingualism, and extensive cul-

tural autonomy for Israel's Arab citizens in regions heavily inhabited by them. This agenda appears to contravene the foundational concept of Israel as a Jewish and democratic state by preferring the latter tenet over the former.

82. Kate Malleson and Peter Russell, eds., *Appointing Judges in an Age of Judicial Power* (Toronto: University of Toronto Press, 2006).
83. See J. Mark Ramseyer and Eric B. Rasmusen, *Measuring Judicial Independence: The Political Economy of Judging in Japan* (Chicago: University of Chicago Press, 2003); and Frank Upham, "Political Lackeys or Faithful Public Servants? Two Views of the Japanese Judiciary," *Law and Social Inquiry* 30 (2005): 421–455.
84. Robert Dahl, "Decision-Making in a Democracy: The Supreme Court as a National Policy-Maker," *Journal of Public Law* 6 (1957): 279–295, 291.
85. Mathew McCubbins and Thomas Schwartz, "Congressional Oversight Overlooked: Police Patrol vs. Fire Alarms," *American Journal of Political Science* 28 (1984): 165–179.
86. See generally Nathalie Bernard-Maugiron, ed., *Judges and Political Reform in Egypt* (Cairo: American University of Cairo Press, 2009).
87. Egyptian law does not allow judges to travel abroad without prior authorization. There was some speculation that this law has been used by the government to prevent activist judges—notably Hisham Bastawissi of the Court of Cassation and Ashraf El-Baroudi, a judge of the Alexandria Court of Appeal—from participating in international human rights meetings overseas.
88. See Hootan Shambayati, "The Guardian of the Regime: The Turkish Constitutional Court in Comparative Perspective," in S. A. Arjomand, ed., *Constitutional Politics in the Middle East* (Oxford: Hart Publishing, 2008), 105.
89. A classic illustration is *Mohammed Ahmed Khan v. Shah Bano Begum,* A.I.R. 1985 S.C. 985, and its tumultuous aftermath, stretching to the court's ruling in *Danial Latifi v. Union of India,* A.I.R. 2001 S.C. 3958. See generally Gary J. Jacobsohn, *The Wheel of Law: India's Secularism in Comparative Constitutional Context* (Princeton, N.J.: Princeton University Press, 2003); S. P. Sathe, *Judicial Activism in India: Transgressing Borders and Enforcing Limits* (New Delhi: Oxford University Press, 2002); Josh Goodman, "Divine Judgment: Judicial Review of Religious Legal Systems in India and Israel," *Hastings International and Comparative Law Journal* 32 (2009): 477–528.
90. *Sarla Mugdal v. Union of India,* A.I.R. 1995 S.C. 1531, paras. 35–36.
91. *John Vallamattom v. Union of India,* A.I.R. 2003 S.C. 384.
92. Special Leave Petition (Civil) 5939/2009 *Mohammad Salim v. Nirmala Convent Higher Secondary School* (Supreme Court of India ruling of Mar. 30, 2009).
93. As one would expect, these comments triggered vocal criticism from Muslim leaders in India. Ultimately, Justice Katju apologized for his controversial "Talibanization" comments, and re-directed the case to another bench, which in September 2009 reversed course and ordered the readmission of the student until further notice. Thus the subtle secularization in a polity where religion and religious affiliation play a central and often politically charged role continues.

94. The combination of these two factors effectively sabotaged the appointment to the Supreme Court of Ruth Gavison, a vocal critic of the Barak court's activism. Barak conducted an unusually outspoken campaign to prevent Gavison's appointment, presumably because of her open criticism of the Barak court's overactivism and ultralenient justiciability rules.
95. The three justice ministers in the Kadima-led government (ousted in the February 2009 elections), Haim Ramon, Tzippi Livni, and most notably Daniel Friedman, were markedly more critical of the court's entanglement with politics than their predecessors. In April 2009 a more moderate route was taken with the appointment of Ya'akov Ne'eman as the justice minister in the newly formed Likud-led Netanyahu government. Ne'eman is an established lawyer of Zionist religious background who acquired his graduate law degree at New York University and who served as justice minister and as minister of finance in the 1990s.
96. Because religious courts in Israel are statutory bodies, employment standards in such courts are subject to general labor-law norms and regulations.
97. See Mark E. Cammack, "The Indonesian Islamic Judiciary," in Feener and Cammack, eds., *Islamic Law in Contemporary Indonesia,* 146–169.
98. *Id.,* 162.
99. *Id.,* 161.
100. Women have served as Islamic court judges in Indonesia since the 1960s. Indonesian religious scholars concluded that women may serve as Islamic court judges in all but criminal cases, which in any event are not tried in the Islamic court system.
101. "Tahani al-Gebali . . . A Journey of Outstanding Success," *Egypt Magazine,* Spring 2003, http://www.sis.gov.eg/public/magazine/iss031e/html/mag09.html.
102. *Id.*
103. See Mark Ramseyer and Eric Rasmusen, "Why Are Japanese Judges So Conservative in Politically Charged Cases?" *American Political Science Review* 95 (2001): 331–343; Gretchen Helmke, "The Logic of Strategic Defection: Court-Executive Relations in Argentina under Dictatorship and Democracy," *American Political Science Review* 96 (2002): 291–303; and Paula Newberg, *Judging the State: Courts and Constitutional Politics in Pakistan* (New York: Cambridge Univerity Press, 1995).
104. See Lisa Hilbink, *Judges beyond Politics in Democracy and Dictatorship: Lessons from Chile* (New York: Cambridge University Press, 2007).
105. See Lawrence Baum, *Judges and Their Audiences: A Perspective on Judicial Behavior* (Princeton, N.J.: Princeton University Press, 2006). See also Richard A. Posner, *How Judges Think* (Cambridge, Mass.: Harvard University Press, 2008).
106. Some empirical evidence supports this assertion. Survey evidence in Herbert McClosky and Alida Brill, *Dimensions of Tolerance: What Americans Believe about Civil Liberties* (New York: Russell Sage Foundation, 1983) shows that when people were asked about civil liberties issues, answers by lawyers, law-enforcement officials, and government officials tended to track Supreme Court doctrine much more closely than those of the other groups.

107. The establishment of an international rule of law in the EU, for example, was driven in no small part by national judges' attempts to enhance their independence, influence, and authority vis-à-vis other courts and political actors. See, e.g., Karen Alter, *Establishing the Supremacy of European Law: The Making of an International Rule of Law in Europe* (New York: Oxford University Press, 2001). See also Joseph H. H. Weiler, "A Quiet Revolution: The European Court of Justice and Its Interlocutors," *Comparative Political Studies* 26 (1994): 510–534.
108. Kevin McGuire and James Stimson, "The Least Dangerous Branch Revisited: New Evidence on Supreme Court Responsiveness to Public Preferences," *Journal of Politics* 66 (2004): 1018–1035.
109. This in a nutshell is the message of the "strategic" approach to judicial behavior. See Pablo T. Spiller and Rafael Gely, "Strategic Judicial Decision-Making," in Keith Whittington et al., eds., *The Oxford Handbook of Law and Politics* (New York: Oxford University Press, 2008), 35–45; and Lee Epstein and Jack Knight, "Towards a Strategic Revolution in Judicial Politics: A Look Back, a Look Ahead," *Political Research Quarterly* 53 (2000): 625–661.
110. See Ran Hirschl, "The Judicialization of Mega-Politics and the Rise of Political Courts," *Annual Review of Political Science* 11 (2008): 93–118.
111. See Gerald Rosenberg, *The Hollow Hope: Can Courts Bring About Social Change?* (Chicago: University of Chicago Press, 2nd ed., 2008); Gerald Rosenberg, "Judicial Independence and the Reality of Political Power," *Review of Politics* 54 (1992): 369–398; Geofrey Garrett et al., "The European Court of Justice, National Governments, and Legal Integration in the European Union," *International Organization* 52 (1998): 149–176; and Lisa Conant, *Justice Contained: Law and Politics in the European Union* (Ithaca, N.Y.: Cornell University Press, 2002).
112. *Employment Division, Dept. of Human Resources v. Smith,* 494 U.S. 872 (1990).
113. In 2006 (*Gonzales v. O Centro Espirita Beneficente Uniao do Vegetal*) the Supreme Court dismissed on free-exercise grounds charges against a church that during a religious ceremony used a sacramental tea that included an otherwise (federally) illegal substance. The Court decisively stated that the federal government must show a compelling state interest in restricting religious freedom.
114. See, e.g., Lee Epstein et al., "The Role of Constitutional Courts in the Establishment and Maintenance of Democratic Systems of Government," *Law and Society Review* 35 (2001): 117–163; and Lee Epstein et al., "Constitutional Interpretation from a Strategic Perspective," in M. Miller and J. Barnes, eds., *Making Policy, Making Law: An Inter-branch Perspective* (Washington, D.C.: Georgetown University Press, 2004).
115. Epstein et al., "Role of Constitutional Courts," 117.
116. See *Id.*; Gretchen Helmke, *Courts under Constraints: Judges, Generals, and Presidents in Argentina* (New York: Cambridge University Press, 2005); George Vanberg, *The Politics of Constitutional Review in Germany* (New York: Cambridge University Press, 2005); and Alexei Trochev, "Fragmentation?

Defection? Legitimacy? Explaining Judicial Behavior in Post-Communist 'Colored Revolutions' " (paper presented at the Sawyer Plenary Seminar on the Dilemmas of Judicial Power, University of California at Berkeley, Nov. 7–8, 2008; on file with author).

117. Recall how President George W. Bush attempted appointment of Harriet Miers to the Supreme Court. Unlike Bush, however, Karzai had to pass far fewer political hurdles in appointing Abdul Salam Azimi to the position of chief justice.

118. Karzai initially claimed to have won the August 2009 elections but later agreed to a runoff election against opponent Abdullah Abdullah when evidence of election fraud and corruption started to surface.

119. After his appointment and until his resignation, Dogar was at the center of at least two corruption allegations, one related to an unregistered loan he allegedly received from the National Bank of Pakistan, and the other related to a rare upward correction of his daughter's national qualification exam scores that lifted her above the threshold cumulative score required for applying to medical schools in Pakistan. See Civil Review Petition 1512 (2008) *Commodore Shamshad v. Federal Board of Intermediate & Secondary Education et al.* (Dec. 19, 2008). In September 2009 Dogar decided to challenge his own removal and Chaudhry's reinstatement.

120. On February 25, 2009, Shahbaz's second term as chief minister of Punjab was terminated when a three-member bench of the Supreme Court of Pakistan, headed by Justice Moosa K. Leghari, declared him ineligible to contest elections, took away his seat in the Punjab Assembly, and thereby removed him from office. See Civil Review Petition 778–779 (2008) *Federation of Pakistan v. Nawaz Sharif et al.* (Feb. 25, 2009); Civil Review Petition 878 (2008) *Federation of Pakistan v. Shahbaz Sharif et al.* (Feb. 25, 2009).

121. Zardari's administration eventually succumbed in March 2009 to immense domestic and international pressure and decided to back the Sharifs' bid to lead Punjab. The government then appealed the court rulings against the brothers, raising the prospect that Shahbaz Sharif could return to office. In May 2009 the Supreme Court reinstated Nawaz and Shahbaz Sharif. See Civil Review Petition 45-48, 5-52, 58-62 (2009) *Federation of Pakistan v. Nawaz Sharif et al.* (May 26, 2009).

122. This reform is part of a larger overhaul that includes fortification of criminal due process rules in Saudi Arabian courts, as well as liberalization of the legal profession that would allow female lawyers to represent clients before the courts in personal status and family law cases.

4. Constitutionalism versus Theocracy

1. The literature on this point is too vast to cite in full. See, e.g., Torsten Persson and Guido Tabellini, *The Economic Effects of Constitutions* (Cambridge, Mass.: MIT Press, 2003); Douglass North and Barry Weingast, "Constitutions and Commitment: The Evolution of Institutions Governing Public Choice in Seventeenth-Century England," *Journal of Economic History* 49 (1989): 803–832; Rafael La Porta et al., "Legal Determinants of External

Finance," *Journal of Finance* 52 (1997): 1131–1150; and Tamir Moustafa, "Law versus the State: The Judicialization of Politics in Egypt," *Law and Social Inquiry* 28 (2003): 883–930.

2. For the nuances of contemporary Egyptian politics and political culture, see Bruce K. Rutherford, *Egypt after Mubarak: Liberalism, Islam, and Democracy in the Arab World* (Princeton, N.J.: Princeton University Press, 2009).
3. As mentioned in Chapter 3, President Mubarak reacted in 1996 to al-Azhar's radical drift by appointing progovernment cleric Muhammad Tantawi, the former grand mufti of Egypt, the new shaykh al-Azhar.
4. Among the reforms introduced is reduced judicial scrutiny of electoral lists, ballots, and procedures, practically meaning more political control over official monitoring and counting of elections.
5. The court was named Supreme Court from 1969 to 1979 and Supreme Constitutional Court from 1979 onward.
6. See Statute of the Supreme Constitutional Court, Law No. 48 (1979).
7. An excellent outline of the court's history, procedures, and political standing is provided in Clark Lombardi, "Egypt's Supreme Constitutional Court: Managing Constitutional Conflict in an Authoritarian, Aspirationally 'Islamic' State," *Journal of Comparative Law* 3 (2008): 234–253.
8. In March 2007, for example, Egypt's president, Hosni Mubarak, and the then chief justice of the Supreme Constitutional Court, Maher Abdel-Wahed, hosted in Cairo the chief justice of Italy's Constitutional Court, Franco Bile. During that visit Bile emphasized that while judicial systems vary among different countries, constitutional ones tend to be similar. Maher Abdel-Wahed said that both courts would work together to preserve the sovereignty of law and protect rights and freedoms in their respective polities.
9. See Lombardi, "Egypt's Supreme Constitutional Court"; and Tamir Moustafa, *The Struggle for Constitutional Power: Law, Politics, and Economic Development in Egypt* (New York: Cambridge University Press, 2007).
10. See generally Clark Lombardi, *State Law as Islamic Law in Modern Egypt: The Incorporation of the Shari'a into Egyptian Constitutional Law* (Leiden: Brill, 2006).
11. See Nathan J. Brown, "Islamic Constitutionalism in Theory and Practice," in Eugene Cotran and Adel Omar Sherif, eds., *Democracy, the Rule of Law and Islam* (New York: Springer, 1999), 496.
12. See, e.g., Noah Feldman, *The Fall and Rise of the Islamic State* (Princeton, N.J.: Princeton University Press, 2008).
13. Brown, "Islamic Constitutionalism in Theory and Practice," 497.
14. In the United States, see *Presbyterian Church v. Mary Elizabeth Blue Hull Memorial Presbyterian Church,* 393 U.S. 440 (1970). See also *Gonzalez v. Roman Catholic Archbishop of Manila,* 280 U.S. 1 (1929).
15. *Riba* [usury or interest] case, Decision No. 20, 1st Judicial Year, and Decision 28, 2nd Judicial Year (May 4, 1985).
16. Clark B. Lombardi, "Islamic Law as a Source of Constitutional Law in Egypt: The Constitutionalization of the Sharia in a Modern Arab State," *Columbia Journal of Transnational Law* 37 (1998): 81, 89.

17. Case No. 7, Judicial Year 8 (May 15, 1993). See Lombardi, *State Law as Islamic Law in Modern Egypt,* 202–218.
18. Case No. 29, Judicial Year 11 (Mar. 26, 1994); Case No. 35, Judicial Year 9 (Aug. 14, 1994). See Lombardi, *State Law as Islamic Law in Modern Egypt,* 218–236.
19. *Wassel v. Minister of Education* (the *niqab* [veil] case), Case No. 8 of the 17th Judicial Year (May 18, 1996); a translation into English is available at *American University International Law Review* 21 (2006): 437.
20. Lombardi, "Islamic Law as a Source of Constitutional Law in Egypt," 111–112.
21. See *Moustafa v. President of the Republic,* Case No. 18 of the 14th Judicial Year (May 3, 1997).
22. *Human Rights Watch World Report 2008,* 470.
23. Egypt's family-law reform project eventually resulted in the passage of three new laws: Law 1 of 2000, Law 10 of 2004, and Law 11 of 2004. Law 1 reformed the terms and procedures of personal-status cases. Four years later, Law 10 introduced the system of family courts; and Law 11 established the Family Insurance Fund, a mechanism through which female litigants could collect court-ordered alimony and child support. See Sherifa Zuhur, "The Mixed Impact of Feminist Struggles in Egypt during the 1990s," *Middle East Review of International Affairs* 5 (Mar. 2001): 78–89; and Mulki Al-Sharmani, "Egypt's Family Courts: Route to Empowerment?" *Open Democracy,* Sept. 7, 2007.
24. Obviously, this new arrangement favors women who are economically well off because it puts them in a better position to buy themselves out of ailing marriages by forfeiting some of their economic rights.
25. *Khul Law* case, Constitutional Case No. 201, 23rd Judicial Year (Dec. 26, 2002). The same interpretive flexibility allowed Habib Bourguiba, the first president and great modernizer of Tunisia, to adopt the Personal Status Code in 1956; this was arguably the most liberal legislation in the field of personal status adopted by a country that is constitutionally committed to the teachings of Islam. On the basis of the same interpretive flexibility, further modernizing revisions were added to the code in 1993. See Amira Mashhour, "Islamic Law and Gender Equality—Could There Be a Common Ground? A Study of Divorce and Polygamy in Shari'a Law and Contemporary Legislation in Tunisia and Egypt," *Human Rights Quarterly* 27 (2005): 562–596.
26. Quoted in "Mubarak's Address to the Parliament: Rule of Law as a Fundamental Approach" (Nov. 21, 2003).
27. Cited in "SCC Counselor Chairman: Mubarak Granted a Distinguished Status for Judiciary" (Aug. 31, 2003).
28. Speech delivered at the Supreme Constitutional Court, Cairo, Mar. 7, 2009, reported by Egypt's State Information Services, http://www.sis.gov.eg/En/Politics/Presidency/President/Speeches/.
29. For an elaboration of some of these liberalizing rulings and their effect on the Egyptian political economy, see Moustafa, *Struggle for Constitutional Power.*
30. Nathan Brown, *The Rule of Law in the Arab World: Courts in Egypt and the Arab States of the Gulf* (Cambridge: Cambridge University Press, 1997), 126.

31. *Id.*
32. Zvi Barel, "How the Muslim World Deals with the Rise of Islamism," *Ha'Aretz*, Oct. 21, 2009.
33. Decision of Oct. 28, 2009.
34. Decision of Oct. 20, 2009.
35. Farzana Shaikh, *Making Sense of Pakistan* (New York: Columbia University Press, 2009).
36. In 2008, under the temporary administration of Chief Justice Abdul Hameed Dogar, the court committed to expedite case hearings and clear the backlog, although as of 2010 this seems an overly ambitious and unrealistic goal.
37. See, e.g., *Zafar Ali Shah v. Pervez Musharraf, Chief Executive of Pakistan*, P.L.D. 2000 S.C. 869; *Benazir Bhutto v. President of Pakistan*, P.L.D. 1998 S.C. 388; *Muhammad Nawaz Sharif v. President of Pakistan*, P.L.D. 1993 S.C. 473; and *Begum Nusrat Bhutto v. Chief of Army Staff*, P.L.D. 1977 S.C. 657.
38. *Zafar Ali Shah v. Pervez Musharraf, Chief Executive of Pakistan*, P.L.D. 2000 S.C. 869.
39. *Id.*, 1219.
40. *Id.*
41. *Id.*, 1223.
42. Constitution Petition 8/2009 *Nadim Ahmed, Advocate v. Federation of Pakistan;* and Constitution Petition 9/2009 *Sindh High Court Bar Association v. Federation of Pakistan* (decisions released July 31, 2009).
43. Constitution Petition No. 76-80/2007 & 59/2009, *Dr. Mobashir Hassan and Others v. Federation of Pakistan* (January 19, 2010) [NRO case]. See also "In Disrepute," *The Economist*, January 23, 2010.
44. "In Disrepute." Constitution Petition No. 76-80/2007 & 59/2009, 160–164.
45. Constitution Petition No. 76-80/2007 & 59/2009, 30.
46. The persecution of the Ahmadiyya sect has certainly not been confined to Pakistan. In June 2008, for example, the government of Indonesia ordered members of the Ahmadiyya sect to cease public religious activities or face up to five years' imprisonment. In September 2008 the South Sumatra provincial government issued a total ban on the sect, claiming that the federal decree did not go far enough. See *Human Rights Watch World Report 2009*, 260–261.
47. See generally Jeffrey A. Redding, "Constitutionalizing Islam: Theory and Pakistan," *Virginia Journal of International Law* 49 (2004): 759–827.
48. Section 20 of the act states that "[n]otwithstanding anything contained in this Act, the rights of women as guaranteed by the Constitution shall not be affected."
49. Section 2A reads: "The Objective Resolution to form part of substantive provisions: The principles and provisions set out in the Objectives Resolution reproduced in the Annex are hereby made substantive part of the Constitution and shall have effect accordingly." It effectively incorporates an entire "Islamization" annex into the constitution.
50. Section 227(3) clarifies that: "Nothing in this Part shall affect the personal law of non-Muslim citizens of their status as citizens."

51. *Hakim Khan v. Government of Pakistan,* P.L.D. 1992 S.C. 595.
52. Ajmal Mian, *A Judge Speaks Out* (Oxford: Oxford University Press, 2004), 135.
53. Osama Siddique and Zahra Hayat, "Unholy Speech and Holy Laws: Blasphemy Laws in Pakistan—Controversial Origins, Design Defects, and Free Speech Implication," *Minnesota Journal of International Law* 17 (2008): 303, 368.
54. This is the essence of the "theory of harmonious construction" that the court has developed over the last twenty years. See, e.g., Constitution Petition 13/2004 and 2/2005 *Pakistan Lawyers Forum v. Federation of Pakistan* P.L.D. 2005 S.C. 719.
55. Constitution Petition 15/2002 *Qazi Hussain Ahmed, Ameer Jamaat-e-Islami Pakistan v. General Pervez Musharraf, Chief Executive & Another,* P.L.D. 2002 S.C. 853.
56. *Zaheerudin v. State,* 26 S.C.M.R. 1718 (S.Ct. 1993).
57. *Federation of Pakistan v. Ms. Farzana Asar,* P.L.D. 1999 S.C. 476. The government of Pakistan introduced the system of *zakat* for the first time in the country through the Ordinance of 1980. The objective behind the system of *zakat* is to assist the needy, the indigent, and the poor, preferably by giving financial assistance to widows and orphans.
58. Andrew Bainham et al., eds., *The International Survey of Family Law* (Bristol, UK: Jordans, 2002), 331.
59. Interestingly, the same holds true in neighboring Bangladesh, where the same MFLO is in effect. See, e.g., *Jesmin Sultana v. Mohammad Elias* (1997) 17 B.L.D. 4, where the Bangladesh Supreme Court upheld a divorced woman's MFLO-based right to *mahr* and maintenance. But in *Md. Hefzur Rahman v. Shamsun Nahar Begum* (1995) 15 B.L.D. 34, a divorcing husband's responsibility to maintain his divorced wife was considered to continue beyond the *idda* period, and a husband was found bound to provide maintenance on a reasonable scale for an indefinite period. However, this progressive and economically consequential ruling was quashed and traditional law reaffirmed upon appeal in 1998.
60. *Dr. Mahmood-ur-Rahman Faisal v. Govt of Pakistan,* P.L.D. 1994 S.C. 607 (SAB). Compare this with the SAB's earlier ruling in *Federation of Pakistan v. Farishta,* P.L.D. 1981 S.C. 120 (SAB).
61. As in many other predominantly religious polities, the struggle to liberalize family law in Pakistan has been an uphill battle. Despite the Islamization pressures, the National Assembly Standing Committee on Law, Justice, and Human Rights recently approved the Family Law (Amendment) Bill, 2007. It enables a woman who has been given in marriage or otherwise in *badal-i-sulh* (negotiated interfamily or interclan compromise, restitution, or truce) to get her marriage dissolved without a protracted trial in the light of the order passed by the Supreme Court of Pakistan on April 24, 2006.
62. Civil Shari'at Review Petition 1/2000 *United Bank Ltd. v. M/S Farooq Brothers & Others;* Civil Shari'at Review Petition 1/2001 *Muhammad Iqbal Zahid v. M/S Farooq Brothers & Others* (June 22, 2002) P.L.D. 2002 S.C. 800. For a

general survey of the legislative initiatives and lower-court rulings leading up to the court's ruling, see Aurangzeb Mehmood, "Islamization of Economy in Pakistan: Past, Present, and Future," *Islamic Studies* 41 (2002): 675–704.

63. *Id.*, 815–816.
64. See Majida Razvi, *Violence against Women—Overcoming the Traditional Resistance to Change and Amending the Hudood Ordinances in Pakistan.*
65. Constitution Petition 23/1999 & 21/2004 *Ch. Muhammad Siddique et al. v. Government of Pakistan* (Nov. 5, 2004).
66. Reference No. 2/2005 *In Re: NWFP Hisba Bill*, P.L.D. 2005 S.C. 873.
67. *Id.*, 101.
68. *Id.*, 36.
69. *Id.*, 47–48.
70. Cited in Osman Bakar, "Malaysian Islam in the Twenty-First Century," in John Esposito et al., eds., *Asian Islam in the 21st Century* (Oxford: Oxford University Press, 2008), 84.
71. This policy is seen as a continuation of previous laws made by the British to protect the indigenous Malay peoples from being overwhelmed by the immigration of Chinese and Indian workers into Malaya. In the years after independence in 1957 the Chinese and Indians were generally rich urban dwellers, while the Bumiputra were mostly poor farmers or manual laborers.
72. In several states conversion from Islam to another religion is a criminal offense that can be punished by a fine or jail term.
73. The other two states controlled by the PAS and the antiestablishment coalition are Kedah and Kelantan, where PAS won by a landslide in the March 2008 elections.
74. Clerics in Egypt issued a similar edict in 2004 that called the practice of yoga "an aberration." Although the council's decisions are not legally binding, they carry tremendous symbolic authority among Muslims. The council's rulings may be used by community leaders to ostracize an offending Muslim from society.
75. Both *hudood* and *qisas* offenses are contained in the set of legislation known as the Syariah Criminal Code Enactment. In Kelantan the law was formally called the Syariah Criminal Code (11) Enactment 1993 and was passed on November 25, 1993. In Terengganu the Syariah Criminal Offences (Hudud and Qisas) Bill was passed on July 8, 2002. The main offenses that were recognized under these enactments as *hudud* offenses were *sariqah* (theft), *hirabah* (robbery), *zina* (illicit intercourse by an unmarried person with another person, which carries a penalty of corporal punishment, and adultery, the punishment for which is death by stoning), *qazaf* (an accusation of *zina* that cannot be proved by four witnesses), *liwat* (sodomy), *syurb* (drinking liquor or other intoxicating beverages), and *irtidad* or *riddah* (apostasy). See Mohammad Hashim Kamali, "Punishment in Islamic Law: A Critique of the Hudud Bill of Kelantan, Malaysia," *Arab Law Quarterly* 13 (1998): 203–234.
76. See, e.g., Kamali, "Punishment in Islamic Law."
77. A good example is in the area of Islamic banking, finance, and insurance, all of which are matters enumerated in the Federal List, items 7 and 8. The

ascertainment whether a particular banking, finance, and insurance (*takaful*) product is compliant with Shari'a falls within item 4(k) and is a federal matter. For this purpose the Malaysian Parliament has established the Syariah Advisory Council; see Section 16B of the Central Bank of Malaysia Act 1958 (Act 519).

78. The Federal Court is Malaysia's highest judicial authority and the final court of appeal. On January 1, 1978, Privy Council appeals in criminal and constitutional matters were abolished, and on January 1, 1985, all other appeals, that is, civil appeals except those filed before that date, were abolished. The Federal Court consists of nine judges: the chief justice (formerly called the lord president), the president of the Court of Appeal, two chief judges of the High Courts in Malaya and in Sabah and Sarawak, and presently four Federal Court judges.
79. *Che Omar bin Che Soh v. Public Prosecutor* [1984] 1 MLJ 113.
80. In 1988 Malaysian lord president Tun Salleh Abas and a number of Supreme Court judges were suspended and later dismissed in reaction to the court's antigovernment position in an electoral crisis in 1987. The constitution was amended to remove direct reference to judicial power. The Malaysian judiciary has been under close political control ever since. The court found itself in political hot water again in 2004 because of its final ruling on the aforementioned Anwar Ibrahim affair.
81. *Teoh Eng Huat v. Kadhi Pasir Mas et al.* [1990] 2 MLJ 300.
82. *Soon Singh a/l Bikar Singh v. Pertubuhan Kebajikan Islam Malaysia (PERKIM) Kedah et al.* [1999] 1 MLJ 489.
83. *Kaliammal Sinnasamy v. Pengarah Jabatan Agama Islam Wilayah Persekutuan et al.* [2006] 1 MLJ 685.
84. *Lina Joy v. Majlis Agama Islam Wilayah Persekutuan* [2007] 4 MLJ 585.
85. Eventually the National Registration Department allowed the name change but continued to refuse the change of Joy's religious affiliation.
86. Subjecting conversion out of Islam to religious jurisdiction makes it harder for women to go through the process successfully. It locks women into Shari'a law in personal-status matters. Because Shari'a-based family law is ordinarily considered less favorable to women, this can be seen as formal gender inequality.
87. *Latifa Mat Zin v. Rosmawati Binti Sharibun and Roslinawati Rosmawati Binti Sharibun* [2007] 5 MLJ 101.
88. *Id.*
89. *Subashini v. Saravanan and Other* [2008] 2 MLJ 147.
90. *Abdul Kahar bin Ahmad v. Kerajaan Negeri Selangor Darul Ehsan* (decision released on May 22, 2008).
91. *Id.*, 7.
92. *Id.*
93. *Latifa Mat Zin v. Rosmawati Binti Sharibun and Roslinawati Rosmawati Binti Sharibun* [2007] 5 MLJ 101.
94. *Id.*
95. *Ismail bin Mohamad v. Wan Khariani binti Wan Mahmood* (decision released on June 9, 2009).

96. *Id.*, 7–8.
97. See Chris Szabla, "No 'Clash of Civilizations' in Malaysia's Courts," *Harvard Law Record,* Nov. 13, 2008.
98. For pertinent general background, see "Sharia Law in Northern Nigeria," *Economist,* Feb. 1, 2007; and Philip Ostien, *Sharia Implementation in Northern Nigeria, 1999–2006: A Sourcebook* (Ibadan, Nigeria: Spectrum Books, 2007). On the rise of Pentacostalism in Nigeria, see Ruth Marshall, *Political Spiritualities: The Pentacostal Revolution in Nigeria* (Chicago: University of Chicago Press, 2009).
99. Amitabha Bose, "Do All Roads Lead To Islamic Radicalism? A Comparison of Islamic Laws in India and Nigeria," *Georgia Journal of International and Comparative Law* 32 (2004):779–812; David Laitin, "The Sharia Debate and the Origins of Nigeria's Second Republic," *Journal of Modern African Studies* 20 (1982): 411–430.
100. The twelve states are Bauchi, Borno, Gombe, Jigawa, Kaduna, Kano, Katsina, Kebbi, Niger, Sokoto, Yobe, and Zamfara.
101. "Nigeria Sharia Architect Defends Law," BBC News, Mar. 21, 2002.
102. M. H. A. Bolaji, "Shari'ah in Northern Nigeria in the Light of Asymmetrical Federalism," *Publius: The Journal of Federalism* 40 (2009): 114–135.
103. *Safiyatu Hussaini Tungar Tudu v. Attorney-General Sokoto State,* Appeal No. SCA/GW/28/2001 (Shari'a Court of Appeal of Sokoto State, Mar. 25, 2002).
104. *Amina Lawal v. The State,* Case No. KTS/SCA/FT/86/2002 (Shari'a Court of Appeal of Katsina State, Sept. 25, 2003).
105. See Jan Michiel Otto, "Rule of Law, Adat Law, and Sharia: 1901, 2001, and Monitoring the Next Phase," *Hague Journal on the Rule of Law* 1 (2009): 15–20.
106. Paul Marshall, "Nigeria: Shari'a in a Fragmented Country," in Paul Marshall, ed., *Radical Islam's Rules* (Lanham, Md.: Rowman and Littlefield, 2005), 126.
107. See Andrew Ubaka Iwobi, "Tiptoeing through a Constitutional Minefield: The Great Sharia Controversy in Nigeria," *Journal of African Law* 48 (2004): 111–164; and Vincent Obisienunwo Orlu Nmehielle, "Sharia Law in the Northern States of Nigeria: To Implement or Not to Implement, the Constitutionality Is the Question," *Human Rights Quarterly* 26 (2004): 730–759.
108. Enyinna S. Nwauche, "Law, Religion and Human Rights in Nigeria," *African Human Rights Law Journal* 8 (2008): 568–595, 576.
109. S.C. 26/2006 *Attorney-General of Kano State v. Attorney-General of the Federation* (2007) 3 NILR 23 (Mar. 2, 2007).
110. *Id.*, 1.
111. *Id.*, 2.
112. The resolution stated: "The constitution shall be composed of individual chapters in such a manner that each of them shall constitute a basic law in itself. The individual chapters shall be brought before the Knesset . . . and all the chapters together will form the State Constitution."
113. Shas grew from 4 Knesset seats in 1984 (63,600 votes) to 10 seats in 1996 (260,000 votes) and 17 seats in 1999 (430,000 votes). In both the 2006 and

2009 elections it received approximately 300,000 votes, which translated into 12 seats.

114. For a detailed account of this transformation and its role in Israel's "constitutional revolution," see Ran Hirschl, *Towards Juristocracy: The Origins and Consequences of the New Constitutionalism* (Cambridge, Mass.: Harvard University Press, 2004).
115. CA 6821/93 *United Mizrahi Bank v. Migdal Cooperative Village,* 49(4) P.D. 221 (1995).
116. See Ran Hirschl and Ayelet Shachar, "Constitutional Transformation, Gender Equality, and Religious/National Conflict in Israel: Tentative Progress through the Obstacle Course," in Beverly Baines and Ruth Rubio-Marin, eds., *The Gender of Constitutional Jurisprudence* (Cambridge, U.K.: Cambridge University Press, 2005), 205–229.
117. See generally Anat Scolnicov, "Religious Law, Religious Courts and Human Rights within Israeli Constitutional Structure," *International Journal of Constitutional Law* 4 (2006): 732–740.
118. On the state and status of Islamic law in Israel, see Moussa Abou Ramadan, "The Shari'a in Israel: Islamization, Israelization, and the Invented Islamic Law," *UCLA Journal of Islamic and Near Eastern Law* 5 (2006): 81–129.
119. See, e.g., HCJ 232/81 *Vilozni v. Great Rabbinical Court* 36(2) P.D. 733 (1982).
120. HCJ 1000/92 *Bavli v. The Great Rabbinical Court,* 48(2) P.D. 6 (1995). On Shari'a court jurisdiction, see CA 3077/90 *Plonit ("Jane Doe") v. Ploni ("John Doe"),* 49(2) P.D. 578 (1996).
121. See, e.g., HCJ 3269/95, *Katz v. Jerusalem Reg'l Rabbinical Court,* 50(4) P.D. 590 (2000); HCJ 9734/03 *Yemini v. Great Rabbinical Court,* 59(2) P.D. 295 (2004); HCJ 5227/97 *David v. Great Rabbinical Court,* 55(1) P.D. 453 (1998); HCJ 293/00 *Plonit ("Jane Doe") v. Great Rabbinical Court,* 55(3) P.D. 318 (2001); HCJ 2222/99 *Gabai v. Great Rabbinical Court,* 54(5) P.D. 401 (2000); and HCJ 2274/99 *Shafir v. Regional Rabbinical Court,* 56(1) P.D. 673 (2002).
122. HCJ 8928/06 *Plonit ("Jane Doe") v. The Great Rabbinical Court* (decision released on Oct. 8, 2008).
123. HCJ 5416/09 *Plonit ("Jane Doe") v. Ploni ("John Roe")* (decision released on Feb. 10, 2010).
124. The two early classics of this thread of judgments are HCJ 72/62 *Rufeisen v. Minister of the Interior,* 16 P.D. 2428 (1962) (case of Brother Daniel), holding that any Jew converting to another religion (Catholicism in this case) would lose his or her preferential access to Israeli citizenship. But in *Shalit* (1969) the court ruled (5–4) after nearly two years of deliberation in favor of Shalit's claim that the government could not use the test of Halakha alone to define a person's nationality. See HCJ 58/68 *Shalit v. Minister of Interior,* 23(2) P.D. 477 (1969). Whereas in the first case the court opted for a more formal (or narrow) interpretation of "Who is a Jew," in the later case it favored a somewhat more substantive (or pluralistic) definition.
125. HCJ 264/87 *Sepharadi Torah Guardians, Shas Movement v. Population Registrar,* 43(2) P.D. 723 (1989).

126. HCJ 1031/93 *Pessaro (Goldstein) et al. v. Ministry of Interior,* 49(4) P.D. 661 (1995).
127. HCJ 5070/95 *Conservative Movement v. Minister of Religious Affairs,* 1 TakEl 634 (2002).
128. HCJ 2597/99 *Thais-Rodriguez Tushbaim v. Minister of Interior,* [2005] IsrSC 59(6) ("Leap Conversions" case).
129. See Nathan Jeffay, "Rabbinical Court Puts Thousands of Converts in Legal Limbo: Ruling Reopens Fractious Debate over 'Who Is a Jew?' " *Forward—The Jewish Daily,* May 8, 2008.
130. HCJ 7052/03 *Adalah v. Minister of Interior,* [2006] 2 TakEi 1754 (Citizenship Law/Family Unification case).
131. Because both Justice Michael Cheshin, who wrote the main majority opinion in the 2006 ruling, and Chief Justice Aharon Barak, who wrote the main dissenting opinion, have now retired, it will be interesting to see which direction the decisions on these follow-up petitions will take, and who, if any, will emerge as the new "philosopher-king" judge on the SCI.
132. Cairo Administrative Court, Ruling of May 19, 2009. Because of a major recession in Egypt in the late 1980s and early 1990s, several thousand Egyptian citizens sought work in Israel. Several hundred of them married Israeli spouses (mainly Arab-Israeli) and continue to live in Israel.
133. HCJ 3872/93 *Meatrael Ltd. v. Prime Minister and Minister of Religious Affairs,* 47(5) P.D. 485 (1993); HCJ 5009/94 *Meatrael Ltd. v. The Council of the Chief Rabbinate of Israel,* 48(5) P.D. 617 (1994); HCJ 4676/94, *Meatrael Ltd. v. The Knesset,* 50(5) P.D. 15 (1996).
134. HCJ 7203/00 *Aviv Osoblanski Ltd. v. The Council of the Chief Rabbinate of Israel,* 56(2) P.D. 196 (2001).
135. This interpretive approach seems to have filtered down to lower courts as well. For example, in a recent ruling (*State of Israel v. Terminal 21 et al.,* Apr. 3, 2008) the Jerusalem Municipal Affairs Court ruled that private businesses may sell leavened products on Passover because this does not constitute a violation of the Prohibition of Leaven Law, 1986, better known as the "Hametz ['Leaven' in Hebrew] Law." In response, the Shas Party publicly vowed to pass a law prohibiting any sales of leavened products during Passover. As of March 2010, such a law has not been formally passed although a legislative proposal has been tabled, and most Jewish parties have taken a position with respect to it.
136. HCJ 1067/08 *Noar Ke'Halacha v. Ministry of Education* (decision released Aug. 6, 2009).
137. See Edna Ullman-Margalit, "Removing Hypocrisy," in *Ha'Aretz,* Aug. 12, 2009.
138. Curiously, the newly established United Kingdom Supreme Court has recently drawn on the same general logic in a case that raised analogous issues to those addressed in this Israeli Supreme Court decision. See *R. (E) v. Governing Body of JFS* [2009] UKSC 15, discussed in Chapter 5.
139. Hannah Arendt and Karl Jaspers, *Correspondence 1926–1969* (Orlando, Fla.: Harcourt Brace, 1993), 443.

140. Esra Özyürek, *Nostalgia for the Modern: State Secularism and Everyday Politics in Turkey* (Durham, N.C.: Duke University Press, 2006), 13–14.
141. For an early account of such attempts see Metin Heper, "Islam and Democracy in Turkey: Toward a Reconciliation?" *Middle East Journal* 51 (1997): 32–45.
142. Reported by the Turkish newspapers *Milliyet* and *Radikal* (translated by the Jamestown Foundation, http://www.jamestown.org).
143. See Özyürek, *Nostalgia for the Modern.*
144. The show, called *Tovbekarlar Yarisiyor* (Penitents Compete), features a Muslim imam, a Catholic priest, a Jewish rabbi, and a Buddhist monk attempting to persuade ten atheists of the merits of their religion, according to CNN-Turk. If they succeed, the contestants are rewarded with a pilgrimage to one of their chosen faith's most sacred sites—Mecca for Muslims, Jerusalem for converts to Judaism, a trip to Tibet for Buddhists, and the chance to visit Ephesus and the Vatican for Christians. Contestants are said to be judged by a panel of religious experts before going on the show to make sure that their lack of faith is genuine.
145. In March 2009, for example, the ruling AKP censored a major article celebrating the 150th anniversary of Darwin's *Origin of Species* that was about to appear in the country's *National Geographic*–like popular science magazine *Science and Technology* (*Bilim ve Teknik*). The magazine's editor was fired.
146. In September 2004 the AKP-led parliament attempted to adopt legal provisions that would have criminalized adultery. The so-called adultery law was shelved following signals from EU authorities that the passage of such a law would seriously jeopardize Turkey's EU admission chances. Adultery had been decriminalized in Turkey in 1996. Under the proposed law of 2004, men and women would have been prosecuted on equal terms and would have faced the same three years in prison.
147. See "The Enduring Popularity of Recep Tayyip Erdogan," *Economist,* Mar. 21, 2009, 59–60. In September 2009 Turkey's tax authorities imposed an astronomic fine of no less than $2.5 billion on Dogan's media conglomerate—a fine that is roughly equivalent to the company's cumulative capital. Eager to portray Turkey as unfit to join the EU and agnostic at best toward the AKP's redistributive agenda, European authorities expressed grave concern over the fine and portrayed it as a serious threat to freedom of the press.
148. Turkey 1982 Const., art. 143.
149. See Hootan Shambayati, "The Guardian of the Regime: The Turkish Constitutional Court in Comparative Perspective," in S. A. Arjomand, ed., *Constitutional Politics in the Middle East* (Oxford: Hart Publishing, 2008), 99–121.
150. TCC Decision 4/2009 (DTP Party Dissolution case), Dec. 11, 2009.
151. TCC Decision 1/1998 (Welfare [Refah] Party Dissolution case), Jan. 16, 1998; and TCC Decision 57/2001 (Virtue [Fazilet] Party Dissolution case), June 21, 2001. See generally Dicle Kogacioglu, "Dissolution of Political Parties by the Constitutional Court in Turkey: Judicial Delimitation of the Political Domain," *International Sociology* 18 (2003): 258–276; Dicle Kogacioglu,

"Progress, Unity, and Democracy: Dissolving Political Parties in Turkey," *Law and Society Review* 38 (2004): 433–462.

152. Cited in Kogacioglu, "Dissolution of Political Parties," 268.
153. *Id.*
154. *Id.*
155. Susanna Dokupil, "The Separation of Mosque and State: Islam and Democracy in Modern Turkey," *West Virginia Law Review* 105 (2002): 53, 123–124.
156. *Refah Partisi (The Welfare Party) and Others v. Turkey,* ECtHR, Feb. 13, 2003, Application Nos. 41340/98; 41342/98; 41343/98; 41344/98.
157. *Id.*, paragraph 72.
158. *Id.*, paragraph 123.
159. Consequently, Gül was elected president on August 28, 2007.
160. Under constitutional rules adopted in 2001 a minimum of seven votes (three-fifths of the eleven TCC judges) are needed to order the dissolution of a party (Article 149).
161. Note, however, that only days after the TCC's ruling President Abdullah Gül assigned twenty-one new deans to all government universities, many or all of whom support lifting the headscarf ban (see the discussion of this ban in the following paragraphs). In August 2008 Edibe Sozen, an AKP parliament member, proposed establishing a prayer section in all schools, as well as a ban on sales of pornographic images to anyone under the age of sixteen and restrictions on the purchase of such material by anyone over sixteen.
162. TCC Decision 52/2009 (Civil Prosecution of Military Personnel case), Jan. 21, 2010. At issue was the scope of Article 145 of the constitution that defines the meaning of "military justice" and the jurisdictional boundaries of military tribunals.
163. TCC Decision 652/1989 (Mar. 7, 1989).
164. See Hillal Elver, "Gender Equality from a Constitutional Perspective: The Case of Turkey," in Beverly Baines and Ruth Rubio-Marin, eds., *The Gender of Constitutional Jurisprudence* (Cambridge, U.K.: Cambridge University Press, 2005), 278–305.
165. See *Karaduman v. Turkey* (European Commission of Human Rights, Application No. 16278/90, decision released May 3, 1993).
166. *Dal and Ozen v. Turkey* (European Court of Human Rights, Application No. 45379/99, decision released Oct. 3, 2002); and *Baspinar v. Turkey* (European Court of Human Rights, Application No. 45631/99, decision released Oct. 3, 2002).
167. *Leyla Şahin v. Turkey,* 19 BHRC 590 [2006] ELR 73 [European Court of Human Rights]. As the discussion in Chapter 5 indicates, the prominence of constitutional courts as secularizing agents in countries where popular support for theocratic governance is high is, of course, not limited to the Middle East. National high courts in Germany (e.g., the *Ludin* case, 2003), Britain (*Shabina Begum,* 2006), and France (the Conseil d'État ruling in the *Faiza M* case, 2008) have recently addressed the hotly contested question of differentiated citizenship and the wearing of religious attire in the public education system. The Supreme Court of India has also advanced a secularist

agenda against the backdrop of one of the most religious societies in the world.

168. TCC Decision 116/2008 (decision released June 5, 2008; legal reasoning released Oct. 22, 2008).
169. Some works suggest that constitutional politics in democratic and authoritarian regimes are qualitatively different from each other. I subscribe to the view that to a large extent the differences are of degree, not qualitative. See, e.g., Tom Ginsburg and Tamir Moustafa, "Introduction: The Functions of Courts in Authoritarian Politics," in Tom Ginsburg and Tamir Moustafa, eds., *Rule by Law: The Politics of Courts in Authoritarian Regimes* (New York: Cambridge University Press, 2008), 1–22. For a more integrative view, see Duncan Kennedy, "Three Globalizations of Law and Legal Thought," in David Trubek and Alvaro Santos, eds., *The New Law and Economic Development: A Critical Appraisal* (New York: Cambridge University Press, 2006), 19–73.

5. Courts as Secularizing Agents in the Nontheocratic World

1. See, e.g., Tom Ginsburg and Tamir Moustafa, eds., *Rule by Law: The Politics of Courts in Authoritarian Regimes* (New York: Cambridge University Press, 2008); and Peter Solomon, "Courts and Judges in Authoritarian Regimes," *World Politics* 60 (2007): 122–145.
2. Aristide Zolberg and Long Litt Woon, "Why Islam Is like Spanish," *Politics and Society* 27 (1999): 5–38.
3. See Renáta Uitz, *Freedom of Religion in European Constitutional and International Case Law* (Strasbourg: Council of Europe Publishing, 2007), 124–125.
4. BVerfGE 93, 1 1 BvR 1087/91 [1995] (Classroom Crucifix case).
5. *Id.*, cited in Donald Kommers, *The Constitutional Jurisprudence of the Federal Republic of Germany* (Durham, N.C.: Duke University Press, 1997), 475.
6. BverfG, 2 BvR 1436/02 (Sept. 24, 2003), paras. 2ff (*Ludin* case).
7. *Id.*, para. 43.
8. *Id.*, para. 45.
9. *Id.*, para. 46.
10. *Id.*, paras. 78ff.
11. *Dahlab v. Switzerland*, ECtHR, Feb. 15, 2001, Application No. 42393/98.
12. *Id.* In an earlier case, the ECtHR held that the freedom manifest one's religion or beliefs may be subject to restrictions. See, *Kokkinakis v. Greece*, May 25, 1993, Application No. 14307/88.
13. *Leyla Şahin v. Turkey*, ECtHR, Nov. 10, 2005, Application No. 44774/98. For an illuminating commentary, see Kathryn Boustead, "The French Headscarf Law before the European Court of Human Rights," *Journal of Transnational Law and Policy* 16 (2007): 167.
14. *Leyla Şahin v. Turkey*, paras. 36–37.
15. *Id.*, paras. 14–28.
16. *Id.*, paras. 76–78.
17. *Id.*, paras. 79–83.

18. *Id.*, paras. 94–98.
19. *Id.*, para. 99.
20. *Id.*, paras. 100–102.
21. *Id.*, para. 103.
22. *Id.*, paras. 104–123.
23. *Id.*, para. 121.
24. Quoted from *Id.*, para. 161; paras. 152–162.
25. *Id.*, Concurring Opinion.
26. *Id.*, Dissenting Opinion, paras. 1–20.
27. *R. (on the Application of Shabina Begum) v. Headteacher and Governors of Denbigh High School* [2006] UKHL 15.
28. *Id.*, paras. 3–19.
29. *Id.*, para. 23.
30. *Id.*, para. 25.
31. *Id.*, para. 86.
32. *Id.*, para. 41.
33. *Id.*, paras. 92–94.
34. *Id.*, para. 34.
35. *Id.*, para. 64.
36. *Azmi v. Kirklees Metropolitan Borough Council* (EAT) (Apr. 2, 2007).
37. *R. (on the application of Playfoot) v. Millais School Governing Body* [2007] EWHC 1698 (Admin).
38. See *R. (E) v. Governing Body of JFS* [2009] UKSC 15. For a powerful critique of the ruling see Joseph H.H. Weiler, "Discrimination and Identity in London: The Jewish Free School Case," *Jewish Review of Books* 1 (2010).
39. Elisa T. Beller, "The Headscarf Affair: The Conseil d'Etat on the Role of Religion and Culture in French Society," *Texas International Law Journal* 39 (2004): 581, 584.
40. T. Jeremy Gunn, "Religious Freedom and Laicité: A Comparison of the United States and France," *Brigham Young University Law Review* 419, 459–462 (2004).
41. *Id.*
42. Décision du Conseil d'État N° 286798 (June 28, 2008).
43. *Id.*
44. *Id.*, "Conclusions: Mme Prada Bordenave, Commissaire du Gouvernement," http://www.conseil-etat.fr/ce/jurispd/conclusions/conclusions_286798.pdf.
45. *Lautsi v. Italy*, ECtHR, Nov. 3, 2009, Application No. 30814/06.
46. Rex Murphy, "Crucifix Out, Warming In," *Globe and Mail*, Nov. 6, 2009.
47. *Id.*
48. See, e.g., the ruling of the Spanish Constitutional Court in S.T.C. 53/1985. See also Ruth Rubio-Marin, "Engendering the Constitution: The Spanish Experience," in Beverley Baines and Ruth Rubio-Marin, eds., *The Gender of Constitutional Jurisprudence* (New York: Cambridge University Press, 2005), 271–272. Antiabortion positions continue to be quite common in Spain. The queen of Spain, Doña Sofia Margarita Victoria Frederica, made headlines in her country after she was quoted as denouncing abortion, euthanasia, and gay marriage

in a book based on interviews with her (*The Queen Up Close*, Barcelona: Planeta, 2008).

49. See, e.g., the Irish Supreme Court's ruling in *A. G. v. X* [1992] IESC 1; [1992] 1 IR 1 (Mar. 5, 1992). See more generally Jennifer E. Spreng, *Abortion and Divorce Law in Ireland* (Jefferson, N.C.: McFarland, 2004).
50. See Miguel Schor, "An Essay on the Emergence of Constitutional Courts: The Cases of Mexico and Colombia," *Indiana Journal of Global Legal Studies* 16 (2009): 173–194, 181.
51. For a comprehensive case outline and analysis, see Rebecca Cook, "Foreword," in *Women's Link Worldwide,* 2007, http://www.womenslinkworldwide.org/pdf_pubs/pub_c3552006.pdf.
52. Case No. C-355/2006 (May 10, 2006). The Constitutional Court's communication on the case (Spanish) is available at http://www.reddesalud.org/english/datos/ftp/corteconstitucional.pdf.
53. Reported in the *New York Times,* May 11, 2006.
54. *Id.* In Colombia, where one-quarter of pregnancies are terminated, unsafe abortion is the third-leading cause of maternal mortality.
55. The discussion of this case draws on Rebecca Cook et al., "Healthcare Responsibilities and Conscientious Objection," *International Journal of Gynecology and Obstetrics* 104 (2009): 249–252.
56. Case T-209/2008 (Feb. 15, 2008) (Constitutional Court of Colombia, Denial of Lawful Abortion case).
57. Colombian State Council, Administrative Chamber, Decision 2002 00251 01 (June 5, 2008) ("Morning-After Pill" case).
58. Reported by Angela Castellanos, "Colombian High Court Rules Emergency Contraception Is Not Abortion," *RH Reality Check: Information and Analysis for Reproductive Health,* Aug. 11, 2008.
59. See Stephen Zamora and José Ramón Cossío, "Mexican Constitutionalism after Presidencialismo," *International Journal of Constitutional Law* 4 (2006): 411–437.
60. In the Latin American context this is a very progressive law. Cuba and Guyana are the only countries in the region that currently allow abortion for all reasons in the first trimester, as the United States allows. Nicaragua voted in November 2006 to ban abortion in all cases. El Salvador and Chile also have some of the region's most restrictive policies.
61. Reported in Sara Miller Llana, "Mexico's Supreme Court Upholds Abortion Law," *Christian Science Monitor,* Aug. 29, 2008.
62. *T. S. c. Gobierno de la Ciudad de Buenos Aires*, s/amparo, judgment of 11–1–2001, Fallos 324:05 (Supreme Court of Argentina, 2001). See Rebecca Cook et al., "Prenatal Management of Anencephaly," *International Journal of Gynecology and Obstetrics* 102 (2008): 304–308, 306.
63. Supreme Court of Brazil, Ruling of May 29, 2008 (Law of Biosecurity case). See Rodrigo Squizato, "Brazilian Court Decision Eases Scientists' Stem Cell Worries," *Nature Medicine* 14 (2008): 699.
64. Supreme Court of Bolivia, Ruling of Oct. 17, 2008 (Abortion case). This tendency has been reflected in other parts of the world as well. In December 2007

the Constitutional Court of the Slovak Republic confirmed that the Slovak Act on Artificial Interruption of Pregnancy (Abortion Act), which allows abortion on request during the first twelve weeks of pregnancy, is in compliance with the Slovak Constitution, particularly Article 15 (the right-to-life provision). The decision was the result of a legal challenge brought by conservative members of Parliament who argued, in part, that the permissive Abortion Act violates the right to life of fetuses, which should be protected by Article 15 of the constitution from the moment of conception. The court decided that the act is in compliance with the Slovak Constitution (art. 15). A few months later, on the other side of the planet, in August 2008 Nepal's Supreme Court dismissed a petition that had aimed to overturn the country's abortion law, which allows abortion upon request up to twelve weeks. The law was challenged in 2005 on the grounds that it discriminates against men because it allows a woman to terminate a pregnancy without requiring the consent of her husband. However, the court was convinced that a requirement of spousal consent for abortion would violate women's human rights under international law and Nepal's Constitution.

65. Decision of Apr. 4, 2008.
66. See Bruce Ryder, "The Canadian Conception of Equal Religious Citizenship," in Richard Moon, ed., *Law and Religious Pluralism in Canada* (Vancouver, BC: UBC Press, 2008), 87; and Will Kymlicka, *Multicultural Citizenship: A Liberal Theory of Minority Rights* (New York: Oxford University Press, 1995), 31. Kymlicka here refers to the category of "ethnic groups" rather than "national minorities." The tribunal's advocates would fit under the former rather than the latter definition in Kymlicka's typology.
67. My use of the term "citizenry" refers to all those residing permanently within the boundaries of the territorial state, irrespective of their formal membership status.
68. See S. Afr. Const. 1996 §§ 15, 30, 31 (addressing religion, culture, and cultural, religious, or linguistic communities, respectively). Sections 39(3) and 211(3) hold that courts are required to apply customary law "subject to the Constitution and any legislation that specifically deals with customary law."
69. Statistics South Africa, Census 2001 Key Results, http://www.statssa.gov.ca.
70. *Ex Parte Chairperson of the Constitutional Assembly: In re Certification of the Constitution of the Republic of South Africa* 1996 (4) SA 744 (CC) at 200 (S. Afr.).
71. S. Afr. Const. 1996, § 1; see also §§ 9–10.
72. See South African Law Commission, "The Harmonisation of the Common Law and the Indigenous Law: Customary Marriages," Discussion Paper 74 (1997); and Monique Deveaux, "A Deliberative Approach to Conflicts of Culture," *Political Theory* 31 (2003): 780–807.
73. David L. Chambers, "Civilizing the Natives: Marriage in Post-apartheid South Africa," *Daedalus* 129 (2000): 101, 113.
74. *Id.*, 114; see also Penelope E. Andrews, "'Big Love'? The Recognition of Customary Marriages in South Africa," *Washington and Lee Law Review* 64 (2007): 1485, 1486.

75. The commission's members are appointed by the president and are assigned the task of making recommendations for the "renewal and improvement of the law of South Africa on a continuous basis."
76. South African Law Commission, "Customary Law of Succession," Discussion Paper 93 (2000); South African Law Commission, "Customary Law: Administration of Estates," Discussion Paper 95 (2001).
77. See South African Law Commission, "Customary Law of Succession," ¶ 1.2.2; see also Nelson Tebbe, "Inheritance and Disinheritance: African Customary Law and Constitutional Rights," *Journal of Religion* 88 (2008): 466, 467.
78. See Tebbe, "Inheritance and Disinheritance," 468.
79. *Mthembu v. Letsela* 1997 (2) SA 936 (TPD) (S. Afr.); *Mthembu v. Letsela & Another* 1998 (2) SA 675 (T) (S. Afr.); *Mthembu v. Letsela & Another* 2000 (3) SA 867 (SCA) (S. Afr.).
80. *Mthembu v. Letsela & Another* 2000 (3) SA 867 (SCA), ¶ 33.
81. *Id.*, ¶ 8.
82. See Gardiol van Niekerk, "Indigenous Law and Narrative: Rethinking Methodology," *Comparative and International Law Journal of Southern Africa* 32 (1999): 208, 211, 218–226.
83. See Chuma Himonga and Craig Bosch, "The Application of African Customary Law under the Constitution of South Africa: Problems Solved or Just the Beginning?" *South African Law Journal* 117 (2000): 306, 319–336.
84. See Victoria Bronstein, "Reconceptualizing the Customary Law Debate in South Africa," *South African Journal of Human Rights* 14 (1998): 388.
85. *Id.*, 403.
86. *Bhe & Others v. Magistrate, Khayelitsha, & Others* 2005 (1) SA 580 (CC) (S. Afr.). In the earlier case *Moseneke & Others v. Master of the High Court* 2001 (2) SA 18 (CC) (S. Afr.), the court ordered the government to expedite its harmonization efforts and granted it two years to accomplish that goal.
87. See Repeal of the Black Adminstration Act of 2005.
88. *Shilubana & Others v. Nwamitwa* 2009 (2) SA 66 (CC) (S. Afr.).
89. *Id.*, ¶ 56.
90. *Id.*, ¶ 81.
91. See Tebbe, "Inheritance and Disinheritance," 469, citing Chritelle Terreblanche, "Woman's Battle to Be Chief Pits Traditional Leaders against Their Past," *Sunday Independent* (South Africa), May 6, 2007.
92. *Gumede v. Pres. of the Rep. of S. Afr. & Others* 2009 (3) BCLR 243 (CC) (S. Afr.).
93. In the United States the doctrinal sex-equality standard is "intermediate scrutiny," whereas in South Africa gender classification is treated, in American constitutional law terminology, as a "suspect category," thus inviting strict scrutiny.
94. Canada's official multiculturalism policy was introduced in 1971, predating the charter. Today it finds statutory expression at the federal level, as well as in several provincial acts. These policy goals are also enacted through the Canadian Multiculturalism Act of 1985. Canada's vision of multiculturalism generally places a premium on culture rather than religion. See Will Kymlicka,

Finding Our Way: Rethinking Ethnocultural Relations in Canada (Oxford, U.K.: Oxford University Press, 1998).

95. For concise overviews, see generally Ryder, "Canadian Conception of Equal Religious Citizenship," 87–109; and Benjamin L. Berger, "Law's Religion: Rendering Culture," *Osgoode Hall Law Journal* 45 (2007): 277–314. For an illuminating discussion of the differences and similarities between the United States and Canada in accommodating religious freedoms, see Christopher L. Eisgruber and Mariah Zeisberg, "Religious Freedom in Canada and the United States," *International Journal of Constitutional Law* 4 (2006): 244–268.
96. *Syndicat Northcrest v. Amselem,* [2004] 2 S.C.R. 551 (Can.).
97. *Multani v. Marguerite-Bourgeoys (Comm'n scolaire),* [2006] 1 S.C.R. 256 (Can.).
98. *Id.,* ¶ 71.
99. *R. v. Jones,* [1986] 2 S.C.R. 284 (Can.).
100. *Alberta v. Hutterian Brethren of Wilson Colony*, [2009] 2 S.C.R. 567 (Can.).
101. *Wisconsin v. Yoder,* 406 U.S. 205 (1972).
102. See Austin Sarat and Roger Berkowitz, "Disorderly Differences: Recognition, Accommodation, and American Law," *Yale Journal of Law and the Humanities* 6 (1994): 285–316.
103. Briefly, the idea was to rely on a preexisting legal framework, the Arbitration Act, which at that time permitted a wide array of family-law disputes to be resolved under its extensively open-ended terms.
104. Syed Mumtaz Ali, "Establishing an Institute of Islamic Justice (Darul Qada)," Canadian Society of Muslims News Bulletin, Oct. 2002, http://muslim-canada.org/news02.html.
105. *Id.*
106. These changes were implemented with the passage of the Arbitration Act, S.O. ch. 1, § 1(2) (2006) (incorporated into section 2.2 of the 1991 Arbitration Act) and 2007 regulations pursuant to this legislation.
107. See Ayelet Shachar, "Religion, State, and the Problem of Gender: New Modes of Citizenship and Governance in Diverse Societies," *McGill Law Journal* 50 (2005): 49, 61–77.
108. *Hartshorne v. Hartshorne,* [2004] 1 S.C.R. 550 (confirming and reinstating the legal validity of a "domestic contract" that was defined by legal counsel as an "unfair agreement" to the wife, allowing the parties to stray away from statutory equitable default rules found in governing family-law statutes).
109. *Bruker v. Marcovitz,* [2007] 3 S.C.R. 607 (Can.).
110. Canada's Divorce Act requires parties to remove religious barriers to remarriage. For an illuminating analysis of the Divorce Act's effects on Canada's Jewish women, see Lisa Fishbayn, "Gender, Multiculturalism, and Dialogue: The Case of Jewish Divorce," *Canadian Journal of Law and Jurisprudence* 21 (2008): 71–96.
111. *Bruker v. Marcovitz,* [2007] 3 S.C.R. 607, ¶ 92 (emphasis added).
112. *Id.,* ¶ 1 (emphasis added).
113. *Id.,* ¶ 2.

114. Robert M. Cover, "The Supreme Court 1982 Term—Foreword: *Nomos* and Narrative," *Harvard Law Review* 97 (1983): 4.

6. Yin and Yang?

1. See, generally, Nancy Maveety, ed., *The Pioneers of Judicial Behavior* (Ann Arbor: University of Michigan Press, 2003).
2. See Robert P. George, "Natural Law," in Keith Whittington et al., eds., *The Oxford Handbook of Law and Politics* (Oxford, U.K.: Oxford University Press, 2008), 399–413.
3. Max Lerner, "Constitutions and Courts as Symbols," *Yale Law Journal* 46 (1937): 1290, cited in Jamal Greene, "On the Origins of Originalism" *Texas Law Review* 88 (2009): 79.
4. Lerner, "Constitutions and Courts as Symbols," 1294–1295.
5. Jaroslav Pelikan, *Interpreting the Bible and the Constitution* (New Haven, Conn.: Yale University Press, 2004), cited in Greene, "On the Origins of Originalism," 80.
6. Sanford Levinson, *Constitutional Faith* (Princeton, N.J.: Princeton University Press, 1988).
7. Mitchell Meltzer, *Secular Revelations: The Constitution of the United States and Classical American Literature* (Cambridge, Mass.: Harvard University Press, 2005), 1–3.
8. Daniel Lazar, "America the Undemocratic," *New Left Review* 232 (1998): 3, 21.
9. Stuart Scheingold, *The Politics of Rights: Lawyers, Public Policy, and Politics* (New Haven, Conn.: Yale University Press, 1974), 34.
10. See, e.g., Tomoko Masuzawa, *The Invention of World Religions* (Chicago: University of Chicago Press, 2005); Talal Asad, *Formations of the Secular: Christianity, Islam, Modernity* (Stanford, Calif.: Stanford University Press, 2003); Hans G. Kippenberg, *Discovering Religious History in the Modern Age* (Princeton, N.J.: Princeton University Press, 2001); and Timothy Fitzgerald, *The Ideology of Religious Studies* (Oxford: Oxford University Press, 2000).
11. See, e.g., *British Columbia (A.G.) v. Christie,* [2007] 1 S.C.R. 873; *Auton (Guardian ad litem of) v. British Columbia (A.G.),* [2004] 3 S.C.R. 657, 659 (determining that the government's decision not to fund a medically required treatment did not infringe on the petitioners' equality rights); *Gosselin v. Quebec (A.G.),* [2002] 4 S.C.R. 429, 430 (dismissing appellant's claim that a different welfare base payment for individuals above and below the age of thirty violated the Charter of Rights and Freedoms and the Quebec Charter of Human Rights and Freedoms); and *R. v. Prosper,* [1994] 3 S.C.R. 236, 237 (permitting the government to appeal a dismissal that was based on a constitutional challenge to law-enforcement conduct and, particularly, the officers' inadequate efforts to inform a criminal defendant of his rights).
12. See, e.g. *Olga Tellis v. Bombay Municipal Corporation,* A.I.R. 1986 S.C. 180; and *Unni Krishnan, JP v. State of Andhra Pradesh,* A.I.R. 1993 S.C. 2178.

Note that in 2002 a new § (21A) was added to the Indian Constitution. It states that "[t]he State shall provide free and compulsory education to all children of the age of six to fourteen years in such manner as the State may, by law, determine."

13. The term "Lamarckism" comes from eighteenth-century French biologist Jean-Baptiste Lamarck, who is known for the evolutionary theory that acquired characters are inheritable, or that modifications resulting from an organism's development of particular habits may be passed on to that organism's offspring under the appropriate conditions.
14. Zachary Elkins et al., *The Endurance of National Constitutions* (New York: Cambridge University Press, 2009).
15. For an insightful discussion of these similarities, see Pelikan, *Interpreting the Bible and the Constitution,* 48–75.
16. Menachem Elon, "The Legal Systems of Jewish Law," *New York University Journal of International Law and Politics* 17 (1985): 221–243, 227.
17. *Id.,* 231.
18. *Id.,* 232.
19. Louis Jacobs, *A Tree of Life: Diversity, Flexibility, and Creativity in Jewish Law* (Oxford: Littman, 2000), 117.
20. Scientific progress is another catalyst of change in both constitutional and religion law. Just as scientific progress pushes toward interpretive innovation in constitutional law—for example, the emergence of new information technologies and the right to free expression, or the amniogenetic test and the extension of the first trimester in abortion jurisprudence—it has been a catalyst of religious innovation and adaptation. A fascinating example of such adjustment is how close-knit Ashkenazi (European Jewish) ultra-Orthodox communities have changed their matchmaking practices to overcome the problem of Tay-Sachs disease, an often-fatal genetic, recessively inherited disorder of increased prevalence in the Eastern European Jewish population.
21. Mahmoud A. El-Gamal, "Interest and the Paradox of Contemporary Islamic Finance," *Fordham International Law Journal* 27 (2004): 108–149.
22. Clement M. Henry and Rodney Wilson, eds., *The Politics of Islamic Finance* (Edinburgh: Edinburgh University Press, 2004); Munawar Iqbal and Philip Molyneux, *Thirty Years of Islamic Banking: History, Performance, and Prospects* (New York: Palgrave, 2005).
23. Bart D. Ehrman, *Misquoting Jesus: The Story behind Who Changed the Bible and Why* (San Francisco: Harper, 2005).
24. See generally, Gershom Scholem, *Sabbatai Sevi: The Mystical Messiah: 1626–1676* (Princeton, N.J.: Princeton University Press, 1973).
25. Thomas Grey, "The Constitution as Scripture," *Stanford Law Review* 37 (1984): 1–25.
26. The political science and sociology literature on this period is meager at best. The main primary sources are Flavius Josephus's *The Jewish War* (published circa 75 C.E.) and *Antiquities of the Jews* (published circa 94 C.E.). For more recent socio-religious accounts, see Richard A. Horsley, *Scribes, Visionaries, and the Politics of Second Temple Judea* (Louisville, Ky.: Westminster John

Knox Press, 2007); Anthony Saldarini, *Pharisees, Scribes, and Sadducees in Palestinian Society* (Wilmington, Del.: Michael Glazier Inc., 1988); J. W. Lightley, *Jewish Sects and Parties in the Time of Jesus* (Peterborough, UK: Epworth Press, 1925); and Julius Wellhausen, *The Pharisees and the Sadducees: An Examination of Internal Jewish History* (Macon, Ga.: Mercer University Press, 2001 [1874]).

27. For a resourceful survey of the academic research on this theory, see Edna Ullman-Margalit, *Out of the Cave: A Philosophical Inquiry into the Dead Sea Scrolls Research* (Cambridge, Mass.: Harvard University Press, 2006).
28. Josephus, *The Jewish War*, Book 1, Chapter 5, 112.
29. Aharon Shemesh, *Halakhah in the Making: The Development of Jewish Law from Qumran to the Rabbis* (Berkeley: University of California Press, 2009), 7–11.
30. See Evan F. Kuehn, "Instruments of Faith and Unity in Canon Law: The Church of Nigeria Constitutional Revision of 2005," *Ecclesiastical Law Journal* 10 (2008): 161–173.
31. *Lawrence v. Texas,* 539 U.S. 558 (2003); *Roper v. Simmons,* 543 U.S. 551 (2005). In *Atkins v. Virginia*, 536 U.S. 304 (2002), the majority opinion referred to an amicus brief by the European Union.
32. Norman Dorsen, "The Relevance of Foreign Legal Materials in U.S. Constitutional Cases: A Conversation between Justice Antonin Scalia and Justice Stephen Breyer," *International Journal of Constitutional Law* 3 (2005): 519–541. See generally Vicki Jackson, *Constitutional Engagement in a Transnational Era* (New York: Oxford University Press, 2010).
33. Those who oppose reference to foreign jurisprudence make what seem to be at least five additional arguments: (1) the constitution constitutes the nation, and so reference to foreign rulings infringes on a nation's constitutional sovereignty; (2) as a matter of principle, constitutional change is better accomplished through amendment and legislation, not through other means such as flexible interpretation or reference to foreign sources; (3) foreign court judges have not been appointed or confirmed by the president and Congress and so bear no accountability or authority vis-à-vis the American people; (4) there are serious methodological problems in reference to foreign cases, for example, problems of "cherry-picking" favorable cases, out-of-context analysis, and selective designation of relevant sources (why certain countries but not others are considered legitimate sources to borrow from); and (5) the onus of proof in this debate should be on those who advocate reference to foreign rulings because historically the practice has been not to refer to such rulings.
34. Max Weber, *The Protestant Ethic and the Spirit of Capitalism* (Wiley-Blackwell, 2002 [1905]); Max Weber, *Economy and Society: An Outline of Interpretive Sociology* (Berkeley: University of California Press, 1978 [1914]).
35. Robert Barro and Rachel McCleary, "Religion and Economic Growth across Countries," *American Journal of Sociology* 68 (2003): 760–781.
36. See, e.g., Lisa A. Keister, "Conservative Protestants and Wealth: How Religion Perpetuates Asset Poverty," *American Journal of Sociology* 113 (2008): 1237–

1271. Religion may also account for attitudes toward redistribution. See, e.g., Kenneth Scheve and David Stasavage, "The Political Economy of Religion and Social Insurance in the United States, 1910–1939," *Studies in American Political Development* 20 (2006): 132–159.

37. Douglass North and Robert Thomas, *The Rise of the Western World: A New Economic History* (New York: Cambridge University Press, 1973).
38. *Id.*, 2–3.
39. Douglass North and Barry Weingast, "Constitutions and Commitment: The Evolution of Institutions of Public Choice in Seventeenth-Century England," *Journal of Economic History* 49 (1989): 803–832.
40. See, e.g., Rafael La Porta et al., "Law and Finance," *Journal of Political Economy* 106 (1998): 1113–1155; Rafael La Porta et al., "The Quality of Government," *Journal of Law, Economics and Organization* 15 (1999): 222–279; and Paul Mahoney, "The Common Law and Economic Growth: Hayek Might Be Right," *Journal of Legal Studies* 30 (2001): 503–525.
41. Avner Greif, "Reputation and Coalitions in Medieval Trade: Evidence on the Maghribi Traders," *Journal of Economic History* 49 (1989): 857–882; Avner Greif, "Contract Enforceability and Economic Institutions in Early Trade: The Maghribi Traders' Coalition," *American Economic Review* 83 (1993): 525–548. See generally Avner Greif, *Institutions and the Path to the Modern Economy: Lessons from Medieval Trade* (New York: Cambridge University Press, 2006).
42. Barak Richman, "How Communities Create Economic Advantage: Jewish Diamond Merchants in New York," *Law and Social Inquiry* 31 (2006): 383–420.
43. See, e.g., Nurit Bird-David, "The Giving Environment: Another Perspective on the Economic System of Gatherer-Hunters," *Current Anthropology* 31 (1990): 189–196; Marshall D. Sahlins, "The Original Affluent Society," in *Stone Age Economics* (Hawthorne, N.Y.: Aldine de Gruyter, 1972), 1–39; Richard B. Lee, *The !Kung San: Men, Women, and Work in a Foraging Society* (Cambridge: Cambridge University Press, 1979).
44. Beshara Doumani, "Endowing Family: *Waqf*, Property Devolution, and Gender in Greater Syria, 1800 to 1860," *Comparative Studies in Society and History* 40 (1998): 3–41.
45. *Id.*, 19.
46. My own favorite example here is the World Changers Church International, led by Pastor Creflo A. Dollar (yes, Dollar), who advances a theory of material prosperity as reflective of religious belief. As Jean Comaroff notes, the Christian exercise chain Lord's Gym promises to build body and soul without compromising on Christian atmosphere; its logo, she reports, is a pumped-up Jesus, bench-pressing a huge cross under the message "His Pain, Your Gain." See Jean Comaroff, "The Politics of Conviction: Faith and Neoliberal Frontier" (paper presented at the University of Bergen, Norway, Nov. 3, 2006).
47. See, e.g., Robert B. Ekelund et al., *Sacred Trust: The Medieval Church as an Economic Firm* (Oxford, U.K.: Oxford University Press, 1996). Lisa Keister ("Conservative Protestants and Wealth: How Religion Perpetuates Asset

Poverty," *American Journal of Sociology* 113, 5 [March 2008]: 1237–1271) notes that sixteen of the thirty-eight parables and 10 percent of New Testament verses address money or finances. Whereas there are approximately five hundred verses each on prayer and faith, there are more than two thousand that deal with money and finances.

48. Maureen Purcell, *Papal Crusading Policy: The Chief Instruments of Papal Crusading Policy and Crusade to the Holy Land from the Final Loss of Jerusalem to the Fall of Acre, 1244–1291* (Leiden: Brill, 1975), cited in Robert Goodin, "Selling Environmental Indulgences," *Kyklos* 47 (1994): 573–596, 577.
49. Ekelund et al., *Sacred Trust,* 155.
50. See Robert Ekelund et al., *The Marketplace of Christianity* (Cambridge, Mass.: MIT Press, 2006), 84–93.
51. See generally Alice Moore-Harell, *Gordon and the Sudan: Prologue to the Mahdiyya, 1877–1880* (London: Frank Cass Publishers, 2001).
52. See "Unleashing the Counter-reformation," *Economist,* Oct. 22, 2009.
53. *Id.*
54. Mark R. Cohen, "The 'Convivencia' of Jews and Muslims in the High Middle Ages," in Moshe Ma'oz, ed., *The Meeting of Civilizations* (Eastbourne, UK: Sussex Academic Press, 2009), 54–65, 58.
55. This equilibrium broke down in the mid-twelfth century when the fundamentalist Muslim Berber Almohads emerged from the periphery of northern Africa to successfully challenge the hegemony of the Moorish Empire. Entire Jewish communities were destroyed, and numerous non-Muslims were forced to accept Islam.
56. David Laitin, *Hegemony and Culture: Politics and Change among the Yoruba* (Chicago: University of Chicago Press, 1986).
57. Steven I. Wilkinson, *Votes and Violence: Electoral Competition and Ethnic Riots in India* (Cambridge: Cambridge University Press, 2006).
58. Ashutosh Varshney, *Ethnic Conflict and Civic Life: Hindus and Muslims in India* (New Haven, Conn.: Yale University Press, 2002).
59. El-Gamal, "Interest and the Paradox of Contemporary Islamic Finance."
60. See Dale Eickelman and James Piscatori, *Muslim Politics* (Princeton, N.J.: Princeton University Press, 2004), 80–107.
61. See Judith Tucker, *Women, Family, and Gender in Islamic Law* (Cambridge: Cambridge University Press, 2008), 224.
62. Several scholars suggest that women have made less progress in the Middle East than in most other regions, not because of the prevalence of Islam in that region, but because oil production is so fundamental to the region's economy. Oil (and other mineral) production reduces the number of women in the labor force as these industries depend on hard physical labor and on suitable infrastructure (pipelines, railroads, ports, etc.), a traditionally male-dominated economic sector. As a result, oil-producing countries are left with atypically strong patriarchal norms, law, and political institutions. Because women are less essential to the workforce, female political representation is relatively weak. See, e.g., Michael Ross, "Oil, Islam, and Women," *American Political Science Review* 101 (2008): 107–123.

63. In some branches of Judaism bat mitzvah may be performed for Jewish girls as well, at the age of either twelve or thirteen. This, however, has not gained a canonical status, as bar mitzvah has, and is not endorsed by Israel's Orthodox establishment.
64. See R. H. Tawney, *Religion and the Rise of Capitalism* (New Brunswick, N.J.: Transaction Publishers, 1998 [1922]). See also Mushtaq Husain Khan, "The Political Economy of Secularism and Religion in Bangladesh," in S. Basu and S. Das, eds., *Electoral Politics in South Asia* (Kolkata, India: K. P. Bagchi, 2000), 181–185.
65. The formal split between the Eastern and Western churches and the establishment of the Eastern Orthodox Church took place in 1054, but it was not until the Protestant Reformation that the hegemony of the Catholic Church was challenged in a more far-reaching and direct fashion. Although many historical and theological accounts of that challenge have been written, far fewer works have taken a hard look at the economic aspects of these transformations. See, e.g., Ekelund et al., *Marketplace of Christianity;* and John T. Gilchrist, *The Church and Economic Activity in the Middle Ages* (New York: St. Martin's Press, 1969).
66. Eli Berman, "Hamas, Taliban and the Jewish Underground: An Economic View of Radical Religious Groups," Working Paper No. 10004, National Bureau of Economic Research (Sept. 2003). See also Eli Berman and David Laitin, "Religion, Terrorism and Public Goods: Testing the Club Model," *Journal of Public Economics* 92 (2008): 1942–1967.
67. See, e.g., Malika Zeghal, "Participation without Power," *Journal of Democracy* 19 (2008): 31–36.
68. For attempts to map and analyze possible links between socioeconomic status and political values and behavior in the Arab world, see, e.g., *UNDP Arab Human Development Reports* (various years); Mark Tessler and Eleanor Gao, "Democracy and the Political Culture Orientations of Ordinary Citizens: A Typology for the Arab World and Perhaps Beyond," *International Social Science Journal* 192 (2009): 197–207; Mark Tessler, "Islam and Democracy in the Middle East: The Impact of Religious Orientations on Attitudes toward Democracy in Four Arab Countries," *Comparative Politics* 34 (2002): 237–254; Mark Tessler, "The Origins of Popular Support for Islamist Movements: A Political Economy Analysis," in John Entelis, ed., *Islam, Democracy, and the State in North Africa* (Bloomington: Indiana University Press, 1997), 93–125.

Conclusion

Epigraph source: John H. Wigmore, "Comparative Law: Jottings on Comparative Legal Ideas and Institutions," originally published in 6 *Tul. L. Rev.* 50 (1931), Reprinted with the permission of the Tulane Law Review Association, which holds the copyright.

1. See Mark Tushnet, "Interpreting Constitutions Comparatively: Some Cautionary Notes, with Reference to Affirmative Action," *Connecticut Law Review* 36 (2004): 649–663.

2. One of my favorite examples here is Richard Lee's meticulous ethnographic work on patterns of food gathering and consumption among the !Kung San in the Kalahari. His work led to the expansion of the "homo economicus" thesis to the least likely of settings, and ultimately to a paradigm shift in our understanding of the economic and political organization of hunter-gatherer societies. See, e.g., Richard B. Lee, *The !Kung San: Men, Women, and Work in a Foraging Society* (Cambridge: Cambridge University Press, 1979).
3. Ran Hirschl, *Towards Juristocracy: The Origins and Consequences of the New Constitutionalism* (Cambridge, Mass.: Harvard University Press, 2004).
4. Ran Hirschl, "The Judicialization of Mega-politics and the Rise of Political Courts," *Annual Review of Political Science* 11 (2008): 93–118.
5. Michael Mandel, "A Brief History of the New Constitutionalism, or 'How We Changed Everything So That Everything Would Remain the Same,'" *Israel Law Review* 32 (1998): 250.
6. See, e.g., Charles Taylor, *A Secular Age* (Cambridge, Mass.: Belknap Press of Harvard University Press, 2007); and Graeme Smith, *A Short History of Secularism* (London: I. B. Tauris, 2008).

Acknowledgments

WRITING A BOOK of this scope on comparative constitutional law and politics in the infrequently explored, religion-laden world is not an easy undertaking to say the least. It must be informed by big ideas from law, religion, political science, and economics alongside close acquaintance with various constitutional settings. Not too many studies, we can safely assume, juxtapose, let alone aim to proficiently examine, interpretive debates in Second Temple Judaism alongside constitutional jurisprudence from Canada, Britain, or South Africa; jurisdictional wars in medieval Europe alongside contemporary constitutional politics in Malaysia, Egypt, Nigeria, Israel, or Pakistan. And these are only a handful of the dozens of destinations, near and far, where this scholarly journey, literal or figurative, has taken me.

Writing this book and thinking about its themes has been a true labor of love for me; however, it could not have been completed without the support of many friends and colleagues who provided valuable references, pinpoint citations, insightful examples, thoughtful new directions, or simply overall good advice. My University of Toronto colleagues David Cameron, Janice Stein, and Rob Vipond created an institutional environment that is conducive to original thinking and quality scholarship. The Canada Research Chair program provided essential research funding without which this project could not have been completed. My work on this book began while I was a Fellow at the Center for Advanced Study in the

Behavioral Sciences, Stanford University. It is my hope that a distant echo of the Center's intellectual legacy and grandeur may still be heard in these pages. I thank Mike Aronson of Harvard University Press for his confidence in this project from the outset. I benefited tremendously from questions and comments by participants in workshops and conferences held at the University of California–Berkeley Boalt Hall Law School, Princeton Center for Human Values, University of Maryland Law School, College of William & Mary School of Law, Georgetown Law Center, University of Southern California Gould School of Law, Harvard Divinity School, and the University of Chicago School of Law. Charles Eberline, MaryAnne Kneif, Kate Brookson-Morris, Howard Kislowicz, and Tom Rowe helped at various stages with dedicated research assistance or with meticulous editorial comments and suggestions. I am indebted to Steven Bernstein, Rebecca Cook, Andrew Harding, Gary Jacobsohn, Baber Johansen, Steve Macedo, Jack Rakove, Hootan Shambayati, Peter Solomon, Alexei Trochev, Jeff Tulis, Ernest Weinrib, and Malika Zeghal for their insightful suggestions and responses to my queries, pointed or broad as they might have been. Mark Graber and Sanford Levinson—outstanding scholars and mentors—read a crude draft of the entire manuscript and provided detailed comments and sage advice that made the final product a distinctly better one.

I am grateful to the following journals for their publishing my earlier articles related to the issues and topics discussed in this book, including: "The New Wall of Separation: Permitting Diversity, Restricting Competition" (coauthored with Ayelet Shachar), *Cardozo Law Review* 30 (2009): 2535–2560; "The Socio-Political Origins of Israel's Juristocracy," *Constellations* 16 (2009): 476–492; "Juristocracy vs. Theocracy? Constitutional Courts and the Containment of 'Sacred Law,'" *Middle East Law & Governance* 1 (2009): 129–165; "The Theocratic Challenge to Constitution Drafting in Post-Conflict States," *William & Mary Law Review* 49 (2008): 1179–1121; and "The Rise of Constitutional Theocracy," *Harvard International Law Journal* 49 (2008): 72–82.

Naomi Ernst-Hirschl, Tmima Shachar, and Arie Shachar instilled a culture of high expectations and true cosmopolitanism, for which I am grateful. Most of all, I thank my much better half, Ayelet Shachar, and our dazzling son, Shai, for their infinite wisdom, contagious laughs, invaluable support, and constant inspiration.

Index

www.ingramcontent.com/pod-product-compliance
Lightning Source LLC
LaVergne TN
LVHW091517200926
848483LV00005B/444/J
* 9 7 8 0 6 7 4 0 4 8 1 9 5 *